MW01536516

INCLUDING LEARNERS WITH LOW-INCIDENCE DISABILITIES

INTERNATIONAL PERSPECTIVES ON INCLUSIVE EDUCATION

Series Editor: Chris Forlin

Recent Volumes:

Volume 1: Emotional and Behavioural Difficulties in Mainstream Schools – Edited by John Visser, Harry Daniels, and Ted Cole

Volume 2: Transforming Troubled Lives: Strategies and Interventions for Children with Social, Emotional and Behavioural Difficulties – Edited by John Visser, Harry Daniels and Ted Cole

Volume 3: Measuring Inclusive Education – Edited by Chris Forlin and Tim Loreman

Volume 4: Working with Teaching Assistants and other Support Staff for Inclusive Education – Edited by Dianne Chambers

INTERNATIONAL PERSPECTIVES ON INCLUSIVE EDUCATION VOLUME 5

INCLUDING LEARNERS WITH LOW-INCIDENCE DISABILITIES

SERIES EDITOR

CHRIS FORLIN

Hong Kong Institute of Education, Hong Kong

VOLUME EDITOR

ELIZABETH A. WEST

University of Washington, USA

United Kingdom – North America – Japan
India – Malaysia – China

Emerald Group Publishing Limited
Howard House, Wagon Lane, Bingley BD16 1WA, UK

First edition 2015

British Library Cataloguing in Publication Data
A catalogue record for this book is available from the British Library

ISBN: 978-1-78441-251-7
ISSN: 1479-3636 (Series)

CONTENTS

LIST OF CONTRIBUTORS

Vicki Barnitt	Florida Inclusion Network, University of South Florida, Department of Teaching and Learning, Tampa, FL, USA
Jody Marie Bartz	Department of Educational Specialties, Northern Arizona University, Flagstaff, AZ, USA
Grace I. Blum	Curriculum and Instruction, University of Washington, Seattle, WA, USA
Pei-Yu Chen	Department of Special Education, National Taipei University of Education, Taipei City, Taiwan (R.O.C.)
Chun-Yu Chiu	Department of Special Education, National Taipei University of Education, Taipei City, Taiwan (R.O.C.)
Debra L. Cote	Department of Special Education, California State University Fullerton, Fullerton, CA, USA
Anne E. Crylen	Special Education, University of Washington, Seattle, WA, USA
Carol Ann Davis	Special Education, University of Washington, Seattle, WA, USA
Robin Drogan	Department of Exceptionality Programs, Bloomsburg University of Pennsylvania, Bloomsburg, PA, USA
Jeremy Erickson	Special Education, University of Washington, Seattle, WA, USA
Michael Gutierrez	Special Education, University of Washington, Seattle, WA, USA

Young Hyuk Hong	Secondary Special Education Teaching, Federal Way School District, Federal Way, WA, USA
Erica Howell	Department of Special Education, California State University Fullerton, Fullerton, CA, USA
Andrea D. Jasper	Department of Counseling and Special Education, Central Michigan University, Mount Pleasant, MI, USA
Phyllis Jones	Department of Teaching and Learning, University of South Florida, Tampa, FL, USA
Vita L. Jones	Department of Special Education, California State University Fullerton, Fullerton, CA, USA
Kyungsook Kang	Secondary Special Education, Wonkwang University, Seoul, Korea
Jennifer Kurth	Department of Special Education (SPED), University of Kansas, Lawrence, KS, USA
Penny Lacey	Department of Disability, Inclusion and Special Educational Needs, School of Education, University of Birmingham, Birmingham, UK
Meaghan M. McCollow	Department of Counseling and Special Education, Central Michigan University, Mount Pleasant, MI, USA
Kinga M. Ober	Department of Child Psychopathology, Adam Mickiewicz University, Poznan, Poland
Daniel Östlund	Department of Teacher Education, Kristianstad University, Kristianstad, Sweden
Charles Peck	Special Education, University of Washington, Seattle, WA, USA

Darlene Perner	Department of Exceptionality Programs, Bloomsburg University of Pennsylvania, Bloomsburg, PA, USA
Melinda R. Pierson	Department of Special Education, California State University Fullerton, Fullerton, CA, USA
Richard Rose	Centre for Education and Research, University of Northampton, Northampton, UK
Jeanette Scull	John F Kennedy Special Needs Academy, London, UK
Michael Shevlin	Department of Education, Trinity College Dublin, Dublin, Ireland
Jordan Shurr	Department of Counseling and Special Education, Central Michigan University, Mount Pleasant, MI, USA
Daphne Thomas	Department of Teaching and Learning, University of South Florida, Tampa, FL, USA
Andrzej Twardowski	Department of Child Psychopathology, Adam Mickiewicz University, Poznan, Poland
Matthew Wangeman	Institute for Human Development, Northern Arizona University, Flagstaff, AZ, USA
Elizabeth A. West	Special Education, University of Washington, Seattle, WA, USA

INTRODUCTION

This volume provides a focus on including learners with low-incidence disabilities. Few books are published with content relating to low-incidence disabilities and inclusion. In addition, the contribution of an international perspective offers a unique insight which is rarely heard.

This volume is divided into two sections. The first section provides the reader with an insight into strategies to facilitate inclusion for learners with low-incidence disabilities who have extensive support needs. Examples of good practice are provided for practitioners to employ to improve teaching and learning in their school or classroom for students and their families who continue to struggle to gain appropriate supports and services. The chapter "Moving toward Inclusion" serves as an introduction and other chapters build on this foundation. The chapter "Beyond Access: Moving toward Increased Participation, Membership, and Skills in the Inclusive Classroom" provides a conceptual framework for inclusive education for learners with low incidence disabilities grounded in the argument that increased access and participation in socially valued roles, activities, and settings is both the most fundamental goal of the inclusive education process and also the primary means in which that goal is achieved. The chapter "Best Practices in Teacher Training and Professional Development for Including Learners with Low-Incidence Disabilities" examines and provides recommendations for pre-service teacher preparation and in-service teacher professional development related to inclusion for learners with low-incidence disabilities. The chapter "Including Learners with Severe Intellectual Disabilities: System Planning and Support for Greater Inclusive Practices" presents an assessment tool which can support a facilitated review and subsequent action planning for greater inclusive practices. The chapters "Facilitating Systems of Support" and "Facilitating Supports and Services for Learners with Low-Incidence Disabilities" relate to influences that are fundamental to facilitating a system of support for inclusive education and provide examples of models of service and support delivery. The chapter "Providing Appropriate Individualized Instruction and Access to the General Education Curriculum for Learners with Low-Incidence Disabilities" provides the reader with an overview and a framework for making individualized and curriculum choices for learners with low-incidence disabilities and cognitive deficits, focusing on embedded instruction. The last chapter in this section highlights the socio-emotional support needs for re-entry to school after traumatic brain injury. Case studies and insider perspectives are woven throughout these chapters to further illustrate concepts and to offer implications for practice.

The second section offers a wide variety of perspectives from seven countries that illuminate the state of inclusion within their context. Many of these chapters center on policies, practices, and perspectives. In addition, several chapters highlight what works within those contexts for learners with low-incidence disabilities, and include learners own reflection on what worked for them. Developing partnerships among countries with different cultures, levels of expertise, and existing service infrastructure is critical. This content is important as we learn from each other and promote inclusion for those learners who have been historically marginalized in many ways.

The rich diversity of contributors to the book is one of its defining elements. A number of experienced researchers and practitioners were invited to contribute chapters to this book and I am so grateful to all of them for their thoughtful contributions.

This text will be of value to those engaged in similar endeavors around the globe who seek to move inclusion for learners with low-incidence disabilities forward. This volume will be useful to academics, teachers, families, and to those enrolled in teacher preparation programs. This book makes a significant contribution to the limited literature available that supports learners with low-incidence disabilities, especially in a global context.

Elizabeth A. West
Editor

ACKNOWLEDGMENTS

A special thank-you to Clyde and Sharon West and Gabriel for your continued love and support.

SECTION I
STRATEGIES AND SUPPORTS FOR INCLUSION

MOVING TOWARD INCLUSION

Elizabeth A. West

ABSTRACT

This chapter provides an overview of inclusion for learners with low-incidence disabilities and highlights related terminology. Special education is detailed as a service and not a place. A comprehensive definition of the term low-incidence disabilities is provided. The chapter concludes with potentials and challenges related to the least restrictive environment and inclusion.

Keywords: Inclusion; low-incidence disabilities; least restrictive environment; special education

INTRODUCTION

The right to education is universal and extends to all learners with disabilities, including learners who have low-incidence disabilities. It is not only important that each child receives education but it is also critical that it is of high quality. We must remove barriers to accessing education and learning for learners with low-incidence disabilities. Since 1975, federal law has required that students with disabilities have access to school and free appropriate public education. The U.S. Congress enacted the Education

Including Learners with Low-Incidence Disabilities
International Perspectives on Inclusive Education, Volume 5, 3–12

ISSN: 1479-3636/doi:10.1108/S1479-363620140000005001

for All Handicapped Children Act of 1975 to ensure that all children with disabilities had access to public education. Provisions of this act provided that all children with disabilities have equal access to free appropriate public education in the least restrictive environment (LRE), including learners with low-incidence disabilities.

Although the Education for All Handicapped Children Act of 1975 mandated the LRE, implementation in the schools was inconsistent. During the next 10 years, several lawsuits were brought to the federal courts by parents to obtain integration of their children with disabilities into a regular school environment. Students with disabilities were still not placed in the same classroom, but it was thought that their closer proximity to children without disabilities would help with the integration. At this point, the students with disabilities participated only in nonacademic classes such as lunch and recess.

In December 2004, Congress reformed and renamed the law. The law, Individuals with Disabilities Education Improvement Act (IDEA, 2004), continues to require school districts to educate children in the LRE. This law places an emphasis on the general education curriculum which necessitates a shift in attention to the accommodations and modifications necessary to enable learners with low-incidence disabilities to access this curriculum in meaningful ways.

Special education is a contested field. There are major controversies about the nature of disability, who has a disability, the best ways to serve students with disabilities, and the goals of special education. There is considerable critique both within and from outside the profession. There are many technical solutions proposed (evidenced-based practices), and while it is necessary to understand these technical solutions, in and of themselves the technical solutions are not sufficient to assure positive outcomes for students with disabilities. There are also many laws governing the definition of disability and how individuals deemed to have a disability should be served. While it is imperative that these laws be followed, total compliance with the laws will not resolve the fundamental issues surrounding disabilities.

It took the United States nearly 10 years to have all states come into compliance with its national law to support individuals with disabilities (Raver, 2001). Change is happening at a rapid pace in many countries, and many teachers across the world echo a sentiment of anxiety (Bradshaw, Tennant, & Lydiatt, 2004) and concern over perceived competence (Forlin, 2005). In many countries teachers are also being asked to ensure that all their students achieve, regardless of background (Dyson, 2001). The doors have been opened but many countries are now grappling with how to prepare teachers to meet the needs of such a heterogeneous population.

WHO ARE LEARNERS WITH LOW-INCIDENCE DISABILITIES?

Over the past few decades, both professional literature and actual practice have supported alternative approaches for defining and classifying students with low-incidence disabilities. Students with disabilities can be classified in many ways. IDEA (2004) continues to recognize disabilities in the form of more or less discrete diagnostic categories. Other approaches to classification include categorizing individuals with disabilities by degree of severity of their needs or by how atypical an individual may be when compared to a norm. Still other approaches may emphasize the level of intensity of supports necessary for an individual to function optimally in home, school, community, and work settings.

IDEA retains the use of specific disability categories for eligibility determination and classification. A major portion of special education today is driven by the Federal Law, IDEA (2004). This law specifies the types of children who are classified as having a disability, the criteria to be so classified, and the procedural guidelines schools must follow. For a student to be placed in special education the student must meet the criteria of one of the disability categories and there must be evidence that the disability has had an adverse effect on the student's educational achievement. IDEA lists 13 different disability categories under which 3- through 21-year-olds may be eligible for services. The disability categories listed in IDEA are

- autism;
- deaf-blindness;
- deafness;
- emotional disturbance;
- hearing impairment;
- intellectual disability;
- multiple disabilities;
- orthopedic impairment;
- other health impairment;
- specific learning disability;

- speech or language impairment;
- traumatic brain injury; or
- visual impairment (including blindness).

It is important to know that, under IDEA, states and local educational agencies (LEAs) can use the term "developmental delay" with children aged three through nine.

None of the disabilities listed under low-incidence disabilities generally exceed 1% of the school-aged population at any given time. The federal definition of the term low-incidence disability includes: (a) a visual or hearing impairment or simultaneous visual and hearing impairments; (b) a significant cognitive impairment; or (c) any impairment for which a small number of personnel with highly specialized skills and knowledge are needed in order for children with that impairment to receive early intervention services or a free appropriate public education (IDEA, 2004).

WHAT IS SPECIAL EDUCATION?

Special education is an instruction that is specially designed to meet the unique needs of a child with a disability. This means education that is individually developed to address a specific child's needs that result from his or her disability. Special education should be considered a service, not a place. While this idea is the foundation of most professionals who write about the philosophy of special education, in the view of many, special education is a place and as such is a negative connotation. The key concept of special education, before the law was passed, and embedded in the heart of the law, is individualization. The basic idea is that the students classified as disabled are so diverse that each needs an individualized educational experience. In the law this has been codified though the Individualized Education Plan (IEP). The IEP is a legal document that specifies the disability, the adverse educational impact of the disability, and the plan for delivering specially designed instruction (what the special education teachers will provide to address the disability). The IEP must be agreed upon by the IEP team (special education teacher, general education teacher, a representative of the school or district, an individual who can interpret the instructional implications of the child's evaluation results, other specialists, the parents/guardian, and the student).

LEAST RESTRICTIVE ENVIRONMENT AND INCLUSION

IDEA does not use the term "inclusion." However, IDEA does require school districts to place students in the LRE. LRE means that, to the maximum extent appropriate, school districts must educate students with disabilities in a regular classroom with appropriate aids and supports, referred to as "supplementary aids and services," along with their nondisabled peers in the school they would attend if not disabled, unless a student's IEP requires some other arrangement. IDEA does not require that every student with a disability be placed in regular classrooms regardless of individual abilities and needs. This recognition that regular class placement may not be appropriate for every disabled student is reflected in the requirement that school districts make available a range of placement options, known as a continuum of alternative placements, to meet the unique educational needs of students with disabilities. This requirement for the continuum reinforces the importance of the individualized inquiry, not a "one size fits all" approach, in determining what placement is the LRE for each student with a disability.

As a consequence of a 2004 change in federal law, children with disabilities are much more often educated with typically developing children. However, students with low-incidence disabilities are more likely to be served in less inclusive settings (such as in special classes, separate schools, and residential facilities) than are students with high-incidence disabilities. Ryndak et al. (2014) identify that "Students with significant disabilities continue to be among the most segregated in school" (p. 65).

The extent to which an individual student participates in a regular education setting with the use of supplementary aids and services is determined on a case-by-case basis by the IEP team. This requires an examination of the unique educational needs of each student so that the team can determine the possible range of aids and supports that would enable the student to be educated satisfactorily in the general education environment before a more restrictive placement is considered.

Both Federal and State law indicate a clear preference for educating students with disabilities in general education classrooms with their typical peers. This preference has become recognized as inclusion. While there is no legal definition of inclusion or inclusive education, many organizations and advocacy groups have developed their own definitions. A comprehensive definition of inclusion was developed by the National Center on Educational Restructuring and Inclusion (NCERI) (Table 1).

Table 1. Key Terms and Explanation of Inclusion Definition.

Key Terms	Explanation
Supplementary aids and support services	Assistive technology, environmental adaptations, specialized instructional strategies, peer supports, curricular adaptations or modifications, and collaborative teaching
Age appropriate classroom	All students within one to two years of the same chronological age
Neighborhood school	The school the student would attend if he or she did not have an exceptionality label

Source: Adapted from NCERI definition.

> Providing to all students, including those with significant disabilities, equitable opportunities to receive effective educational services, with the needed supplementary aids and support services, in age appropriate classrooms in their neighborhood schools, in order to prepare students for productive lives as full members of society. (1995, p. 99)

WHY INCLUSION?

Inclusion is one way to build a stronger society through the explicit valuing of difference among the members of that society. When inclusive education is fully embraced, we abandon the idea that children have to become "normal" in order to contribute to the world. We begin to look beyond typical ways of becoming valued members of the community, and in doing so, begin to realize the achievable goal of providing all children with an authentic sense of belonging (Kunc, 1992, pp. 38–39).

Some research has shown that inclusion may improve learning and academic performance for all students (Salend & Duhaney, 1999; Walter-Thomas, Bryant, & Land, 1996). Children also have an opportunity to learn to accept individual differences and to overcome misconceptions about disabilities. Inclusion provides opportunities for socialization and friendships to develop (Carter, Hughes, Guth, & Copeland, 2005; Cole & Meyer, 1991). It provides a sense of belonging and appropriate modeling of social, behavioral, and academic skills, including children with disabilities in general education classes models acceptance of diversity. Separate is not equal.

POTENTIALS AND CHALLENGES

Students with low-incidence disabilities possess highly complex needs and may be uniquely challenging to serve in local schools. Required personnel, materials, and technological resources are all highly specialized and may be difficult to acquire and maintain, which may hinder access for these students within the general education classroom. The relative rarity of students with low-incidence disabilities in public schools may pose a challenge for schools struggling to meet their needs. Since they encounter these students so infrequently, most local schools may have little knowledge on how to best educate these students, of what technologies are available to assist them, and of how to obtain needed and appropriate support services. There is little controversy surrounding the specialized skills and knowledge necessary to provide services for students with LID. Of key importance is the preparation of teachers, both general and special educators. Designing specialized instruction requires focused collaboration among team members, particularly general educators, special educators, and related services personnel. The general educator has the knowledge of the general curriculum and its alignment with state- and district-wide standards. Special education personnel possess knowledge of the implications of disability and the elements of adaptive instruction.

The extent to which accommodations and modifications are designed into curriculum at the outset of the planning process can have an enormous impact upon access, participation, and progress for students with disabilities. The first section of this book will provide details around strategies and supports to facilitate inclusion for learners with low-incidence disabilities highlighting the potentials and challenges. The second section of the book offers an international perspective on including learners with low-incidence disabilities. This set of chapters presents context-specific information that highlight the status of inclusion for those learners with low-incidence disabilities. It offers insights that are interesting to consider in the discourse around inclusion and learners with low-incidence disabilities.

CONCLUSION

Students with LID have been historically excluded and continue to be marginalized in the dual education systems of special and general education. Special education is at a fork in the road. One road leads to a more separate system of special education charged with meeting the educational needs of youth with disabilities. The other meanders into a public space where the special education and general education system merge into a system that meets the needs of all students. Which road is eventually followed will largely depend on decisions deliberated in schoolhouses, professional meetings, legislative halls, and commission offices. Teachers, as well as policy makers, will have a major role in these deliberations. We can choose to dwell on the obstacles that lie in our path; however, the choice that will propel us forward is one of optimism. Individuals with low-incidence disabilities have the same right to education as everyone else. However, it must be ensured that this education is individualized, appropriate, and of high quality. There is no doubt that many challenges face the field of special education, but the future is full of promise. The future of this field is in the hands of those who have promoted the progress begun under IDEA. We have flourished from the pre-1970s when millions of children with disabilities received inadequate or inappropriate special education services from public school and another one million children were excluded from school altogether (U.S. Department of Education, 2004).

Stainback and Stainback (1996) stated "... it should be emphasized that saying restructuring can be done is not the same as saying it is easy to do. Segregation has been practiced for centuries, and there are entrenched attitudes, laws, policies, and educational structures that work against achieving inclusion of all students on a widespread basis" (p. 385). Thus, achieving the inclusion of all students is hard work, especially when new legislative requirements make the task daunting. However, the goal of inclusion is far too important to not accept or ignore the challenge. The goal of universal inclusive education is within our reach and many previously segregated learners have benefited from the movement toward inclusion. This book contributes to the dialogue as authors provide unique insights into effective strategies and supports that can move the field in productive ways. In addition, the international perspective provides a lens from which to examine the development of inclusion in other cultures.

KEY TERMS

Low-incidence disabilities – The federal definition of the term low-incidence disability includes (a) a visual or hearing impairment, or simultaneous visual and hearing impairments; (b) a significant cognitive impairment; or (c) any impairment for which a small number of personnel with highly specialized skills and knowledge are needed in order for children with that impairment to receive early intervention services or a free appropriate public education (IDEA, 2004).

Special education – Special education is an instruction that is specially designed to meet the unique needs of a child with a disability.

Individualized Education Plan (IEP) – The IEP is a legal document that specifies the disability, the adverse educational impact of the disability, and the plan for delivering specially designed instruction (what the special education teachers will provide to address the disability).

Least Restrictive Environment (LRE) – LRE means that, to the maximum extent appropriate, school districts must educate students with disabilities in regular classrooms with appropriate aids and supports, referred to as "supplementary aids and services," along with their nondisabled peers in the school they would attend if not disabled, unless a student's IEP requires some other arrangement.

REFERENCES

Bradshaw, K., Tennant, L., & Lydiatt, S. (2004). Special education in the United Arab Emirates: Anxieties, attitudes and aspirations. *International Journal of Special Education, 19*(1), 49–55.

Carter, E. W., Hughes, C., Guth, C. B., & Copeland, S. R. (2005). Factors influencing social interaction among high school students with intellectual disabilities and their general education peers. *American Journal on Mental Retardation, 110*, 366–377.

Cole, D. A., & Meyer, L. H. (1991). Social integration and severe disabilities: A longitudinal analysis of child outcomes. *Journal of Special Education, 25*(3), 340–351.

Dyson, A. (2001). Varieties of inclusion. Paper presented at conference of VI Jornadas Cientificas de Investigacion sobre Personas con Discapacidad, March, Salamanca, Spain, pp. 17–19.

Forlin, C. (2005). Sustaining inclusive practices in primary school communities. In C. Newell & T. R. Parmenter (Eds.), *Disability in education: Context, curriculum and culture* (pp. 13–21). Deakin West, Australian Capital Territory: Australian College of Educators.

Individuals with Disabilities Education Act, 20 U.S.C. § 1400 (2004).

Kunc, N. (1992). The need to belong: Rediscovering Maslow's hierarchy of needs. In R. Villa, J. Thousand, W. Stainback, & S. Stainback (Eds.), *Restructuring for caring & effective education: An administrative guide to creating heterogeneous schools* (pp. 25–40). Baltimore, MD: Brookes.

National Center on Educational Restructuring and Inclusion. (1995). *National study of inclusive education*. New York, NY: City University of New York.

Raver, S. A. (2001). India: Training teachers for children with mental retardation. *International Journal of Special Education, 16*(1), 54–66.

Ryndak, D. L., Taub, D., Jorgensen, C. M., Gonsier-Gerdin, J., Arndt, K., ... Allock, H. (2014). Policy and the impact on placement, involvement, and progress in general education: Critical issues that require rectification. *Research and Practices for Persons with Severe Disabilities, 39*(1), 65–74.

Salend, S. J., & Duhaney, L. G. (1999). The impact of inclusion on students with and without disabilities and their educators. *Remedial & Special Education, 20*(2), 114–127.

Stainback, S., & Stainback, W. (1996). *Inclusion: A guide for educators.* Baltimore, MD: Brookes Publishing.

U.S. Department of Education. (2004). *Twenty-sixth annual report to Congress on the implementation of the Individuals with disabilities education act.* Washington, DC: Author.

Walter-Thomas, C. S., Bryant, M., & Land, S. (1996). Planning for effective co-teaching: The key to successful inclusion. *Remedial and Special Education, 17*(4), 255–264.

BEYOND ACCESS: MOVING TOWARD INCREASED PARTICIPATION, MEMBERSHIP, AND SKILLS IN THE INCLUSIVE CLASSROOM

Grace I. Blum, Michael Gutierrez and Charles Peck

ABSTRACT

This chapter provides a conceptual framework for inclusive education for learners with low-incidence disabilities grounded in the argument that increased access *and* participation in socially valued roles, activities, and settings *are both the most fundamental goals of the inclusive education process and also the primary means in which these goals are achieved. By challenging traditional views of learning development as merely the acquisition of skills, the proposed framework largely considers the social contexts in which the development of new skills takes place. Through the presentation of three case illustrations, the authors describe ways in which the framework may be relevant to designing and evaluating programs of inclusive education that are responsive to the*

Including Learners with Low-Incidence Disabilities
International Perspectives on Inclusive Education, Volume 5, 13–36

ISSN: 1479-3636/doi:10.1108/S1479-363620140000005006

needs of diverse communities, including those in a variety of international contexts.

Keywords: Inclusion; skills; participation; relationships; membership

AHMED

At the end of every school day, the students in Ms. Ali's Kindergarten class spend time cleaning the classroom and preparing it for the next day. Every student is given a job and often they work in pairs to accomplish their given tasks. This week, Ahmed is given the honored task of cleaning the blackboard. Ahmed, a student with severe developmental delays, works together with Chinar, his typically developing friend, to get supplies to clean the board. Chinar runs to get a bucket of water and washcloths from Ms. Ali while Ahmed waits at the chalkboard. Chinar returns, dips the cloths in the water, and gives one to Ahmed. Ahmed motions to the bottom of the board, where he will start cleaning. Chinar nods and begins to wipe down the top of the chalkboard. They eagerly wipe down the chalkboard, making sure not to miss any spots. In the process, they both get some chalk and water on their cloths. Realizing how silly they both look, they begin to laugh hysterically. Hearing the laughter, Ms. Ali approaches the students. Admiring their work she says, "Why, this is the cleanest the board has been all year! Thank you my dear students!" When Ahmed's mother picks him up at the end of the day she asks, "Ahmed, how was your day?" Ahmed enthusiastically replies, "It was wonderful! Can we invite Chinar's family to our home for tea?"

INTRODUCTION

International education policies have brought about various country/context-specific interpretations and progress toward inclusive education. In particular, Education for All (EFA) has articulated the inclusion agenda through a variety of international declarations and projects sponsored by a coalition of national governments, civil society groups, and international organizations such as UNESCO and the World Bank. Inclusive education, as understood within this particular policy context, has focused on ensuring that a variety of students from traditionally excluded groups have *access* to a variety of opportunities to learn in formal school environments. Yet, despite growing consensus around definitions of inclusive education, there is a tremendous diversity across the contexts in which these policies are intended for implementation (Artiles, Kozleski, & Waitoller, 2011). As we approach the 2015 target year for EFA, many countries are currently assessing their progress toward creating and sustaining inclusive school environments. As UNICEF reports, still over 57 million school-aged children are currently excluded from receiving a primary education because of ethnicity, ability level, language background, social class, and gender (UNICEF, 2013). While the challenges for many developing nations around inclusion still center mainly around issues of *access* and *completion*, many developed nations are facing issues largely surrounding equity in *participation* and *outcomes* for diverse groups of learners (Artiles et al. 2011). The purpose of this chapter is to describe a conceptual framework that may be used to clarify the goals and guide the implementation of inclusive education across these highly diverse settings.

In this chapter, the authors argue that increased *access* and *participation in socially valued roles, activities, and settings* are both the most fundamental goals of the inclusive education process and also the primary means in which these goals are achieved. This perspective challenges historical views of learning development that focus primarily on the acquisition of skills – a view widely accepted in the field of special education for individuals with severe disabilities. Of course, skill acquisition is not considered to be insignificant. However, the authors broaden their analysis to consider how students with severe disabilities come to be more competent and participatory members of their communities by including more focused consideration of the social contexts in which the development of new skills takes place.

The main argument draws upon a conceptual framework originally developed by Staub, Peck, Gallucci, and Schwartz (2000), the Inclusive Education Outcome Framework, which is grounded in an expanded view of inclusive education integrating various perspectives on the outcomes of inclusion. Through the presentation of three case studies, the authors describe ways in which the model may be relevant to designing and evaluating programs of inclusive education that are responsive to the needs of diverse communities, including those in a variety of international contexts.

THEORETICAL FRAMEWORK

The Inclusive Education Outcome Framework draws upon sociocultural learning theory in framing the nature of learning as inherently both social and cultural in nature (Rogoff, 2003; Vygotsky, 1980). In this theoretical perspective, learning is always situated within certain cultural, historical, and social contexts. In particular, several key assumptions of sociocultural learning theory are drawn from the work by Lave and Wenger (1991): (1) learning is always *situated* within a particular community or culture, (2) learning occurs through the medium of social interaction, and (3) participation is always negotiated within a community of practice. Although conventional views of learning characterize this process as the transmission of knowledge or skills, sociocultural theorists view the process of learning as essentially a social practice where knowledge is co-constructed with participants within a particular sociocultural context (Lave & Wenger, 1991).

Learning is further viewed as a process in which all participants change through their mutual negotiation of actions, roles, and relationships. Lave and Wenger conceptualize this process as one of "legitimate peripheral participation" (LPP). LPP foregrounds changes in the ways in which learners participate in "communities of practice." "Newcomers" at the periphery transition to fully participating "oldtimers" as they become members of a community with shared goals and expectations. As newcomers gain the skills to become more involved within the core practices of the community, they move from the periphery to full membership within the community. In turn, the community of practice is affected, as changes are negotiated in the roles, expectations, and relationships of those involved.

Taken together, these core assumptions of sociocultural learning theory underscore the importance of conceptualizing both the learning process and the ultimate outcomes of inclusive education, in ways that expand the field's historical focus on skills. Ultimately, achieving increased participation in valued roles, activities, and settings within local cultures is the outcome of inclusion. In the following sections, the authors provide a description of several specific ways in which educators in diverse cultural settings can create opportunities, not only for teaching new skills but also for building the kinds of social relationships and experiences of membership that are close to the heart of what we mean by "inclusion."

The vignette with which we began our chapter illustrates a number of ways in which the social dimensions of class participation are considered valuable outcomes of the inclusive classroom and contribute to Ahmed's own development. First, Ahmed's interactions with his friend Chinar are an important context where he learns new skills. Chinar models language and behavior that are appropriate for participating in similar social situations. In addition, Ahmed's participation in the classroom routines allows opportunities for Ahmed to follow directions in a large group, observe what the group is doing as a cue for what is expected of him, and make choices that regulate his own behavior, independent of adult intervention. All of these can be considered important skills for competent participation in a variety of activities, roles, and settings within Ahmed's local culture.

Second, the special friendship that Ahmed and Chinar have provides both personal support and a meaningful context for participation in the activity. For example, Chinar provides needed and appropriate support for Ahmed in learning how to carry out the shared task. From Ahmed's perspective, the new cognitive, language, and social skills required by this social situation constitute, in part, the means by which she can participate in a relationship she values greatly. Hence, the task of cleaning the blackboard, the behaviors required to participate, and the social relationships that underlie all of it, form a web of connections that make the activity meaningful to Ahmed, Chinar, and the rest of the class. This web of connection between context, behavior, and social relationships is extremely important for teachers struggling to address the challenge of making learning meaningful for their students. Viewing "skills" as a set of discrete behaviors rather than complex context-behavior relationships exacerbates this challenge of creating meaningful learning experiences in the classroom.

Third, the vignette illustrates how Ahmed's participation in the inclusive classroom may impact his peers. For example, Chinar's mother and teachers often comment about how much she has learned and benefited through her friendship with Ahmed, in which she plays the role of a leader and nurturer. Not only do these comments make Chinar feel good about herself but they also have a positive impact on Ahmed's development. As Chinar learns more about the ways in which Ahmed communicates, the situations with which he struggles, the things he enjoys, and the things they enjoy in common, Chinar becomes able to better support Ahmed's participation in a variety of activities, including many that they enjoy together. Chinar and her mother begin to invite Ahmed over after school regularly, and the two students begin to enjoy playdates to the park and to other students' homes together. These experiences create multiple opportunities for Ahmed to participate in new activities, roles, and settings – and all demand that he learn new skills. Viewed in this way, we recognize that Ahmed's development is intertwined with Chinar's in many important ways.

THE OUTCOME FRAMEWORK

In the following paragraphs, the authors draw upon the framework developed by Staub et al. (2000) to more clearly articulate the complex dynamics of the inclusive education process. Staub et al. outline three specific outcome domains that individually and together contribute to increased participation in culturally valued roles, activities, and settings (Fig. 1).

The first domain, "*skills*," tends to be the traditional focus of special education outcome assessment. For students with significant developmental disabilities, this can include *functional skills* like learning to tie shoes or balancing a checkbook, *social skills* like having a conversation or asking for help from a peer, or *academic skills* like math and reading. Skill acquisition, particularly social and communicative skills, can have a large effect on the amount of time students with severe disabilities are able to participate in a variety of social roles, activities, and settings. However, it is important to note that skill acquisition by itself does not exclusively determine the extent to which a student can participate with his peers. In order for the skill acquisition to be truly meaningful, it must be learned within the context of the various social activities and settings in which the student regularly participates. This is where the next two domains come into play.

"*Relationships*" refer to the wide variety of personal relationships that the students have with one another. While friendships remain a high priority for both individuals with and without disabilities, other important relationships exist as well. These include play/companion, helper (giver), helpee (receiver), and conflictual – all of which provided unique learning opportunities to

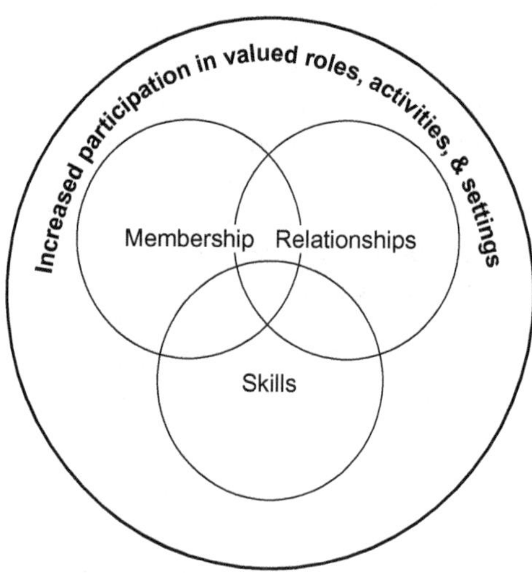

Fig. 1. The Inclusive Education Outcome Framework.

support the social growth of the student. Examples include regularly playing a game with a friend during recess, helping a student enter and exit school each day, receiving help from another student clean up a mess before beginning class work, or resolving a dispute on the playground. The following three case illustrations provide a richer, more contextualized scenario where the students navigate relationships in their own unique ways.

The third domain, *membership*, refers to the phenomological sense of belonging to a social group such as a classroom, a teacher/peer led work group, or a friendship group. Although membership is difficult to observe directly, it is possible to note the extent in which a student is treated through the accommodations other group members make to help the student be included. Furthermore, a student can be a member of a group of individuals within a classroom, community, or social network. Some examples include being part of a multiple-friend group, being included in community activities, belonging to a friend "clique," or membership within a club or community activity. In the three cases below, each student achieved membership that was unique to their individualized context.

The following experiences illustrate three students with moderate or severe disabilities in culturally diverse inclusive settings. These examples focus on the critical functions that social relationships play in providing opportunities to learn new skills, to achieve a sense of membership or "belonging" to valued social groups, and as a means of supporting participation in valued roles, activities, and settings.

THREE CASE ILLUSTRATIONS

Mateo

Mateo was born without a disability. When he was almost a year old, he contracted spinal meningitis. The brain damage resulted in early paralysis and severe seizures. In his 3rd grade, his intense health and behavior challenges resulted in his placement within a self-contained special education classroom. Mateo displayed strong social initiation skills, and his expressive vocabulary was growing rapidly during that year. However, while in this self-contained classroom, he displayed problematic behaviors in the form of aggressive tantrums, loud disruptions, and mimicking other students with special needs. When Mateo was in 6th grade, his parents and teachers agreed that he would benefit greatly if moved to a classroom with typically developing peers.

Mateo's Day in School

Each morning, Mateo's friend and neighbor Andreas, meets him at his home and walks with him to school. Growing up as neighbors, Mateo and Andreas have spent many hours outside of school playing and hanging around the neighborhood. Naturally, when Mateo's teacher asked Andreas to be a peer mentor to assist Mateo when he needed help with certain parts of his school day, he enthusiastically agreed. Mateo and Andreas line up outside of their school in the morning waiting for their teacher to meet them. When all the students are quietly lined up, their teacher walks with them to their classroom. In the classroom, Andreas and Mateo put their bags and books away and sit together at their desks in the front of the classroom.

The first subject of the day is Math. When Math starts, Mateo goes to the back of the room and works with a teacher assistant (TA) on a counting activity. The assignment has been modified to suit Mateo's current level of academic performance and Mateo works through the activity with the TA's help. When he finishes, the teacher reminds the class that the next subject they will study is grammar. The TA repeats to Mateo what the teacher has announced to the class. Mateo walks to his desk and takes out his grammar textbook.

"Mateo, you forgot to push in your chair," a peer tells him. Mateo sticks his tongue out at him, but pushes in his chair anyway.

When grammar time begins, Mateo sits with the TA again at the back of the room. He lets the teacher know that he is feeling tired and does not want to copy the words down from the chalkboard. After the activity, Mateo's teacher asks Mateo to collect all the grammar books. Mateo complains that he is still too tired. Another student, Pablo volunteers to take on that role and is rewarded by the teacher.

At the end of the day, Mateo meets Andreas and she walks him to his home. They walk with a group of other boys from their school. Occasionally, Mateo likes to run in front of them leading the boys in which direction they should go. He enjoys walking them to their homes and continuing on his way with Andreas.

Relationships

This vignette exemplifies the various ways in which Mateo participates in valued roles, activities, and settings in his class and school. Whether it's walking to the school every morning, helping his classmates walk home, or being reminded to take out his book, the relationships that Mateo has with his peers span the variety of social contexts in which he participates, and form the *medium* through which he receives assistance in carrying out various tasks. The quality and extent of his relationships are directly related to the opportunities he has to learn new skills.

Membership

Mateo takes part in group activities, follows the same schedule as his peers, and has defined roles just like his peers. His peers expect him to participate in these activities in the same way they are expected to – which reflects their sense that "he is one of us." Even though there are some occasions where Mateo is unable to follow-through with his role, another student is eager to help Mateo fulfill his duty and is rewarded for that behavior.

Skills

Within both of these contexts, opportunities for skill development are apparent throughout Mateo's school day. For activities that Mateo demonstrates the highest level of need, he is given increased assistance for the duration of time necessary. While this assistance is necessary, it is offered in the context of the relationships Mateo has and his membership within the group.

Joon-Young

Joon-Young is a quiet 6th grade boy of average size, who generally chooses to observe, rather than actively participate in the activities around him. He will respond to both adults and peers at school but rarely initiates conversation. He tends to have a rather unkempt appearance and casts his eyes downward as he walks along or sits in class. When given the opportunity to interact, such as at lunch or recess, Joon-Young will most often choose to eat or play alone. The initiations which he does attempt with peers tend to be awkward and socially inappropriate. His challenging behavior includes running around the room, crawling under the table, and grabbing things. Joon-Young was diagnosed with autism when he was two years old. At the age of three, he began a self-contained special education program, which continued until 5th grade. By this time, he was spelling words and sentences using facilitated communication with his older sister. The level of communication and the experience of being integrated into a typical classroom setting at the middle school seemed to open a new world for Joon-Young. He began the school year with a full-time facilitator participating in the regular 6th grade curriculum. The changes that had taken place for him in the span of three to four months were immense. For the following three years, a collection of narrative observation records were gathered and interviews were conducted to track Joon-Young's progress as he participated in an inclusive classroom.

Joon-Young's Day in School

As part of her math lesson, Ms. Kim asks her class of 6th grade students to work together in small groups to solve a word problem. She divides her class into groups of three and intentionally groups Joon-Young with Hyun-Jae. Knowing that they have worked well together in the past, Joon-Young, Hyun-Jae, and Yoon-Kyung get started on the word problem that is written on the board. Hyun-Jae starts by reading the problem out loud for Joon-Young and Yoon-Kyung to hear. Joon-Young whispers to Hyun-Jae and laughs. Hyun-Jae laughs, then quiets down quickly. Hyun-Jae then tells Joon-Young to pay attention to the teacher as she's giving further instruction. Joon-Young quietly watches the teacher for a few minutes, then turns to whisper to Yoon-Kyung. Yoon-Kyung laughs. Hyun-Jae intentionally bumps Joon-Young's elbow and tells Joon-Young to stop whispering again and pay attention. Joon-Young bumps back Hyun-Jae's elbow, smiles, and looks toward the teacher again. After the teacher finishes her instructions, the group continues to work on the math problem. When their group is called on to report on their work, Hyun-Jae tells Joon-Young: "Just watch me and do what I do."

Relationships

For Joon-Young, the social interactions with his typically developing peers have been his greatest support. Working in small groups with students such as Hyun-Jae and Yoon-Kyung has allowed Joon-Young to receive varied support in his academic work. Hyun-Jae and Yoon-Kyung both provided accommodations to include Joon-Young in the activity, and gave feedback about appropriate social behavior as needed. Joon-Young also developed several lasting friendships outside of class. He was a "helper" for a younger student with disabilities in the same school.

Membership

Joon-Young was perceived as an important member of his class and an important contributor to his small group activity. His group made accommodations so that he could participate and contribute to their group work in a meaningful way. Because he often worked in small groups with assigned roles, Joon-Young's contribution was critical to the group work.

Skills

At the end of the year, Joon-Young showed growth and improvement in all skill outcome areas. Ms. Kim commented on how he exhibited more appropriate social skills with peers and that he was making verbal requests with adults more frequently. Joon-Young showed academic improvement in both math and reading. In terms of functional skills, Joon-Young became more responsible at home and at school. Joon-Young's mother commented on how his communication skills had improved greatly at home.

Nisa

Nisa is a nine-year-old with Down syndrome. She is a shy, hesitant student who has difficulties making transitions and often appears to be uncomfortable in her surroundings. Academically, Nisa functions close to grade level in areas of reading and writing. She has some difficulty with abstract concepts in math but is able to participate in the general class math curriculum with adaptations. Although she is verbal, she has some speech difficulties. On first impression, one would expect Nisa to have clumsy and delayed gross motor skills. However, she is quite agile and able to imitate fairly sophisticated dance steps and movements. Her years of participation in community dance lessons have no doubt contributed to her skills in this area. When Nisa was in 1st grade, she was placed in an inclusive setting. In this placement, her growth, development, and participation over the course of four years related to her outcomes in areas of membership, relationships, and skill acquisition were observed.

Nisa's Day at School

"Nisa, will you eat lunch with me and Sunny today?" Maya asks. Nisa nods enthusiastically, and the three girls skip in line to the school cafeteria. Nisa and her two typically developing peers from class sit together in the cafeteria during lunch. At one point during the conversation, all the students discuss how many years they have been in class together with certain people. Sunny exclaims, "I've been in class with Nisa for two years." Nisa smiles, and Sunny continues "And next year it will be three years, at least I hope you'll still be here next year Nisa!" Maya chimes in, "Yeah, Nisa. I hope so too. Because you have lots of people here that like you and care about you!"

Relationships
Nisa had a system of buddies that helped her daily when she first arrived in the classroom, recess, lunch, and some academic periods throughout the day. Two typically developing girls, Sunny and Maya, felt particularly connected to Nisa and took on a nurturing role to help her. While many of these peer supports were initially encouraged by Nisa's teacher, Nisa's peers soon took responsibility and initiated interactions with Nisa.

Membership
Nisa was considered a key member of her class and her school. Nisa was often included in small groups with her peers where her participation was supported by her peers. Nisa enjoyed participating in activities outside of school, in particular, the traditional dance classes offered at the local community center. Nisa took great pride in participating in the traditional dance performance with her classmates at the annual holiday celebration.

Skills
Nisa's skill development continued to grow throughout the year. Over the course of the year, Nisa learned to participate in a variety of large group activities. She learned how to make her way through the routine and schedule of the school day. Her most significant growth has been in social communication. She learned how to interact more appropriately with her peers, how to share, and how to wait for her turn patiently. Nisa also initiated more social interactions with her typically developing peers, asking her classmates to play together at recess and to sit together during class.

RELATIONSHIPS AND LEARNING

These vignettes about Mateo, Joon-Young, and Nisa demonstrate how critical social participation in inclusive classrooms is in each of the students' lives as related to their learning. Their opportunities to interact with their typically developing peers are one of the strongest motivations to participate in classroom activities. Teachers for these students comment on how other students understand their attempts toward communication, make accommodations to enable their participation in activities, and give them constructive feedback and prompts about their behavior.

In the following section, the authors present a variety of curriculum goals related to participation in inclusive settings, as well as intervention strategies for addressing them. In suggesting these, the authors propose an intentional move from the traditional curriculum focus of specific skill acquisition toward a more holistic view of student learning and development in which valued outcomes are defined by increased student participation in roles, activities, and settings.

Strategies for Intervention

Meyer, Park, Grenot-Scheyer, Schwartz, and Harry (1998) developed a set of guidelines for intervening in the social lives of students with disabilities. They suggest that interventions should be:

1. Doable in context. Interventions must be based on an understanding of the "average" classroom and what are practical and reasonable expectations.
2. Feasible with available resources. A careful analysis of long-term available resources should precede the implementation of an intervention.
3. Sustainable over time. Time for sharing ideas and expertise is essential for sustaining the life and quality of an intervention.
4. Constituent-owned and operated. Interventions created, facilitated, and supported by the individuals carrying them out are more likely to be implemented and sustained over time.
5. Culturally inclusive. Interventions must be consistent with and respectful of the values, behaviors, and beliefs of the ones implementing and receiving them.
6. Intuitively appealing. Does the intervention make good, common sense? Is it appealing to the recipients and the ones carrying it out?

One approach to developing intervention strategies that reflect many of these guidelines is to identify practices that teachers, specialists, and others have found successful within inclusive classrooms (Peck, Gallucci, & Staub, 2002; Salisbury, Gallucci, Palombaro, & Peck, 1995). In our experience as educators and researchers within inclusive classrooms in the United States, we have had the opportunity to observe and record a variety of classroom practices associated with positive outcomes for students with and without disabilities. Although these practices have not been subject to rigorous experimental analysis, they are perhaps considered as "best practice" for classroom teachers and special educators that others may find of value in developing their interventions for their respective classroom contexts. Although, these suggestions for classroom practice are organized according to specific themes within our conceptual framework, many of these practices are likely to have a simultaneous effect on all three of the outcome domains (social relationships, membership, and skills).

Recognizing and Supporting Membership

Outcomes related to the domain termed "membership" refer to the sense of belonging which students with disabilities experience in a variety of formal and informal group contexts in inclusive environments. An important consideration in planning supports for students with disabilities in this domain is that the perception of adults regarding who is and who is not a member of the group may not always be consistent with the perceptions held by students. In this context, teacher should listen carefully to what students have to say about their social experiences in the classroom and school (Grenot-Scheyer, Staub, Peck, & Schwartz, 1998; Locke, Ishijima, Kasari, & London, 2010).

The following are five contexts in which teachers, parents, and students viewed membership as an important outcome for students with disabilities.

Small Group Membership (Teacher Developed)

Perhaps the most critical strategy for supporting membership of students with disabilities within the small group is the quality of the group work itself. There is a great amount of research literature supporting the design and implementation of successful group work amongst students from diverse backgrounds and abilities (Cohen & Lotan, 2014; Putnam, 1998). An important aspect of cooperative learning methods within small group contexts is the provision for each student to make a substantial contribution to the group without having to make the same contribution. In order for some students with severe disabilities to participate as members within small groups, teachers may need to make accommodations in the activities.

Small-Group Membership (Peer-Developed)

This outcome theme refers to formal and informal groups organized by students themselves, such as teams for soccer at recess or groups of students playing a game during their free time in the classroom. Teachers can support membership in these groups by creating unstructured situations for play and exploration. Teachers can also plan ahead for facilitating classroom discussions about how classmates with disabilities can be included in student-directed activities.

Class Membership

This theme refers to the student's belonging to the class as a social group. Examples of class membership can include students with disabilities having special roles in special classroom events such as assemblies or class celebrations. Strategies for supporting class membership center on developing an overall sense of community that prevails through the classroom. Classroom meetings are one way in which a stronger sense of community can be achieved (Nelsen, Lott, & Glenn, 2000). Classroom meetings can be conducted in a variety of ways but have the common goal of creating opportunities for students to have a voice in decisions about how the class is conducted and in setting norms and expectations for behavior in the classroom community.

School Membership

Membership outcomes at the school level can be observed by the student's participation in school-wide activities, the accommodations made by adults and other students to support such participation, by the display of symbols of membership (such as school logos, clothing, and other artifacts), and by their presence in special settings such as school-wide meetings and events. Opportunities for students to participate in school events that reflect and contribute to a sense of school memberships are often present in schools. In many schools though, the importance of these opportunities is not readily recognized for students with severe disabilities. Teachers, administrators, and parents who appreciate the value of students' experience of belonging at school can include students with disabilities in active roles at school, such as taking turns making the school-wide announcements of the loud speaker or taking tickets at a school soccer game. In addition, membership can be promoted by planning necessary supports and accommodations to ensure that students with disabilities can participate in school-wide celebrations such as graduation.

Friendship Groups/Cliques

Membership within a friendship group/clique refers to a student belonging to a group of mutual friends whether or not there is a close relationship with any individual within the group. As any parent knows, a student's membership in a friendship clique is one of the most valued experiences in a student's life. If it doesn't occur naturally, it is one of the most difficult outcomes to create. While it may be difficult for teachers to "program" membership in friendship cliques for their students with severe disabilities, there are things that can be done to facilitate the creation of groups from which these cliques may spring. For example, teachers can create a regular meeting time for peers to discuss issues of inclusion which may result in continued development of supports for classmates with disabilities.

Recognizing and Supporting a Range of Relationships

Social relationships between students with severe disabilities and their typically developing peers can take a wide variety of forms. We identify four major types of peer relationships in the lives of students: (1) play/companionship, (2) helpee, (3) helper, and (4) conflictual. Each of these relationships offers somewhat different opportunities for development. In the following section, we present examples of each type of relationship and describe strategies to support students' learning in each.

Play/Companion Relationships

These relationships revolve around the mutual enjoyment of an activity or interaction. We believe these kinds of relationships are extremely important for students as contexts for the development of social and communication skills and as pathways for achieving membership in larger social groups. Educators cannot force students' friendships. What they can do is build connections that may foster friendships between and among their students. Teachers can implement practices that encourage student participation, provide opportunities for free-time activities that encourage playful interactions, and model caring, respectful, attitudes toward the students. The following are some strategies supporting play/companion relationships:

- *Time and opportunity*. Students with moderate and severe disabilities and their typically developing peers need frequent, consistent, and varied opportunities to interact with each other. Students with disabilities who spend the majority of their school day in inclusive classrooms need to be engaged in activities that encourage frequent peer interaction and general social skills development. Positive social relationships are more likely to develop when students are given multiple opportunities to work together in a variety of small and large groups, talk with each other about the work in which they are engaged, and assist one another with classroom activities (Salisbury et al., 1995; Salisbury & Palombaro, 1998). For example, the richness of Joon-Young's relationships with his peers during his 6th grade year was directly related to his teacher's design of a classroom environment with these characteristics. In contrast, classrooms that are dominated by teacher talk, individual seat work, and activities in which helping one another is viewed negatively (and sometimes viewed as "cheating") are less suited for peer interactions of any kind.

- *Classroom climate.* The significance of the general emotional tone or climate of a classroom on students' feelings and performance is well documented (Janney & Snell, 1996, 1997) While many benefits for students with and without disabilities derive from the existence of a warm and caring classroom environment (Hedeen, Ayres, & Tate, 2001), the emergence of play/companion relationships between students with severe disabilities and their typically developing classmates is likely to be particularly affected. In an environment in which students feel themselves particularly vulnerable and subject to judgment, rejection, and exclusion, they are unlikely to take social risks inherent in affiliating themselves with peers who are obviously different in ways that are devalued in our culture. In order to make the classroom a place where typically developing students could develop positive personal relationships with their most vulnerable peers, it must be made a safe place for all kinds of differences to be acknowledged and accepted. The establishment of such a climate may not be an easy task in schools and communities in which some students experience judgment and exclusion related to race, social class, gender, or ethnicity. Hence, the task of cultivating safe and supportive classroom climates for students with disabilities is inextricably linked with making these contexts safe and supportive for all students (Meyer et al., 1998).
- *Cooperative group structures.* Scholars have noted that classrooms using cooperative goal structures may help generate friendships and foster the development of a variety of social and communicative skills that are important for all students (Bryant, 1998; Putnam, 1993; Sapon-Shevin, 1992). However, merely setting up cooperative group activities does not in itself ensure that positive interactions, relationships, an academic outcomes will occur (Ohtake, 2003). The success of such arrangements is dependent on thoughtful planning, guidance, and support from the teacher (Cohen & Lotan, 2014). In cooperative activities that include students with severe disabilities, considerable creativity is required to ensure

their meaningful participation. While teachers must be careful to not delegate too much responsibility to their typically developing students for creating accommodations for students with disabilities. Peers can often be a valuable source of creative ideas (Salisbury et al., 1995).

- *Classroom structures: physical considerations.* The physical arrangement of a classroom may impact student interactions and the development of social relationships. Flexibility of seating arrangements, amount of space available to carry out activities, and placement of the teacher's desk are all factors that influence interactions in the classroom setting (Epstein & Karweit, 1983).
- *Teachers as models.* Studies suggest that students are more likely to acquire positive attitudes and behaviors when they experience warm and affectionate relationships with their teachers (Grenot-Scheyer, Fisher, & Staub, 2001; Lipsky & Gartner, 1998). We believe that nondisabled students are extremely sensitive to the ways in which the classroom teacher and other adults respond to students with disabilities. The extent to which they see acceptance and caring modeled by the teacher impacts their own interpretation of being "different" in the classroom not only for their peer with disabilities but also for themselves.

"Helpee" Relationships

This type of relationship refers to contexts in which students with disabilities receive assistance from peers. It often develops organically in the context of social settings in which students need special support for participation. There is a large body of literature on typically developing peers providing support to students with disabilities. Increases in social skills and improvements in academic skill development for students with severe disabilities at the elementary and secondary levels have all been associated with peer support programs.

Relationships in which students with severe disabilities receive help from peers are perhaps the most frequent and naturally occurring. However, there is a tremendous difference between classrooms in which these relationships are intentionally supported by adults and those in which students are left to themselves to figure out when and how to help. Also, there are several limitations of these types of relationships, especially when they become the predominant mode of relationship. Following are some strategies for structuring and supporting helpee relationships:

- *Classwide helping procedures.* Teachers can support all students to have a voice in how the classroom is conducted, addressing issues of providing "help" to each other in ways that do not take over the activity. Teachers can also discuss with their students the kinds of help peers with disabilities may require. If these discussions take place with the context of all students helping each other, more naturalized systems of support may develop.

- *Peer tutoring programs.* Teachers can set up structured systems, such as peer tutoring or peer buddy programs. An important component of these programs can include frank and open discussions at the beginning of the school year that gives students opportunities to learn about differences among people. During discussions, students can express fears or misconceptions they may have regarding disability. Also, peer tutoring programs can include "helping" opportunities with friendly opportunities for interaction. For example, student helpers and students with disabilities could go on outings in the community or play games together during recess.

Helper Relationships

This theme refers to relationships and interactions in which the student with disabilities provides support or assistance to another child. This type of relationship is relatively unusual for students with disabilities but serves as an important function in educating others about the many ways in which individuals with disabilities can make meaningful contributions to the welfare of others.

Teachers and other adults must plan opportunities for students with disabilities to help others. These opportunities may be focused on helping individuals, or they may be group focused, such as having a student regularly pass out materials to their classmates. With support from teachers, many older students with severe disabilities may be able to develop meaningful helper relationships with younger students. In schools with preschool programs or childcare programs for younger students, they may be many useful contexts in which students with disabilities can develop relationships win which they are the "helper." Often, the possibility and value of such relationships fail to be recognized by adults.

Conflictual Relationships

Students with severe disabilities, like other students, have occasional conflict with peers. Conflictual relationships, although unpleasant, provide important learning opportunities. Teacher can help in problem-solving and teach conflict resolution skills in hopes that students will learn from the conflicts with their peers. In some cases, students may learn to independently use structured strategies to solve problems with each other. In other cases, group discussion and collective brainstorming during class meetings may be used to address problems with individuals, small groups, or the entire classroom community (Nelsen et al., 2000).

Recognizing and Supporting Skill and Knowledge

This domain is where most of the effort of traditional special education has focused. When special educators discuss specially designed instruction, they mostly identify discrete, objective, and measurable behaviors. It is important that special educators do not lose focus on discrete skills. One purpose of the outcome framework is to help educators consider how and when the skills being taught are being used. By considering how skills facilitate group membership and individual relationships (and how these relationships create a context for development of new skills), teachers can better identify target skills that will yield meaningful outcomes for students.

There are a number of effective strategies for teaching discrete social skills to students with severe disabilities. Brown and his colleagues (Brown, Odom, & Conroy, 2001) present a model for social skills interventions that include interventions that range in intensity and focus. The model begins with interventions that address all the students in a classroom that are less intensive and increase in intensity to interventions that are developed for a specific child. The less-intensive interventions, such as environmental design and affective interventions to influence attitudes, help establish the classroom climate and set the stage for social interaction. These interventions are directed to all the students in the classroom. The next level of intervention targets students who may be at risk for social problems and increases the intensity of the intervention. This level of intervention includes strategies such as incidental teaching of social skills and group instruction. These interventions require more planning and intervention on the part of the teacher and include fewer students directly. Finally, the most intensive interventions are developed in response to the needs of individual students and are presented to single students or small groups of students. All levels of interventions as proposed by Brown and colleagues can help facilitate the skills that result in improved peer relationships.

What about Nondisabled Students?

While research related to social relationships between students with severe disabilities and their nondisabled peers has focused almost exclusively on the impact on the students with disabilities (Haring, 1991; Meyer et al., 1998; Strully & Strully, 1985), the cultural construction of disability as a deficiency (McDermott, 1993) has obscured the contributions that individuals with disabilities may have in the lives of nondisabled peers and to larger society (Wolfensberger, 2004). The positive value that many nondisabled students possess with their severely disabled peers benefits themselves, their parents, and their teachers in a multitude of ways. These include:

1. Increased understanding of how other people feel
2. Increased acceptance of differences in appearance and behavior
3. Increased sense of self-worth in contributing to the lives of others
4. Increase sense of commitment to personal principles of social justice.

In addition, evidence shows that academic progress of nondisabled students is not harmed by the inclusion of students with severe disabilities in regular classes (Peck, Staub, Gallucci, & Schwartz, 2004; Sharpe, York, & Knight, 1994). Perhaps the most mutually beneficial outcomes of these relationships include (a) warm and caring relationships, (b) increase in social cognitions and self-concept, and (c) the development of personal principles and an increased sense of belonging (Staub, 1998; Wolfberg, 2009)

CONCLUSION

This chapter highlights the importance of social participation in inclusive settings in the lives of students. Three illustrative cases of culturally and linguistically diverse students in varying international contexts are provided in the hopes that readers can elicit connections to their own relevant contexts. By emphasizing the importance of a more holistic approach toward understanding the outcomes of inclusive education, the authors are not making the argument against the use of "pull-out" models of intervention. Rather, a re-orientation toward viewing increased access and participation in socially valued roles, activities, and settings as the ultimate goal of inclusion, and of education in general is proposed. In this context, the pull-out and self-contained models of instruction utilized widely in special education should be used only to the extent that they contribute clearly and directly to these larger goals. The Inclusive Education Outcome Framework and corresponding strategies provide ideas and tools for educators in this important capacity.

KEY TERMS

Inclusion – The assurance that all students, including those from traditionally excluded groups, have *access* to a variety of opportunities to learn in formal school environments. Furthermore, the authors argue that increased *access* and *participation in socially valued roles, activities, and settings* are both the most fundamental goals of the inclusive education process and also the primary means in which these goals are achieved.

Membership – The phenomenological sense of belonging to a social group such as a classroom, a teacher/peer led work group, or a friendship group.

Relationships – The wide variety of personal relationships that the students have with one another.

Skills – The traditional focus of special education outcome assessment. For students with significant developmental disabilities, this can include *functional skills* like learning to tie shoes or balancing a checkbook, *social skills* like having a conversation or asking for help from a peer, or *academic skills* like math and reading.

Sociocultural learning theory – A theory of learning which situates the learning process within cultural and historical contexts.

REFERENCES

Artiles, A. J., Kozleski, E. B., & Waitoller, F. R. (2011). *Inclusive education: Examining equity on five continents*. Cambridge, MA: Harvard Education Press.

Brown, W. H., Odom, S. L., & Conroy, M. A. (2001). An intervention hierarchy for promoting preschool children's peer interactions in natural environment. *Topics in Early Childhood Special Education, 21*, 162–175.

Bryant, B. K. (1998). Children's coping at school: The relevance of failure and cooperative learning for enduring peer and academic success. In L. H. Meyer, H. S. Park, M. Grenot-Scheyer, I. S. Schwartz, & B. Harry (Eds.), *Making friends: The influences of culture and development* (pp. 353–368). Baltimore, MD: Paul H. Brookes.

Cohen, E. G., & Lotan, R. A. (2014). *Designing groupwork: Strategies for the heterogeneous classroom* (3rd ed.). New York, NY: Teachers College Press.

Epstein, J. L., & Karweit, N. (1983). *Friends in school: Patterns of selection and influence in secondary schools*. New York, NY: Academic Press.

Grenot-Scheyer, M., Fisher, M., & Staub, D. (2001). *At the end of the day: Lessons learned in inclusive education*. Baltimore, MD: Paul H. Brookes.

Grenot-Scheyer, M., Staub, D., Peck, C. A., & Schwartz, I. S. (1998). Reciprocity and friendships: Listening to the voices of children and youth with and without disabilities. In L. H. Meyer, H. S. Park, M. Grenot-Scheyer, I. S. Schwartz, & B. Harry (Eds.). *Making friends: The influences of culture and development* (pp. 149–168). Baltimore, MD: Paul H. Brookes.

Haring, T. G. (1991). Social relationships. In L. Meyer, C. Peck, & L. Brown (Eds.), *Critical issues in the lives of people with severe handicaps* (pp. 195–217). Baltimore, MD: Paul H. Brookes.

Hedeen, D., Ayres, B., & Tate, A. (2001). Charlotte's story: Getting better, happy day, problems again! In M. Grenot-Scheyer, M. Fisher, & D. Staub (Eds.), *At the end of the day: Lessons learned in inclusive education*. Baltimore, MD: Paul H. Brookes.

Janney, R., & Snell, M. (1996). How teachers use peer interactions to include students with moderate and severe disabilities in elementary general education classes. *Journal of the Association for Persons with Severe Handicaps, 21*, 72–80.

Janney, R. E., & Snell, M. E. (1997). How teachers include students with moderate and severe disabilities in elementary classes: The means and meaning of inclusion. *Journal of the Association for Persons with Severe Handicaps, 22*, 159–169.

Lave, J., & Wenger, E. (1991). *Situated learning: Legitimate peripheral participation*. Cambridge: Cambridge University Press.

Lipsky, D., & Gartner, A. (1998). Taking inclusion into the future. *Educational Leadership, 56*(2), 78–81.

Locke, J., Ishijima, E. H., Kasari, C., & London, N. (2010). Loneliness, friendship quality and the social networks of adolescents with high functioning autism in an inclusive school setting. *Journal of Research in Special Educational Needs, 10*(2), 74–81.

McDermott, R. (1993). The acquisition of a child by a learning disability. In S. Chaiklin & J. Lave (Eds.), *Understanding practice: Perspectives on activity and context*. New York, NY: Cambridge University Press.

Meyer, L. H., Park, H. S., Grenot-Scheyer, M., Schwartz, I. S., & Harry, B. (1998). Participatory research approaches for the study of the social relationships of children and youth. In L. H. Meyer, H. S. Park, M. Grenot-Scheyer, I. S. Schwartz, & B. Harry (Eds.), *Making friends: The influences of culture and development* (pp. 3–30). Baltimore, MD: Paul H. Brookes.

Nelsen, J., Lott, L., & Glenn, H. S. (2000). *Positive discipline in the classroom: Developing mutual respect, cooperation, and responsibility in your classroom*. Roseville, CA: Prima Publishing.

Ohtake, Y. (2003). Increasing class membership of students with severe disabilities through contribution to classmates' learning. *Research and Practice for Persons with Severe Disabilities, 28*, 228–231.

Peck, C. A., Gallucci, C., & Staub, D. (2002). Children with severe disabilities in regular classroom: Risk and opportunity for creating inclusive communities. In G. Furman (Ed.), *Schools as community: From promise to practice* (pp. 217–231). Albany, NY: State University of New York Press.

Peck, C. A., Staub, D., Gallucci, C., & Schwartz, I. (2004). Parent perception of the impacts of inclusion on their nondisabled child. *Research and Practice for Persons with Severe Disabilities, 29*(2), 135–143.

Putnam, J. (Ed.). (1993). *Cooperative learning and strategies for inclusion*. Baltimore, MD: Paul H. Brookes.

Putnam, J. W. (1998). The process of cooperative learning. *Cooperative Learning and Strategies for Inclusion*, 17–47.

Rogoff, B. (2003). *The cultural nature of human development*. New York, NY: Oxford University Press.

Salisbury, C., & Palombaro, M. M. (1998). Friends and acquaintances: Evolving relationships in an inclusive elementary school. In L. H. Meyer, H. S. Park, M. Grenot-Scheyer, I. S. Schwartz, & B. Harry (Eds.), *Making friends: The influences of culture and development* (pp. 81–104). Baltimore, MD: Paul H. Brookes.

Salisbury, C. L., Gallucci, C. L., Palombaro, M. M., & Peck, C. (1995). Strategies that promote social relations among elementary students with and without severe disabilities in inclusive schools. *Exceptional Children, 62*, 125–137.

Sapon-Sheven, M. (1992). Student support through cooperative learning. In W. Stainback & S. Stainback (Eds.), *Support networks for inclusive schooling* (pp. 65–80). Baltimore, MD: Paul H. Brookes.

Sharpe, M. N., York, J. L., & Knight, J. (1994). Effects of inclusion on the academic performance of classmates without disabilities. *Remedial and Special Education, 15*, 281–287.

Staub, D. (1998). *Delicate threads: Friendships between children with and without special needs in inclusive settings*. Bethesda, MD: Woodbine House.

Staub, D., Peck, C. A., Gallucci, C., & Schwartz, I. (2000). Peer relationships. In M. Snell & F. Brown (Eds.), *Instruction of students with severe disabilities* (pp. 381–408). New York, NY: Merrill.

Strully, J., & Strully, C. (1985). Friendship and our children. *Journal of the Association for Persons with Severe Handicaps, 10*, 224–227.

UNICEF. (2013). *State of the world's children 2013*. New York, NY: UNICEF, 2013.

Vygotsky, L. S. (1980). *Mind in society: The development of higher psychological processes*. Cambridge, MA: Harvard University Press.

Wolfberg, P. J. (2009). *Play and imagination in children with autism*. AAPC Publishing.

Wolfensberger, W. (2004). Social role valorization. *Special Educational Needs and Inclusive Education: Systems and contexts, 1*(6), 42.

BEST PRACTICES IN TEACHER TRAINING AND PROFESSIONAL DEVELOPMENT FOR INCLUDING LEARNERS WITH LOW-INCIDENCE DISABILITIES

Meaghan M. McCollow, Jordan Shurr and Andrea D. Jasper

ABSTRACT

A shift from a medical model to a social model of including learners with disabilities has occurred over the past 25 years (Stella, Forlin, & Lan, 2007). This shift has impacted both preservice teacher preparation and in-service teacher professional development. This chapter utilizes a conceptual framework built on the work of Forlin and colleagues (Forlin, Loreman, Sharma, & Earle, 2009; Sharma, Forlin, Loreman, & Earle, 2006; Stella et al., 2007) to guide teacher preparation and professional development. This conceptual framework provides a model for (1) addressing attitudes and perceptions*; (2) increasing* knowledge *of disability policies, laws, and evidence-based practices for providing instruction in inclusive settings; (3) and increasing* experiences *with individuals with*

Including Learners with Low-Incidence Disabilities
International Perspectives on Inclusive Education, Volume 5, 37–62

ISSN: 1479-3636/doi:10.1108/S1479-363620140000005002

disabilities, including experiences within inclusive settings. In addition, the framework incorporates aspects of the context within which inclusion is to occur. Implications include recommendations for teacher training and professional development to improve inclusive education for learners with LID.

Keywords: Preservice teacher training; in-service professional development; inclusion; essential elements for inclusive schooling

INTRODUCTION

A shift from a medical model of providing services to learners with disabilities to a social model of including learners with disabilities has occurred over the past 25 years (Stella, Forlin, & Lan, 2007). This shift has impacted both preservice teacher training and in-service teacher professional development. This chapter utilizes a conceptual framework built on the work by Forlin and colleagues (Forlin, Loreman, Sharma, & Earle, 2009; Sharma, Forlin, Loreman, & Earle, 2006; Stella et al., 2007) to guide teacher preparation and professional development. This conceptual framework (Fig. 1) provides a model for (1) addressing *attitudes and perceptions* toward individuals with disabilities; (2) increasing *knowledge* of disability policies, laws, and evidence-based practices for providing instruction in inclusive settings; (3) and increasing *experiences* with individuals with disabilities, including experiences within inclusive settings. In addition, the framework incorporates aspects of the *context* within which inclusion is to be implemented. Throughout this chapter, the authors use this framework to describe ways in which preservice teacher candidates and in-service teachers can be supported in their implementation of inclusion in a variety of settings. The chapter focuses on best practices in teacher training for preservice teacher candidates as they prepare for providing education in inclusive settings as well as professional development for in-service teachers from a global perspective. This chapter is structured around these key questions:

1. What are the current issues and challenges in inclusive education for learners with low-incidence disabilities?
2. What are best practices for inclusive education in preservice teacher training?
3. What are best practices for inclusive education for in-service professional development and the essential elements for inclusive schooling?

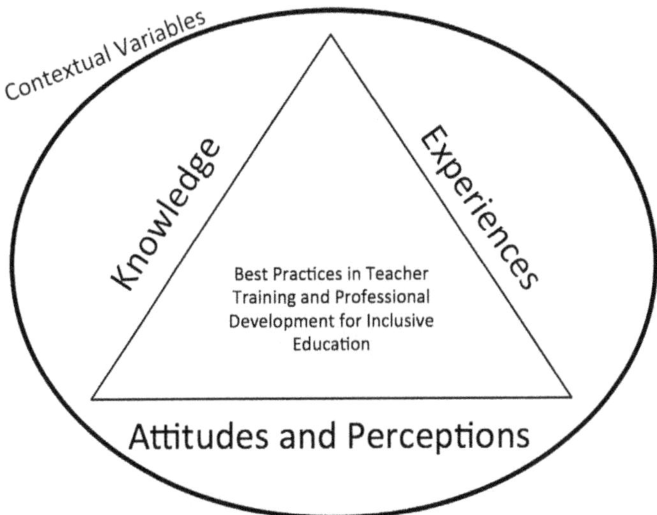

Fig. 1. Conceptual Framework for Teacher Training and Professional Development in Inclusive Education.

This chapter begins with a brief background on inclusion, focusing on the impact of moving from a medical model of providing services to learners with low-incidence disabilities (LID) to that of a social model of including learners with LID. Next, the authors describe a conceptual framework for best practices in teacher training and professional development for inclusive education. Followed by a discussion on best practices for preservice teacher candidates and in-service teachers, giving an illustration on how the conceptual framework can be utilized to ensure well-rounded preservice and in-service educators prepared for inclusive teaching. The chapter ends with future directions in inclusive education for learners with LID.

BACKGROUND

At the core of inclusion is the idea of social justice that represents the belief that all learners, regardless of disability, should be afforded the opportunity for equal access to education (Sharma et al., 2006). Social justice calls not for every learner to be treated the same but for a responsive learning environment that recognizes the different needs of all learners. Social justice seeks to place responsibility on the education system to change and adapt to meet the needs of all learners, rather than expecting learners to adapt and change to fit the educational system (Lawerence-Brown & Sapon-Shevin, 2014). Within a cultural and international framework, social justice has not only become an issue of equal access but also of creating a society in which individuals with disabilities are enabled to participate in typical daily life, including participating in educational systems (Polat, 2011). But, what do we mean by "inclusion?" Many definitions have been used to express the practice of inclusion. These definitions include "educating children and youth with disabilities in general education classrooms with their nondisabled peers" (Blecker & Boakes, 2010; Peters, 2007, p. 99) and "the right of all learners to a quality education that meets basic learning needs and enriches lives" (Kim & Linderberg, 2012, p. 97) to defining inclusion as "a process toward school systems that welcomes all learners despite their background, disability, or other personal characteristics" (Malinen, Savolainen, & Xu, 2012, p. 526). For the purposes of this chapter, we chose to define inclusion as educating and integrating children and youth with disabilities in classrooms with their peers without disabilities, with full access to content and context, including access to general educators, peers, activities, and curriculum.

Inclusion Shift

At its earliest conception, special education was intended to provide special curriculum to a special population in a special setting (Wehmeyer, 2013; Zigmond, Kloo, & Volonino, 2009). The shift toward more inclusive practices at the inception of P.L. 94-142 (the predecessor to the Individuals with Disabilities Education Act in the United States) was intended for all learners, with the exception of learners with the most severe disabilities, to receive their education in the general education setting, with pullout supports (i.e., taking a student out of a classroom to provide services) only when needed and with the special educator providing guidance to the general education teacher (Zigmond et al., 2009). In the 1990s in the United States, inclusion became an increasing priority for learners with all needs, including those with low-incidence, or severe, disabilities (Brownell, Sindelar, Kiely, & Danielson, 2010). Progress, however, has been slow. Ryndak, Moore, Orlando, and Delano (2008) point to the need for "educators … to accept too great a paradigm shift related to instructional practice" (p. 201) as a key problem with the widespread acceptance of inclusion on a large scale. Indeed, there are certainly pockets of hope, but overall inclusive efforts across the United States are still local and fragmented. Additionally, instruction and materials available to learners with LID have been deemed overall to be of low quality (Giangreco, 2011). While there is a consensus between general and special educators on the benefits of inclusion for all learners, the methods of achieving inclusive contexts are often at odds (Blecker & Boakes, 2010). At this point in time, we, as professionals, have many resources for inclusion and understand the necessity and benefits of inclusion for all learners (Sharma & Loreman, 2013). However, more emphasis needs to be placed on how inclusive education is incorporated into preservice teacher training and in-service teacher professional development.

Access to General Education

In addition to the conversation on inclusion and what it means for learners with LID, *access* to the general education curriculum for learners with LID is also a central component of the inclusive education discourse. What is access to the general education curriculum and what does that access look like? Definitions of access differ between general educators and special educators (Dymond, Renzaglia, Gilson, & Slagor, 2007). For instance, many general educators tend to see access as learners with disabilities being exposed to the same content in the general education classroom supported by special education-related staff. Consequently, this definition focuses on location, with content being the same for both learners with and without disabilities. In contrast, many special educators have described access as access to adapted content that is meaningful to and ultimately functional for learners' daily and future life, which may or may not occur in the general education classroom (Dymond et al., 2007). While definitions of access differ between general and special educators, both agree that access is important for learners with disabilities (Dymond et al., 2007). However, there is a need for a shared understanding of the term *access to the general education curriculum* for learners with LID, otherwise, as is currently the case, the definition of access is left up to the learner's individualized education program (IEP) team (Dymond et al., 2007; Jackson, Ryndak, & Wehmeyer, 2008). Indeed, placement decisions for learners with LID, has been described by Norwich (2008) as "one of the most challenging decisions in the field" (p. 288).

Physical access to the general education classroom, while important, is not enough. Access goes beyond location to include access to curriculum (Brownell et al., 2010). Access to the general curriculum consists of physical access, involvement in the curriculum within the typical context, as well as meaningful progress within the general education curriculum (Ryndak et al., 2008). In fact, with the proper supports, access to the general curriculum is possible for learners with LID (Agran, Cavin, Wehmeyer, & Palmer, 2006). Additionally, research evidence on engagement, "indicates [that] learners with extensive support needs are more engaged when in general education contexts than in self-contained settings" (Ryndak et al., 2008, p. 201). While general education access is a critical component for inclusive education it does not necessarily exclude access to functional living curricula (Dymond et al., 2007) nor does it exclude access to the continuum of services, which are intended to meet specific support needs of individual students (Brownell et al., 2010).

In order to provide successful access to the general education curriculum for learners with disabilities, special educators need to know the curricular content and how to best present it, know characteristics of disability and related assessments and instructional strategies, and understand how to successfully integrate appropriate academic and behavioral support technologies (Brownell et al., 2010). In addition, general educators need to not only welcome learners with LID into their classrooms but to also provide access in the same way, through content, context, and high expectations (Cook, 2001).

Conceptual Framework

There are four key elements that can be used to conceptualize both the current issues and the best practices for teacher training and professional development, including *attitudes and perceptions*, *knowledge*, *experiences*, and *context*. These elements have been combined into a framework for identifying best practices for teacher training and professional development. This framework draws upon the four assumptions from the Salamanca Statement that describes an inclusive education system as one that "provides high expectations and standards, quality academic curriculum and instruction that are flexible and relevant, an accessible environment, and teachers who are well prepared to address the educational needs of all students" (Peters, 2007, p. 99). Fig. 1 provides a visual illustration of the conceptual framework utilized in this chapter. Each element of the framework is discussed below.

Attitudes and Perceptions

Research literature investigating educators' perspectives on inclusion have found that, overall, the more severe the disability, the less apt an educator is to perceive inclusion as appropriate and/or positive (Avramidis & Norwich, 2002). More specifically, research has indicated that both preservice teachers and in-service teachers hold beliefs and attitudes toward inclusion that depend on disability type. For example, an international group of preservice teachers described learners with social disabilities (i.e., internalizing behaviors such as depression) as more in need of inclusion than learners with behavior challenges (i.e., externalizing behaviors such as aggression) (Loreman, Forlin, & Sharma, 2007). In addition, the same group of preservice teachers were divided on whether learners with physical disabilities should be included or not (Loreman et al., 2007). In some cases, attitudes and perceptions toward including learners with disabilities hinge on the subject matter or course. Content areas with higher perceived levels of academic rigor (e.g., math, science), were perceived as less appropriate contexts for inclusion than school subjects with less perceived academic rigor (e.g., art, humanities) (Ellins & Porter, 2005). While negative attitudes and perceptions do exist toward including learners with LID, many educators have positive beliefs about inclusion. Consequently, educator attitudes and perceptions toward including learners with LID is a critical element in implementing inclusive education (Stella et al., 2007). Persistence of negative attitudes on behalf of educators negates the possibility of successful inclusion, regardless of supports, training, and resources available (Baglieri & Shapiro, 2012).

Knowledge

In addition to focusing on creating more positive attitudes and perceptions toward including learners with LID, a focus on increasing knowledge and skills related to policies and evidence-based practices for inclusive teaching must be considered. Inclusive teaching is often in contrast to traditional instruction and approaches to education (Kim & Linderberg, 2012). Learners with LID most often require additional supports and considerations in instructional planning that are unfamiliar to general education teachers (Cook, 2001; De Bortoli, Balandin, Foreman, Arthur-Kelly, & Mathisen, 2012). Similarly, special education teachers often have limited knowledge and skills in collaborative teaming for sustaining successful inclusionary placements (Downing, Eichinger, & Williams, 1997).

An additional component to the influence of teacher knowledge regarding inclusive education can be found in the research on teacher self-efficacy (i.e., the confidence in one's abilities). Research has demonstrated that high levels of teacher self-efficacy are correlated with positive attitudes (Ahsan, Sharma, & Deppeler, 2012), indicating higher levels of knowledge and skills have an impact on attitudes and perceptions toward including learners with LID. Both general educators and special educators must be equipped with instructional strategies and knowledge on including learners with disabilities in the classroom culture and in assessments (Brown, Welsh, Hill, & Cipko, 2008; Little & Evans, 2012). Addressing gaps in knowledge and skills may serve to address feelings of being ill-equipped and unprepared to teach in inclusive settings (Lambe & Bones, 2006).

Experiences

There is a potential for any educator, but especially beginning educators, to become daunted with the idea of inclusion on top of their substantial demands of learning the profession as well as a lack of specific support in the area (Forlin, Douglas, & Hattie, 1996). Negative attitudes toward inclusion as well as feelings of unpreparedness can often be formed by a lack of sufficient and successful experiences in inclusive education (Hay, Smit, & Paulsen, 2006; Loreman et al., 2007). Teacher training should include practical exposure and experiences as well as training in skills related to inclusive education (Rodrìguez, 2012). Experiential and field-based learning opportunities have been found to increase positive attitudes toward inclusion as well as boost an educators' own beliefs in their capacity to support inclusion in the classroom (Forlin et al., 2009). Indeed, "experience in working with children and youth with disabilities [is] associated with a more positive view about the benefits of inclusion and with fewer concerns about behavior difficulties in inclusive classrooms" (Romi & Leyser, 2006, p. 99).

Context

Currently, there is tension and confusion in education due to the top-down approach to implementing inclusive education. Using the top-down approach, policies and mandates are initiated at the "top" (i.e., administrative) levels with the expectation that these policies and mandates will be implemented at the "bottom" (i.e., classroom) levels. There is a need for emphasis on preparing teachers and schools for inclusion before mandating that inclusion occur without proper training or resources (Forlin, 2012). To be sure, forcing inclusion without proper training and resources often has the unintended consequence of creating disfavor toward inclusion due to bad experiences (Forlin, 2012).

In addition, many educators feel that they lack the resources to adequately implement inclusion, though they are, overall, in favor of inclusive education (Memisevic & Hodzic, 2011). Other educators have expressed that inclusion of learners with LID has not been sufficiently supported by resources or necessary staff and, therefore, is not always the best option as the benefits do not seem to outweigh the extraordinary challenges (De Bortoli et al., 2012).

BEST PRACTICES IN TEACHER TRAINING

Throughout the literature on preservice teacher training in inclusive education, the three key elements from the conceptual framework are repeated: *attitude and perceptions* toward learners with disabilities, *knowledge* of policies regarding and characteristics of learners with disabilities, and *experiences* working with learners with disabilities (e.g., Loreman et al., 2007; Ryndak, Alper, & Hughes, & McDonnell, 2012; Stella et al., 2007; Van Reusen, Shoho, & Barker, 2000). These elements have a significant relationship toward attitudes on inclusive education, including previous exposure and instruction, understanding of special education/inclusion-related law, and self-confidence in instructing learners with disabilities (Loreman et al., 2007). The following section has been formatted around these three essential elements of teacher training in inclusive education: attitudes and perceptions, knowledge, and experiences.

Attitudes and Perceptions

Attitude affects behavior (Van Reusen et al., 2000). When attitudes toward learners with disabilities are negative, the benefits of inclusive education cannot be realized (Baglieri & Shapiro, 2012). Stella and colleagues (2007) put it this way, "It is clear from the international literature that attitudes play an important role on teachers' capacity to engage in inclusive education practices" (p. 162). For preservice educators, research has demonstrated that even a single course on special education can affect attitudes and perceptions toward teaching learners with disabilities (Shade & Stewart, 2001). In addition, self-efficacy, or confidence in abilities, in inclusive education directly impacts attitudes toward inclusion. That is, preservice teachers who believe they will be good inclusive teachers also had a positive attitude toward inclusion. The reverse is true as well, teachers who believed they would not be good inclusive teachers did not have positive attitudes toward learners with disabilities being included in general education (Malinen et al., 2012). These findings highlight the importance of addressing attitudes toward learners with disabilities and inclusion at the teacher training level. Indeed, if attitudes toward inclusion remain negative as a preservice teacher moves into the profession, it is less likely that those negative attitudes will change (Sharma et al., 2006).

Knowledge

Closely linked to attitudes and perceptions toward learners with disabilities and inclusion is knowledge about working with learners with disabilities. Indeed, providing preservice teachers with only knowledge about specific disabilities may result in the over-generalization of disability characteristics as well as perpetuate lower expectations for learners with particular disability labels (Sharma & Loreman, 2013). While preservice teachers need to know about special education laws and policies as part of their preparation for inclusive teaching (Loreman et al., 2007), this information should be coupled with discussion on appropriate attitudes and perceptions toward and experiences with learners with disabilities. Indeed, preservice instruction should contain an emphasis on building self-efficacy of teacher candidates in collaboration, behavior management, and instructional strategies to increase their future success in inclusion (Malinen et al., 2012).

Knowledge should focus on building preservice teacher self-efficacy for both general and special education teacher candidates. Embedding special education content (e.g., assessment and instructional adaptations) into general education teacher preparation courses can improve teacher candidate confidence and abilities in including learners with disabilities in their classrooms (Browder, Karvonen, Davis, Fallin, & Courtade-Little, 2005; Brown et al., 2008).

Experiences

Research demonstrates that experiences working with learners with disabilities lead to positive views about the benefits of inclusion as well as a decrease in concerns about negative behavior in inclusive classrooms (Romi & Leyser, 2006). While one special education course in a teacher education program may result in some change in attitudes and perspectives toward inclusive education, Romi and Leyser (2006) suggest general education preparation should include field experiences in settings that have learners both with and without disabilities in order to make a significant impact in preteachers inclusion training and self-efficacy. The same can be said for special education preparation, where preservice special educators need to have field experiences that include settings with learners both with and without disabilities in order to provide experiences in supporting general educators within inclusive settings (Romi & Leyser, 2006). Field experiences for preservice special educators should include the full continuum as directed under the least restrictive environment provisions (Recchia & Puig, 2011).

In addition to specific emphasis within teacher training programs for both general and special educators, it is important to infuse collaboration between general and special education teacher candidates, providing opportunities to plan instruction and work within teams throughout teacher training programs (Leyser Zeiger, & Romi, 2011; Malinen et al., 2012). There is a need for preservice teacher candidates to experience success in inclusion while still in teacher training programs as success increases confidence, which in turn can lead to successful implementation of inclusive education once in the field (Loreman et al., 2007).

Research indicates that teacher candidates who received practical, experiential training as a substantial component of their training were more likely to obtain employment in their field and to feel prepared to teach in their area (Boe, Shin, & Cook, 2007). Indeed, the combination of learning facts through traditional instructional delivery (e.g., lecture) and practical off-site exchanges with various disability stakeholders was found to positively influence preteachers perspectives of disability as well as their understanding and perspective of inclusive education (Campbell, Gilmore, & Cuskelly, 2003). One study investigated the impact of a combination of coursework and field experiences on teacher candidates' views of including learners with Down syndrome. Initially, the teacher candidates viewed learners with Down syndrome stereotypically but following the combination of coursework and field experiences, teacher candidates' views of working with learners with Down syndrome shifted to a more accurate portrait of learners with Down syndrome (Campbell et al., 2003). In addition, teacher candidates viewed inclusion for learners with Down syndrome much more favorably than prior to instruction and field experiences (Campbell et al., 2003). This study highlights the need for knowledge coupled with experiences. Coursework alone is not sufficient to alter preservice teacher candidates' perspectives on inclusive education; instead there is a need for coursework to be coupled with intensive practice and experiential learning in inclusive education (Leyser et al., 2011).

Knowledge and experiences foster positive attitudes toward working with learners with disabilities. Leaving teacher education with negative attitudes fosters continued negative attitudes that are difficult to change. However, changing those attitudes during preservice teacher training fosters continued positive attitudes (Sharma et al., 2006).

Supporting Implementation

Implementation of best practices in teacher education for inclusion involves contextual variables at the higher education level including providing experiences and modeling collaboration and providing postgraduation support including teaching self-directed learning strategies and postgraduation programs. The following section provides specific information on each of these strategies for supporting implementation of inclusive education in teacher training.

There is a duty to teacher educators, in both general and special education, to "ensure new teachers are effectively prepared to teach within inclusive classrooms" (Forlin, 2012, p. 5). Indeed, there is a need for training institutions to adapt more quickly to the changing reality of today's classrooms (Forlin, 2012). While it can be difficult to find sufficient exemplary inclusive education models in which to place teacher candidates to experience inclusive education, teacher educators can start small by seeking out one inclusive placement to use as a model for teacher candidates and then work toward building more placements (Delano, Keefe, & Perner, 2008). While differences in practicum placements can lead to "cognitive disequilibrium as [students] attempt to reconcile what they have been taught at university with what they see in the field" (Sharma & Loreman, 2013, p. 171), these moments are opportunities for teacher educators to discuss the dissonance teacher candidates are experiencing. Rather than ignore the disequilibrium that occurs when training (i.e., coursework) clashes with experiences (i.e., practicum), teacher educators must be prepared to discuss the realities of the teaching profession with teacher candidates.

In addition to providing positive experiences in inclusive classrooms and schools and tying those experiences to coursework, teacher educators need to model professional collaboration with related fields (Delano et al., 2008; Florian, 2012; Forlin, 2012). In order to provide this collaborative model, teacher education faculty need training in skills and knowledge on inclusive education for effective incorporation into teacher training coursework in both general and special education (Brown et al., 2008; Forlin, 2012). Currently, special education preparation programs place much more of an emphasis on inclusion than their general education counterparts (Brownell, Ross, Colón, & McCallum, 2005). Due to the prevalence of response-to-intervention (RTI) in schools, it is essential for teacher training to integrate both general and special education content into teacher training as roles often overlap and rely on common knowledge of evidence-based practices and identification of academic difficulties (Brownell et al., 2010), while providing necessary skills and knowledge in a specific and targeted manner (i.e., specific special education coursework).

Special education is a very dynamic, ever changing system, leading to support the idea of self-directed professional development. Teacher training should include training on continuing and self-managing one's own professional development (Gerber, 2012). Indeed, it is not unusual for teachers of learners with LID to be the only special educator in a school building; therefore, it is essential these educators have tools for directing their own professional development (Shurr, Hirth, Jasper, McCollow, & Heroux, 2014). Establishing the expectation that educators working in inclusive contexts may need to be more self-directed in their professional learning can occur at the teacher training level by infusing these expectations into coursework and field experiences.

In addition to providing appropriate field experiences, modeling collaboration, and establishing self-directed learning as a quality of an effective educator, higher education should seek to provide support to graduates of preservice teacher training programs. Providing support to graduates of preservice programs would benefit both the newly graduated and the continuing growth and development of the university programs (Sharma & Loreman, 2013). Indeed, beliefs in teachers' own preparedness for inclusive instruction does not always indicate effective practice once in the field (Cook, 2002) though this may be overcome by offering continuous support following graduation. This, then, would solve the barrier to finding appropriate inclusive placements for preservice teacher candidates. If higher

Table 1. Components of Best Practice for Teacher Training in Including Learners with LID.

• Specific special education-related coursework including law, policy, collaboration, behavior management, instructional strategies, assessment, technology integration, as well as attitudes and perception of disability and inclusion
• Integration of special education concepts in general education coursework
• Supported field experience teaching students with and without disabilities
• Opportunities for general and special teacher education students to collaborate in planning and instruction

education teacher educators are more involved in providing support for graduates, ongoing connections to schools will be possible and schools can improve while preservice teacher candidates can experience evidence-based practices in their training programs (Fox & Williams, 1992). Fox and Williams (1992) have stated:

> Graduates from programs who embrace values that are not consonant with the school programs in which they are employed, who find themselves working in programs with teachers who are untrained, or who work within school programs that implement outdated practice are at risk of isolation and frustration. As students are being trained, teacher educators must prepare them to engage in behaviors that will help them maintain their values and skills and apply them to new situations. (p. 105)

While this is not a new idea, the need for continued education, support, and mentorship for practicing teachers is still being echoed across the decades as a much needed support (Forlin, 2012). It is essential that newly graduated teacher candidates receive the support they need to be effective educators for all learners both at the very beginning and throughout their career. See Table 1 for a summary of the components of best practices in teacher training.

BEST PRACTICES IN TEACHER PROFESSIONAL DEVELOPMENT

The expectation of in-service professional development is "changes in the day-to-day practices of teachers will reform the system" (Stowitschek, Cheney, & Schwartz, 2000, p. 152). However, we know that hoping practices learned in a one-day workshop will result in a change in practice is an inefficient model of professional development (Odom, 2009). Educators have described the need for further training, experience, and support to better include their learners with LID. This training could include activities such as mentorship, structured experiences, fieldwork, observations, specific coursework, or web-based resources (De Bortoli et al., 2012). The key, however, is in including specific elements in the professional development experiences. The essential elements described in teacher training can be further developed for teacher professional development. The following section expands upon the three essential elements from the previous section to focus on ways in which *attitude and perceptions*, *knowledge*, and *experience* can be further enhanced through teacher professional development.

Attitude

While at first apprehensive, educators have often been found to change their beliefs on the importance and feasibility of inclusion in the schools (Avramidis, & Norwich, 2002). Indeed, in regards to identifying the major issues with the inclusion of learners with disabilities, educators identified disability awareness and community attitudes as the most important (Bradshaw, 2009). While policy and law can help to remove structural barriers to inclusion, they do little to change the attitudes of key stakeholders, general educators included, who are essential to the success of inclusive education (Little & Evans, 2012). Though the previous section on teacher training emphasized the need for positive attitudes to be fostered during preservice teacher training, it is possible to shift attitudes and perceptions toward learners with disabilities once an educator is in the field (e.g., attending a webinar on people first language).

Knowledge

General educators are in need of training on working with learners with LID (West, Jones, & Stevens, 2006). General educators, in particular, are at risk for negative feelings toward inclusion, which may be related to a lack of skills and training in behavior management and instructional strategies (Cook, Cameron, & Tankersley, 2007; Lohrmann & Bambara, 2006). A positive attitude toward inclusion can be a good starting point for general educators as many of the good general education teaching strategies can be applied to learners who have disabilities, and making this clear as a starting point for general educators may result in a higher perception of ability in working with learners with disabilities (Giangreco, Carter, Doyle, & Suter, 2010). For special educators, there is a need for explicit and ongoing training in providing adaptations and collaborating for successful inclusion (Downing et al., 1997). Indeed, all educators need to continually develop as new knowledge and evidence-based practices are identified (Giangreco et al., 2010).

Experience

Incorporating hands-on experience into in-service professional development enhances the learning and subsequent implementation that occurs following an in-service professional development (Stowitschek et al., 2000). Experiences also impact attitudes toward including learners with disabilities (Romi & Leyser, 2006). Even when negative feelings are held toward including learners with disabilities, direct experience in inclusive classrooms can help to change the perspectives of general educators toward a more positive outlook on inclusion (Giangreco, Dennis, Cloninger, Edelman, & Schattman, 1993), and more experience has resulted in changes toward more positive attitudes toward including learners with disabilities (Malinen et al., 2012).

Training educators using on-the-job training and feedback on how to use inclusion strategies (e.g., instructional adaptations, assessment adaptations) has been demonstrated to increase implementation of strategies in an inclusive setting (Schepis, Reid, Ownbey, & Parsons, 2001). In addition to training prior to the implementation of an inclusion program, educators who were supported through observations and constructive feedback throughout the program reported higher self-efficacy in using inclusive practices (McDonnell, Mathot-Buckner, & Thorson, 2001).

Supporting Implementation

Implementation of inclusive education involves a wide variety of contextual variables. Supporting implementation of inclusive education involves collaboration among stakeholders and support from administrators. The following section will explore each of these factors – collaboration and support – in further detail.

Collaboration

A mutual relationship between general educators and special educators must be established (Silverman, 2007). Collaboration both in instruction as well as instructional planning should be stressed not only in teacher education programs but also in in-service training and support efforts (Malinen et al., 2012). Indeed, collaboration among educators has been rated higher than instructional and behavioral strategies as a concern for in-service teachers in regards to inclusive education (Malinen et al., 2012). Educators have also indicated a desire for "interpersonal support," someone, such as a mentor, who can help them emotionally cope with difficulties and pressures that can result in changing instructional methods within the context of inclusive education (Lohrmann & Bambara, 2006). Indeed, the entire school system must be involved and evolve to initiate and sustain inclusion (Kim & Linderberg, 2012). This being a concern for educators, it is critical that support for collaboration is provided and roles are clearly defined. Inclusive teachers, whether they be trained as general or special educators, should have the following characteristics: be a member of both their profession and surrounding community, be focused on individual needs of learners, be knowledgeable and capable in differentiated instruction for learners from diverse backgrounds, and be supported by an experienced and supportive mentor teacher for guidance (Rodrìguez, 2012).

General Educators

General educators have a critical role to play in the inclusive education process. Their role includes knowing learners' current performance and progress toward goals, providing direct instruction to each student, taking a lead role in lesson planning, helping to supervise paraprofessionals, and to continually develop their inclusive education proficiency (Giangreco et al., 2010).

Special Educators

Special educators act as more than support to general educators. There are six general roles and responsibilities within inclusive education special educators fulfill. These include general problem solving, adapting/modifying general education curriculum, demonstrating multiple formats for instruction, encouraging and supporting peer interactions between learners with and without disabilities, supervising and supporting paraprofessionals, and keeping up to date on educational advances (Giangreco et al., 2010).

Paraprofessionals

As the support provider who may spend the bulk of the day with a student, paraprofessionals also play a critical role in inclusion. The duties of paraprofessionals include supporting the planning and instruction of a student as well as supporting peer interactions (Causton-Theoharis & Malmgren, 2005; Giangreco et al., 2010). While paraprofessionals are often relied on too frequently to translate messages to and from learners with disabilities (De Bortoli et al., 2012), it has been demonstrated that paraprofessionals serving beyond their support roles may hinder, rather than support, inclusive education (Giangreco et al., 1993). Therefore, it is critical that paraprofessionals have appropriate support, training, and clarity in classroom duties (Giangreco et al., 2010) as well as in supporting interactions between learners with and without disabilities (Causton-Theoharis & Malmgren, 2005) without getting "in the way" of natural interactions to successfully support inclusive education.

Related Service Providers

Related service providers (e.g., physical therapists, occupational therapists, speech-language pathologists, nurses, orientation and mobility specialists) can support inclusive education by focusing on supporting educationally related behaviors. Roles and responsibilities of related service providers include assessment and implementation of necessary adaptive equipment, training classroom staff on relevant related service needs (e.g., stretching, positioning), family support and information, and integrating discipline knowledge to academic support needs for student (Giangreco et al., 2010).

Administrators

Administrators are key personnel in regards to creating and maintaining inclusive education. Administrator support is required for successful inclusion and involves creating opportunities for collaboration among special and general educators as well as other professionals involved in service delivery, arranging for pertinent training, and effectively managing appropriate and manageable educator workload in regards to inclusion (Giangreco et al., 2010). Research indicates a need for emphasis on effective training in inclusive education for educational leaders, to provide effective support and delivery (Forlin, 2012).

Unsurprisingly, the majority of educators are for inclusion, the "trick," however, is in how inclusion is implemented and in what ways inclusion is supported by the organization (i.e., school administration). Several factors affect attitudes, namely, supportive leadership from administration that encourages innovation and collaboration but does not threaten autonomy, has been found to be positively correlated with educator self-efficacy, which is tied to positive attitudes toward inclusion (Wehmeyer, 2006). Educators need both global school support for an inclusive school context and

Table 2. Components of Best Practice for Professional Development and In-Service Support Including Learners with LID.

- School-wide commitment to inclusion
- Administrative support for inclusion
- Ongoing teacher mentorship and support
- Guidance and constructive feedback for improvement of teacher practices in inclusion
- Experiential training and support in behavior management, instructional strategies, adaptation, and collaboration
- Opportunities for interpersonal support
- Teacher involvement in professional as well as community membership

context-specific inclusionary support for their daily classroom inclusive needs (Lohrmann & Bambara, 2006). Administrators must be prepared for the initial apprehension or anxieties that come with a newly implemented inclusion program and recognize the progression from a newly implemented program to full adoption (Fixsen, Naoom, Blase, Friedman, & Wallace, 2005). The organizational climate affects educators' self-efficacy related to inclusion (Wehmeyer, 2006) and supports, including professional development and ongoing in-class support, have the ability to increase educator buy-in for inclusion (Forlin et al., 1996; Lohrmann & Bambara, 2006). See Table 2 for a summary of components of best practices in professional development.

FUTURE DIRECTIONS

One distinct difficulty underlying discussion on inclusive education is the varying definitions of what comprises an "inclusive school" (Salisbury, 2006). For a future direction, it is clear that clarity is needed in defining what is meant by "inclusive education," including the parameters of and measures for inclusive education.

While this chapter sought to define supports that can be put in place to support implementation within the contexts of teacher training and teacher professional development, further exploration of what implementation of inclusion looks like in a variety of schools is warranted. Indeed, as the field of implementation grows, it will be useful to consider the ways in which schools might successfully implement inclusion.

Further research is also needed to focus on the multidimensional nature of access to general curriculum, "including instructional practice, preparation of special educators, alignment of IEP goals with the general education curriculum, and location" (Ryndak et al., 2008, p. 210). In addition, the importance of measuring the social validity of inclusive practices cannot be understated. Quality of life, particularly quality of life postschool, for learners with LID must be considered within the context of inclusive schooling. In order to determine the long-term effects of inclusive education for this population of learners, social validity measures must be incorporated in a much more systematic way. Early research was focused on providing evidence this population of learners was capable of learning rather than the usefulness of the tasks being learned (Ryndak et al., 2012). Future research must move beyond early research and examine the meaningfulness of inclusive education for learners with LID.

CONCLUSION AND SUMMARY

This chapter explored the shift from a medical model to a social model for including learners with disabilities, providing both a historical and international context for including learners with LID. Best practices for teacher training and teacher professional development highlighted three essential elements – attitude, knowledge, and experiences – as being critical elements upon which to base teacher training and professional development. Without addressing each of these elements, something is left out of the equation when providing inclusive education to learners with LID. While much has been learned over the decades on what comprises an inclusive education, much is still left to learn. Definitions of "inclusive schooling" are still vague, implementation of inclusive education remains inconsistent, and research has not yet made the transition to providing evidence-based practices that have been studied within the context of inclusive settings.

KEY TERMS

Access to general education – beyond physical access to access to content (e.g., curriculum) as well as context, including general educators, instruction, peers, materials, activities, and high expectations.

Best practice – practices recommended by experts combined with support from research literature.

Collaboration – working with others to accomplish a task and achieve a shared goal or goals.

Continuum of services – refers to the scope of services made available to learners with disabilities under the US Individuals with Disabilities Education Act (IDEA) (see *least restrictive environment*).

Evidence-based practice – practices informed by sound valid and rigorous research.

Implementation science – scientific study of the process in which organizations take up practices, including evidence-based practices, to incorporate those practices into routine practice.

Inclusion – educating and integrating children and youth with disabilities in classrooms with their peers without disabilities, with full access to content and context, including access to general educators, peers, activities, and curriculum.

Integration – combining into a unified system, class, or school; desegregation of classes, schools, and/or settings.

Least restrictive environment – one of the principles of the US Individuals with Disabilities Education Act (IDEA) that states learners with disabilities have the opportunity to be educated with their nondisabled peers to the fullest extent possible.

Low-incidence disability (LID) – moderate to severe disability that impacts a small portion of the school population, usually less than 1%.

Medical model – describes disability as a result from an individual's physical or mental limitations, unconnected from environment or context.

Professional development – a variety of activities, including workshops, coaching, webinars, and conferences, intended to enhance knowledge and skills of practicing educators.

Self-efficacy – one's belief in one's ability to succeed; for educators, this is the belief and confidence in one's ability to plan instruction and utilize instructional strategies.

Social model – describes disability as a consequence of environment, including social and attitudinal barriers, which prevent individuals from participating to their fullest extent.

Teacher training – methods designed to prepare future teachers with the necessary knowledge, attitudes, skills, and behavior required to perform in their profession as educators.

REFERENCES

Agran, M., Cavin, M., Wehmeyer, M., & Palmer, S. (2006). Participation of students with moderate to severe disabilities in the general curriculum: The effects of the self-determined learning model of instruction. *Research and Practice for Persons with Severe Disabilities*, *31*(3), 230–241.

Ahsan, M. T., Sharma, U., & Deppeler, J. M. (2012). Exploring pre-service teachers' perceived teaching-efficacy, attitudes and concerns about inclusive education in Bangladesh. *International Journal of whole schooling*, *8*(2), 1–20.

Avramidis, E., & Norwich, B. (2002). Teachers' attitudes towards integration/inclusion: A review of the literature. *European Journal of Special Needs Education*, *17*(2), 129–147.

Baglieri, S., & Shapiro, A. (2012). *Disability studies and the inclusive classroom: Critical practices for creating least restrictive attitudes*. New York, NY: Routledge.

Blecker, N. S., & Boakes, N. J. (2010). Creating a learning environment for all children: Are teachers able and willing? *International Journal of Inclusive Education*, *14*(5), 435–447.

Boe, E. E., Shin, S., & Cook, L. H. (2007). Does teacher preparation matter for beginning teachers in either special or general education? *The Journal of Special Education*, *41*(3), 158–170.

Bradshaw, K. (2009). Teachers' attitudes and concerns towards integrating students with special needs in regular classrooms: A United Arab Emirates perspective. *The Journal of the International Association of Special Education*, *10*(1), 49–55.

Browder, D. M., Karvonen, M., Davis, S., Fallin, K., & Courtade-Little, G. (2005). The impact of teacher training on state alternate assessment scores. *Exceptional Children*, *71*(3), 267–282.

Brown, K. S., Welsh, L. A., Hill, K. H., & Cipko, J. P. (2008). The efficacy of embedding special education instruction in teacher preparation programs in the United States. *Teaching and Teacher Education*, *24*(8), 2087–2094.

Brownell, M. T., Ross, D. D., Colón, E. P., & McCallum, C. L. (2005). Critical features of special education teacher preparation a comparison with general teacher education. *The Journal of Special Education*, *38*(4), 242–252.

Brownell, M. T., Sindelar, P. T., Kiely, M. T., & Danielson, L. C. (2010). Special education teacher quality and preparation: Exposing foundations, constructing a new model. *Exceptional Children*, *76*(3), 357–377.

Campbell, J., Gilmore, L., & Cuskelly, M. (2003). Changing student teachers' attitudes towards disability and inclusion. *Journal of Intellectual and Developmental Disability*, *28*(4), 369–379.

Causton-Theoharis, J. N., & Malmgren, K. W. (2005). Increasing peer interactions for students with severe disabilities via paraprofessional training. *Exceptional Children*, *71*(4), 431–444.

Cook, B. G. (2001). A comparison of teachers' attitudes toward their included students with mild and severe disabilities. *The Journal of Special Education, 34*(4), 203–213.

Cook, B. G. (2002). Inclusive attitudes, strengths, and weaknesses of pre-service general educators enrolled in a curriculum infusion teacher preparation program. *Teacher Education and Special Education, 25*(3), 262–277.

Cook, B. G., Cameron, D. L., & Tankersley, M. (2007). Inclusive teachers' attitudinal ratings of their students with disabilities. *The Journal of Special Education, 40*(4), 230–238.

De Bortoli, T., Balandin, S., Foreman, P., Arthur-Kelly, M., & Mathisen, B. (2012). Mainstream teachers' experiences of communicating with students with multiple and severe disabilities. *Education and Training in Autism and Developmental Disabilities, 47*(2), 236.

Delano, M. E., Keefe, L., & Perner, D. (2008). Personnel preparation: Recurring challenges and the need for action to ensure access to general education. *Research and Practice for Persons with Severe Disabilities, 33*(4), 232–240.

Downing, J. E., Eichinger, J., & Williams, L. J. (1997). Inclusive education for students with severe disabilities comparative views of principals and educators at different levels of implementation. *Remedial and Special Education, 18*(3), 133–142.

Dymond, S. K., Renzaglia, A., Gilson, C. L., & Slagor, M. T. (2007). Defining access to the general curriculum for high school students with significant cognitive disabilities. *Research and Practice for Persons with Severe Disabilities, 32*(1), 1–15.

Ellins, J., & Porter, J. (2005). Departmental differences in attitudes to special educational needs in the secondary school. *British Journal of Special Education, 32*(4), 188–195.

Fixsen, D. L., Naoom, S. F., Blase, K. A., Friedman, R. M., & Wallace, F. (2005). *Implementation research: A synthesis of the literature*. Tampa, FL: University of South Florida, Louis de la Parte Florida Mental Health Institute, The National Implementation Research Network (FMHI Publication #231).

Florian, L. (2012). Teacher education for inclusion: A research agenda for the future. In C. Forlin (Ed.), *Future directions for inclusive teacher education: An international perspective* (pp. 212–220). New York, NY: Routledge.

Forlin, C. (2012). Responding to the need for inclusive teacher education: Rhetoric or reality? In C. Forlin (Ed.), *Future directions for inclusive teacher education: An international perspective* (pp. 3–12). New York, NY: Routledge.

Forlin, C., Douglas, G., & Hattie, J. (1996). Inclusive practices: How accepting are teachers? *International Journal of Disability, Development and Education, 43*(2), 119–133.

Forlin, C., Loreman, T., Sharma, U., & Earle, C. (2009). Demographic differences in changing pre-service teachers' attitudes, sentiments and concerns about inclusive education. *International Journal of Inclusive Education, 13*(2), 195–209.

Fox, L., & Williams, D. G. (1992). Preparing teachers of students with severe disabilities. *Teacher Education and Special Education, 15*(2), 97–107.

Gerber, M. (2012). Emerging issues in teacher education for inclusion in the United States. In C. Forlin (Ed.), *Future directions for inclusive teacher education: An international perspective* (pp. 71–80). New York, NY: Routledge.

Giangreco, M. F. (2011). Educating students with severe disabilities: Foundational concepts and practices. In M. E. Snell & F. Brown (Eds.), *Instruction of students with severe disabilities* (7th ed., pp. 1–30). Upper Saddle River, NJ: Pearson.

Giangreco, M. F., Carter, E., Doyle, M. B., & Suter, J. C. (2010). Supporting students with disabilities in inclusive classrooms: Personnel and peers. In R. Rose (Ed.), *Confronting obstacles to inclusion: International responses to developing inclusive schools* (pp. 247–263). New York, NY: Routledge.

Giangreco, M. F., Dennis, R., Cloninger, C., Edelman, S., & Schattman, R. (1993). I've counted Jon: Transformational experiences of teachers educating students with disabilities. *Exceptional Children, 59*(4), 359–372.

Hay, J. F., Smit, J., & Paulsen, M. (2006). Teacher preparedness for inclusive education. *South African Journal of Education, 21*(4), 213–218.

Jackson, L. B., Ryndak, D. L., & Wehmeyer, M. L. (2008). The dynamic relationship between context, curriculum, and student learning: A case for inclusive education as a research-based practice. *Research and Practice for Persons with Severe Disabilities, 33*(4), 175–195.

Kim, G., & Linderberg, J. (2012). Inclusion for innovation: The potential for diversity in teacher education. In C. Forlin (Ed.), *Future directions for inclusive teacher education: An international perspective* (pp. 93–101). New York, NY: Routledge.

Lambe, J., & Bones, R. (2006). Student teachers' perceptions about inclusive classroom teaching in Northern Ireland prior to teaching practice experience. *European Journal of Special Needs Education, 21*(2), 167–186.

Lawerence-Brown, D., & Sapon-Shevin, M. (2014). Examining perspectives on inclusive education. In D. Lawerence-Brown & M. Sapon-Shevin (Eds.), *Condition critical: Key principles for equitable and inclusive education* (pp. 219–227). New York, NY: Teachers College Press.

Leyser, Y., Zeiger, T., & Romi, S. (2011). Changes in self-efficacy of prospective special and general education teachers: Implication for inclusive education. *International Journal of Disability, Development and Education, 58*(3), 241–255.

Little, C., & Evans, D. (2012). Conceptualizing social inclusion within teacher education. In C. Forlin (Ed.), *Future directions for inclusive teacher education: An international perspective* (pp. 141–150). New York, NY: Routledge.

Lohrmann, S., & Bambara, L. M. (2006). Elementary education teachers' beliefs about essential supports needed to successfully include students with developmental disabilities who engage in challenging behaviors. *Research and Practice for Persons with Severe Disabilities, 31*(2), 157–173.

Loreman, T., Forlin, C., & Sharma, U. (2007). An international comparison of pre-service teacher attitudes towards inclusive education. *Disability Studies Quarterly, 27*(4). Retrieved from http://dsq-sds.org/article/view/53/53

Malinen, O. P., Savolainen, H., & Xu, J. (2012). Beijing in-service teachers' self-efficacy and attitudes towards inclusive education. *Teaching and Teacher Education, 28*(4), 526–534.

McDonnell, J., Mathot-Buckner, C., & Thorson, N. (2001). Supporting the inclusion of students with moderate and severe disabilities in junior high school general education classes: The effects of classwide peer tutoring, multi-element curriculum, and accommodations. *Education & Treatment of Children, 24*(2), 141–160.

Memisevic, H., & Hodzic, S. (2011). Teachers' attitudes towards inclusion of students with intellectual disability in Bosnia and Herzegovina. *International Journal of Inclusive Education, 15*(7), 699–710.

Norwich, B. (2008). Dilemmas of difference, inclusion and disability: International perspectives on placement. *European Journal of Special Needs Education, 23*(4), 287–304.

Odom, S. L. (2009). The tie that binds evidence-based practice, implementation science, and outcomes for children. *Topics in Early Childhood Special Education, 29*(1), 53–61.

Peters, S. J. (2007). "Education for all?" A historical analysis of international inclusive education policy and individuals with disabilities. *Journal of Disability Policy Studies, 18*(2), 98–108.

Polat, F. (2011). Inclusion in education: A step towards social justice. *International Journal of Educational Development, 31*(1), 50–58.

Recchia, S. L., & Puig, V. I. (2011). Challenges and inspirations: Student teachers' experiences in early childhood special education classrooms. *Teacher Education and Special Education, 34*(2), 133–151.

Rodrìguez, H. (2012). Seven essential components for teacher preparation programs for inclusion. In C. Forlin (Ed.), *Future directions for inclusive teacher education: An international perspective* (pp. 102–113). New York, NY: Routledge.

Romi, S., & Leyser, Y. (2006). Exploring inclusion preservice training needs: A study of variables associated with attitudes and self-efficacy beliefs. *European Journal of Special Needs Education, 21*(1), 85–105.

Ryndak, D. L., Alper, S., Hughes, C., & McDonnell, J. (2012). Documenting impact of educational contexts on long-term outcomes for students with significant disabilities. *Education and Training in Autism and Developmental Disabilities, 47*(2), 127–138.

Ryndak, D. L., Moore, M. A., Orlando, A. M., & Delano, M. (2008). Access to the general curriculum: The mandate and role of context in research-based practice for students with extensive support needs. *Research and Practice for persons with Severe Disabilities, 33*(4), 199–213.

Salisbury, C. L. (2006). Principals' perspectives on inclusive elementary schools. *Research and Practice for Persons with Severe Disabilities, 31*(1), 70–82.

Schepis, M. M., Reid, D. H., Ownbey, J., & Parsons, M. B. (2001). Training support staff to embed teaching within natural routines of young children with disabilities in an inclusive preschool. *Journal of Applied Behavior Analysis, 34*(3), 313–327.

Shade, R. A., & Stewart, R. (2001). General education and special education preservice teachers' attitudes toward inclusion. *Preventing School Failure, 46*(1), 37–41.

Sharma, U., Forlin, C., Loreman, T., & Earle, C. (2006). Pre-service teachers' attitudes, concerns and sentiments about inclusive education: An international comparison of the novice pre-service teachers. *International Journal of Special Education, 21*(2), 80–93.

Sharma, U., & Loreman, T. (2013). Teacher educator perspectives on systemic barriers to inclusive education. In P. Jones (Ed.), *Bringing insider perspectives into inclusive teacher learning: Potentials and challenges for educational professionals* (pp. 168–177). New York, NY: Routledge.

Shurr, J., Hirth, M., Jasper, A. D., McCollow, M., & Heroux, J. (2014). Another tool in the belt: Self-directed learning for teachers of students with moderate and severe disabilities. *Physical Disabilities: Education and Related Services, 33*(1), 17–38.

Silverman, J. C. (2007). Epistemological beliefs and attitudes toward inclusion in pre-service teachers. *Teacher Education and Special Education, 30*(1), 42–51.

Stella, C. S. C., Forlin, C., & Lan, A. M. (2007). The influence of an inclusive education course on attitude change of preservice secondary teachers in Hong Kong. *Asia Pacific Journal of Teacher Education, 35*(2), 161–179.

Stowitschek, J. J., Cheney, D. A., & Schwartz, I. S. (2000). Instigating fundamental change through experiential inservice development. *Teacher Education and Special Education, 23*(2), 142–156.

Van Reusen, A. K., Shoho, A. R., & Barker, K. S. (2000). High school teacher attitudes toward inclusion. *The High School Journal, 84*(2), 7–20.

Wehmeyer, M. L. (2006). Beyond access: Ensuring progress in the general education curriculum. *Research and Practice for Persons with Severe Disabilities*, *31*(4), 322–326.

Wehmeyer, M. L. (Ed.). (2013). *The story of intellectual disability*. Baltimore, MD: Paul H. Brookes.

West, E., Jones, P., & Stevens, D. (2006). Teachers of students with low incidence disabilities talk about their own learning: An international insight. *Research and Practice for Persons with Severe Disabilities*, *31*(2), 186–195.

Zigmond, N., Kloo, A., & Volonino, V. (2009). What, where, and how? Special education in the climate of full inclusion. *Exceptionality*, *17*(4), 189–204.

INCLUDING LEARNERS WITH SEVERE INTELLECTUAL DISABILITIES: SYSTEM PLANNING AND SUPPORT FOR GREATER INCLUSIVE PRACTICES

Vicki Barnitt, Phyllis Jones and Daphne Thomas

ABSTRACT

This chapter explores a US state-endorsed tool for reviewing district, school, and classroom inclusive practices. The Best Practices for Inclusive Education (BPIE) assessment tool was developed through a collaborative initiative between state personnel, University faculty, and representatives from a federally funded technical assistance project, Florida Inclusion Network. The tool supports a facilitated review and subsequent action planning for greater inclusive practices that includes learners with severe intellectual disabilities. This chapter describes the BPIE process and offers examples of its application in districts across

Including Learners with Low-Incidence Disabilities
International Perspectives on Inclusive Education, Volume 5, 63–87

ISSN: 1479-3636/doi:10.1108/S1479-363620140000005003

Florida with particular reference to practices that support learners with severe intellectual disabilities.

Keywords: Best Practices for Inclusive Education; systems change; shared decision making; leadership; least restrictive environment

INTRODUCTION

The Best Practices for Inclusive Education assessment (BPIE) was developed as a comprehensive instrument and process to assess the capacity to plan, implement, support, and improve inclusive best practices at the district and school levels. Engaging in the BPIE assessment process allows district and school leaders to focus on systems that ensure students with disabilities make progress in general education contexts with the appropriate services and supports. The BPIE explicitly refers to students with disabilities across the continuum of intensity, thereby including students with low-incidence disabilities. The assessment instrument measures the degree of implementation of district- and school-wide inclusive educational practices based on current data and other supporting evidence, including outcome data for students with extensive support needs. The BPIE is designed as an improvement planning process and tool requiring districts to identify and prioritize critical areas of need to facilitate inclusive practices in schools where all students with disabilities achieve to their highest potential and enjoy a life of meaning and value (BPIE, Florida Department of Education, 2013). When implemented with fidelity, the BPIE is a powerful catalyst for systems change across the school district. This chapter describes the importance of systems change for greater inclusive practices, development of the BPIE, and offers examples of the BPIE in supporting whole school development for greater inclusive practices.

Thus, the aims of this chapter are the following:

- To examine the role of systems change in supporting the development of greater inclusive practices.
- To present and discuss the BPIE tool.
- To discuss emerging key lessons learned from the application of the BPIE tool.

SYSTEMS CHANGE AND INCLUSION

Integral to the support of more inclusive schools is the recognition that the system of the classroom, school, and district create the context for teachers' developments of teaching and learning opportunities for learners with diverse learning needs. This context can help, hinder, or maintain current practices of inclusive or noninclusive pedagogy, where pedagogy refers to the beliefs, understandings, and practices surrounding teaching and learning. It is argued that educating students with severe intellectual disabilities (SInD) cannot be approached through a single pedagogy (Silverman, Hong, & Trepanier-Street, 2010) and that the integration of individual learning profiles and curricular demands requires a holistic and comprehensive approach that mirrors the complexity of pupil needs (Ryndak, Ward, Alper, Storch, & Montgomery, 2010). This calls for teachers to engage in sophisticated pedagogical decision making, where they balance individual personal pathways in the context of general education curricular and inclusive schooling opportunities. A tall order calls for a supportive professional context where teachers are able to develop their pedagogical repertoires. Attention to the system of schooling as a whole and how this translates to changes in classroom pedagogical practices is referred to as systems or systemic change and recognized as integral to the development of greater inclusive practices (Roach & Salisbury, 2006). The development of greater inclusive school policies and practices are influenced by the implicit and explicit expectations, supports, practices, and accountability for students who learn differently. It follows that international attention has been paid to the connection between school systems development and the evolution of best practices in inclusive schools (Grimes & Sayarath, 2007; Jones, Forlin, & Gillies, 2013; Jorgensen, McSheehan, & Sonnenmeier, 2009). This effort to develop comprehensive systems around inclusive developments has received much attention in research (Ainscow, 2005; Burrello, Sailor, & Kleinhammer-Tramill, 2013; Jones, Carr, & Fauske, 2011; Losert, 2010). However, the practice of systems change can be very challenging and demands ongoing attention to the nurturing of holistic and coherent contexts for the development of professional policies and practices. In response to this, tools that support the evaluation of systems of schooling have been developed (Booth & Ainscow, 2002; Florida Department of Education, 2007; Jorgensen et al., 2009). This chapter focuses upon the Best Practices for Inclusive Education (BPIE) assessment tool (Florida Department of Education, 2007) developed to support school systems' development for more inclusive schooling. The BPIE explicitly refers to students with severe disabilities and shares this focus with the Program Quality Measurement Tool (PQMT) (Cushing, Carter, Clark, Wallis, & Kennedy, 2008). Both the BPIE and PQMT are examples of tools developed to support systems change intended to impact practice by generating "program information specific enough to be acted on by administrators and educators" (Cushing et al., 2008, p. 2). The BPIE recognizes that students with severe disabilities benefit academically from inclusive educational strategies, particularly when there are documented high levels of active student engagement (Hunt, Soto, Maier, & Doering, 2003).

HISTORY OF BPIE

The BPIE was initially published in 2007 by the Florida Department of Education/Florida Inclusion Network (FIN). FIN is a state technical assistance project funded to increase and improve inclusive practices throughout the state. Many factors led to the development of the BPIE. In 2001, special education administrators from school districts across Florida gathered at a state-sponsored event to identify common concerns, barriers, and needs related to the implementation of inclusive practices, especially for students with extensive support needs. During the two-day event, a common thread emerged from the group dialogue: The need for systemic change that would maximize existing district and school resources to support inclusive education. Underlying this need was the assumption that improving outcomes for students with and without disabilities would require the alignment and integration of actions across district divisions and resources (Telfer, 2011). Additionally, district leaders agreed that change efforts should be driven by the continuous analysis and monitoring of data to assess the impact of student outcomes associated with inclusive practices. A final recommendation of the group was to develop a common assessment tool that could be used to assess the fidelity of implementation of inclusive practices across all the state's districts and schools. Administrators believed that measuring best practice indicators would drive decision-making related to the allocation of resources and supports for inclusive educational practices, including those for students with extensive support needs. Thus, the BPIE was conceptualized and a workgroup formed to develop the instrument and process. Members of the BPIE workgroup included FIN staff, university experts and researchers, and a district-level inclusion specialist. The workgroup members conducted an extensive review of research and literature related to inclusive best practices. Members also drew upon their collective years of experience working with districts and schools across Florida and other states. The workgroup convened during an 18-month period to develop the district and school-level assessment tools. Development activities included discussion of evidence-based practices, writing, editing, and revising the BPIE content and process.

Upon completion of the district and school BPIEs, the content was further examined through expert review and feedback from national experts and authors in the field of inclusive education, district and school administrators, special and general education teachers, professional development practitioners, and family members. Finally, the Florida Department of Education provided content review and approval prior to dissemination and use of the tool across the state.

Nearly a decade later, in July 2013, Florida lawmakers enacted §1003.57(f), Florida Statutes (F.S.), which includes the following provisions for the use of the BPIE at the district and school levels:

> Once every 3 years, each school district and school shall complete a Best Practices in Inclusive Education (BPIE) assessment with a Florida Inclusion Network facilitator and include the results of the BPIE assessment and all planned short-term and long-term improvement efforts in the school district's exceptional student education policies and procedures. BPIE is an internal assessment process designed to facilitate the analysis, implementation, and improvement of inclusive educational practices at the district and school team levels. (§1003.57(f), Florida Statutes (F.S.), 2013)

Pursuant to this new legislation, the Florida Department of Education collaborated with the Florida Inclusion Network to revise the initial BPIE tool and process. This decision was based on two conditions. First, the initial BPIE, published in 2007, needed updates to reflect (a) current literature and research on inclusive best practices and (b) current language related to educational policies and instructional pedagogy (e.g., Florida Standards and a Multi-Tiered System of Support). Second, feedback received from districts completing the initial BPIE indicated the tool and processes were overly meticulous, requiring a minimum of a full day for a team to complete. It was determined that the extensive amount of time required to complete the BPIE and subsequent action plan was a barrier to districts' and schools' engagement in the assessment process.

THE BPIE

The *revised* district and school BPIE (hereafter referred to as BPIE) has been developed as a tool to assess the level of implementation of inclusive practices and develop common improvement goals. Goals are aligned with other district and school improvement efforts, with the allocation of resources focused on implementing and sustaining inclusive practices over time (Newmann, Smith, Allensworth, & Bryk, 2011). Specifically, the BPIE is designed to:

- facilitate a self-assessment for districts and schools to evaluate current status of inclusive best practices,
- initiate data-driven discussion among district and school leaders and stakeholders to identify priority needs for improvement,
- develop measurable goals and action steps to increase or improve inclusive best practices in the district and schools,
- identify, align, and organize resources to improve and expand inclusive practices in all schools,
- validate areas of strength in the implementation of best practices for inclusive education for all students with disabilities,
- Monitor and report progress toward the implementation and ongoing improvement of inclusive best practices at the district and school level, and
- analyze data from districts and schools to determine the status of inclusive practices across the state.

The assessment process was also designed for a team to complete within four hours, thereby making the process less time-intensive.

Inclusion can be defined as "a philosophy that undergirds the entire educational system" (Roach & Salisbury, 2006, p. 282). A key feature of the BPIE assessment process is to "be intentional about broadening representation at the table" (Salisbury, Strieker, Roach, & McGregor, 2001, p. 7). A vital component of the BPIE assessment process is the identification and involvement of key individuals who have knowledge and evidence of current practices related to all or some of the indicators in the instrument. Other stakeholder groups who provide significant perspectives during the self-assessment process are also represented on the BPIE assessment team, including parents and school-based general and special education personnel. Bringing the right people together to engage in the BPIE process results in implementation of inclusive practices founded on these leadership elements:

- Creation of a context for developing a shared vision
- Creation of a context for shared ownership of development
- Development of processes for shared decision-making

- Use of focused questions to bring in different voices, knowledge, and experience
- Development of consensus decision-making (Jones et al., 2013, p. 64).

The district and school BPIE instruments include 30 and 34 indicators, respectively, categorized in three domains: Leadership and Decision-making, Instruction and Student Achievement, and Communication and Collaboration. Each indicator includes three possible ratings: not yet implemented, partially implemented, and fully implemented.

The criteria for each of these ratings are as follows:

- *NY – Not yet implemented*: There is no evidence that the district or school has put in place actions to address this indicator or implement the practice.
- *P – Partially implemented*: There is some evidence that the indicator is practiced in some instances or in some schools or classrooms. The practice is not implemented consistently across the entire district or school, and further action or improvement is needed.
- *F – Fully implemented:* There is clear evidence that this indicator is consistently practiced and in place across the entire district or school.

Each indicator includes a list of specific examples or samples of evidence of the practice when in place or implemented. The examples are provided to add clarity to the language and intent of each indicator and to stimulate thinking about specific examples of practices (e.g., including students with intellectual disabilities) that reflect varying levels of implementation in each district or school. The examples are not provided as individual measures of each indicator but rather as a means to assist team members in rating the extent to which the practice is or is not in place.

It is important to note that, throughout the rating process, the facilitator maintains the groups focus on inclusive practices for *all* students, including those with low-incidence disabilities. It is not uncommon for teams to overlook inclusive practices for students with significant and/or multiple disabilities when they analyze and discuss data during the decision-making process. A critical role of the person(s) facilitating the assessment process is to ensure *all* students with disabilities are at the forefront of discussions around data and inclusive practices. During the rating process, team members refer to current, available, and specific data (e.g., district and school data on least restrictive environment) and tangible evidence (e.g., school board policies, district documents, bus schedules) to determine and support their rating for each indicator. Data sources and evidence of practice are used to guide team discussion and reach consensus on a final rating for each indicator. Following are samples of the district and school indicators, ratings, and examples.

Table 1 shows a sample District BPIE indicator and its associated examples or evidence of practice. This indicator addresses the issue of student transportation schedules and locations of service for students with disabilities. It is included in the District BPIE in response to the current and predominant practice of districts that develop separate bus schedules and drop-off locations for students with significant and low-incidence disabilities. It is not uncommon to find these students, some with serious medical conditions, to ride specially scheduled buses for longer periods of time as

Table 1. District BPIE: Leadership and Decision-Making Indicator 9.

Indicator	Examples or Evidence of Practices	Rating			Data Sources/ Supporting Evidence
		NY	P	F	
9. District policies and student transportation schedules indicate all students with disabilities (SWDs) arrive and leave schools and district facilities at the same time, in the same place and on the same daily schedule as students without disabilities, except for those SWDs who have an IEP indicating a shortened school day.	• All SWDs are provided transportation to and from school or school-related activities in the same manner as students without disabilities. • Transportation schedules for all SWDs are the same as those for students without disabilities attending the same school or district event (e.g., extracurricular activity bus, field trips). • SWDs do not spend more time on the bus getting to school than their peers without disabilities. • SWDs do not lose instructional time getting to and from school on the bus. • SWDs arrive and leave school and district facilities in the same location as students without disabilities.				

Source: Reprinted with permission from the Florida Department of Education (2013).

the bus picks up students who are bused to special school locations to receive educational services. Often, these buses arrive at school later and leave earlier than those of students without disabilities, leading to the loss of instructional time during a shortened school day. Additionally, students with mobility support needs often exit buses in a separate location from other buses and students, further isolating those students from their peers without disabilities.

Table 2 presents a sample indicator from the School BPIE assessment tool. It refers to administrative support for the use of resources (people,

Table 2. School BPIE: Leadership and Decision-Making Indicator 8.

Indicator	Examples or Evidence of Practices	Rating			Data Sources/ Supporting Evidence
		NY	P	F	
8. School administrators facilitate the use of resources, by school personnel, to implement best practices for inclusive education for all SWDs.	• School administrators obtain and allocate resources (e.g., personnel and materials) to implement effective inclusive practices. • School administrators provide and monitor the use of resources across all school teams, such as: o Supplemental materials for core subject areas related to all academic standards; o Text sets with differentiated reading levels; o Accessible instructional materials, (e.g., textbook set for homework and textbooks with alternate formats: audio/electronic, braille, large print); o Assistive technologies, supports and services; o Time for instructional planning; and • Allocation of personnel aligned with in-class support needs of students (e.g., reading and math coaches, paraprofessionals, therapists).				

Source: Reprinted with permission from the Florida Department of Education (2013).

money, and materials) to support the implementation of inclusive best practices. This indicator measures the extent to which school administrators distribute and use funds to support instructional teams as they collaborate to include and teach students with disabilities in general education classrooms and other natural contexts across the school day. This includes the allocation of resources, such as accessible instructional materials and equipment, to support students with low-incidence disabilities and extensive support needs.

Table 3 presents another sample indicator from the School BPIE assessment tool. This indicator specifically refers to the use of general education standards as the basis of all instruction for students with significant

Table 3. School BPIE: Instruction and Student Achievement Indicator 19.

Indicator	Examples or Evidence of Practice	Rating			Data Sources/ Supporting Evidence
		NY	P	F	
19. General and special education teachers use the Florida Standards as the foundation for instruction of all SWDs, including those with a significant cognitive disability.	• IEP goals and objectives for all SWDs are aligned to the general education standards. • General and special education teachers can articulate what all students need to know, understand, and be able to do in relation to the Florida Standards. • The instructional goals and learning targets of students with a significant cognitive disability are based on access points. • Teachers modify learning goals and instruction for students with a significant cognitive disability using the same, or similar, age-appropriate materials as those used by students without disabilities.				

Source: Reprinted with permission from the Florida Department of Education (2013).

cognitive disabilities. It measures the extent to which general and special education teachers develop learning goals and targets using the same standards and curriculum as those students without disabilities, with modifications as appropriate.

The final analysis of ratings, data sources, and information obtained through the BPIE leads to the development of an action plan, including measurable goals, action steps, timelines, persons responsible, and evaluation criteria. Action plan goals are identified through team discussion and prioritization of specific indicators. For example, based on the indicator ratings, the team may identify four to five high-impact indicators, that if *partially* or *fully* implemented, could also influence desired outcomes related to other indicators. For instance, it may be assumed that, when administrators allocate human and fiscal resources to support inclusive practices (Indicator 8), increased access to general education *and* student achievement will result over time.

While the action planning process is a team approach, the team meeting is scheduled for a future time to allow leaders to (a) collect additional data and (b) schedule other team members, as appropriate, per each specific indicator selected. District and school leaders are urged to embed action plan steps and goals into ***existing*** district and school action plans (e.g., the district strategic plan or school improvement plan) so that inclusive practices become a shared responsibility among district and school departments, leaders, practitioners, and stakeholders. When organizational divisions unite, inclusive practices become part of integrated improvement efforts where all departments, grade levels, and adults understand their roles and align resources to reach common goals (Telfer, 2011).

APPLICATION TO PRACTICE: HOW DISTRICTS ARE USING BPIE TO DRIVE CHANGE

During the fall of 2013, the District BPIE process was first implemented in a very large district in Florida. The fourth largest in the United States, the district serves over 390 schools across a culturally diverse and large geographic area. While the district has many resources to support schools, district special education administrators were eager to conduct the BPIE, identify priority goals, and align internal and external resources to increase inclusive practices. During the BPIE assessment process, a team of district and school-level administrators, curriculum specialists, family members, and other service providers (e.g., school-to-work adult service agencies) gathered to discuss and rate each of the 30 indicators. After the rating process, the team selected three priority indicators to focus their district improvement efforts for the coming three-year period. The priority indicators selected were as follows:

District Indicator 5: District-level administrators allocate special education units and resources to all schools and grade levels based on student need and flexible service delivery models.

District Indicator 7: District has key personnel with expertise in a multi-tiered system of support and positive behavior intervention plans that provides ongoing professional development and technical assistance to schools.

District Indicator 12: Data reflect students with disabilities receive most or all of their education and related services in age- and grade- appropriate general education classes.

The District BPIE process was facilitated by trained facilitators from FIN who provided an overview of the process and shared district data on least restrictive environment (LRE); facilitated the reading, discussion, and rating of each indicator; and guided the team's prioritization of indicators for continued action plan development. In the following weeks, the special education administrator gathered a smaller team to develop action steps based on the priority indicators selected by the district team. These goals included measurable targets and activities to (a) increase the percent of students with disabilities included in general education more than 80% of the week and (b) increase the percentage of students with disabilities graduating from high school.

Many activities occurred during the school year related to the district's goals: FIN and district special education staff collaborated to provide school-based needs assessments, including analysis of each school's LRE rates, in 57 identified "high need" schools. High need schools were identified as those with less than 72% of students with disabilities in general education more than 80% of the week. As a result of school-based assessments, data-driven professional development was developed and delivered to schools, including the creation and coordination of online professional learning modules for teachers to improve inclusive models of support, for example, co-teaching models of instruction. Through the site-based assessment process, the district also identified schools in need of more intensive supports from the district and service providers. Intensive supports included school-based instructional coaching, classroom demonstration and modeling, and ongoing progress monitoring and team problem solving to meet individual school LRE goals. The district and FIN also developed a structure for continuous communication to coordinate follow-up activities and ensure the fidelity of implementation of inclusive practices in schools.

Nine months after the introduction of the new district level BPIE; an additional 23 districts had engaged teams of district administrators and other key stakeholders in the completion of the assessment and action planning process, with assistance and support from FIN. When prioritizing specific indicators, trend data show that over 50% of those districts completing the District BPIE selected the following indicators for their action plan priority goals:

Indicator 14: District provides job-embedded professional development and technical assistance to schools to integrate individual educational plan (IEP) goals in general education standards and classes.

Indicator 15: District provides professional development and technical assistance to all school leaders on the implementation of flexible scheduling and collaborative teaching models.

Indicator 24: District provides information and resources about the use of person-first language in all communication.

Additionally, trend data revealed that over 30% of the 23 districts selected the following indicators for their action plan priority goals:

Indicator 5: District-level administrators allocate special education units and resources to all schools and grade levels based on student need and flexible service delivery models.

Indicator 11: District and schools use job interview questions to appraise knowledge and beliefs about inclusion and diversity.

Indicator 13: District and school leaders receive information and professional development about best practices for inclusive education.

Indicator 17: District provides job-embedded professional development and technical assistance to school-based personnel to implement best practices for inclusive education, including instruction and assessment, based on the Florida Standards.

Themes emerging from these data indicate a strong need for expanded professional development and technical assistance tailored to the needs of district and school staff. Specifically, districts desired support for increasing knowledge and practice in the areas of (a) administrative level support for inclusive best practices, (b) aligning student IEP goals with general education standards when planning instruction in general education classrooms, and (c) implementation of a student-centered scheduling process and the subsequent use of collaborative instructional models when serving students with and without disabilities in general education classrooms. Furthermore, districts targeting indicators 11 and 24 as priorities reflect the intention to shift attitudes and beliefs about inclusion among district staff. Subsequent improvement goals were developed by districts completing the BPIE and embedded into existing district strategic plans. A sample of goals and action steps are provided as follows:

Goal: Identify a feeder pattern of schools (elementary, middle and high school) to establish and support inclusive practices, increasing the percentage of students with disabilities (including those with intellectual disabilities) receiving instruction in the general education environment to over 72% by September 2014.

Action Steps: Provide training for each school on the use of a flexible scheduling process to

- identify and plan for individual support needs of students with disabilities in general education classrooms,
- create a master schedule for teachers and paraprofessionals providing instructional supports in general education classrooms, and
- ensure common planning time for collaborative teacher teams.

Goal: Provide all district-level administrators and staff with ongoing and current information on inclusive best practices, including methods to promote and expand inclusion of *all* students with disabilities in all district schools.

Action Steps: Schedule and provide training and follow-up to district and school administrators, faculty, and staff on inclusive best practices using the eLearning module *Building Inclusive Schools*.

- Participants will complete a reflection guide upon completion of the training, including steps to promote and expand inclusive practices in schools and the resources needed to complete those steps.

- District staff will schedule and provide training to selected schools, in collaboration with FIN staff, on inclusive best practices and collaborative models of in-class support to students with disabilities.
- District administrators will distribute a quarterly climate survey to selected schools for on-going feedback and needs assessment.

Goal: Provide targeted schools with training and ongoing technical assistance on the implementation of collaborative models of instruction (e.g., co-teaching) in inclusive classrooms.

Action Steps: Schedule and provide training and follow-up to selected teacher teams on collaborative models of instruction, including co-teaching and partial in-class supports for students with disabilities in general education classrooms.

- District staff will collaborate with FIN to provide an overview of collaborative models of instruction and support to all school administrators.
- District staff will identify, using school LRE data, those schools with the highest level of need for establishing collaborative models of instruction for students with disabilities.
- District staff will co-train with FIN staff to provide online training on collaborative service delivery models.
- District staff will collaborate with FIN to schedule and provide school-based instructional coaching and classroom demonstration or modeling for ongoing implementation and improvement of instruction.

Following the completion of the district-level BPIE and development of action plans, the district is responsible for ensuring that each school completes the school-level BPIE assessment process. Each school's indicator ratings and priority goals will be used, along with student outcome data, to drive decision-making at the district level and to ensure that schools receive the necessary services and support to meet their priority indicator goals and targets. School priority goals and action steps are included in each school's annual school improvement plan to ensure allocation of resources and services across the whole school. As districts analyze school improvement plan goals and strategies, including those related to inclusive practices, they can identify, organize, and unify a multi-tiered scope of district and state resources to meet the needs of all schools.

LESSONS LEARNED FROM THE APPLICATION OF THE BPIE

From the application of the revised BPIE there are some interesting issues emerging that require further attention, these include building support for systemic change, capacity building at the state and district levels, and challenges of implementation. Developing and applying an effective and multi-tiered system of support is critical to systems change and improvement efforts. In this context, a multi-tiered system of support (MTSS) is defined as an integrated system of providing effective levels of services and support to districts and schools, based on evidence of need (student data), to improve outcomes for *all* students with disabilities, including those with intellectual disabilities. The MTSS involves data-based decision-making to ensure the systematic use and alignment of resources to accelerate the performance of *all* students in the appropriate districts and schools (Florida's MTSS, 2012). When used appropriately, the BPIE, and other assessment tools, can inform schools, districts, and state agencies in the identification and alignment of resources and services across multiple tiers. The organization of such resources may include training, technical assistance, print or electronic resources, sharing of evidence-based practices, instructional technology, and policy development. Multiple tiers of supports are identified, delivered, and evaluated across the following three levels:

- *Tier One:* Core, universal supports that are more effective than those currently provided to meet improvement goals and targets leading to improved student results in all schools and districts.
- *Tier Two:* Effective, focused, and frequent supports, in addition to and aligned with Tier One supports, provided to meet improvement goals and targets in some districts and schools.
- *Tier Three:* Specific, more intensive supports and services, in addition to and aligned with Tier One and Two supports, provided to meet improvement goals selected districts and schools.

Within an effective systems change process, resources and supports cannot be provided in a vacuum. They must be purposeful, organized, and consist of interrelated and interdependent elements and factors that continually influence one another in order to achieve the goal of the system (Businessdictionary.com, 2014). That state, district, and school systems must build internal capacity for change and improvement is inherent in systems change. Using a MTSS as a systems change and improvement framework involves the development of infrastructures that support the implementation and sustainability of inclusive practices in all schools and for all students, including those with intellectual disabilities. In the state of Florida, state-level leaders use the MTSS framework to align all state-level resources to respond to and support the specific, data-driven needs of districts and schools. During the spring of 2013, state leaders developed state-level workgroups to develop a five-year, state strategic plan to identify needs, develop action steps, and align state resources. These resources include service providers with the requisite knowledge and experience to support coordination and implementation of key evidence-based practices across districts and schools in the following specialized areas: Positive behavior intervention and support; school-based response-to-intervention and problem-solving; services to students with emotional and behavioral disorders; kindergarten readiness; student achievement and instructional pedagogy; inclusive practices; parent and community involvement; and post-secondary school transition. The state strategic plan was developed with the goal of building capacity within districts and schools to ensure all students with disabilities, *including those with low-incidence disabilities*, graduate from high school ready for postsecondary and continuing education and/or meaningful careers. Within the 2013 state plan were action steps that included the revision of the district and school BPIE. Members of several strategic plan workgroups were involved in the development of specific indicators to ensure alignment of inclusive practices to other evidence-based practices supporting inclusive education, such as positive behavior intervention and supports, student achievement and instructional pedagogy, and post-secondary school transition.

Alignment of state, district, and school resources stemming from the BPIE is beginning to show promise for students with disabilities. Districts that have completed the BPIE are collaborating to plan and implement multi-tiered efforts to improve inclusive practices for *all* students with disabilities, not just those previously regarded as "ready for inclusion." Both general and special education administrators at the district and school levels are sharing their commitment to support inclusive practices in schools and classrooms. One district special education administrator shared his belief in the BPIE assessment process: *"By engaging even the most reticent participants, a wide variety of stakeholders were involved in a meaningful discussion pertinent to best practices in supporting students with disabilities to be included in all aspects of school and community. Subsequent feedback from community, general education, other support services, and exceptional student education representatives in attendance highlighted the power of the collaborative process for identifying and meeting student needs."* (Email correspondence, April, 2014). Equally important, the voices of families are being heard as part of the collaborative BPIE assessment team. One parent shared her perspectives on the assessment tool: *"I'm hopeful it will raise awareness and improve outcomes for students with disabilities in Florida—including my daughter—a bright and curious kindergartener who also happens to have Down syndrome. I can see what a difference these measures would make if consistently implemented in schools."* (Email correspondence, March, 2014).

As reflected in the sample action plan goals and steps above, districts are adopting and employing new ways to build capacity among district and school staff. Administrators and stakeholders alike acknowledge the importance of sustaining inclusive practices over time. They understand that people and resources may come and go, but the focus of each district and school is to ensure all students, including those with intellectual and other disabilities, graduate from high school ready for a successful, productive, and happy adult life.

While many districts and schools are moving forward to assess needs and implement change efforts, a number of factors can contribute to the lack of engagement by some districts. One factor is the lack of belief in inclusive practices by special and general education leaders. Despite recent research showing a significant relationship between access to general education contexts and student achievement (Cosier, Causton-Theoharis, & Theoharis, 2013), many leaders hesitate to move beyond traditional and segregated approaches to educating students with disabilities. Efforts to collaborate and make decisions are often stalled by individual "gate keepers" who hold a large share of decision-making power and allocate resources to support other district goals or initiatives. Often, there is a tug of war for district funds and resources to satisfy competing priorities. Sadly, for those districts without clear vision and top-down leadership, inclusion is often placed low on the district list of priorities, and worse, not placed on the list at all. At best, efforts to support inclusive practices across such districts and their schools remain superficial and tentative. Another factor contributing to unsuccessful improvement efforts is a lack of resources, including money, people, materials, and time. Many larger districts have an array of resources to support schools and are skilled at collaborating with external resources (e.g., state-level service providers and resources from local colleges and universities) to meet student needs. Other, smaller districts often lack people and funding resources to meet even the most basic of needs in schools and classrooms. While external resources may be available to assist such districts, leaders lack understanding of and vision for capacity building at the school level.

For districts and schools with a clear vision and plan for building inclusive schools, other challenges may exist that can prevent desired results. When districts engage in the BPIE or other needs assessment process, it is critical to make decisions based on current and accurate student data. Districts may need guidance and support to obtain data from local as well as state-level sources. District teams may lack resources and techniques for the analysis and use of data, leading to erroneous decisions about district, school, and student or family needs. If improvement goals are based on flawed data and decisions, then they can become a waste of precious time and resources. Goals and action steps based on accurate and appropriate student data, however, are more than ideas on a piece of paper – they must be measurable and monitored for progress throughout the year. When goals are developed without specific measures of desired student outcomes, it is impossible to monitor the fidelity of implementation of action steps. Likewise, without appropriate and measurable follow-up aligned with each action step, it is not uncommon to see efforts miss the mark or subside over time.

CONCLUSION

This chapter set out to examine the role of systems change in supporting the development of greater inclusive practices, presented and discussed the BPIE tool and discussed the emerging key lessons learned from the application of the BPIE tool. From the application of the revised BPIE, interesting issues emerged including building support for systemic change, capacity building at the state and district levels and challenges of implementation. Some interesting ways to proactively respond are as follows:

- Constantly check that school discussions actually encompass learners with LI disabilities in a meaningful and realistic way.

- Use data-based needs assessments and problem-solving processes to identify goals and respond to the needs of students with disabilities in general education classrooms.
- Create policies to align state, district, and school resources and services to students with disabilities in general education classrooms, driven by measured needs rather than diagnostic labels or categories (Sailor & Burrello, 2009).
- Build capacity of district and school staff to sustain inclusive practices through data-based decision-making and progress monitoring.

  Example: When district lacks available personnel to provide support, district leaders should identify and engage external, state-level technical assistance providers. Outside organizations and groups can provide guidance, training, and resources for schools to build the knowledge, understanding, and capacity of teachers and teacher leaders.
- Critical key support from outside the district: the identification of roles and responsibilities of external organization/staff (state or other non-profit) to take a lead role in coordinating and facilitating the BPIE process in each district.
- Involve all stakeholders in the assessment and decision-making process for change. The implementation of inclusive practices across the system begins with breaking down the barriers between general and special education to promote inclusive policies, structures, and practices.
- Maintain a clear focus on inclusive practices for students with low-incidence disabilities throughout the change process. For example, during the BPIE assessment process, leadership teams would rate specific indicators as *fully implemented.* However, when asked by the facilitator if the practice was fully in place across the district for *all students with disabilities* (including those with low-incidence disabilities), teams rarely produced evidence of such practice, thereby compelling the group to re-rate the indicator as *partially implemented or not yet implemented.* Keeping students with low-incidence disabilities at the forefront of conversations and decisions is vital to ensuring inclusive education is not only in place for a select group of students with disabilities.
- Provide examples of how to build change from the school level (if you have a district administrator who does not support inclusion). School administrators, parents, and advisory councils need to advocate at all levels (superintendent, community, media, etc.).

The BPIE is proving to be an interesting tool for schools and districts to consider to support systems development for greater inclusive policies and practices for all students, including students with low incidence disabilities. While the work of the BPIE was focused on districts in Florida, the authors believe the tool and assessment process are universal and applicable to all countries.

KEY TERMS

Access points – Academic expectations written specifically for students with significant cognitive disabilities. As part of the Florida Standards, access points reflect the essence or core intent of the standards that apply to all students in the same grade but at reduced levels of complexity.

Age appropriate – Describes materials, activities, and experiences that are useful and suitable for persons of a particular age. For example, age-appropriate books for a teenager are different than age-appropriate books for a seven-year-old, even if the teenager reads on a second-grade level.

Collaborative service delivery models (models of support): Support facilitation – Two teachers, one general and one special education Exceptional Student Education (ESE) teacher (grades K-12), plan and provide instruction in the general education classroom. The ESE teacher provides services to individual or small groups of students on an individualized basis within the general education classroom for a limited time of day or week.

Co-teaching – Two teachers, one general education and one special education (ESE) teacher, share responsibility for planning, delivering, and evaluating instruction for all students in a class/subject for the entire class period.

Flexible scheduling – A team-planning process to schedule supports for students with disabilities in inclusive, general education classrooms. Students are scheduled for services and supports in general education classrooms based on their individual needs rather than their disability label. The flexible scheduling process results in teacher master schedules that allow services to be provided where and when supports are needed.

Inclusion (as defined in s. 1003.57, Florida Statutes [F.S.]) – A student with a disability receiving education in a general education regular class setting, reflecting natural proportions and age-appropriate heterogeneous groups in core academic and elective or special areas within the school community; a student with a disability is a valued member of the classroom and school community; the teachers and administrators support universal education and have knowledge and support available to enable them to effectively teach all children; and a student is provided access to technical assistance in best practices, instructional methods, and supports tailored to the student's needs based on current research.

Individual educational plan (IEP) – A written plan that describes the individual learning needs of a student with disabilities and the ESE services, supports, aids and accommodations, and modifications that will be provided to that student.

Least restrictive environment (LRE) – The Individuals with Disabilities Education Act (IDEA) entitles all students with disabilities to a free, appropriate education in the least restrictive environment. This means that, to the maximum extent possible, children with disabilities are to be educated with children who are not disabled. Special classes, separate schooling or other ways of removing children with disabilities from the regular educational environment should only occur when the nature or severity of the disability is such that education in regular classes cannot be achieved satisfactorily with the use of supplementary aids and services.

Low-incidence (L1) disabilities – Students with a particular disability or combination of disabilities, such as blindness, low vision, deafness, hard-of-hearing, dual sensory impairment, significant cognitive disability, complex health issues, serious physical impairment, multiple disability, traumatic brain injury, and autism spectrum disorder, that generally do not exceed one percent of the school population.

Multi-tiered system of support (MTSS) – MTSS uses a data-based, problem-solving process that matches the intensity of support with student needs to most efficiently allocate resources to improve learning and behavior for all students. Effective core instruction and interventions are provided for all students, including students with disabilities, who need various levels of supports to master all academic standards. Three tiers describe the level and intensity of the instruction/interventions provided across a continuum of support: Tier One – core, universal instruction; Tier Two – supplemental intervention; and Tier Three – intensive intervention.

Positive behavior intervention and support (PBIS) – The application of evidence-based strategies and systems to increase academic performance, increase safety, decrease problem behavior, and establish positive school cultures.

Problem-solving/response to intervention or instruction (PS/RtI) – RtI is a problem-solving process that matches resources to individual student's needs. It involves understanding where the student is struggling; designing a way to help the student (an intervention); monitoring how the student responds to the intervention; and changing, decreasing, or increasing the intensity of the intervention depending on how the student responds.

Stakeholder groups – Administrators, general education teachers, special education teachers, related services personnel (speech/language therapist, occupational therapist, physical therapist), other certified personnel (e.g., guidance, academic and non-academic coaches), noninstructional personnel (e.g., paraprofessionals, front office staff, cafeteria staff), families of students with disabilities, families of students without disabilities.

Technical assistance (TA) – The provision of targeted and customized supports by a professional or teacher, with subject matter and adult learning knowledge and skills to develop or strengthen processes, knowledge application, or implementation of services by recipients.

REFERENCES

Ainscow, M. (2005). Developing inclusive education systems: What are the levers for change? *Journal of Educational Change*, *2005*(6), 109–124.

Booth, T., & Ainscow, M. (2002). *Index for inclusion: Developing learning and participation in schools*. London: Centre for Studies on Inclusive Education (CSIE).

Burrello, L. C., Sailor, W., & Kleinhammer-Tramill, J. (Eds.). (2013). *Unifying educational systems: Leadership and policy perspectives*. New York, NY: Rutledge.

Businessdictionary.com. (2014). *System*. Retrieved from http://www.businessdictionary.com/definition/system.html#ixzz34d9oyxfk. Accessed on May, 2014.

Cosier, M., Causton-Theoharis, J., & Theoharis, G. (2013). Does access matter? Time in general education and achievement for students with disabilities. *Remedial and Special Education*, *34*(6), 323–332.

Cushing, L., Carter, E., Clark, N., Wallis, N., & Kennedy, C. (2008). Evaluating inclusive educational practices for students with severe disabilities using the program quality measurement tool. *Journal of Special Education*, OnlineFirst, published on May 13, 2008. doi:10.1177/0022466907313352

Florida Department of Education. (2007). *Best practices for inclusive education (BPIE)*. Tallahassee, FL: Bureau of Exceptional Education and Student Services, Florida Inclusion Network.

Florida Department of Education. (2013). *Best practices for inclusive education (BPIE): District level*. Tallahassee, FL: Bureau of Exceptional Education and Student Services, Florida Inclusion Network.

Florida's MTSS. (2012). *A multi-tiered system of supports implementation components: Ensuring common language and understanding*. Tallahassee, FL: Florida Department of Education. Retrieved from http://www.florida-rti.org/educatorResources/MTSS_Book_ImplComp_012612.pdf. Accessed on May 2013.

Florida Statutes (F.S.). (2013). *Exceptional students instruction*. § 1003.57(f). Retrieved from http://www.leg.state.fl.us/statutes/index.cfm?mode=View%20Statutes&SubMenu=1&App_mode=Display_Statute&Search_String=1003.57&URL=1000-1099/1003/Sections/1003.57.html. Accessed on May, 2014.

Hunt, P., Soto, G., Maier, J., & Doering, K. (2003). Collaborative teaming to support students at risk and students with severe disabilities in general education classrooms. *Exceptional Children*, *69*, 315–332.

Jones, P., Carr, J. F., & Fauske, J. (Eds.). (2011). *Leading for Inclusion*. New York, NY: Teachers College Press.

Jones, P., Forlin, C., & Gillies, A. (2013). The contribution of facilitated leadership to systems development for greater inclusive practices. *International Journal of Whole Schooling*, *9*(1), 60–74.

Jorgensen, C. M., McSheehan, M., & Sonnenmeier, R. M. (2009). *Essential best practices in inclusive schools*. Durham, NH: University of New Hampshire, Institute on Disability. Retrieved from http://www.tash.org/wp-content/uploads/2011/03/Essential-Best-Practices-for-Inclusive-Schools.pdf. Accessed on June 2012.

Losert, L. (2010). *Best practices in inclusive education for children with disabilities: Applications for program design in the Europe and Eurasia region*. Washington, DC: United States Agency for International Development (USAID). Retrieved from http://transition.usaid.gov/locations/europe_eurasia/dem_gov/docs/best_practices_in_inclusive_ed_final_040110.pdf. Accessed on July 2013.

Newmann, F. M., Smith, B., Allensworth, E., & Bryk, A. S. (2011). Instructional program coherence: What it is and why it should guide school improvement policy. *Educational evaluation and policy analysis*, *23*(4), 297–321.

Roach, V., & Salisbury, C. (2006). Promoting systemic, statewide inclusion from the bottom up. *Theory into Practice*, *45*(3), 279–286.

Ryndak, D. L., Ward, T., Alper, S., Storch, J. F., & Montgomery, J. (2010). Long-term outcomes of services in inclusive and self-contained settings in a one-building school district for brothers with comparable diagnoses. *Education and Training in Developmental Disabilities*, *45*(1), 38–53.

Sailor, W., & Burrello, L. (2009). Best practices in taking inclusive education to scale. *TASH Congressional Briefing on Inclusive Education*, July 9, 2009.

Salisbury, C., Strieker, T., Roach, V., & McGregor, G. (2001). *Pathways to inclusive practices: Systems oriented, policy-linked, and research-based strategies that work*. Chicago, IL: Erikson Institute/Consortium on Inclusive School Practices.

Silverman, K., Hong, S., & Trepanier-Street, M. (2010). Collaboration of teacher education and child disability health. *Journal of Early Childhood Education, 37*, 461–468.

Telfer, D. M. (2011). *Moving your numbers: Five districts share how they used assessment and accountability to increase performance for students with disabilities as part of district-wide improvement*. Minneapolis, MN: University of Minnesota, National Center on Educational Outcomes.

FACILITATING SYSTEMS OF SUPPORT

Robin Drogan and Darlene Perner

ABSTRACT

This chapter describes the influences that are fundamental to facilitating a system of support for inclusive education for students with low-incidence disabilities. Some of the major factors are values and beliefs, rights, relationships and a sense of belonging, policy, and effective practices (Smith, 2006; Walther-Thomas, Korinek, McLaughlin, & Williams, 2000). Within each of the features, collaboration is inherent and essential. A summary of literature on each feature is provided with examples to support the importance for students with low-incidence disabilities. The effective practices of Universal Design for Learning (UDL), co-teaching, peer supports, and school-based teams are highlighted. In order to move forward, educators and administrators need to take responsibility for all children. Effective leadership models are characterized by collaborative efforts that foster a shared responsibility of the team, emphasize thoughtful planning, and identify and allocate the necessary resources and supports.

Keywords: Systems change; supports; inclusion; inclusive education; rights; effective practices

Including Learners with Low-Incidence Disabilities
International Perspectives on Inclusive Education, Volume 5, 89–110

ISSN: 1479-3636/doi:10.1108/S1479-363620140000005004

INTRODUCTION

An inclusive educational setting is a place where everyone belongs, is valued, is supported, and is accepted. Facilitating inclusive education involves a concerted effort from a team of committed members to ensure quality programming and inclusive practices are implemented and sustained. There are a number of major features that facilitate a system of support for students with low-incidence disabilities. In this chapter, some of the factors that influence the practice of inclusive education will be highlighted. The features are values and beliefs, rights, relationships and a sense of belonging, policy, effective practices, and school community and culture (Smith, 2006; Walther-Thomas, Korinek, McLaughlin, & Williams, 2000). Within each of the features, collaboration is inherent and essential.

The following questions will guide the discussion in this chapter:

1. Why is it important to understand the history and law as they relate to the facilitation of a system of supports for inclusive practices for students with low-incidence disabilities?
2. What major features are necessary to create a system that supports inclusive education for students with low-incidence disabilities?
3. How is collaboration (e.g., taking collective responsibility) an essential component of the features that facilitate a system of support for students with low-incidence disabilities in inclusive education?

Historical Background

This section will provide a historical perspective of inclusive education. It is important to consider how history facilitates change and is used to inform practice. In the era of creation of public education and prior to the Education for All Handicapped Children Act of 1975 (PL 94-142), children with low-incidence disabilities were generally denied access to educational services and were segregated to large state institutions (Stainback & Stainback, 1996). While students without disabilities were educated in public schools, there was an overwhelming view of people with disabilities as being involved with crime and being seen as less than human-based on their disability (Stainback & Stainback, 1996). This dehumanization justified the mistreatment and separate system of schooling for people with disabilities. A shift occurred with the *Brown vs. Board of Education* 1954 decision that challenged the notion of separate but equal. The Brown vs. Board of

Education case concluded that it was no longer justifiable to have students of color in separate locations even if their curriculum was considered equitable. The interpretation of this decision created an opportunity for change for people with disabilities.

Following the Brown vs. Board of Education decision years later, federal legislation (Education for All Handicapped Children Act of 1975; Education of the Handicapped Children Act Amendments of 1986; Education of the Handicapped Children Act Amendments of 1990) was enacted requiring that students with disabilities are educated with students without disabilities in integrated environments. The Education for All Handicapped Children Act of 1975 (PL 94-142) had significant implications because it was the first law to explicitly state that all children had the right to a free and appropriate education in the least restrictive environment. The reauthorization of the Individuals with Disabilities Education Act of 1997 (IDEA) and Individuals with Disabilities Education Improvement Act of 2004 (IDEIA) initiated a massive education reform.

At times, the law has proven to be challenging to interpret and implement by individual states and school districts (McLaughlin, 2010). The responsibility for inclusion of students with low-incidence disabilities has been driven by family, professionals, and self-advocacy (Wehmeyer, 2014) and the right to access general education curriculum in integrated settings (Spooner, McKissick, Hudson, & Browder, 2014). Inclusion of students with low-incidence disabilities has become more prevalent (Wehmeyer, 2006). Though at times in practice, special education is seen as a service outside of the general education classroom (Walther-Thomas et al., 2000), there is a growing body of literature and technology concerning the administrative, practical, and curricular practices to facilitate inclusive practices for students with low-incidence disabilities (Hunt, Hirose-Hatae, Doering, Karasoff, & Goetz, 2000). For example, Fisher and Frey (2001) investigated the access to core curriculum for students with low-incidence disabilities in a qualitative study of the use of content-specific accommodations and modifications in inclusive settings. Data were obtained from nine teachers and three students through direct observation and interview. The findings suggest that students need access to the core curriculum using strategies such as peer support networks, general education and special education collaboration, cooperative learning experiences, and a shared responsibility with the students themselves (Spooner et al., 2014).

The movement toward more inclusive practices for all has been met with tension and challenge because there are differences in philosophy and practice that are historically routed (Connor & Ferri, 2007;

Kavale & Forness, 2000). Though research suggests the benefits of inclusive practices for both students with disabilities and students without disabilities (Cole, 2006; Cole, Waldron, & Majd, 2004; Peck, Staub, Gallucci, & Schwartz, 2004), the debate has shown both the pros and cons of including students with disabilities in general education settings (Downing, Eichinger, & Williams, 1997; Spooner, Baker, Harris, Ahlgrim-Delzell, & Browder, 2007). Much of the controversy surrounds educating students with the most significant disabilities. First, many teachers do not feel that access to the general curriculum is a priority for students with low-incidence disabilities, and though parents may support higher standards, they do not know how to promote access (Agran, Alper, & Wehmeyer, 2002; Wakeman, Browder, Meier, & McColl, 2007). Second, quality inclusive strategies are not always used in practice (Downing & Peckham-Hardin, 2007). Third, students with low-incidence disabilities do not have regular access to general education settings or curricular opportunities (Alquraini & Gut, 2012). Fourth, educators and educational leaders have expressed the lack of training, support, and experience regarding teaching students with disabilities in general education settings (Lohrmann & Bambara, 2006; Smith, 2007). In order to move forward, educators and administrators need to take responsibility for all children (Smith, 2007). An opportunity exists at this time to emerge as a unified group with a common purpose.

FACILITATING SYSTEMS OF SUPPORT

This chapter describes the influences that are fundamental to facilitating a system of support. The influences that can support inclusive education are values and beliefs, rights, relationships and a sense of belonging, policy, and effective practices. In addition, the facilitation of systems involves creating a school community and culture that will grow and flourish, encouraging others to take risks, and promoting and opening oneself to the possibilities for change (Hourcade, 2008; Stainback & Stainback, 1996).

Influence of Values and Beliefs

Values and beliefs begin with a shared understanding of respect for each individual that is a respect for diversity, the similarities and differences between us. Everyone has differences; this is a common humanity. The differences need not be considered as a departure from what is perceived as typical but as a part of a person. The consideration and respect for individuals begins with the premise that we value each person as a human. People are not valued or devalued based on inequalities but embraced for their individual accomplishments (Tawney, 2004).

Typically, inclusion is defined as occurring for students with and without disabilities in typical settings and supports individual student needs. In addition, the characteristic of belongingness that includes equal membership, acceptance, and being valued, was added to the inclusion definition created by experts in the field (Jackson, Ryndak, & Billingsley, 2000). Jackson et al. (2000) emphasize that this characteristic is promoted by providing positive examples, clarifying values amongst the participants, implementing inclusionary practices, and fostering community in every educational setting. As educators, we need to understand the relationship between our values and actions as practical movement toward inclusive practices (Booth, 2011). Actions are linked to core values and belief. It is important to consider this link between actions and values in participation, responsibility, collaboration, freedom, rights, and equality (Booth, 2011). When our values spur actions this may be implemented in schools through links being made in the curricula, the relationships that are formed between peers and between children and adults, and within the activities in the school and community. For example, inclusive actions happen when we promote belongingness in schools by supporting students in collaborative activities, supporting staff with peer reviews and reflection, and when administrators are visible in buildings listening and supporting staff and students (Jackson et al., 2000; Perner, 2008).

An inclusive school starts with a shared value or understanding of inclusion (Perner & Porter, 2008). A shift occurs in the attitudes, philosophy, understanding, and is reinforced through the development of practices and policies that demonstrate the groups' collective vision (McMaster, 2013). In order to create a shift in values and culture toward more inclusive practices, opportunities for collaboration are essential. Collaboration entails critical and open reflection, group discussion, shared research, and collective exploration of ideas and action. Participants are encouraged to critically reflect on the values and beliefs they hold and seek interpretation through discussion and visitation of inclusive settings (McMaster, 2013). Often teams develop indicators of inclusive schools and collectively examine the culture and environment in order to identify areas for improvement. An honest examination is frequently charged by a desire to improve and a shared understanding of responsibility and vision for inclusion (McMaster, 2013).

The debate continues on whether to include or not include (Kavale & Forness, 2000; Perner & Gordon, 2008). This is not where the emphasis should be placed. It should not be a decision as to whether inclusion is the value we want to embrace; it is more about what we make of these inclusive practices (Hegarty, Pocklington, & Lucas, 2004; Tomlinson, 2004). Survey respondents, including teachers, parents, and educators, stated that they supported the values of inclusive education, though some educators expressed conflict between their beliefs and the practical day-to-day implementation. Teachers shared uncertainty with their ability to accommodate and create meaningful inclusive opportunities (Downing & Peckham-Hardin, 2007).

Influence of Rights

The outcome of inclusive education is for all individuals to contribute to and participate in the community. We need to consider rights, and how to reduce inequalities. In schools, human rights are encouraged through fostering caring and reciprocal relationships and creating communities in which everyone belongs equally and is respected.

One's rights can be conceptualized into four major goals and ideals that guide our laws and policies (Silverstein, 2000). First, individualization within equity is each person being viewed in terms of her strengths and needs. Educational programs and policies are flexible and respond to the differences in people and do not respond based solely on categories or people as a part of a group. This principle includes equality of rights. It is our responsibility to reduce exclusion, to respond to diversity in ways that value each individual, and to afford equal opportunity (Booth, 2011; Turnbull III, Turnbull, Wehmeyer, & Park, 2003). Second, is the tenant of full participation (e.g., self-determination, choice making). This means persons with disabilities are included in all activities and community engagement as those without disabilities. Adherence to full participation is demonstrated when each person has the opportunity to experience all of the conditions each day that those without disabilities can experience (McLaughlin, 2010). Third, individuals should be economically self-sufficient. An individual with low-incidence disabilities has the right to become independent and self-sustaining. Fourth, the goal of independence includes the consideration of supports, accommodations, and services necessary for independent living and participation.

Booth and Ainscow (2004) share the Index for Inclusion model that was used in the United Kingdom with three interconnected dimensions of school improvement. First, creating inclusive cultures is at the base of the triangular model. Next, producing inclusive policies and evolving inclusive practices form the sides of the triangle. Within the base of creating inclusive culture, we see the key concepts of rights that can be evidenced in multiple ways. This means valuing all students and staff equally. The reduction of exclusion and the value of benefits for all students enhances rights. When barriers are addressed and reduced, the rights of the individual are considered. Valuing the rights of students is acknowledging the rights to quality and meaningful education for all.

Influence of Relationships and Sense of Belonging

Building relationships with other individuals, with and without disabilities, is at the center of building a sustainable inclusive environment. The social experiences that children have with their peers play a significant role in promoting positive learning outcomes, contributing to social emotional competence, and enhancing quality of life (Carter, Sisco, Chung, & Stanton-Chapman, 2010). The quality and quantity of social interactions with peers may be one of the greatest influences on the person's well-being (Prinstein & Dodge, 2008).

Though there have been increases in the amount of time students with disabilities are spending in general education classrooms with their same-aged peers (US Department of Education, 2009), prolonged interactions between students with and without disabilities outside of targeted intervention efforts remain infrequent (Carter et al., 2010; Webster & Carter, 2007). Students with low-incidence disabilities often have limited interaction with others, not allowing for others to get to know them as a person or to feel comfortable in their presence. This may occur because both parties lack the social skills necessary to interact and understand others that are different from themselves. Another reason may be that many students have not had experiences with a diverse group of peers to prepare them for quality social inclusion (Richardson, Tolson, Huang, & Lee, 2009).

Some of the literature on relationships suggests that there may be interference with the peer interaction (Tews & Lupart, 2008). For example, Tews and Lupart (2008) found that opportunities for socialization were compromised at times when participants reported that the majority of their day was spent interacting with a paraprofessional rather than classmates. Similar results were reported to the extent that students who had individual support of an adult were often in separate activities which isolated them from peers and the teachers. In a study by Giangreco and Broer (2005), 15% of the 153 special education paraprofessionals interviewed reported a lack of concern about when their close proximity to students was unnecessary or may interfere with interactions between the student and others. In addition, the paraprofessionals reported that about 86% of their time was spent within three feet of the student with disabilities that they supported. The proximity of adults that may interfere with building social relationships is of concern, especially when the literature suggests that peers are more likely to be in proximity of students with disabilities when paraprofessionals were not in close proximity (Giangreco, Edelman, Broer, & Doyle, 2001).

Students' sense of belonging and success are often encouraged by their relationships with teachers. The evidence is mixed regarding the relationships between students with low-incidence disabilities and teachers. Some literature suggests that students with low-incidence disabilities have limited interactions with general education teachers. For example, students interviewed by Broer, Doyle, and Giangreco (2005) reported that teachers expressed that they did not have time which made the students feel undeserving and devalued.

It is not enough for students to be present in classrooms. Students need to have meaningful experiences that truly encompass the principles of inclusion (Connor & Ferri, 2007). In buildings and classrooms, we need to foster a community that supports students with low-incidence disabilities in being visible or having social impact, being someone that others wish to spend time with or having social preference, and belonging to a group of friends that spend time together or have social network affiliation (Boutot & Bryant, 2005). Strategies that foster positive relationships for students with low-incidence disabilities may include (a) directly teaching social skills to promote friendships including students with and without disabilities (Richardson et al., 2009), (b) sharing positive information about the student, (c) creating an environment where asking for support when necessary is valued (Lohrmann & Bambara, 2006), and (d) fostering respectful interactions and positive relationships between students with and without disabilities.

A culture of inclusive educational practice builds and cultivates relationships within the broader community. Teachers identified three features in their schools' culture of inclusion that helped them to feel that their actions were accepted and valued by the schoolwide community: (a) a common vision for inclusion, (b) a collegial and supportive atmosphere, and (c) the access to resources (e.g., support personnel, training, materials) (Lohrmann & Bambara, 2006). These features together may foster inclusive educational practices that include strong relationships. In isolation, one of these features is not enough. In a research synthesis of almost 10,000 general educators regarding the inclusion of students with disabilities (Scruggs & Mastropieri, 1996), two-thirds of the teachers supported inclusive educational practices. Of those teachers, only a small majority were actually willing to include students within their own classroom. The beliefs and values alone will not create an inclusive educational environment with strong relationships.

In order to facilitate strong social relationships, systems may need focus on adjusting both attitudes and structures. For example, Jordan, Swartz, and McGhie-Richmond (2009) investigated that relationship between beliefs and practices. Several sources of data were analyzed including teacher observation and teacher report of practice. The findings suggest that teachers who believe that they have the responsibility to instruct students with disabilities are more effective in the classroom overall with all of the students than those teachers who do not (Jordan et al., 2009). Effective teachers engage students in learning and develop teacher-student relationships that promote higher level learning for all students. This is especially important when we recognize the limited interactions between general educators and students with low-incidence disabilities (Broer et al., 2005). The facilitation of effective inclusionary practice with strong relationships for students with low-incidence disabilities depends on the development of both the beliefs of the teachers on inclusion of students and about the teachers' roles and responsibility in meeting the students' educational needs. The challenge is to provide teachers and preservice teachers with peer models to support effective inclusive practice. In addition, teacher preparation programs should incorporate organized collaborative opportunities to inquire, experiment, and work toward sustained practice (Jordan et al., 2009; Lohrmann & Bambara, 2006; Richardson et al., 2009). Students need to be provided with opportunities that foster positive interactions and positive interpersonal relationships with peers and adults (Lohrmann & Bambara, 2006).

In the inclusive school setting, relationships exist outside the classroom a student attends. Both general and special educators, school staff, administrators, and peers with and without disabilities are involved in a collaborative effort to support every person in their school. Inclusive communities are designed to surround all individuals (students and teachers alike) with support. Teachers of students with low-incidence disabilities feel a sense of belonging when they are included and valued like other teachers in their school. Children feel a sense of belonging when they are valued and included in instruction and activities with their peers without disabilities. Teachers make accommodations to facilitate inclusion for all students. They ensure opportunities are provided that allow students with low-incidence disabilities to participate in the day-to-day activities experienced by all students. Teachers model acceptance to create a sense of community within the classroom (Jordan et al., 2009) and the school. They create welcoming environments as a place where students and adults are encouraged to learn with each other through interactions. Systems of support are established to enhance belonging and friendships. Effective systems of support include (a) using cooperative grouping, (b) facilitating natural peer support networks, and (c) utilizing person-centered planning (Fisher & Frey, 2001).

Influence of Policy

The policies and procedures that are set act as a guide for programming in schools. Our history was marred with exclusion from education for individuals with disabilities. As a result of advocacy and recognition of the rights of people with disabilities, laws have been passed with the intent to ensure equal access to educational programming and services. Even with the passage of laws to protect individuals' rights, there is variation in the interpretation of the laws at the state and district levels and therefore inconsistencies in implementation.

The PL 94-142 and now, the Individuals with Disabilities Education Improvement Act 2004, intended the fundamental understanding that students have the right to an education appropriate to their unique needs and that students with disabilities are educated to the maximum extent possible with students without disabilities. Though in translation, a range of interpretations are put into practice. For example, parallel systems are commonly used. Students with low-incidence disabilities continue to be pulled out of general education at high rates to be educated without consideration of Least Restrictive Environment (LRE) as defined by law. Another interpretation of the law has focused on full membership in general education classroom or consideration to as much time as possible in the general education setting

The passage of the No Child Left Behind Act (2001) legislation brings forth standards-based reform as an initiative that continues to support the inclusion of all students in the field of special education (Thurlow, 2002). The initiative of standards-based reform is not new but historically low expectations have been held for subgroups of the general population including students with low-incidence disabilities. The inclusion of students with disabilities in the standards-based reform has provided benefit in a way that was intended for all students, through the setting of high expectations and emphasis on student learning of content standards (McDonnell, McLaughlin, & Morison, 1997).

With the reauthorization of the IDEIA (2004), an effort was made to align with NCLB. Both laws established increased accountability for the education of all students. It remains unclear how to reconcile the contention between these laws that for IDEIA, individualized assessments that demonstrate student growth in academic and functional areas and for NCLB, that educational benefits are evidence by academic proficiency in content (Cole, 2006). In fact, that growth which has been shown toward more inclusive practices may have ultimately been undermined by the passage of the No Child Left Behind Act (2001) (Cole, 2006). For example, students with disabilities may be made the scapegoat for a school not reaching annual yearly progress (AYP). The cost of providing support to students not making AYP is a concern and adds to the perception that students with disabilities are taking resources from other students (Cole, 2006). Accountability has placed greater emphasis on standardized tests. This emphasis on content area learning may in turn narrow the offerings of curricular selections that are most appealing and motivating to students with low-incidence disabilities (Cole, 2006). It may be the case that when "high stakes" test scores are being used to determine access to educational opportunities (e.g., selection of classes, promotion or non-promotion, graduation with diploma or certificate) that the decision made can have long lasting implications for the student and family. For example, program options may be limited because students are focusing on remediation in content skill areas (e.g., access to work-related programs, taking elective classes, exposure to career programs) (Cole, 2006). There is a concern that the progress in inclusive practices made over several decades could weaken resulting in increased segregated settings. The practices of educators and administrators will need to move to a more collaborative model that emphasizes the skills, dispositions, attitudes, experiences, and vision to create sustained change toward inclusive education (Smith, 2007).

Influence of Effective Practice

Effective practice includes maximizing participation, attending to diverse learning needs, and making learning meaningful and relevant for all learners (Snell & Brown, 2000). The focus of an effective educational leader is to ensure that their school focuses on powerful learning outcomes for all students (DiPaola, Tschannen-Moran, & Walther-Thomas, 2004). The alignment of IDEIA and NCLB has emphasized the accountability for all students' learning and the use of scientifically based instructional practices to meet student needs. This alignment necessitates a shift of emphasis from curriculum-focused strategies to cover more content with the large group to include student-focused strategies (Browder & Cooper-Duffy, 2003).

NCLB challenges educators to move inclusive practices forward by creating ways and utilizing evidence-based practices to ensure students with low-incidence disabilities can make progress in the general education curriculum (Browder & Cooper-Duffy, 2003). Though we continue to need research on academic outcomes for students with low-incidence disabilities, the literature to date reflects positive academic content outcomes and strategies (Browder, Spooner, Ahlgrim-Delzell, Harris, & Wakeman, 2008; Browder, Wakeman, Spooner, Ahlgrim-Delzell, & Algozzine, 2006). It is important that teachers use instructional supports that have evidence to support students with low-incidence disabilities in making progress and to continue to seek new approaches (Browder & Cooper-Duffy, 2003).

Several effective practices have been used to facilitate inclusive educational practice and are based on the principle of meeting all students' needs. First, Universal Design for Learning (UDL) is a strategy used to plan and implement instruction in a way to meet the needs of diverse student populations (Spooner et al., 2007). Three components are used to create a universal curriculum and environment for all students (i.e., engagement, expression, and representation). Multiple means for engagement refers to how all students may be able to participate in the lesson. For example, the use of cooperative grouping or manipulatives may increase engagement for students with low-incidence disabilities at the same time as other students in the class. Multiple means of expression allows students to have flexibility in showing what they know. For example, students may express knowledge by using technology, using props, or explaining orally or in written form. Multiple means of representation refers to the teachers' variation in how students may access the information presented. Forms of representation may include using digital books, providing guided notes, or adding visual supports (Browder & Spooner, 2011). UDL can reduce barriers to accessing the curriculum while considering individual student needs (Dymond et al., 2006).

Second, co-teaching is an effective inclusive practice that entails collaboration and shared responsibility for teaching by the special and the general educator. Dymond et al. (2006) incorporated the use of UDL and co-teaching in a high school science class including students with low-incidence disabilities. In this model, the curriculum was adapted and designed to meet the needs of diverse learners. The purpose of the case study was to develop a process for the universal design of a science co-taught class and to evaluate the effectiveness of the process supporting students to access the curriculum. During the redesign process, predetermined questions around five core areas (i.e., curriculum, instructional delivery/organization of learning environments, student participation, materials, and assessment) were used to guide the discussion. During implementation, the class teaching was staggered with the first session class using the UDL lessons and the second session class using the traditional lesson plans.

The findings suggest that relationships and interactions were enhanced among students with low-incidence disabilities and other students in the classroom. For example, students with low-incidence disabilities were paired with two students without disabilities and students were assigned roles to increase participation. Students with low-incidence disabilities benefited from increased opportunities for communication, collaborative learning, and for the development of friendships. The UDL redesign successfully incorporated the main concepts in the science curriculum, individualized goals, socialization, and engagement for all students including students with low-incidence disabilities. The redesign incorporated differentiation and increased choice for students to help them succeed.

Important implications were shared from the experiences of Dymond et al. (2006). First, the involvement of all stakeholders led to increased collaboration and shared responsibility. The creation of clear roles and responsibilities was essential to the process. Second, the redesigned lesson plans were important because teachers used them to communicate the UDL changes and ensure greater consistency. Third, it was important that the teachers had the supports available to plan and implement the redesign. Some of the resources that were made available included, time for planning, help with creating materials, and funds to purchase materials. Fourth, at times there were additional structures that needed to be put into place based on student need. For example, students may need support in learning how to work in groups or how to involve students with different needs than their own. With limited research in this area, further investigation of the use of UDL and co-teaching are warranted in order to better understand specific gains in content, attainment of IEP goals, increased participation and socialization.

Third, peer-focused approaches can be used as an effective tool for the promotion of inclusive practices. Peer-focused approaches utilize other students as the interventionists to support the students with low-incidence disabilities (Carter & Kennedy, 2006). There are several types of peer-focused approaches including peer mediation, peer interaction training, peer networks, peer support arrangements, and peer tutoring (Carter et al., 2010). As an example, peer support offers mediated learning opportunities in academics or socialization for students with low-incidence disabilities by one or more same-aged peer without disabilities (Cushing & Kennedy, 2004). An important component of peer support is training for the peers without disabilities to facilitate skill enhancement in a variety of areas (e.g., to reinforce academic skills, to provide frequent feedback and support, to promote communication). Carter, Cushing, Clark, and Kennedy (2005) investigated peer supports with specific attention to the influence of the number of peers used to support students with low-incidence disabilities. Results of this study suggest that with initial training and ongoing assistance for the peers, students with low-incidence disabilities demonstrated higher levels of engagement with the curriculum and social interaction with the addition of a second peer support person. The use of peers as supports for students with disabilities across grade levels and in both participation in academics and promotion of social relationships is an evidence-based practice (Carter et al., 2005; Carter et al., 2010). In addition, peer support strategies appear to be considered feasible and acceptable to practitioners and therefore, a practical approach for inclusive classrooms (Carter & Kennedy, 2006).

Collaboration is an essential component of all of the effective practices. General education and special education teachers are joining together sharing responsibility to provide appropriate accommodations and modifications for students with low-incidence disabilities. In fact, Fisher and Frey (2001) recognized a shift in roles between collaborative teachers where general education teachers developed interesting and motivating lessons and special education teachers had a wider understanding of the general education curriculum. This finding emphasizes the power that successful collaboration can have for students, programs, and communities.

Influence of School Community and Culture

Strong leadership and shared culture influence the facilitation of the systems of support for students with low-incidence disabilities. As school systems continue to move toward more inclusive practices, school leaders are highly influential in shaping school culture and are instrumental in the change process (Sharpe & Hawes, 2003).

There is a growing consensus that we need to support change so that inclusive education can be enhanced. The literature suggests several factors that emerge in schools and contribute to change including values and leaders, commitment and support, and collaboration and training (Burstein, Sears, Wilcoxen, Cabello, & Spagna, 2004). Effective leadership models are characterized by collaborative efforts that foster a shared responsibility of the team, emphasize thoughtful planning, and identify and allocate the necessary resources and supports. Productive leaders and teams create and implement unified systems as a result of team building and shared understanding. Leaders often provide the overall impetus for change. The leader sets forth the movement and builds the values with the school team for continued growth. The school team assesses where the school is in relation to inclusive education and sets a vision and plan for the school.

One of the greatest barriers to the inclusion of students with low-incidence disabilities is the lack of training and knowledge of strategies to support individuals (Fuchs, 2009-2010; Lee et al., 2006). Collaboration and training include knowledge building and knowledge sharing. One way to promote continuous learning is through the establishment of learning communities and school teams. In learning communities and school teams, teachers are encouraged to share ideas and learn from one another (DiPaola et al., 2004).

FUTURE DIRECTIONS

An increasing number of students with low-incidence disabilities are being served in inclusive settings (Carter & Kennedy, 2006; US Department of Education, National Center for Education Statistics, 2013; Wehmeyer, 2006). Several inclusive practices have been identified as effective; however, these practices need to be investigated further in order to establish a stronger evidence base. More research is needed to explain the extent to which evidence-based practices are being implemented and the factors that contribute to the greatest gains for students with low-incidence disabilities (Cushing, Carter, Clark, Wallis, & Kennedy, 2009).

Although there has been a change in practice in many schools to facilitate inclusive education, teachers continue to express that they feel ill-prepared to teach students with low-incidence disabilities (Smith, 2007). There is a continued need to provide training for general educators, special educators, and para-educators. More research is needed to investigate systematic and quality training for professionals that will assist in facilitating inclusive practices for students with low-incidence disabilities.

Facilitation of inclusive education for students with low-incidence disabilities includes a number of major factors (values and beliefs, rights, relationships and a sense of belonging, policy, effective practices, and school community and culture). Many of these features are addressed or implied in school-wide implementation models such as the Index for Inclusion model (Booth & Ainscow, 2004), and the Schoolwide Application Model (SAM) (Sailor & Roger, 2005). For example, SAM incorporates a unified approach to inclusive education. Innovative models and pilot-projects that also include all students need to be developed, implemented, and evaluated for effectiveness such as the school-wide Response To Intervention (RTI) model that incorporates the tiered-level approach for both behavioral and academic intervention (Sailor, 2008-2009). There is a need to investigate systemic models of implementation in order to better understand the relationship between and among a variety of factors that facilitate inclusive education for students with low-incidence disabilities.

CONCLUSION AND SUMMARY

There are a variety of influences that are critical to facilitating a system of support for inclusive practices. These features include values and beliefs, rights, relationships and a sense of belonging, policy, effective practices, and school community and culture. It is our charge to ensure that students with low-incidence disabilities are valued and included in general education and community settings. All students have the right to develop friendships; however, for students with low-incidence disabilities, teachers and para-educators have to provide many opportunities for students to interact with their peers and for peers to interact with students with low-incidence disabilities. This may entail specific strategies that encourage socialization and friendship development. For example, teachers may establish a peer network and use cooperative groupings to foster relationships (Lohrmann & Bambara, 2006) and ensure that adults do not impede opportunities for peer-to-peer socialization. As well, it is important for teachers to create a community within the classroom and school that is welcoming. Laws have been enacted to guide our practice. The laws are intended to ensure the rights of students with low-incidence disabilities to educational access with their peers without disabilities. In addition, legislation has encouraged the commitment to high expectations for all students. The facilitation of inclusive practices involves designing and implementing effective practices that meet the needs of all learners. Co-teaching, school-based teaming, universal design for learning and peer supports are a few examples of interventions that can facilitate inclusive education. Meaningful collaboration within schools is at the core of developing and sustaining systems of support to facilitate inclusive practices for students with low-incidence disabilities. Teachers are central to making change happen. To support teachers in facilitating change, teachers need to be provided with collaborative opportunities, to inquire, experiment, and work toward sustained inclusion of students with low-incidence disabilities (Jordan et al., 2009; Lohrmann & Bambara, 2006; Richardson et al., 2009).

KEY TERMS

Belief – A value or idea which you trust or have confidence in or that you feel is true.

Collaboration – Two or more people working together and sharing interaction in order to achieve a goal.

Co-teaching – A general education teacher and special education teacher with shared responsibility for planning, teaching, and assessment of a group of diverse student learners.

Equality – The rights of each individual are valued.

Inclusion – All students together.

Inclusive education – Participation and involvement in learning of students both with disabilities and without disabilities.

Low-incidence disability – A disability that significantly affects adaptive, communication, learning, motor, and/or social skill development or a combination thereof. Some examples of low-incidence disabilities include intellectual disabilities, multiple disabilities, autism, and significant developmental delay.

Peer support – One or more students provides support in learning academic or social skills to another student.

Policy – A course of action proposed by a person, agency, or government.

Relationships – The way that people relate and connect with each other.

School-based teaming – Pairing a group of teachers (typically four to six teachers) to allow for discussion and collaboration. The composition and structure of teams may vary greatly school to school.

Sense of belonging – The experience of personal involvement in a system so that the person feels an integral part of community.

Supports – To give assistance to.

REFERENCES

Agran, M., Alper, S., & Wehmeyer, M. (2002). Access to the general curriculum for students with significant disabilities: What it means to teachers. *Education and Training in Mental Retardation and Developmental Disabilities*, *37*, 123–133.

Alquraini, T., & Gut, D. (2012). Critical components of successful inclusion of students with severe disabilities: Literature review. *International Journal of Special Education*, *27*, 42–58.

Booth, T. (2011). The name of the rose: Inclusive values into action in teacher education. *Prospects*, *41*, 303–318.

Booth, T., & Ainscow, M. (2004). Index for inclusion. In G. Thomas & M. Vaughn (Eds.), *Inclusive education: Readings and reflections* (pp. 181–187). Berkshire: Open University Press.

Boutot, E. A., & Bryant, D. P. (2005). Social integration of students with autism in inclusive settings. *Education and Training in Developmental Disabilities*, *40*, 14–23.

Broer, S. M., Doyle, M. B., & Giangreco, M. F. (2005). Perspectives of students with intellectual disabilities about their experiences with paraprofessional support. *Exceptional Children*, *71*, 415–430.

Browder, D. M., & Cooper-Duffy, K. (2003). Evidence-based practices for students with severe disabilities and the requirement for accountability in "No Child Left Behind." *The Journal of Special Education*, *37*, 157–163.

Browder, D. M., & Spooner, F. (2011). *Teaching students with moderate and severe disabilities.* New York, NY: Guilford Press.

Browder, D. M., Spooner, F., Ahlgrim-Delzell, L., Harris, A. A., & Wakeman, S. (2008). A meta-analysis on teaching mathematics to students with significant cognitive disabilities. *Exceptional Children*, *74*, 407–432.

Browder, D. M., Wakeman, S. Y., Spooner, F., Ahlgrim-Delzell, L., & Algozzine, B. (2006). Research on reading instruction for individuals with significant cognitive disabilities. *Exceptional Children*, *72*, 392–408.

Brown v. Board of Education of Topeka. (1954). 347 U.S. 483, 74 S. Ct. 686; 98 L. Ed. 873 (U.S.).

Burstein, N., Sears, S., Wilcoxen, A., Cabello, B., & Spagna, M. (2004). Moving toward inclusive practices. *Remedial and Special Education*, *25*, 104–116.

Carter, E. W., Cushing, L. S., Clark, N. M., & Kennedy, C. H. (2005). Effects of peer support interventions on students' access to the general curriculum and social interactions. *Research and Practice for Persons with Severe Disabilities*, *30*, 15–25.

Carter, E. W., & Kennedy, C. H. (2006). Promoting access to the general curriculum using peer support strategies. *Research and Practice for Persons with Severe Disabilities*, *31*, 284–292.

Carter, E. W., Sisco, L. G., Chung, Y. C., & Stanton-Chapman, T. L. (2010). Peer interactions of students with intellectual disabilities and/or autism: A map of the intervention literature. *Research and Practice for Persons with Severe Disabilities*, *35*, 63–79.

Cole, C. (2006, Fall). Closing the achievement gap series: Part III: What is the impact of NCLB on the inclusion of students with disabilities? (Educational Policy Brief). *Center for Evaluation and Education Policy*, *4*, 1–12.

Cole, C. M., Waldron, N., & Majd, M. (2004). Academic progress of students across inclusive and traditional settings. *Mental Retardation*, *42*(2), 136–144.

Connor, D. J., & Ferri, B. A. (2007). The conflict within: Resistance to inclusion and other paradoxes in special education. *Disability & Society*, *22*, 63–77. doi:10.1080/09687590601056717

Cushing, L. S., Carter, E. W., Clark, N. M., Wallis, T., & Kennedy, C. H. (2009). Evaluating inclusive educational practices for students with severe disabilities using the program quality measurement tool. *The Journal of Special Education*, *42*, 194–208. doi:10.1177/0022466907313352

Cushing, L. S., & Kennedy, C. H. (2004). Facilitating social relationships in general education settings. In C. H. Kennedy & E. M. Horn (Eds.), *Including students with severe disabilities* (pp. 206–216). Boston, MA: Allyn & Bacon.

DiPaola, M., Tschannen-Moran, M., & Walther-Thomas, C. (2004). School principals and special education: Creating the context for academic success. *Focus on Exceptional Children*, *37*(1), 1–10.

Downing, J. E., Eichinger, J., & Williams, L. J. (1997). Inclusive education for students with severe disabilities comparative views of principals and educators at different levels of implementation. *Remedial and Special Education*, *18*, 133–142.

Downing, J. E., & Peckham-Hardin, K. D. (2007). Inclusive education: What makes it a good education for students with moderate to severe disabilities? *Research & Practice for Persons with Severe Disabilities*, *32*, 16–30.

Dymond, S. K., Renzaglia, A., Rosenstein, A., Chun, E. J., Banks, R. A., Niswander, V., & Gilson, C. L. (2006). Using a participatory action research approach to create a universally designed inclusive high school science course: A case study. *Research & Practice for Persons with Severe Disabilities*, *31*, 293–308.

Education for All Handicapped Children Act of 1975, Pub. L. 94-142, 20 U. S. C. § 1400, 89 Stat 773.

Education of the Handicapped Children Act Amendments of 1986, Pub. L. 99-457, 20 U. S. C. § 1400, 100 Stat 1145.

Education of the Handicapped Children Act Amendments of 1990, Pub. L. 101-476, 20 U. S. C. § 1400, 104 Stat. 1103.

Fisher, D., & Frey, N. (2001). Access to the core curriculum: Critical ingredients for students' success. *Remedial and Special Education, 22*, 148–157. doi:10.1177/074193250102200303

Fuchs, W. W. (2009-2010). Examining teachers' perceived barriers associated with inclusion. *SRATE Journal, 19*, 30–35.

Giangreco, M. F., & Broer, S. M. (2005). Questionable utilization of paraprofessionals in inclusive schools: Are we addressing symptoms or causes? *Focus on Autism and Other Developmental Disabilities, 20*, 10–26. doi:10.1177/10883576050200010201

Giangreco, M. F., Edelman, S. W., Broer, S. M., & Doyle, M. B. (2001). Paraprofessional support of students with disabilities: Literature from the past decade. *Exceptional Children, 68*, 45–63.

Hegarty, S., Pocklington, K., & Lucas, D. (2004). Educating pupils with special needs in ordinary schools. In G. Thomas & M. Vaughn (Eds.), *Inclusive education: Readings and reflections* (pp. 66–68). Berkshire: Open University Press.

Hourcade, J. J. (2008). Collaboration in the schools: Enhancing success for students with developmental disabilities. In P. Parette, G. Peterson-Karlan, & R. Ringlaben (Eds.), *Research-based in developmental disabilities* (2nd ed., pp. 589–610). Austin, TX: PRO-ED.

Hunt, P., Hirose-Hatae, A., Doering, K., Karasoff, P., & Goetz, L. (2000). "Community" is what I think everyone is talking about. *Remedial and Special Education, 21*, 305–317.

Individuals with Disabilities Education Act of 1997, Pub. L. 105-117, 20 U. S. C. § 1400.

Individuals with Disabilities Education Improvement Act of 2004, Pub. L. 108-446, 20 U. S. C. § 1400.

Individuals with Disabilities Education Improvement Act, 20. U.S.C. § 1400 *et seq.* (2004).

Jackson, L., Ryndak, D. L., & Billingsley, F. (2000). Useful practices in inclusive education: A preliminary view of what experts in moderate to severe disabilities are saying. *The Journal of the Association for Persons with Severe Handicaps, 25*, 129–141.

Jordan, A., Swartz, E., & McGhie-Richmond, D. (2009). Preparing teachers for inclusive classrooms. *Teaching and Teacher Education, 25*, 535–542. doi:10.1016/j.tate.2009.02.010

Kavale, K. A., & Forness, S. R. (2000). History, rhetoric, and reality: Analysis of the inclusion debate. *Remedial and Special Education, 21*, 279–296. doi:10.1177/074193250002100505

Lee, S., Amos, B. A., Gragoudas, S., Lee, Y., Shogren, K. A., Theoharis, R., & Wehmeyer, M. L. (2006). *Education and Training in Developmental Disabilities, 41*, 199–212.

Lohrmann, S., & Bambara, L. M. (2006). Elementary education teachers' beliefs about essential supports needed to successfully include students with developmental disabilities who engage in challenging behaviors. *Research and Practice for Persons with Severe Disabilities, 31*, 157–173.

McDonnell, L. M., McLaughlin, M. J., & Morison, P. (1997). *Educating one and all: Students with disabilities and standards-based reform.* Washington, DC: National Academy Press.

McLaughlin, M. J. (2010). Evolving interpretations of educational equity and students with disabilities. *Exceptional Children, 76*, 265–278.

McMaster, C. (2013). Building inclusion from the ground up: A review of whole school re-culturing programmes for sustaining inclusive change. *International Journal of Whole Schooling, 9*(2), 1–24.

No Child Left Behind Act of 2001, Pub. L. No. 107-110, 115 Stat. 1425 (2002).

Peck, C. A., Staub, D., Gallucci, C., & Schwartz, I. (2004). Parent perception of the impacts of inclusion on their nondisabled child. *Research & Practice for Persons with Severe Disabilities, 29*, 135–143.

Perner, D. (2008). Creating inclusive schools: Strategies for change, administrators and teachers. In P. Parette, G. Peterson-Karlan, & R. Ringlaben (Eds.), *Research-based in developmental disabilities* (2nd ed., pp. 543–565). Austin, TX: PRO-ED.

Perner, D., & Porter, G. (2008). Creating inclusive schools: Changing roles and strategies. In P. Parette, G. Peterson-Karlan, & R. Ringlaben (Eds.), *Research-based practices in developmental disabilities* (2nd ed., pp. 521–541). Austin, TX: PRO-ED.

Prinstein, M. J., & Dodge, K. A. (Eds.). (2008). *Understanding peer influence in children and adolescents*. New York, NY: The Guilford Press.

Richardson, R. C., Tolson, H., Huang, T. Y., & Lee, Y. H. (2009). Character education: Lessons for teaching social and emotional competence. *Children & Schools, 31*, 71–78.

Sailor, W. (2008-2009). Access to the general curriculum: Systems change or tinker some more? *Research & Practice for Persons with Severe Disabilities, 33*, 249–257.

Sailor, W., & Roger, B. (2005). Rethinking inclusion: Schoolwide applications. *Phi Delta Kappan, 86*, 503–509.

Scruggs, T., & Mastropieri, M. A. (1996). Teacher perceptions of mainstreaming/inclusion 1958–1995: A research synthesis. *Exceptional Children, 63*, 59–74.

Sharpe, M. N., & Hawes, M. E. (2003, July). Collaboration between general and special education: Making it work. *Examining Current Challenges in Secondary Education and Transition, 2*(Issue Brief), 1–6.

Silverstein, R. (2000). Emerging disability frameworks: A guidepost for analyzing public policy. *Iowa Law Review, 85*, 1691–1806.

Smith, A. (2006). Access, participation, and progress in the general education curriculum in the least restrictive environment for students with significant cognitive disabilities. *Research and Practice for Persons with Severe Disabilities, 31*, 331–337.

Smith, P. (2007). Have we made any progress? Including students with intellectual disabilities in regular education classrooms. *Intellectual and Developmental Disabilities, 45*, 297–309.

Snell, M. E., & Brown, F. (2000). *Instruction of students with severe disabilities* (5th ed.). Upper Saddle River, NJ: Merrill/Prentice Hall.

Spooner, F., Baker, J. N., Harris, A. A., Ahlgrim-Delzell, L., & Browder, D. M. (2007). Effects of training in universal design for learning on lesson plan development. *Remedial and Special Education, 28*, 108–116.

Spooner, F., McKissick, B. R., Hudson, M. E., & Browder, D. (2014). Access to general education curriculum in general education classes. In M. Agran, F. Brown, C. Hughes, C. Quirk, & D. Ryndak (Eds.), *Equity & full participation for individuals with severe disabilities* (pp. 217–234). Baltimore, MD: Paul H. Brookes.

Stainback, S. B. E., & Stainback, W. C. (1996). *Inclusion: A guide for educators*. Baltimore, MD: Paul H. Brookes.

Tawney, R. H. (2004). Equality. In G. Thomas & M. Vaughn (Eds.), *Inclusive education: Readings and reflections* (pp. 8–10). Berkshire: Open University Press.

Tews, L., & Lupart, J. (2008). Students with disabilities' perspectives of the role and impact of paraprofessionals in inclusive education settings. *Journal of Policy and Practice in Intellectual Disabilities, 5*, 39–46.

Thurlow, M. L. (2002). Positive educational results for all students. *Remedial and Special Education, 23*, 195–202.

Tomlinson, S. (2004). A sociology of special education. In G. Thomas & M. Vaughn (Eds.), *Inclusive education: Readings and reflections* (pp. 59–65). Berkshire: Open University Press.

Turnbull, H. R., III, Turnbull, A. P., Wehmeyer, M. L., & Park, J. (2003). A quality of life framework for special education outcomes. *Remedial and Special Education, 24*, 67–74.

US Department of Education. (2009). *28th Annual report to Congress on the implementation of the Individuals with Disabilities Education Act, 2006*. Washington, DC: Author.

US Department of Education, National Center for Education Statistics. (2013). *Digest of Education Statistics, 2013* (NCES 2014–015). Retrieved from http://nces.ed.gov/fastfacts/display.asp?id=59

Wakeman, S. Y., Browder, D. M., Meier, I., & McColl, A. (2007). The implications of No Child Left Behind for students with developmental disabilities. *Mental Retardation and Developmental Disabilities Research Reviews, 13*, 143–150. doi:10.1002/mrdd.20147

Walther-Thomas, C., Korinek, L., McLaughlin, V. L., & Williams, B. T. (2000). *Collaboration for inclusive education: Developing successful programs*. Boston, MA: Allyn & Bacon.

Webster, A. A., & Carter, M. (2007). Social relationships and friendships of children with developmental disabilities: Implications for inclusive settings. A systematic review. *Journal of Intellectual and Developmental Disability, 32*, 200–213.

Wehmeyer, M. (2014). Disability in the 21st century: Seeking a future of equity and full participation. In M. Agran, F. Brown, C. Hughes, C. Quirk, & D. Ryndak (Eds.), *Equity & full participation for individuals with severe disabilities* (pp. 3–23). Baltimore, MD: Paul H. Brookes.

Wehmeyer, M. L. (2006). Beyond access: Ensuring progress in the general education curriculum for students with severe disabilities. *Research & Practice for Persons with Severe Disabilities, 31*, 322–326.

FACILITATING SUPPORTS AND SERVICES FOR LEARNERS WITH LOW-INCIDENCE DISABILITIES

Jody Marie Bartz, Jennifer Kurth and Matthew Wangeman

ABSTRACT

Facilitating inclusive supports and services for learners with low-incidence disabilities involves collaborative teaming, understanding the benefits and challenges involved in delivering inclusive supports, and appreciating the diverse and unique needs of this population. In this chapter, we provide families, educators, researchers, academics, related service personnel, and other professionals with examples of models of service and support delivery. Emphasis will be on school-age learners with low-incidence disabilities. Additionally, an insider perspective of the opportunities for, as well as benefits and barriers to, successful implementation of supports and services for learners with low-incidence disabilities is presented. The chapter concludes with future directions for research.

Keywords: Inclusive education; systems of support; service delivery

Including Learners with Low-Incidence Disabilities
International Perspectives on Inclusive Education, Volume 5, 111–136

ISSN: 1479-3636/doi:10.1108/S1479-363620140000005005

INTRODUCTION

Recent decades have witnessed a significant increase in the number of children with disabilities participating in general education settings (McLeskey, Landers, Williamson, & Hoppey, 2012). However, students with low-incidence disabilities are largely excluded from such progress (Kurth, Morningstar, & Kozleski, in press). The rise of inclusive educational placements in the United States has been occurring since the 1970s, when philosophical ideas ushered in the era of "normalization" (Wolfsenberger, 1972) and students with disabilities were placed in general education settings for the first time. However, this movement toward inclusion occurred well before any empirical evidence existed to support the movement (Eaves & Ho, 1997). Some 30 years later, inclusion is gaining research support, with findings ranging from improved cognitive and academic gains (Dessemontet, Bless, & Morin, 2012; Dore, Dion, Wagner, & Brunet, 2002; Fisher & Meyer, 2002; Hedeen & Ayres, 2002; McCleskey, Henry, & Hodges, 1998; Meyer, 2001) to increases in social interactions and peer acceptance (Causton-Theoharis & Malmgren, 2004; Cawley, Hayden, Cade, & Baker-Kroczynski, 2002; Dore et al., 2002; Mastropieri & Scruggs, 2001). Additionally, empirical research has found that typical peers do not "suffer" academically or socially as a result of inclusion (Gandhi, 2007; Kalambouka, Farrell, Dyson, & Kaplan, 2007). Rather, typical peers show academic, social, and behavioral benefits, as do students with disabilities (Heiman, 2001; Johnson & McDonnell, 2004). Finally, the parents of both children with and without disabilities consistently support inclusion (Frazeur-Cross, Traub, Hutter-Pishgahi, & Shelton, 2004; Hanson et al., 2001; Seery, Davis, & Johnson, 2000). Despite these positive trends and research findings, there has been a troubling "regression … or resignation toward, a self-contained setting as a viable placement for students with severe disabilities" (Jackson, Ryndak, & Wehmeyer, 2008–2009, p. 176). Thus, there is a pressing need to describe and advocate for effective inclusive practices, framed around issues of educational equity, presumptions of competence, and the least dangerous assumption. The purpose of this chapter is to describe the various methods of delivering supports and services for students with low-incidence disabilities in inclusive educational settings. Students with low-incidence disabilities are those (a) served under the categories of intellectual disability, multiple disabilities, vision impairment, hearing impairment, deaf-blindness, and autism; (b) who have extensive support needs; and (c) are the 1–2% of U.S. students who are eligible to complete their state's alternate assessment. The following questions guided the discussion in this chapter:

1. How do we provide inclusive supports and services for learners with low-incidence disabilities?
2. What types of support and service model delivery options are available to learners with low-incidence disabilities?
3. What are the benefits and challenges to providing effective and inclusive supports and services for learners with low-incidence disabilities?

After reading this chapter, the reader will

- understand key terms and laws related to facilitating supports and services for learners with low-incidence disabilities,
- differentiate between various service delivery models for learners with low-incidence disabilities,
- identify benefits and challenges of individualized supports and services for learners with significant support needs.

HISTORICAL ROOTS OF INSTITUTIONALIZATION IMPACTING CONTEMPORARY SPECIAL EDUCATION

Students with low-incidence disabilities have been marginalized and segregated throughout much of human history. It was simply assumed that people with low-incidence disabilities are unable to learn or make meaningful contributions to society. These assumptions led to the widespread segregation into institutions and family homes. Even the genetics of people with disabilities have been feared, resulting in forced sterilization and institutionalization (Smith & Wehmeyer, 2012). It was only in 1975 in the United States, with the passage of the *Education of All Handicapped Children Act* (P.L. 94-142), that students with low-incidence disabilities were mandated to receive education services. Prior to this law, students with disabilities were typically discouraged or even prohibited from attending school. The passage of P.L. 94-142 coincided with a movement to deinstitutionalize adults with disabilities. Efforts were made to assist adults to move from large facilities into smaller, more family-like, group homes within communities (Bigby, Kristiansen, Johnson, & Traustadottir, 2005).

Although federal law and the deinstitutionalization movement marked important steps in promoting quality and equitable lives for individuals with disabilities, a long history of institutionalizing and segregating people with disabilities greatly impacts the delivery of special education services today. Following passage of the law, students with disabilities were re-segregated into public and private schools (Winzer, 2007), grouped together in special education classes for much, if not all, of the school day. This segregation of students on the basis of disability was founded on the same assumptions that guided institutionalization and segregation from the earliest days. Namely, that some students could not learn in the "regular" class, and so separating students with unique learning needs from this setting would be beneficial in (a) preventing the "deviant" student from interfering with the learning of "normal" students and (b) preventing an inordinate amount of teacher's time being directed toward this "deviant" student (Heller, Holtzman, & Messick, 1982). As Heller et al. (1982) further report, segregation was purported to benefit those students requiring special education: (a) instruction was provided in smaller class sizes, (b) students in segregated settings would be provided effective teaching at a level that is appropriate to the student, and (c) any assault to the self-esteem of students with disabilities would be prevented, as there would be no opportunity to be compared to "normal" children in a "normal" class. Perhaps as a result of these assumptions and expectations, students with disabilities were educated in segregated settings and in a manner that focused on needs, rather than addressed potential.

While these claims of the benefits of segregation may seem outdated, and despite voluminous evidence supporting the benefits of inclusive education, these assumptions about the benefits of segregating students with disabilities persist to this day. Educators and parents regularly believe that segregated self-contained classrooms deliver educational experiences that are in some way unique or beneficial to students with disabilities, including supporting the claims outlined by Heller and colleagues. These claims, however, have failed to be supported by research evidence. For example, Causton-Theoharis, Theoharis, Orsait, and Cosier (2011) completed a series of observations in six self-contained special education classrooms over the span of seven years, and found that these classrooms failed to deliver on their promises of community, distraction-free environments, specialized curriculum and instruction, and behavioral supports. As these authors concluded, "we found it difficult to argue for fixing or improving these self-contained settings because everything we observed that could have been considered educational could have been transported to inclusive settings without compromising the education these students were receiving" (p. 73). Simply, the instruction delivered in these segregated settings was not different from, or superior to, instruction in the general education setting. However, the persistence of segregated education within and across schools today, particularly for students with low-incidence disabilities, illustrates how these assumptions continue to drive practice (Smith & Kozleski, 2005).

LEGISLATION REGARDING SUPPORTS AND SERVICES

Inclusive education is firmly grounded in federal legal mandates, notably the *Individuals with Disabilities Education Improvement Act* (IDEA, 2004), the most recent reauthorization of P.L. 94-142. IDEA mandates that, to the maximum extent possible, children with disabilities should be educated with their typical peers and that removal of children with disabilities from the general education environment occurs only in exceptional cases. Furthermore, IDEA shifts the focus from mere physical access to general education *settings*, emphasizing instead access to the core general education *curriculum* (Clark, Cushing, & Kennedy, 2004; Jitendra, Edwards, Choutka, & Treadway, 2002). Of significance in the reauthorization of IDEA in 2004 is its close alignment to the *Elementary and Secondary Education Act*, commonly known as the *No Child Left Behind Act*, of 2002 (Moores, 2005; Smith, 2005; Turnbull, 2005). Both laws emphasize academic accountability and results, along with research-based educational practices (Clark et al., 2004).

The IDEA has been further interpreted in case law, with findings strongly supporting that special education services be delivered in inclusive settings, as seen in Table 1. Importantly, these findings not only state that inclusive education is the intent of the law, but that inclusion is about more than just physical placement or geography. Instead, inclusive education entails the provision of appropriate supports and services so students can be meaningfully involved and make progress in, the general education curriculum and activities.

SUPPORTS AND SERVICES

With growing support for inclusive education, schools, families, policy makers, and researchers have identified a number of intervention methods

Table 1. Summary of Legal Cases in Support of Inclusive Education.

Name of Case	Description of Case
Brown v. Board of Education (1954)	Education must be available to all, on equal terms. Separate is inherently unequal.
PARC v. Pennsylvania (1972)	The state provided students without disabilities a free education, and thus the state could not deny students with disabilities this same right.
Board of Education v. Rowley (1982)	Students with disabilities must be provided with an education, including supports and services, that confer a basic educational benefit.
Roncker V. Walter (1983)	A district cannot simply claim that a self-contained program is superior. If the self-contained setting is somehow superior, the court will determine if those supports and services that make the placement superior could be reasonably provided in an inclusive setting (the principle of portability).
Daniel R.R. v. State Board of Education (1989)	Here, the court did not follow the Roncker test, but developed its own. The court must (1) examine whether, with the use of supplementary aids and services, the child can be included in the classroom and (2) if the child cannot be included, if the child was mainstreamed to the maximum extent possible.
Sacramento Unified School District v. Rachel H. (1992)	A four-part test for determining if a student can be included in general education: (1) the educational benefits of the general education classroom; (2) the nonacademic benefits of interaction between students with and without disabilities; (3) the impact of the student with disabilities on the teacher and other students in the classroom; and (4) the cost of supplementary aids and services required for inclusion.
Rafael Oberti v. Clementon School District (1993)	Here, the court found that the school had failed to provide the student with the supports, resources, and appropriate training to be placed in an inclusive setting. The judge found that, "inclusion is a right, not a special privilege for a select few."

to provide access to general education settings and curriculum for students with disabilities. While IDEA (2004) does not define direct and indirect support, it does note that the student's Individualized Education Program (IEP) must include a statement of the special education and related services "to be provided to the child or on behalf of the child" 300.320(a)(4)(i). These supports and services are provided to assist a student in meeting his or her IEP goals and to make progress in the general education curriculum.

Direct Supports and Services

Direct supports and services are provided to the child by a special education teacher or a related services provider (see Fig. 1). They may be provided individually or in small group settings. For example, a speech-language pathologist may work individually with a student to focus on articulation. Similarly, an occupational therapist may work directly on ball handling skills with a small group of students.

Indirect Supports and Services

Indirect supports and services are not provided directly to the child, but are provided to those people who work directly with the child (see Fig. 2). Indirect services may include consultation, collaboration, curricular modifications, and progress monitoring, among others. For example, a behaviorist may observe a student in a classroom and provide specific recommendations for the teacher to implement. Likewise, a special education teacher may provide detailed instructions for a paraeducator to implement when working directly with a student.

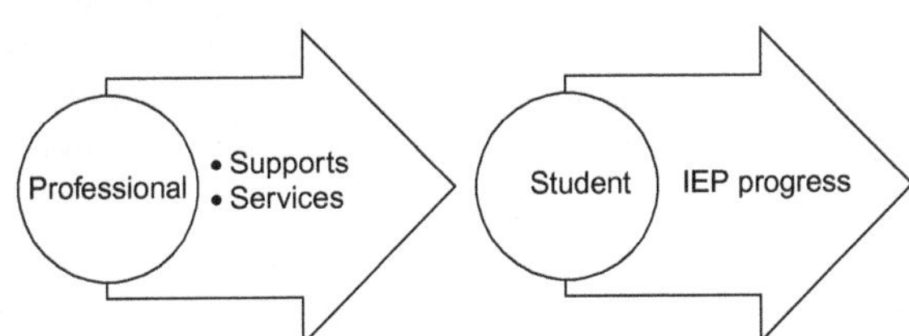

Fig. 1. Direct Supports and Services.

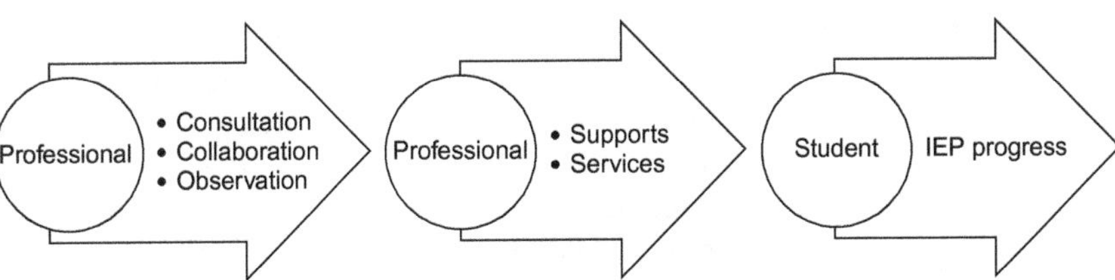

Fig. 2. Indirect Supports and Services.

A SYSTEMS OF SUPPORT FRAMEWORK

The delivery of supports and services for individuals who experience disability, particularly low-incidence disabilities, are always guided by a set of assumptions and values. Those who subscribe to a medical model of disability aim to provide supports and services that "fix" or "cure" disability. In this view, disability resides entirely within an individual. People with disabilities will be able to participate fully in society when they are no longer disabled. A social model takes a different view, namely, that people may experience disability when physical, attitudinal, and institutional barriers prevent a person from participating in society. When a person's personal capabilities closely approximate the demands of the environment, that person experiences little disability. However, when a person's present personal capacity is more different from the demands of the environment, that person experiences more disability. As an example, a wheelchair user who has ready access to ramps and elevators experiences little disability. However, when this person is faced with a staircase and no alternatives, that individual becomes disabled. When we consider designing and implementing supports and services throughout this chapter, we take a social model of disability perspective. We assume that all people are competent and capable of learning and succeeding, but that more and different supports must be provided for some individuals as compared to others to achieve this success (Thompson et al., 2009). Our view of inclusive education is that all students belong and can learn in general education, with some needing more and different supports to ensure meaningful access and participation in general education than others.

Further guiding principles in the delivery of supports and services that facilitate inclusive practices are the principle of equity, the presumption of competence, and the least dangerous assumption. The principle of equity asserts that all students should receive what they need, and what individual students need to learn will vary (Lavoie & Lieberman, 1986). Equity demands of us that we make specific accommodations to enable students to learn together. The presumption of competence and least dangerous assumption complement one another and the principle of equity. The presumption of competence demands of us to see all students as capable of learning and contributing; failure to do so based on a student's learning or physical characteristics risks making a dangerous assumption by underestimating a student and failing to provide high standards and expectations of achievement.

MODELS OF SUPPORT AND SERVICE DELIVERY

When designing inclusive supports and services, educators rely on the principle of equity, presumption of competence, and least dangerous assumption. Together, these inform various models of support and service delivery. These models of support and service are systems of support provided to facilitate student involvement and participation in the full range of general education curriculum and activities (including extracurricular). Each student will necessarily require a different system of support. Through provision of these supports, inclusive education and communities are fostered; we replace the requirement that students conform to general education expectations, and instead design supports that make general education accessible and meaningful. These delivery models of inclusive education include (a) paraeducator supports, (b) consultation and/or collaboration supports from special education teachers, (c) co-teaching of general and special education teachers, (d) peer supports, and (e) inclusive-related services. In practice, these delivery models may overlap. For example, a fully included student may have the support of a paraeducator and her general and special education teachers may collaborate regularly. For purposes of highlighting each type of delivery model, each model is described individually, and strengths and weaknesses of each model are presented in Table 2.

Paraeducator Model

Paraeducators, also called paraprofessionals, teacher assistants, or instructional assistants are school employees who work in an instructional capacity alongside with, and under the supervision of, certified teachers (French, 1999). The use of paraeducators as a primary support for students with disabilities in inclusive settings is rising every year (French & Chopra, 1999). In fact, paraeducators are the dominant approach used by schools to support students' involvement in general education classrooms (Carter, Cushing, Clark, & Kennedy, 2005; Giangreco, Doyle, & Suter, 2012). Assigning paraeducators to work with students with disabilities in general education classrooms allows for individualized instruction and targeting individual student needs, as the paraeducator provides small group or one-to-one instruction for the student with disabilities in the general education context.

However, the use of paraeducators to support students in classrooms is not unanimously supported. In fact, Giangreco and Broer assert that the

Table 2. Summary of Models of Inclusive Education Supports and Services Delivery.

Model	Advantages	Disadvantages

Paraeducator	• Individualized instruction
	• Students more likely to be engaged
	• Small group:
	  • Increase socialization
	  • Increase generalization
	  • Increase communication partners
		• Dependency (1-to-1)
		• Social interference (1-to-1)
		• Lack of teacher involvement
		• Decrease socialization (1-to-1)
		• Decrease communication partners (1-to-1)
		• Decreased generalization (1-to-1)

Co-teaching	• Pooled expertise to benefit student • Decreased student-teacher ratio • Teachers gain professional support • Increased instructional opportunities • Increased opportunity for differentiated instruction • Increased generalization • Increase communication	• Lack of planning time • Lack of individualization • Lack of shared content knowledge • Lack of clear roles • Lack of consistent training
Consultation/ itinerant special education teacher	• Modified curriculum available • Full membership in GE • Collaboration between teachers • Pooled expertise to benefit student • Teacher values many ways of student knowledge/learning	• Unclear as to how accommodations are implemented • Large SE teacher caseload • Teachers unprepared to be consultants • In practice little individualization • GE teacher overwhelmed
Peer tutors	• High engagement • Peers successful in tutoring • Increased social interactions • Decreased problem behaviors • Increased academic achievement • Teachers and peers approve of it • Increased communication • Improved behavior (peer modeling) • Increased generalization	• Questions of oversight • Appropriate feedback and instruction • Availability of peers • Parent and student support unclear

Table 2. (*Continued*)

Model	Advantages	Disadvantages
Inclusive-related services	• Reduces classroom disruption • Maximizes instructional time • Facilitates generalization • Creates more opportunities throughout a day to practice needed skills • Reduces stigmatization • Decreases the number of transitions students must make	• Need to co-plan between teachers and related services providers to develop meaningful opportunities • Many related services providers may be unprepared to work in inclusive settings • Opportunities for "watering down" and inappropriate roles

"extensive reliance on paraeducators, though in widespread use, lacks an educationally defensible foundation from a conceptual, theoretical, or data-based perspective" (2005, p. 25). Furthermore, Giangreco and Broer (2005) notes the risk inherent in a model of education in which by having a disability, a student receives most of their instruction from a paraeducator with uncertain and unguaranteed skills, while students without disabilities receive most of their instruction from highly qualified teachers.

Criticisms of reliance on paraeducators are not limited to issues of fairness. Many drawbacks are associated with the use of paraeducators to implement instruction. For example, use of paraeducators for one-to-one instruction nurtures student dependence, inhibits independence and autonomy, and limits the opportunity to learn vicariously through peers and develop social skills (Giangreco et al., 2012). Additionally, paraeducators may evoke stigmatization toward the student, interfere with peer interactions, and reduce teacher involvement by becoming the primary instructors for students with disabilities (Giangreco & Broer, 2005). In addition, paraeducators can also inadvertently contribute to a student's loss of personal control, loss of gender identity, and interfere with the instruction of other students by engaging in different activities and talking during class activities (Giangreco, Edelman, & MacFarland, 1997). Students themselves report that the constant presence of a paraeducator can be frustrating in that these support personnel interfere with their independence, interactions with teachers, and friendships (Broer, Doyle, & Giangreco, 2005). In addition, when a paraeducator is present, teachers tend to assume that the paraeducator is primarily responsible and thus "disown" the student as their responsibility (Cook, 2004). Teachers also tend to be less engaged with students when paraeducators are present, as demonstrated by having few instructional interactions with students and an absence of planning lessons or activities for students (Giangreco, Broer, & Edelman, 2001). Lastly, many teachers report feeling unprepared to supervise paraeducators (Chopra, Sandoval-Lucero, & French, 2011).

Co-Teaching/Collaborative Team Model

A second delivery model of inclusive education, collaborative or co-teaching, is growing in frequency across the nation (Magiera & Zigmond, 2005; Villa, Thousand, & Nevin, 2004). Co-teaching or collaborative teaching can take several forms, including (a) one teacher teaching with the other assisting; (b) station teaching whereby teachers teach groups of students at the same time, (c) team teaching, (d) parallel teaching, and (e) alternative teaching when teachers take turns teaching the whole class (Murawski, 2012). Regardless of form, both general and special education teachers share an equal responsibility for lesson planning, lesson implementation, and assessment (Strogilos & Tragoulia, 2013) and students with disabilities are full-time, full members of classrooms. As such, this model breaks down the traditional barrier between special and general education and capitalizes on the skills and abilities of both teachers (Noonan, McCormick, & Heck, 2003). When working within this model, teachers share and serve students based on needs rather than labels (Burstein, Sears, Wilcoxen, Cabello, & Spagna, 2004). For example, the general education teacher instructs while the special education teacher circulates and assists students in need of extra help (Friend, Cook, Hurley-Chamberlain, & Shamberger, 2010). Typically the general education teacher is valued as the content expert, whereas the special education teacher is valued as the expert in accommodations and differentiation in this model (Austin, 2001). While the divide between general and special education is minimized, this model does allow the special education teacher to instruct primarily struggling students or students with special needs, while the general education teacher can focus on the larger group (Burstein et al., 2004; Heiman, 2001; Magiera & Zigmond, 2005; Mastropieri & Scruggs, 2001).

The philosophical rationale of the co-teaching model is increasingly supported in the literature (Austin, 2001; Mastropieri & Scruggs, 2001; Murawski & Swanson, 2001). For example, co-teaching provides all students with a wider range of instructional opportunities, reduces student-teacher ratios, and allows teachers to provide professional support to each other (Magiera & Zigmond, 2005). Additionally, teachers find co-teaching valuable and feel benefited by their collaboration with others and the feedback they receive from their partner teacher (Austin, 2001; Villa et al., 2004).

While co-teaching has been gaining popularity among teachers, the benefits to students with disabilities have been questioned when implemented under typical conditions. For example, in co-taught classrooms students received individual instruction 2.2% of the time, whereas in single teacher classrooms students received individual attention 1% of the time (Magiera & Zigmond, 2005). However, the co-teachers in this study worked under "realistic" conditions; that is, they did not share common planning time and thus did not collaborate frequently. Thus, while co-teachers value joint planning, frequently this time is not allocated on a consistent basis (Gürgür & Uzuner, 2010).

Consultation/Itinerant Special Education Teacher Model

A third inclusive delivery model is the consultation method. In this model the special education teacher acts as a consultant to the general education teacher in terms of curriculum adaptation, skills deficit remediation, and assessment modification (Austin, 2001). Again, the student with disabilities is a full-time, fully included member of the classroom. The consultation delivery method is generally associated with other methods (e.g., paraeducator support in class), with an itinerant special education teacher providing consultation to teachers and drop-in support of students (Vlachou & Zoniou-Sideri, 2010). Benefits of consultation include the development of a collaborative relationship among teachers, focusing on an equal interchange between colleagues, shared responsibilities, and a freedom to accept or reject ideas (Eisenman, Pleet, Wandry, & McGinley, 2011). Support for this model stems from the observation that general education teachers typically do not have the same expertise to address the unique needs of children with disabilities as do special education teachers; collaboration and consultation between the two experts is thus essential (Collins, Branson, Hall, & Rankin, 2001).

Coaching Model

Another form of the consultation model is the coaching model, whereby special and general education teachers take turns coaching one another in their areas of curricular and pedagogical expertise (Austin, 2001). Noell and Witt (1999) note that reviews of the consultation literature support the assumption that consultation can be an effective method of delivering services to students in that teachers may consult with one another, devise strategies and ideas, and implement them. In such a model, these authors report that teachers would not be limited to a particular classroom all day but could affect change for a number of students, both for students with disabilities and those at risk, across an entire school.

Regardless of whether the focus is on coaching or collaborating, in this special education delivery model the general education teacher becomes the primary teacher for the student with disabilities, while special education teachers act as support staff, providing ideas and adaptations for use in general education classes and content areas (Dymond & Russell, 2004). As such, the primary responsibility of instruction and educational outcomes for the student with disabilities is placed on the general education teacher (Cook, 2001). Collaboration between general education and special education teachers on learning styles, teaching, and assessment is associated with an increase in teacher ability to recognize and accept diverse learning styles (Foster & Cue, 2009). Furthermore, consultation between general and special education teachers enables schools and teachers to focus on providing an appropriate curriculum for all students (Carrington & Elkins, 2002).

Despite the documented positive effects of consultation by some studies, overall, outcome data in support of this method are limited. Currently, very little data exist to describe what consultative or collaborative practices lead to the implementation of the classroom interventions. In addition, itinerant special education teachers providing consultation services poses further challenges. The possibility of large caseloads in such a model presents the risk that teachers provide little instruction and little individualization (Russ, Chiang, Rylance, & Bongers, 2001). Furthermore, itinerant consulting teachers are generally unprepared in their own teacher training for the consultation model. In a study of itinerant teachers, Dinnebeil, McInerney, Roth, and Ramaswamy (2001) found that itinerant teachers are most comfortable with and spend most of their time in child-directed rather than adult-directed (consultation) activities, and question whether this is an effective service, given the limited time itinerant teachers spend with individual children and adults.

Peer-Tutoring Model

The peer-tutoring model involves utilizing one or more peers to provide academic and social support to classmates with a disability (Fennick &

Royle, 2003). The successes of peer-tutoring have been well documented in the literature (Banda, Hart, & Liu-Gitz, 2010; Carter et al., 2005; Carter & Hughes, 2005; Carter & Kennedy, 2006; Carter, Sisco, Melekoglu, & Kurkowski, 2007). Peers have successfully been taught to complete tasks such as adapting curriculum, providing instruction, implementing behavior plans, providing feedback, and promoting communication (Carter et al., 2005). Furthermore, peers can be taught to effectively do drill and practice from study guides, ask content questions and summarize information, do oral readings of English novels and summarize these for their peer tutee (Mastropieri & Scruggs, 2001). In addition, peers have been successfully taught to implement accommodations, ranging from rewording, paraphrasing questions, breaking assignments into smaller tasks, facilitating partial participation in class activities, and modifying course materials (Carter et al., 2005). The use of peer support in classrooms has been associated with higher levels of engagement for students both with and without disabilities, increases in social interactions, decreases in problem behavior, and improved academic performance (Mastropieri, Scruggs, Spencer, & Fontana, 2003). Furthermore, an arrangement of two peer tutors to work with one student with disabilities increased the social interaction and contact with general education curriculum more than having only one peer tutor, although no peer support configuration has been found to have a detrimental impact on participation in general education (Carter et al., 2005). In sum, cooperative learning and the use of peer tutors have been found to enhance academic achievement and social inclusion of students with disabilities in general education classes (O'Reilly, Lancioni, Gardiner, Tiernan, & Lacy, 2002). Both teachers and peers have positive attitudes about peer-tutoring (Mastropieri et al., 2003).

Inclusive-Related Services

Related services are defined as those services that are required to assist a child with disabilities in benefitting from special education services. Related services include services such as speech and language therapy, interpreting, orientation and mobility, and so on (IDEA 300.34(a)). Providing related services in inclusive settings has been advocated since the passage of P.L. 94-142 in 1975 (Giangreco, 1986). The reasons for this are multiple, including the ramifications of the Rowley (1982) case, as well as the need to support students with disabilities in general education settings. "Simply stated … related services are too important for students, families, and school personnel to be provided in ways that interfere with the education of students with disabilities" (Giangreco, Prelock, Reid, Dennis, & Edleman, 2000, p. 362). When students must leave their classroom and activities to access related services, learning is certainly interfered with, and the opportunities for stigmatization increase. Thus, the provision of related services inside general education classrooms, embedded within natural routines, is preferred.

There are many ways that inclusive-related services can be delivered, including teaming and role release (Giangreco et al., 2000; Giangreco, York, & Rainforth, 1989; York, Giangreco, Vandercook, & Macdonald, 1992). Teaming, in which providers and educators learn new skills to support one another and the student, is useful in providing a holistic approach to delivering related services. Role release, a process in which a therapist trains a core group of team members to implement interventions on a daily basis, is also useful. It is important that the roles of related services providers and classroom teachers are clearly articulated (Giangreco et al., 2000), so that services are not "watered down" when educators or related services providers take on inappropriate roles (Ehren, 2000).

The provision of inclusive-related services further reduces the number of transitions a student must make between activities and settings. As transitioning from one activity or environment to another can be challenging for some students (Sterling-Turner & Jordan, 2007), inclusive-related services can be crucial to facilitating student success. Perhaps for these reasons, classroom teachers indicate a preference for inclusive-related services. For example, teachers report that inclusive-related services provide more opportunities for students' IEP goals to be addressed throughout the day, and that all students in the classroom receive help as needed (Downing & Peckham-Hardin, 2008). Therapists report enjoying working with other members of the IEP team but need support to make collaboration effective (Rainforth & York-Barr, 1997).

VIGNETTE: INSIDE PERSPECTIVE OF THE SOCIAL ASPECTS OF PROVIDING INCLUSIVE SUPPORTS AND SERVICES – MATTHEW WANGEMAN

"In the past ten years, there has been a push for more inclusive educational opportunities for all students with disabilities, even for those with low-incidence disabilities. This trend in education has been very much welcomed by the disability community as a whole and many of the gains in education have been initiated by disability advocates around the world. While the concept of inclusion is now the driving force behind the integration of children with disabilities within our schools, often the social aspects of inclusion are too often glossed over or not even addressed by the IEP team members. As a person with support needs, what I mean by the social aspects of inclusion are the social activities surrounding the act of going to school. Examples are going to the prom, involvement in student clubs and government, going to football games, playing with other children at recess, and many more. For many of us, these social activities defined our school experience more than learning to read or adding two numbers together. These school experiences often marked our entrance into becoming more independent and were pivotal in teaching us how to interact socially. More importantly, these school experiences were the foundation of making us into the adults we are today and provided us the connection to the world around us.

To be clear, I am not suggesting that academics are not important and that we should ignore the teaching aspects of inclusion. However if we deny children the rich experience that these school activities have to offer we unfortunately contribute to the further isolation and segregation of children with disabilities. As a person with a significant disability who grew up in a time when people with disabilities were not included in public schools I applaud the push for inclusion and I have advocated strongly for the inclusion of every student with a disability in our schools. However, I have talked to too many students and parents of students who say that they are not included in the social part of school. Sometime ago I was asked by this staff person at a school in the Phoenix area to talk to a student with a disability who was very depressed and our conversation was around how they felt very isolated and had no friends. This student said he thought about suicide often because he didn't see the point of living if he was not included in the social aspects of school or life. Unfortunately I don't know what happened to this student but his experience in school is not uncommon and it proves that if we only focused on academics we can do much harm.

Studies have shown that inclusion is better for students' mental health – they are less depressed and have higher self-esteem than students in self-contained classrooms (Wiener & Tardif, 2004). This of course makes logical sense and inclusion is better than self-contained classrooms for a myriad of reasons however we just should not assume that inclusion will *fix* everything. We have to work at ensuring that inclusion is done in a holistic manner with both academic and social aspects being addressed equally.

Creating an environment that encourages inclusion to occur naturally within the classroom is paramount. Here are a few strategies: (a) natural supports, (b) paraprofessionals who are not tied to the child with the disability and know how to facilitate social interactions among all students, (c) creating spaces where students teach each other, and (d) figuring out students' strengths and focusing on their abilities instead of their disabilities.

Natural Supports

An example of natural supports would be if a child with a disability needed help reading why not ask the other students to assist the child. In doing this, an environment exists where children learn to naturally assist each other when they need help. This also can lead to outside the classroom where children see it is not a big deal to assist others and they learn that everyone needs help with something.

Paraeducators

Paraeducators need to not be tied to the student with a disability because it inhibits social interaction with the other students. They are there to assist the child with a disability but they should allow them to be independent as much as possible in addition they need to facilitate social interaction between every student. A good paraprofessional should be seen by the students as just a classroom aid for everyone and not just an aid for that student.

Peer-Tutoring

Creating spaces where students teach each other is also important because similar to natural supports it teaches everyone that they have strengths and weaknesses but if everyone works together things can get accomplished. Furthermore it can show the strengths of the student with a disability and prove that they are a valuable person.

Presuming Competence

Lastly, we must focus on the abilities rather than disabilities of the students. For example if the student with a disability is a strong reader but math is difficult we should have them lead a reading group and perhaps have other students help them with math. This will show that everyone has different talents and the world is made up of very diverse people and that is a good thing.

If we can create a school environments where inclusion occurs naturally, this will lead to a more holistic form of inclusion where students are not only included in the academics part of school but they are also included in the social part of school. Unfortunately, we cannot mandate the inclusion of students with disabilities in the social aspects of going to school. However, if everyone involved is aware of both the potential issues as well as the benefits surrounding inclusion then we can work together to ensure that students with low-incidence disabilities have an enriching school experience – both academically and socially."

FUTURE RESEARCH DIRECTIONS

Limited studies exist that examine the effectiveness of inclusive-related services for students with low-incidence disabilities. However, Giangreco (1986) found that when therapy is provided within the natural setting of a student's classroom, the student demonstrates an increase in skill development when compared to direct therapy services that are provided in a separate room. Importantly, inclusive-related services result in increased instructional time and less disruption (Rainforth & York-Barr, 1997). Future research focused on examining inclusive supports and services is warranted.

KEY TERMS

Social model of disability – The social model of disability views people who experience disability as an oppressed group. The social model asserts that disability does not reside in an individual but in environmental contexts that exclude and oppress people (Shakespeare, 2006).

Medical model of disability – The medical model of disability claims that disability rests squarely in an individual, and invests effort in fixing and curing disability, rather than in remediating social barriers, whether they are attitudinal, physical, or institutional.

Educational equity – "Do we treat all students the same, or do we make special accommodations for certain groups? Do we educate all groups of students considered different in the same program, or do we create separate programs for some of them?" (Artiles & Bal, 2008, p. 5). Diversity promotes equity, while benefitting all students. "Diversity makes for a rich tapestry, and we must understand that all the threads of the tapestry are equal in value no matter what their color" (Maya Angelou).

Inclusion or inclusive education – Inclusion is defined as both placement and provision of all needed supports. Inclusion means that a student is full member of a general education setting, not a visitor for certain activities. Inclusion also means that the student is provided the range of supports and services she needs to address her specific needs in that setting. Inclusion, then, is about membership and meaningful access that allows students to make progress in areas that are important for all students.

Least dangerous assumption – "Teacher expectations about students' ability to learn – communicated in both explicit and subtle ways – can be more influential on learning outcomes than the students' inherent abilities or the teachers' instructional methods" (Jorgensen, McSheehan, & Sonnenmeier, 2007, p. 249). These self-fulfilling prophecies can be profoundly detrimental for students with disabilities, who are viewed as a label (e.g., "severe disabilities"), and thus denied opportunities that other similarly aged students are learning. Rather than viewing students through this limiting lens of disability, it is critical to make the least dangerous assumptions, and to presume competence by viewing all students as competent learners and contributors to their classrooms, schools, homes, and communities.

Disability – The World Health Organization defines "disability" as a discrepancy of fit between a person's context (e.g., curriculum, physical space) and a person's present capabilities. (http://www.who.int/topics/disabilities/en/). This view, then, suggests that the person is not disabled, but that the environment is disabling.

Low-incidence disabilities – Students with low-incidence disabilities are served under the categories of intellectual disability, multiple disabilities, vision impairment, hearing impairment, deaf-blindness, and autism, who have significant cognitive impairment; these are also the students 1–2% of U.S. students who are eligible to complete their state's alternate assessment (Kurth et al., in press).

Presuming competence – "Difficulties with demonstrating ability are not be taken as evidence of intellectual incompetence …[Rather,] as a matter of basic sensitivity and good educational practice, educators must presume that the person is intelligent" (Biklen, 1999, p. 50).

Related services – According to IDEA, related services means transportation and such developmental, corrective, and other supportive services as are required to assist a child with a disability to benefit from special education, and includes speech-language pathology and audiology services, interpreting services, psychological services, physical and occupational therapy, recreation, including therapeutic recreation, early identification and assessment of disabilities in children, counseling services, including rehabilitation counseling, orientation and mobility services, and medical services for diagnostic or evaluation purposes. Related services also include school health services and school nurse services, social work services in schools, and parent counseling and training (IDEA, 2004, §300.34).

REFERENCES

Artiles, A., & Bal, A. (2008). The next generation of disproportionality research: Toward a comparative model in the study of equity in ability differences. *Journal of Special Education*, *42*, 4–14.

Austin, V. L. (2001). Teachers' beliefs about co-teaching. *Remedial & Special Education. Special Curriculum Access*, *22*(4), 245–255.

Banda, D. R., Hart, S. L., & Liu-Gitz, L. (2010). Impact of training peers and children with autism on social skills during center time activities in inclusive classrooms. *Research in Autism Spectrum Disoders*, *4*(4), 619–625.

Bigby, C. M., Kristiansen, K., Johnson, K., & Traustadottir, R. (2005). *Deinstitutionalization and people with intellectual disabilities: In and out of institutions.* Philadelphia, PA: Jessica Kingsley Publishers.

Biklen, D. P. (1999). The metaphor of mental retardation: Rethinking ability and disability. In H. Bersani, Jr. (Ed.), *Responding to the challenge: Current trends and international issues in developmental disabilities.* Essays in honor of Gunnar Dybwad. Cambridge, MA: Brookline.

Broer, S. M., Doyle, M. B., & Giangreco, M. F. (2005). Perspectives of students with intellectual disabilities about their experiences with paraprofessional supports. *Exceptional Children*, *71*(4), 415–430.

Brown v. Board of Education. 347 U.S. 483 (1954).

Burstein, N., Sears, S., Wilcoxen, A., Cabello, B., & Spagna, M. (2004). Moving toward inclusive practices. *Remedial & Special Education*, *25*(2), 104–116.

Carrington, S., & Elkins, J. (2002). Bridging the gap between inclusive policy and inclusive culture in secondary schools. *Support for Learning*, *17*(2), 51–57.

Carter, E., Cushing, L. S., Clark, N. M., & Kennedy, C. H. (2005). Effect of peer support interventions on students' access to the general curriculum and social interactions. *Research & Practice for Persons with Severe Disabilities*, *30*(1), 15–25.

Carter, E. W., & Hughes, C. (2005). Increasing social interaction among adolescents with intellectual disabilities and their general education peers: Effective interventions. *Research & Practice for Persons with Severe Disabilities*, *30*(4), 179–193.

Carter, E. W., & Kennedy, C. (2006). Promoting access to the general curriculum using peer support strategies. *Research & Practice for Persons with Severe Disabilities*, *31*(4), 284–292.

Carter, E. W., Sisco, L. G., Melekoglu, M. A., & Kurkowski, C. (2007). Peer supports as an alternative to individually assigned paraprofessionals in inclusive high school classrooms. *Research & Practice for Persons with Severe Disabilities*, *32*(4), 213–227.

Causton-Theoharis, J. N., & Malmgren, K. W. (2004). Increasing interactions between students with severe disabilities and their peers via paraprofessional training. *Exceptional Children*, *71*, 431–444.

Causton-Theoharis, J. N., Theoharis, G. T., Orsait, F., & Cosier, M. (2011). Does self-contained special educatino deliver on its promises? A critical inquiry into research and practice. *Journal of Special Education Leadership*, *24*(2), 61–78.

Cawley, J., Hayden, S., Cade, E., & Baker-Kroczynski, S. (2002). Including students with disabilities into the general education science classroom. *Exceptional Children*, *68*(4), 423–435.

Chopra, R. V., Sandoval-Lucero, E., & French, N. K. (2011). Effective supervision of paraeducators: Multiple benefits and outcomes. *National Teacher Education Journal*, *4*(2), 15–26.

Clark, N. M., Cushing, L. S., & Kennedy, C. H. (2004). An intensive onsite technical assistance model to promote inclusive educational practices for students with disabilities in middle school and high school. *Research & Practice for Persons with Severe Disabilities*, *29*(4), 253–262.

Collins, B. C., Branson, T. A., Hall, M., & Rankin, S. W. (2001). Teaching secondary students with moderate disabilities in an inclusive academic classroom setting. *Journal of Developmental & Physical Disabilities*, *13*(1), 41–59.

Cook, B. G. (2001). A comparison of teachers' attitudes toward their included students with mild and severe disabilities. *Journal of Special Education*, *34*(4), 203–213.

Cook, B. G. (2004). Inclusive teachers' attitudes toward their students with disabilities: A replication and extension. *Elementary School Journal*, *104*(4), 307–320.

Daniel R.R. v. State Board of Education. 874 F.2d 1036 (1989).

Dessemontet, R. S., Bless, G., & Morin, D. (2012). Effects of inclusion on the academic achievement and adaptive behaviour of children with intellectual disabilities. *Journal of Intellectual Disability Research*, *56*(6), 579–587.

Dinnebeil, L., McInerney, W., Roth, J., & Ramaswamy, V. (2001). Itinerant early childhood special education services: Service delivery in one state. *Journal of Early Intervention*, *24*(1), 35–44.

Dore, R., Dion, A., Wagner, S., & Brunet, J. (2002). High school inclusion of adolescents with mental retardation: A multiple case study. *Education & Training in Mental Retardation & Developmental Disabilities*, *37*(3), 253–261.

Downing, J. E., & Peckham-Hardin, D. (2008). Inclusive education: What makes it a good education for students with moderate to severe disabiltiies? *Research & Practice for Persons with Severe Disabilities, 32*(1), 16–30.

Dymond, S. K., & Russell, D. L. (2004). Impact of grade and disability on the instructional context of inclusive classrooms. *Education & Training in Developmental Disabilities, 39*(2), 127–140.

Eaves, L., & Ho, H. (1997). School placement and academic achievement in children with autistic spectrum disorders. *Journal of Developmental & Physical Disabilities, 9*(4), 277–291.

Ehren, B. (2000). Maintaining a therapeutic focus and sharing responsibility for student success: Keys to in-classroom speech-language services. *Language, Speech, and Hearing Services in Schools, 31*, 219–229.

Eisenman, L. T., Pleet, A. M., Wandry, D., & McGinley, V. (2011). Voices of special education teachers in an inclusive high school: Redefining responsibliities. *Remedial & Special Education, 32*(2), 91–104.

Fennick, E., & Royle, J. (2003). Community inclusion for children and youth with developmental disabilities. *Focus on Autism & Other Developmental Disabilities, 18*(1), 20–27.

Fisher, M., & Meyer, L. H. (2002). Development and social competence after two years for students enrolled in inclusive and self-contained educational programs. *Research & Practice for Persons with Severe Disabilities, 27*(3), 165–174.

Foster, S., & Cue, K. (2009). Roles and responsibilities of itinerant specialist teachers of deaf and hard of hearing students. *American Annals of the Deaf, 153*(5), 435–439. doi:10.1353/aad.0.0068

Frazeur-Cross, A., Traub, E., Hutter-Pishgahi, L., & Shelton, G. (2004). Elements of successful inclusion for children with significant disabilities. *Topics in Early Childhood Special Education, 24*(3), 169–184.

French, N. (1999). Paraeducators: Who are they and what do they do? *Teaching Exceptional Children, September*, 65–69.

French, N., & Chopra, R. (1999). Parent perspectives on the roles of paraprofessionals. *Journal of the Association of People with Severe Disabilities, 24*(4), 259–272.

Friend, M., Cook, L., Hurley-Chamberlain, D., & Shamberger, C. (2010). Co-teaching: An illustration of the complexity of collaboration in special education. *Journal of Educational & Psychological Consultation, 20*(1), 9–27. doi:10.1080/10474410903535380

Gandhi, A. (2007). Context matters: Exploring relations between inclusion and reading achievement of students without disabilities. *International Journal of Disability, Development, and Education, 54*(1), 91–112.

Giangreco, M. (1986). Effects of integrated therapy: A pilot study. *JASH, 11*(3), 205–208.

Giangreco, M., & Broer, S. M. (2005). Questionable utilization of paraprofessionals in inclusive schools: Are we addressing symptoms or causes? *Focus on Autism & Other Developmental Disabilities, 20*(1), 10–26.

Giangreco, M., Doyle, M. B., & Suter, J. C. (2012). Constructively responding to requests for paraprofessionals: We keep asking the wrong questions. *Remedial and Special Education, 33*(6), 362–373.

Giangreco, M., Prelock, P., Reid, R., Dennis, R., & Edleman, S. (Eds.). (2000). *Roles of related services personnel in inclusive schools* (2nd ed.). Baltimore, MD: Paul H. Brookes.

Giangreco, M., York, J., & Rainforth, B. (1989). Providing related services to learners with severe handicaps in educational settings: Pursuing the least restrictive option. *Pediatric Physical Therapy*, *1*(2), 55–63.

Giangreco, M. F., Broer, S. M., & Edelman, S. W. (2001). Teacher engagement with students with disabiliteis: Differences based on paraprofessional service delivery models. *Journal of the Association for Persons with Severe Handicaps*, *26*, 75–86.

Giangreco, M. F., Edelman, S. W., & MacFarland, S. (1997). Helping or hovering? Effects of instructional assistant proximity on students with disabilities. *Exceptional Children*, *64*(1), 7–18.

Gürgür, H., & Uzuner, Y. (2010). A phenomenological analysis of the views on co-teaching applications in the inclusion classroom. *Kuram ve Uygulamada Eğitim Bilimleri*, *10*(1), 311–331.

Hanson, M., Horn, E., Sandall, S., Beckman, P., Morgan, M., Marquart, J., ... Chou, I. (2001). After preschool inclusion: Children's educational pathways over the early school years. *Exceptional Children*, *68*(1), 65–83.

Hedeen, D. L., & Ayres, B. J. (2002). "You Want Me to Teach Him to Read?" Fulfilling the intent of IDEA. *Journal of Disability Policy Studies*, *13*(3), 180–189.

Heiman, T. (2001). Inclusive schooling – Middle school teachers' perceptions. *School Psychology International*, *22*(4), 451–462.

Heller, K. A., Holtzman, W. H., & Messick, S. (Eds.). (1982). *Placing children in special education: A strategy for equity*. Washington, DC: National Academy Press.

Hendrick Hudson District Board of Education v. Rowley. 458 U.S. 176 (1982).

Individuals with Disabilities Education Improvement Act. H.R. 1350, Pub. L. No. P.L. 108-446 (2004).

Jackson, L., Ryndak, D. L., & Wehmeyer, M. L. (2008–2009). The dynamic relationship between context, curriculum, and student learning: A case for inclusive education as a research-based practice. *Research & Practice for Persons with Severe Disabilities*, *33–4*(4–1), 175–195.

Jitendra, A. K., Edwards, L. L., Choutka, C. M., & Treadway, P. S. (2002). A collaborative approach to planning in the content areas for students with learning disabilities: Accessing the general curriculum. *Learning Disabilities Research & Practice*, *17*(4), 252–267.

Johnson, J. W., & McDonnell, J. (2004). An exploratory study of the implementation of embedded instruction by general educators with students with developmental disabilities. *Education and Treatment of Children*, *27*(1), 46–63.

Jorgensen, C. M., McSheehan, M., & Sonnenmeier, R. M. (2007). Presumed competence reflected in the educational programs of students with IDD before and after the beyond access professional development intervention. *Journal of Intellectual & Developmental Disability*, *32*, 248–262.

Kalambouka, A., Farrell, P., Dyson, A., & Kaplan, I. (2007). The impact of placing pupils with special educational needs in mainstream schools on the achievement of their peers. *Educational Research*, *49*(4), 365–382.

Kurth, J. A., Morningstar, M. E., & Kozleski, E. (in press). The persistence of highly restrictive special education placements for students with low-incidence disabilities. *Research & Practice for Persons with Severe Disabilities*.

Lavoie, R. D., & Lieberman, L. M. (1986). Toward developing a philosophy of education: A re-examination of competition, fairness and the work ethic. *Journal of Learning Disabilities*, *19*(1), 62–63.

Magiera, K., & Zigmond, N. (2005). Co-teaching in middle school classrooms under routine conditions: Does the instructional experience differ for students with disabilities in co-taught and solo-taught classes? *Learning Disabilities Research & Practice*, *20*(2), 79–85.

Mastropieri, M. A., & Scruggs, T. E. (2001). Promoting inclusion in secondary classrooms. *Learning Disability Quarterly*, *24*(4), 265–274.

Mastropieri, M. A., Scruggs, T. E., Spencer, V., & Fontana, J. (2003). Promoting success in high school world history: Peer tutoring versus guided notes. *Learning Disabilities Research & Practice*, *18*(1), 52–65.

McLeskey, J., Henry, D., & Hodges, D. (1998). Inclusion: Where is it happening? *Teaching Exceptional Children*, *30*, 4–10.

McLeskey, J., Landers, E., Williamson, P., & Hoppey, D. (2012). Are we moving toward educating students with disabilities in less restrictive settings? *Journal of Special Education*, *46*(3), 131–140.

Meyer, L. H. (2001). The impact on inclusion on children's lives: Multiple outcomes, and friendship in particular. *International Journal of Disability, Development & Education*, *48*, 9–31.

Moores, D. F. (2005). The no child left behind and the individuals with disabilities education acts: The uneven impact of partially funded federal mandates on education of deaf and hard of hearing children. *American Annals of the Deaf*, *150*(2), 75–80.

Murawski, W. W. (2012). 10 tips for using co-planning time more efficiently. *Teaching Exceptional Children*, *64*(4), 8–15.

Murawski, W. W., & Swanson, H. L. (2001). A meta-analysis of co-teaching research: What are the data? *Remedial & Special Education*, *22*, 258–267.

Noell, G., & Witt, J. (1999). When does consultation lead to intervention implementation? Critical issues for research and practice. *Journal of Special Education*, *33*, 29–35.

Noonan, M. J., McCormick, L., & Heck, R. H. (2003). The co-teacher relationship scale: Applications for professional development. *Education & Training in Developmental Disabilities*, *38*(1), 113–120.

O'Reilly, Lancioni, G., Gardiner, M., Tiernan, R., & Lacy, C. (2002). Using a problem-solving approach to teach classroom skills to a student with moderate intellectual disabilities within regular classroom settings. *International Journal of Disability, Development & Education*, *49*(1), 95–104.

PARC v. Pennsylvania. 334 F. Supp. 279 (1972).

Rafael Oberti v. Clemonton School District. 995 F.2d 1204 (1993).

Rainforth, B., & York-Barr, J. (1997). *Collaborative teams for students with severe disabilities: Integrating therapy and educational services* (2nd ed.). Baltimore, MD: Paul H. Brookes Publishing Co.

Roncker v. Walter. 700 F.2d 1058 (1983).

Russ, S., Chiang, B., Rylance, B., & Bongers, J. (2001). Caseload in special education: An integration of research findings. *Exceptional Children*, *67*(2), 161–172.

Sacramento Unified School District v. Rachel H. C 786 F. Supp. 874 (1992).

Seery, M., Davis, P., & Johnson, L. (2000). Seeing eye-to-eye: Are parents and professionals in agreement about the benefits of preschool inclusion? *Remedial and Special Education*, *21*(5), 268–278.

Shakespeare, T. (2006). The social model of disability. In L. J. Davis (Ed.), *The disability studies reader* (pp. 197–204). London: Routledge.

Smith, A., & Kozleski, E. (2005). Witnessing brown: Pursuit of an equity agenda in American education. *Remedial & Special Education*, *26*, 270–280.

Smith, J. D., & Wehmeyer, M. L. (2012). *Good blood, bad blood: Science and nature and the myth of the Kalikaks*. Washington, DC: American Association on Intellectual and Developmental Disabilities.

Smith, T. C. (2005). IDEA 2004: Another round in the reauthorization process. *Remedial and Special Education*, *26*(6), 314–319.

Sterling-Turner, H. E., & Jordan, S. S. (2007). Interventions addressing transition difficulties for individuals with autism. *Psychology in the Schools*, *44*, 681–690.

Strogilos, V., & Tragoulia, E. (2013). Inclusive and collaborative practices in co-taught classrooms: Roles and responsibilities for teachers and parents. *Teaching and Teacher Education*, *35*, 81–91. doi:10.1016/j.tate.2013.06.001

Thompson, J. R., Bradley, V. J., Buntinx, W. H. E., Schalock, R. L., Shogren, K., Snell, M., ... Yeager, M. H. (2009). Conceptualizing supports and the support needs of people with intellectual disability. *Intellectual and Developmental Disabilities*, *47*(2), 135–146. doi:10.1352/1934-9556-47.2.135

Turnbull, H. R. (2005). Individuals with disabilities education act reauthorization: Accountability and personal responsibility. *Remedial and Special Education*, *26*(6), 320–326.

Villa, R., Thousand, J. S., & Nevin, A. (2004). *A guide to co-teaching: Practical tips for facilitating student learning*. Thousand Oaks, CA: Corwin Press.

Vlachou, A., & Zoniou-Sideri, A. (2010). Inclusive education and collaborative practices between general and special education teachers. *Hellenic Journal of Psychology*, *7*(2), 180–204.

Weiner, J., & Tardif, C. (2004). Social and emotional functioning of children with learning disabilities: Does special education placement make a difference? *Learning Disabilities Research & Practice*, *19*(1), 20–32.

Winzer, M. A. (2007). Confronting difference: An excursion through the history of special education. In L. Florian (Ed.), *The SAGE handbook of special education*. Thousand Oaks, CA: Sage.

Wolfsenberger, W. (1972). *The principle of normalization in human services*. Toronto: National Institute on Mental Retardation.

York, J., Giangreco, M., Vandercook, T., & Macdonald, C. (1992). *Integrating support personnel in the inclusive classroom*. Baltimore, MD: Paul H. Brookes Publishing Co.

PROVIDING APPROPRIATE INDIVIDUALIZED INSTRUCTION AND ACCESS TO THE GENERAL EDUCATION CURRICULUM FOR LEARNERS WITH LOW-INCIDENCE DISABILITIES

Jeremy Erickson and Carol Ann Davis

ABSTRACT

In the United States, the mandate to provide access to general education curriculum standards for all learners is clear. This chapter provides an overview and a framework for making individualized and curriculum choices for learners with low-incidence disabilities and cognitive deficits. Topics covered include reconciling an ecological curriculum model with a standards-based framework and an expanded discussion on embedding individualized learning targets within the ongoing lessons, routines, and activities of inclusive classrooms. Carefully planned and implemented embedded instruction can provide a match between a student's need

Including Learners with Low-Incidence Disabilities
International Perspectives on Inclusive Education, Volume 5, 137–158

ISSN: 1479-3636/doi:10.1108/S1479-363620140000005007

for individualized instruction and the everyday practices of inclusive classrooms.

Keywords: Embedded instruction; systematic instruction; ecological curriculum; standards-based curriculum; partial participation; individualized instruction

INTRODUCTION

Successfully including students with low-incidence disabilities in general education classrooms can be a difficult task. In the United States, the legal mandates are clear: provide all learners with access to the general education curriculum (Individuals with Disabilities Education Improvement Act [IDEIA], 2004; NCLB, 2002). The Individualized Education Program (IEP) is designed to enhance and ensure access to the general curriculum for learners with disabilities, not to replace it as an individualized curriculum (Nolet & McLaughlin, 2000). For most learners with low-incidence disabilities, extensive planning, work, and collaboration are required just to ensure that they are making adequate progress on their individualized learning goals and objectives from their IEP. Balancing individual needs with general curriculum standards is a significant undertaking for many educators. To assist with this challenge, teachers need adequate frameworks to utilize when selecting learning targets and instructional practices to meet the unique needs of their learners. This chapter will provide a framework for planning appropriate curriculum and then detail the practice of utilizing embedded instruction (EI) as a relevant and evidence-based practice to teach learning goals.

Many learners with low-incidence disabilities require more intensive and frequent instructional trials than other learners to acquire, maintain, and generalize skills targeted for instruction. This is especially true for individuals with low-incidence disabilities including cognitive deficits. It has long been suggested that students with significant cognitive disabilities struggle to make adequate progress on learning targets when instruction is presented through curricula based largely on a time-determined progression (i.e., covering multiplication of fractions for two weeks) (Brown et al., 1983). Learners with low-incidence disabilities and cognitive deficits frequently learn more slowly than their peers and have a difficult time maintaining information that has been learned. There is a legitimate concern that many learners with low-incidence disabilities require frequent practice of skills under natural conditions to promote skill maintenance (i.e., so skills are not forgotten and so the learning targets will be applied when needed). This belief has historically justified segregated learning environments and instructional practices for students with low-incidence disabilities. As the learning needs of these students have generally been considered an inappropriate match for the instructional practices of general education classrooms, embedded instruction is one instructional approach that may help bridge the gap between the needs of students with low-incidence disabilities and the practices of general education classrooms.

This chapter provides an overview and a framework for making individualized and curriculum choices for learners with low-incidence disabilities and cognitive deficits (from here on referred to as low-incidence disabilities). This chapter focuses on practices to meet the needs of learners with cognitive deficits, although the practices discussed may be useful for a larger range of learners with low-incidence disabilities, and includes an expanded discussion of embedded instructional (EI) practices in the context of inclusive settings. The following questions guide the discussion in this chapter:

1. In what manner should curriculum decisions and instructional choices be made for meeting the needs of learners with low-incidence disabilities participating in inclusive classrooms and settings?
2. How are learning targets for learners with low-incidence disabilities best represented as a continuum of individualization?
3. What is embedded instruction for students with low-incidence disabilities?
4. How does embedded instruction align with systematic instruction?
5. How can embedded instruction be utilized to meet the learning needs of individuals with low-incidence disabilities in inclusive settings?

HISTORICAL BACKGROUND

With the reauthorization of IDEIA (2004) and NCLB (2002), the mandate to schools to provide access to the general education curriculum for all learners, including students with low-incidence disabilities, is clear. So while there is an ongoing debate in the field on the best curriculum framework (particularly an ecological vs. standards-based model), teachers are required by law to meet the individual needs of learners with low-incidence disabilities including access to the general education curriculum. When the Public Law 94-142, The Education for all Handicapped Children Act, was passed in 1975, learners were guaranteed access to a free and appropriate public education. Educators unfamiliar with serving students with low-incidence disabilities were confronted with the responsibility to provide meaningful instruction for all. One common approach to instruction was based on normal developmental sequences. That is, educators would focus instruction around content appropriate to the "mental age" of the learner using the normal developmental sequence as the guide for what to teach. While this approach is intuitive and logical, students with disabilities that impacted their progression through the developmental sequence were quickly left behind, or stuck working on skills that were not appropriate to their age, or skills that were grossly inadequate to participate in activities and settings with same aged peers. As teachers taught to developmental sequences, they were commonly teaching skills appropriate for early childhood classrooms to adolescents and adults (Baumgart et al., 1982).

The field of special education quickly turned to a framework for instruction that focused not on teaching skills on a developmental sequence but instead on the critical skills that would promote access to meaningful current and future environments. This framework is commonly referred to as an ecological framework. Educators in collaboration with families and students would select current and relevant future environments that the learner might access or that would be meaningful to access, and focus on selecting and teaching the skills necessary to fully or partially participate within them. For young children the focus was on teaching the skills necessary to access their neighborhood school and other relevant community settings, and for older learners, the focus was on teaching skills necessary to access and participate in regular community settings and activities (independent living, social interaction, vocational, and leisure skills). This framework centered on the community as the natural ecology for individuals with severe or low-incidence disabilities. It was guided by the criterion of ultimate functioning, defined as, "an ever changing, expanding, localized, and personalized cluster of factors that each person must possess in order to function as productively and independently as possible in socially, vocationally, and domestically integrated adult community environments" (Brown, Nietupski, & Hamre-Nietupski, 1976, p. 8).

As the field embraced an ecological framework for planning instruction, which centered on access to and participation in regular community settings and neighborhood schools, learners with low-incidence disabilities were increasingly integrated into these environments. Considering the legal mandates on Least Restrictive Environments (LRE) and accountability toward standards, current practice in the field has increasingly shifted beyond mere integration into general education settings, with a greater emphasis and attention being placed on instruction and progress in the general curriculum. With the passing of No Child Left Behind Act of 2001 (NCLB, 2002), states are required to assess all learners regarding their progress toward state standards. The majority of states in the U.S. have adopted curriculum standards known as the Common Core State Standards (CCSS). The accountability requirements of NCLB and national standards represented by the CCSS have resulted in a new focus and discussion in the special education field around a standards-based framework.

There is an ongoing debate and concern in the field that instruction around grade-level content standards may be detrimental to postschool outcomes for learners with low-incidence disabilities. Such an approach may mirror the shortcomings of a developmental model by focusing on teaching students content standards that are not immediately relevant to independent functioning, future adult outcomes, and quality of life (Ayres, Douglas, Lowery, & Sievers, 2011; Brown, 2013; Lowery, Drasgow, Renzaglia, & Chezan, 2007; Ryndak, Alper, Hughes, & McDonnell, 2012). Some leaders and thinkers in the field have responded that both frameworks are necessary; that standards relate to equal educational opportunities and that the critics of grade-level content standards risk perpetuating the myth that learners with low-incidence disabilities are not capable of progressing toward the learning standards that are valued for all students (Courtade, Spooner, Browder, & Jimenez, 2012). In the midst of the ongoing debate, there is a shared underlying agreement in the field that instructional content for learners with low-incidence disabilities should lead to increased independence, participation in valued activities and settings, and result in skill development that is meaningful and functional to the learner. Many agree that work is needed to reconcile the ecological framework with a standards-based approach (Hunt, McDonnell, & Crockett, 2012; McDonnell, Hunt, Jackson, & Ryndak, 2013; Ward, Van De Mark, & Ryndak, 2006). "The need for direct, repeated instruction on highly prioritized and specific skills contrasts sharply with the brisk pace and breadth of content of the general curriculum. The need exists to find ways to teach target skills that have utility across this rapidly moving curriculum" (Browder et al., 2007. p. 7).

In this call for reconciliation, it has been suggested that instructional practices and paradigms that fully consider the needs of all learners are necessary. The concepts of Universal Design for Learning (UDL) (Hall, Meyer, & Rose, 2012; Jimenez, Graf, & Rose, 2007) and differentiated instruction (Broderick, Mehta-Parekh, & Reid, 2005; Trela & Jimenez, 2013) have been recommended as frameworks that require upfront planning and consideration of the learning needs and abilities of all learners included in classroom settings and activities. These frameworks are relatively new and theoretical and have yet to be demonstrated in large-scale studies. A long standing and evidence-based practice, largely from the early childhood literature, is embedded instruction. Several researchers have recommended the use of embedded instruction as a viable means for teaching academic content and individually relevant functional skills for students included in general education classrooms and activities (Copeland & Cosbey, 2010; McDonnell et al., 2013; Ward, 2009).

CONTINUUM OF INSTRUCTION AND INSTRUCTIONAL CONTENT DECISION MAKING

In examining the instructional and support needs of learners with low-incidence disabilities, it is helpful to consider instruction for students with low-incidence disabilities as a continuum of options (see Fig. 1). These options range from participating in the general curriculum (activity or lesson) without individualization, to explicit, student-focused instruction specially designed one-on-one or small group instruction unrelated to the on-going classroom-wide activities. At each step up the continuum, there is an increasing level of individualization for both instruction and learning targets.

In meeting the needs of learners with low-incidence disabilities, teachers must consider what level of instruction and individualization is necessary for their students to participate and make progress in the general curriculum and on their IEP goals and objectives. As students in inclusive classrooms typically engage in a wide variety of activities and lessons, only providing explicit, student-focused instruction for students is not a good match for the everyday practices of inclusive classrooms. Historically, this type of instruction is frequently provided through pull out or pull aside services (Collins, Hager, & Galloway, 2011). Providing adequate instruction for students with low-incidence disabilities often requires that teachers provide a mix of modifications and accommodations, embedded instruction, and explicit, student-focused instruction.

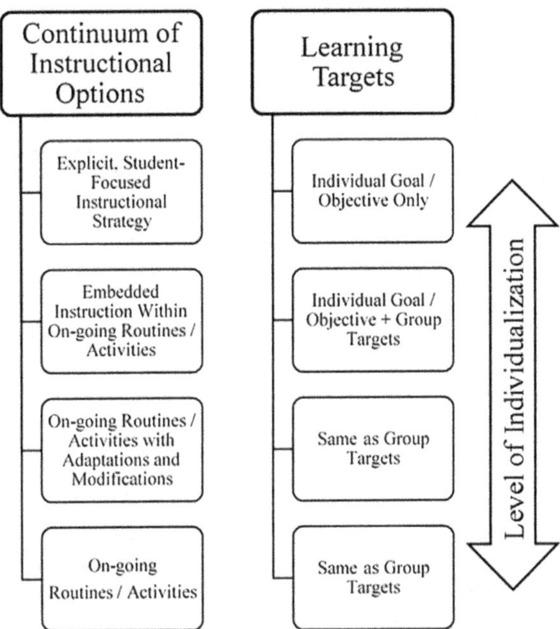

Fig. 1. Continuum of Instruction. *Source*: Adapted from Sandall et al. (2008).

Continuum of Learning Targets

One side of the continuum represents the range of options for where a student's learning targets are aligned with general education settings. These targets are largely focused on aligning instruction for the individual with low-incidence disabilities in meaningfully participating in the same outcomes and objectives as the group. Within this framework, the learning targets may be exactly aligned with or without adaptations and modifications to instructional practices that support access and participation for the learner with low-incidence disabilities.

The continuum is intended to be used in a more fluid rather than static manner. That is, Ms. Zan may decide that Susan can participate in math with targets that are the same as the classroom and reading targets that are individual goal only. In many instances, teachers may see the need or opportunity to address multiple learning targets, including some aspects of the group learning target and an individual learning goal or objective.

This level of instruction is where embedded instructional practices are meaningfully applied. That is, teachers provide systematic instructional practices and learning opportunities for individually relevant and referenced learning targets within the ongoing class activity or routine which supports a larger group learning target. Conversely, within instances where individualized instruction is provided outside the context of general education activities and settings, it is possible to provide embedded instruction on learning targets from a standards-based content into explicit, student-focused instructional strategies. There may be cases where individually relevant instruction is happening through community-based instruction or individualized instructional activities where general education learning targets can be meaningfully applied (e.g., including a learning target on a science standard related to the states of matter in a job training site where the student is preparing a meal and boiling water or melting butter).

An important consideration in applying embedded instructional targets is that the learning target should relate to or expand on the routine or activity in a relevant way. It is believed that embedded instruction that is relevant to the activity and that expands on the relevant stimuli and context will support the maintenance and generalization of the targeted skills (Baumgart & Ferguson, 1991). Embedded instructional approaches as discussed in the early childhood literature emphasize that EI "expands, modifies, or is integral to the activity or event in a meaningful way" (Pretti-Frontczak & Bricker, 2004, p. 40). Instructional trials on concepts that are unrelated to the immediate activity or setting are less likely to be meaningful to the learner with low-incidence disabilities.

The continuum of learning targets includes individualized learning targets and goals in isolation from group learning targets. While there is a growing body of research demonstrating the efficiency and effectiveness of EI, the studies to date on the practice have only included small numbers of embedded learning targets (typically, between one and five) and generally within a small number of routines or activities. There is insufficient evidence in current research to show that school staff serving students with low-incidence disabilities in general education classrooms can successfully manage teaching all of a student's individualized learning targets through EI. In discussing embedded response prompting strategies, Wolery and Schuster (1997) warned, "we do not know whether teaching several different behaviors embedded into several different activities at the same time will result in effective instruction" (p. 72).

Continuum of Instructional Practices

As described above, the focus of the framework is related to learning targets that apply to all students. That is, the students with low-incidence disabilities will be expected to participate in and learn the same instructional content as the rest of the class. Often for a student with disabilities, some form of adaptation or modification will be necessary for the learner to participate with the class and access the group-learning target. Janney and Snell (2006) suggest applying two criteria for judging the appropriateness of individual adaptations: "(a) they facilitate social and instructional participation in class activities and (b) they do so using means that are *only as special as necessary*" (p. 216). These authors also recommend that adaptations should be decided on collaboratively between general education and special education staff after carefully considering the needs of the individual and the typical practices of the classroom. It is also important to utilize direct observation of the student in the setting while participating in the activities that are being considered for adaptations. Observation can help staff ensure that the adaptations are relevant and only as specialized as needed for the student (Janney & Snell, 2006). In a recent paper by Wakeman, Karvonen, and Ahumada (2013), the authors outline several relevant adaptations or modifications which may be considered to increase independence and foster meaningful participation. Some of these suggestions include changes to the complexity of responses or how the response is made; adjusting the complexity of the content; making content less abstract; reduction to the number of steps in the task; and reducing the amount of information presented. Staff should also carefully consider if any environmental modifications, technology tools, or peer assistance supports are available to facilitate participation in targeted learning activities.

The concept of partial participation is critical in regards to meeting the needs of learners with low-incidence disabilities and using embedded instruction (Baumgart et al., 1982). Partial participation revolves around the idea that individuals with disabilities require access to age appropriate activities and settings and that independent functioning within these settings and activities should not be a prerequisite for meaningful access and participation. Systematic instruction should be provided to increase meaningful partial and independent participation in activities and environments that result in improved membership within the community for the individual with disabilities.

The continuum of instructional practices is intended to also be used in a fluid rather than static manner. For some students and depending on the objective, they can participate in ongoing routines and have the same learning targets as the group or classroom. Others may have individual learning targets that occur within on-going routines while still another student may have an individual goal or objective that is implemented with explicit instruction.

MAKING CURRICULUM AND INSTRUCTIONAL CHOICES FOR LEARNERS WITH LOW-INCIDENCE DISABILITIES

Current legislation in the United States requires educators of students with low-incidence disabilities to provide access to the general education curriculum while at the same time considering the curricular and instructional needs necessary to prepare learners to be productive and independent adults. The IDEIA 2004 states:

> (5)(A) having high expectation for such children and ensuring their access to the general education curriculum in the regular classroom, to the maximum extent possible, in order to (i) meet developmental goals and, to the maximum extent possible, the challenging expectations that have been established for all children; and (ii) be prepared to lead productive and independent adult lives, to the maximum extent possible (20 U.S.C. § 1400(c)(5)).

This mandate is aligned with the call from experts in the field to reconcile an ecological curricular framework with a standards-based framework. To successfully accomplish this reconciliation, education teams must take steps to make individualized curriculum and instructional choices that are directly related to both access to general education curriculum and independence as adults. To guide this process, educators should always consider what is personally relevant to the learner (Trela & Jimenez, 2013).

Guiding Principles from an Ecological Framework

Hunt et al. (2012) explain that a guiding question within the ecological framework asks:

> What can we teach students and how can we arrange educational environments to increase quality of life outcomes; connect the students to their worlds of home, school,

> and community; and increase postschool outcomes of full access and social participation, employment, and independent living? (p. 141)

Established methods of identifying high-priority quality-of-life outcomes, and the skills needed for meaningful postschool outcomes in the community, include ecological inventories (Brown et al., 1979), family interviews (Giangreco, Cloninger, & Iverson, 2011), and formal person-centered planning (Falvey, Forest, Pearpoint, & Rosenberg, 1997) procedures. All of these assessment and planning practices focus on the needs of the individual with low-incidence disabilities by referencing current and future environments, and the unique strengths, needs, and desires of the student and their family.

Some form or combination of these practices should be utilized to identify valued priority life goals across broad domains including communication and social skills; independent functioning in the home, school, community, and vocational routines; self-determination, goal setting, and problem-solving skills. Beyond identifying broad domain area goals that are aligned with the functional outcome of independence and participation, assessment procedures should be expanded to include the consideration and prioritization of general knowledge areas that are of personal interest to the student (science, reading, writing, mathematics, and the arts) (Hunt et al., 2012). These general knowledge domains should be examined in relation to student interest and their connection to the specific functional quality-of-life domains identified in the assessment process. That is, if there are general knowledge skills that are likely to motivate the individual, that are foundational and enrich participation in current and future environments.

It is critical that educational teams and families identify priority domains and outcomes that can guide curriculum and instructional choices. To ensure that individuals with low-incidence disabilities are able to participate in the general curriculum to the maximum extent possible, while at the same time being prepared for successful postschool outcomes, educators must make instructional choices that align closely with identified priority goals. Instructional practices that focus on skills that are valued by the student and their family and that are likely to be achieved and put into regular use by the student will have a greater likelihood of promoting meaningful participation in the general curriculum and result in a better quality of life after school. As we know that learners with low-incidence disabilities are capable of learning many things when given high-quality instruction (including grade-level content standard) (Courtade et al., 2012), we also know that without opportunities to regularly practice and apply those skills in meaningful ways, they can be forgotten or lost (Brown, 2013; Horner, Williams, & Knobbe, 1985).

While some of the details of the general curriculum are forgotten by nearly all students with or without disabilities (few individuals remember the details of their first persuasive essay or the results of their early lab reports), the core skills addressed in the general curriculum are rarely centered on details. Instead, the focus is on the ability to apply knowledge through multiple means, such as writing to support an argument, or to use the scientific method to answer a question. The learner without disabilities most often has the ability to acquire, maintain, and generalize these skills with enough practice in the classroom. In contrast, the learner with low-incidence disabilities frequently requires more intensive practice and support and enough opportunities to apply the learned skills across the classroom, home, and community settings for it to be of lasting value.

Guiding Questions for Selecting Content from General Curriculum

Once valued, priority life goals have been identified, teams should work together to look at the general curriculum standards and select learning targets to be considered for inclusion or alignment to the IEP. These should be components of the general curriculum standards that the team feels aligns with the goals and domains prioritized earlier in the ecological assessment process, and that will likely require specially designed instruction to be mastered and applied by the student. It should be noted that selection of these learning targets from the general curriculum does not preclude teams from including students with low-incidence disabilities in opportunities participate in or be exposed to activities or instruction focused on other learning targets from the general curriculum.

There are many instances in the inclusive classroom for students to fully or partially participate in activities that may or may not be centered on learning targets that have been identified for specially designed instruction. Teachers will want to consider the learning targets across the continuum of instruction for all activities and routines that the student participates in, and then determine the relevant learning targets to be addressed. Identified individual learning targets can regularly be embedded into instructional activities that provide exposure to the larger general curriculum learning targets that are the focus of the ongoing instruction in the classroom.

To assist the team with identifying learning targets from the general curriculum for inclusion as individualized goals, it is helpful for the team to consider the following questions:

- Is the skill aligned to the valued, priority life goals identified through ecological assessments?
- Will the student have opportunities for regular practice of the skill?
- Will the skill apply to functional activities and environments?
- Is the skill foundational (will it create more opportunities to access the general curriculum)?
- Does this skill link in critical ways to other opportunities to access the ongoing routines and activities of a general education classroom?
- Will the skill increase social integration, dignity, and competence of the student?
- Does achievement of the skill seem likely given the student's prior knowledge, skills, and response to systematic instruction?
- Can instruction be incorporated into or coordinated with current activities? (adapted from Rainforth, Giangreco, & Dennis, 1989)

The process of examining the general curriculum standards should be completed with the support of general education staff members familiar with the grade-level content. Their insights into the scope and sequence of the curriculum and activities in the inclusion classroom will be necessary to select the foundational skills that will be repeatedly practiced and built upon in the course of the school year and subsequent grades.

EMBEDDED INSTRUCTION WITHIN ON-GOING ROUTINES AND ACTIVITIES

EI and student-focused instructional strategies represent critical components of instruction for students with low-incidence disabilities within the continuum of instruction. In the context of inclusive classrooms, EI may be the best fit for providing explicit, systematic instruction on IEP goals/objectives and in providing meaningful access to the general curriculum or group learning targets. Since it is common that students with low-incidence disabilities require a high degree of individualization or modifications and adaptations to participate in on-going routines, activities, or lessons, it is important that school personnel can successfully evaluate when and what additional individualization is necessary to promote adequate progress toward learning goals. Teachers that carefully evaluate and implement the necessary level of support for everyone can enhance student learning in an efficient and effective manner. Identifying opportunities for meaningful participation and progress on learning goals without exclusively providing explicit, student-focused instruction can save teachers time and effort and promote independence for the learner with low-incidence disabilities.

PLANNING AND IMPLEMENTING EMBEDDED INSTRUCTION

Knowing that teachers of students with low-incidence disabilities struggle to find a balance between providing appropriate individualized instruction, and access to the general education curriculum, it is critical to identify instructional practices to address both needs. Embedded Instruction (EI) is one promising and increasingly common practice for providing socially valid, systematic instruction for students with disabilities. There is a growing research base supporting EI as a manageable and effective model for instructing students with disabilities in inclusive classrooms.

Various labels have been used to describe practices that emphasize an embedded instructional approach. These labels include Individualized Curriculum Sequencing (ICS) (Holvoet, Guess, Mulligan, & Brown, 1980; Sailor & Guess, 1983), activity-based instruction (ABI) (Bricker & Cripe, 1992), milieu teaching (Kaiser, Yoder, & Keetz, 1992), and naturalistic instruction (Hepting & Goldstein, 1996; Rule, Losardo, Dinnibeil, Kaiser, Rowland, 1988). While there is not an agreed upon definition of EI in the research literature, the term commonly refers, "to explicit, systematic instruction designed to distribute instructional trials within on-going routines and activities" (McDonnell, Johnson, & McQuivey, 2008, p. 1). EI typically occurs in natural environments without disrupting the flow of the routine, activity, or lesson.

Embedded Instruction in the Research Literature

EI has been shown to be an effective practice across several research studies. Researchers have examined EI implemented by general education teachers within ongoing classroom activities in inclusive classrooms (Johnson, McDonnell, Holzwarth, & Hunter, 2004; Wolery, Anthony,

Snyder, Werts, & Katzenmeyer, 1997). Other studies have shown successful EI implemented by paraeducators (Collins, Hager, & Galloway, 2011; McDonnell, Johnson, Polychronis, & Riesen, 2002), and peers (Hudson, Browder, & Jimenez, 2014; Jameson, McDonnell, Polychronis, & Riesen, 2008; Jimenez, Browder, Spooner, & Dibiase, 2012). These studies have demonstrated that embedded instruction can be utilized to teach learning targets focused on grade-level content standard and functional skills.

Embedded Instruction and Systematic Instruction

It is a commonly held belief that students with low-incidence disabilities are unlikely to learn without planned systematic instruction (Downing, 2010; Halle, Chadsey, Lee, & Renzaglia, 2004). For this reason, educators frequently provide instruction on controlled environments through one-on-one or small-group discrete trial instruction. Common instructional practices for students with low-incidence disabilities share several key components including breaking down tasks into parts, and teaching these parts using carefully designed antecedent and consequence strategies to assist the learner in focusing on the relevant parts of the task, and thereby enabling them to respond as intended. A final critical feature of systematic instruction is the frequent measurement of student progress on the identified learning targets. Well-designed EI includes the same key components.

When carefully planned and implemented, EI can be an effective means for teaching targeted skills to students with low-incidence disabilities. EI can provide a match between a student's need for individualized instruction and the everyday practices of inclusive classrooms thereby promoting inclusion, access to the general education curriculum, and appropriate instruction on IEP goals and objectives.

PLANNING AND IMPLEMENTING EMBEDDED INSTRUCTION

Identify Learning Targets

As mentioned earlier, it is important to match the learning target with targets in inclusive settings. Students with low-incidence disabilities will have identified annual goals and short-term objectives as a part of their individualized education program (IEP). Many IEP goals are well suited for EI. Matching a very individualized learning target with appropriate targets that are available in the inclusive setting can take many forms as expressed in Fig. 1. For example, social interaction goals can frequently be addressed by using EI in the context of naturally occurring activities with frequent peer-to-peer interactions. Lunch, recess, and group work all provide excellent opportunities to systematically teach skills during routines in which such interactions are typical. In addition, an individualized reading target may be paired with a social interaction target and match the learning targets in a cooperative learning group with a general education classroom. Communication learning targets are best addressed across settings, activities, and communicative partners; learning trials should be distributed across multiple opportunities for communication to promote the generalization and maintenance of communication skills under natural conditions. Ms. Galloway at Eastridge High School plans multiple opportunities for her student Charles to work on his communication skills by planning trials for him to request food items at lunch, balls during gym, and a card game during home room. While the items being requested, the settings, and peers vary by location, the communication learning target is consistent across the trials. Targeting communication and social interactions does not substantially interfere with the student's ability to access the group learning targets or the flow of the routines or activities in which this skill is being embedded.

Learning targets geared directly at valued priority, quality-of-life goals and postschool success can often be embedded into regularly scheduled mathematics, language arts, science, or social studies periods. At Eastridge High School, Charles is working on an IEP goal around neatly and accurately completing a job application with his personal information. Ms. Galloway has created a template that requires his full name, address, email, and phone contacts. Working with Charles' social studies and homeroom general education teachers, they have agreed to provide Charles with daily class assignments printed on the template. These teachers hand out class assignments on a regular basis, and Charles has the opportunity to practice his targeted writing goal at the same time his classmates are completing their daily written assignments.

Determine When, Where, and How Much Embedded Instruction

At this stage the educational team has selected a small number of skills to target within on-going activities, routines, and lessons in the student's day. The next step for the team is to decide when and where these skills will be taught. Activity matrices can be helpful in planning for EI. Activities and times of day should be selected in which the targeted skill can be addressed in the context of the regular activity. Teachers should consider the impact of the EI procedures on the activity. EI works best for teachers when it is provided without substantively interrupting the flow of the general activity or lesson. Teachers should question whether adding EI disrupts instruction for others during the lesson, and does EI interfere with the student's potential for learning the group target(s). Embedded learning targets are generally considered supplemental to the more global learning target(s).

The number of instructional trials necessary to teach skills with embedded instruction is highly individualized. We do know that student's progress improves with high levels of engagement and when embedded instruction is carefully implemented to ensure that each learning trial is complete (includes stimulus presentation, prompting, and feedback) (VanDerHeyden, Snyder, Smith, Sevin, & Longwell, 2005). It is also known that students learn faster when they are provided with more opportunities to respond (Mastropieri & Scruggs, 2002). Research has shown that learning is enhanced for students with cognitive disabilities when tasks are varied during an instructional period (avoiding mass trialing of the same learning target), and when tasks include a mix of new and previously mastered skills (Wolery & Schuster, 1997). It is important that students have multiple opportunities to respond and be engaged with their learning during instruction. Care should be taken to avoid repeatedly presenting the same request and only targeting new or difficult skills. Teams should consider the student's history of learning similar skills, the structure of the general activity or routine, and the complexity of the skill being taught when deciding on the number of instructional trials to embed.

A reasonable starting point for EI is to provide at least 10 planned instructional trials per learning target a day when planning for learners with low-incidence disabilities (McDonnell et al., 2008). Ms. Galloway plans to have Charles in gym playing volleyball and requesting the ball. She anticipates that he will get about four opportunities to ask for the ball as he rotates through to the server position. During lunch, Charles will have three opportunities to request food items from the cafeteria staff, and two opportunities to request dessert items from a peer tutor or paraeducator. Finally, Ms. Galloway plans for Charles to request at least one game during homeroom period. If during planning, the team decides it is not possible to provide at least 10 learning trials during regular lessons and activities, then teachers may think about providing some degree of explicit, student focused instructional strategies to add more opportunities to learn and practice the skill. McDonnell et al. (2008), suggest that supplemental trials be provided across or within on-going instructional activities. "Supplemental embedded instructional trials look and feel much like the discrete trials presented to students during traditional one-to-one or small group instruction" (p. 29). Supplemental trials may be presented during natural breaks or transitions during group lessons or activities (such as when the teacher is turning on the smart board, when students are gathering materials for an activity, or during the transition from lecture to seat work). On the days when Charles does not have an opportunity to request the ball in P.E., Ms. Galloway has planned additional opportunities to request a favorite sensory item from peers during the passing period between lunch and his 4th period class to ensure at least 10 trials a day on his communication target.

FINAL THOUGHTS

Special education practices for students with low-incidence disabilities have progressed significantly in the United States. Laws that prohibit the exclusion of students with low-incidence disabilities from our public schools now exist, and they encourage and mandate inclusive practices and participation in the general education curriculum. For educational teams, successfully including students with low-incidence disabilities and providing them meaningful access to the general curriculum while at the same time ensuring students are mastering the skills they need to be independent adults functioning in the community, is a large expectation. The task of reconciling curriculum and instruction between a standards-based model and an ecological model is largely new territory in the schools. For all learners with low-incidence disabilities, the first step is for teams to take a person-centered planning approach to developing meaningful goals and learning targets. When combined with careful planning, and quality implementation, embedded instruction can be an extremely valuable tool for teachers including students with low-incidence disabilities.

More research is needed to examine the successful application of embedded instruction to address a wider number of learning targets. Additionally, there is a need for studies that look at the adult outcomes and social validity of providing instruction through a combined standards based/ecological model of curriculum. It will be important to know if educators that provide a large portion of their students' instruction through an embedded approach are in fact supporting improved outcomes for their students. These outcomes should include meaningful progress toward the individualized quality-of-life goals, and productive postschool educational and vocational pursuits.

KEY TERMS

Ecological framework – Curricular model centered on identifying and teaching routines, activities, and skills directly related to participating in current and future school, home, vocational, and community settings.

Embedded instruction – Targeted, systematic instructional trials distributed within on-going routines and activities.

Partial participation – Principle that individuals with disabilities can acquire many skills that will foster participation, at least in part, across a wide variety of school and community environments and activities.

Person-centered planning – An individually focused approach for planning that is structured around the unique values, strengths, preferences, capacities, needs, and desired outcomes or goals of the individual.

Standards-based curriculum – Curriculum based on specific criteria defining what students are expected to learn and be able to perform.

REFERENCES

Ayres, K. M., Douglas, K. H., Lowery, K. A., & Sievers, C. (2011). I can identify Saturn, but I can't brush my teeth: What happens when the curricular focus for students with severe disabilities shifts. *Education and Training in Autism and Developmental Disabilities*, *46*(1), 11–21.

Baumgart, D., Brown, L., Pumpian, I., Nisbet, J., Ford, A., Sweet, M., & Schroeder, J. (1982). Principle of partial participation and individualized adaptations in educational programs for severely handicapped students. *Journal of the Association for the Severely Handicapped*, *7*(2), 17–27.

Baumgart, D., & Ferguson, D. L. (1991). Personnel preparation: Directions for the next decade. In *Critical issues in the lives of people with severe disabilities* (pp. 313–352). Baltimore, MD: Paul H. Brookes.

Bricker, D. D., & Cripe, J. J. (1992). *An activity based approach to early intervention*. Baltimore, MD: Paul H. Brookes.

Broderick, A., Mehta-Parekh, H., & Reid, D. K. (2005). Differentiating instruction for disabled students in inclusive classrooms. *Theory into Practice*, *44*(3), 194–202.

Browder, D. M., Wakeman, S. Y., Flowers, C., Rickelman, R. J., Pugalee, D., & Karvonen, M. (2007). Creating access to the general curriculum with links to grade-level content for students with significant cognitive disabilities an explication of the concept. *The Journal of Special Education*, *41*(1), 2–16.

Brown, L. (2013). Educational standards for students with significant intellectual disabilities. *TASH Connections*, *38*(4), 7–19.

Brown, L., Branston, M. B., Hamre-Nietupski, S., Pumpian, I., Certo, N., & Gruenewald, L. (1979). A strategy for developing chronological-age-appropriate and functional curricular content for severely handicapped adolescents and young adults. *The Journal of Special Education*, *13*(1), 81–90.

Brown, L., Nietupski, J., & Hamre-Nietupski, S. (1976). Criterion of ultimate functioning. In M. A. Thomas (Ed.), *Hey, don't forget about me! Education's investment in the severely, profoundly, and multiply handicapped* (pp. 2–15). Reston, VA: Council for Exceptional Children.

Brown, L., Nisbet, J., Ford, A., Sweet, M., Shiraga, B., York, J., & Loomis, R. (1983). The critical need for nonschool instruction in educational programs for severely handicapped students. *Journal of the Association for the Severely Handicapped*, *8*(3), 71–77.

Collins, B. C., Hager, K. L., & Creech Galloway, C. (2011). Addition of functional content during core content instruction with students with moderate disabilities. *Education and Training in Autism and Developmental Disabilities*, *46*(1), 22.

Copeland, S. R., & Cosbey, J. (2010). Making progress in the general curriculum: Rethinking effective instructional practices. *Research and Practice for Persons with Severe Disabilities*, *33*(4), 214–227.

Courtade, G., Spooner, F., Browder, D., & Jimenez, B. (2012). Seven reasons to promote standards-based instruction for students with severe disabilities: A reply to Ayres, Lowrey, Douglas, & Sievers (2011). *Education and Training in Autism and Developmental Disabilities*, *47*(1), 3.

Downing, J. (2010). *Academic instruction for students with moderate and severe intellectual disabilities in inclusive classrooms*. Thousand Oaks, CA: Corwin Press.

Falvey, M., Forest, M., Pearpoint, J., & Rosenberg, R. (1997). *All my life's a circle: Using the tools – Circles, MAPS and PATH*. Toronto, ON: Inclusion Press.

Giangreco, M. F., Cloninger, C. J., & Iverson, V. S. (2011). *COACH 3: Choosing outcomes and accommodations for children* (3rd ed.). Baltimore, MD: Paul H. Brookes.

Hall, T. E., Meyer, A., & Rose, D. H. (Eds.). (2012). *Universal design for learning in the classroom: Practical applications*. New York, NY: Guilford Press.

Halle, J. W., Chadsey, J., Lee, S., & Renzaglia, A. (2004). Systematic instruction. In C. H. Kennedy & E. Horn (Eds.), *Including students with severe disabilities* (pp. 54–77). Boston, MA: Pearson Education.

Hepting, N. H., & Goldstein, H. (1996). What's natural about naturalistic language instruction? *Journal of Early Intervention*, *20*, 250–265.

Holvoet, J., Guess, P., Mulligan, M., & Brown, F. (1980). The individualized sequencing model (II): A teaching strategy for severely handicapped students. *Journal of the Association of the Severely Handicapped*, *5*, 337–351.

Horner, R. H., Williams, J. A., & Knobbe, C. A. (1985). The effect of "opportunity to perform" on the maintenance of skills learned by high school students with severe handicaps. *Journal of the Association for Persons with Severe Handicaps, 10*, 172–175.

Hudson, M. E., Browder, D. M., & Jimenez, B. (2014). Effects of a peer-delivered system of least prompts intervention and adapted science read-alouds on listening comprehension for participants with moderate intellectual disability. *Education and Training in Autism and Developmental Disabilities, 49*, 60–77.

Hunt, P., McDonnell, J., & Crockett, M. A. (2012). Reconciling an ecological curricular framework focusing on quality of life outcomes with the development and instruction of standards-based academic goals. *Research and Practice for Persons with Severe Disabilities, 37*(3), 139–152.

Individuals with Disabilities Education Improvement Act of 2004, 20 U.S.C. 1400 et seq. (2004). (reauthorization of the Individuals with Disabilities Education Act of 1990).

Jameson, J. M., McDonnell, J., Polychronis, S., & Riesen, T. (2008). Embedded, constant time delay instruction by peers without disabilities in general education classrooms. *Intellectual and Developmental Disabilities, 46*(5), 346–363.

Janney, R. E., & Snell, M. E. (2006). Modifying schoolwork in inclusive classrooms. *Theory into Practice, 45*(3), 215–223.

Jimenez, B. A., Browder, D. M., Spooner, F., & Dibiase, W. (2012). Inclusive inquiry science using peer-mediated embedded instruction for students with moderate intellectual disability. *Exceptional Children, 78*(3), 301–317.

Jiménez, T. C., Graf, V. L., & Rose, E. (2007). Gaining access to general education: The promise of universal design for learning. *Issues in Teacher Education, 16*(2), 41–54.

Johnson, J. W., McDonnell, J., Holzwarth, V., & Hunter, K. (2004). The efficacy of embedded instruction for students with developmental disabilities enrolled in general education classes. *Journal of Positive Behavioral Interventions, 6*, 214–227.

Kaiser, A. P., Yoder, P. J., & Keetz, A. (1992). Evaluating milieu teaching. In S. F. Warren & J. Reichle (Eds.), *Causes and effects in communication and language intervention* (pp. 9–47). Baltimore, MD: Paul H. Brookes.

Lowery, K. A., Drasgow, E., Renzaglia, A., & Chezan, L. (2007). Impact of alternate assessments on curricula for students with severe disabilities: Purpose driven or process driven. *Assessment for Effective Intervention, 32*, 244–253.

Mastropieri, M. A., & Scruggs, T. E. (2002). *Effective instruction for special education.* Boston, MA: Allyn & Bacon.

McDonnell, J., Hunt, P., Jackson, L., & Ryndak, D. (2013). Educational standards for students with significant intellectual disabilities: A response to Lou Brown. *TASH Connections, 38*(4), 30–34.

McDonnell, J., Johnson, J. W., & McQuivey, C. (2008). *Embedded instruction for students with developmental disabilities in general education classrooms.* DDD Prism Series.

McDonnell, J., Johnson, J. W., Polychronis, S., & Riesen, T. (2002). Effects of embedded instruction on students with moderate disabilities enrolled in general education classes. *Education and Training in Mental Retardation and Developmental Disabilities, 37*(4), 363–377.

No Child Left Behind (NCLB) Act of 2001, Pub. L. No. 107-110, § 115, Stat. 1425 (2002).

Nolet, V., & McLaughlin, M. J. (2000). *Accessing the general curriculum.* Thousand Oaks, CA: Corwin Press.

Pretti-Frontczak, K., & Bricker, D. (2004). *An activity-based approach to early intervention* (3rd ed.). Baltimore, MD: Paul H. Brookes.

Rainforth, B., Giangreco, M., & Dennis, R. (1989). Motor skills. In A. Ford (Ed.), *Syracuse community-referenced curriculum guide for students with moderate and severe disabilities.* Pacific Grove, CA: Paul H. Brookes.

Rule, S., Losardo, A., Dinnibeil, L., Kaiser, A., & Rowland, C. (1988). Translating research on naturalistic instruction into practice. *Journal of Early Intervention, 21*, 283–293.

Ryndak, D. L., Alper, S., Hughes, C., & McDonnell, J. (2012). Documenting the impact of educational contexts on long-term outcomes for students with significant disabilities. *Education and Training in Autism and Developmental Disabilities, 47*, 127–138.

Sailor, W., & Guess, D. (1983). *Severely handicapped students; An instructional design.* Boston, MA: Houghton-Mifflin.

Sandall, S., Schwartz, I. S., Joseph, G. E., Odom, S, Wolery, R. A., Lieber, J., Horn, E. M., & Chou, H. (2008). *Building blocks for teaching preschoolers with special needs.* Baltimore, MD: Paul H. Brookes.

Trela, K., & Jimenez, B. A. (2013). From different to differentiated: Using "ecological framework" to support personally relevant access to general curriculum for students with significant intellectual disabilities. *Research and Practice for Persons with Severe Disabilities, 38*(2), 117–119.

VanDerHeyden, A. M., Snyder, P., Smith, A., Sevin, B., & Longwell, J. (2005). Effects of complete learning trials on child engagement. *Topics in Early Childhood Special Education, 25*(2), 81–94.

Wakeman, S., Karvonen, M., & Ahumada, A. (2013). Changing instruction to increase achievement for students with moderate to severe intellectual disabilities. *Teaching Exceptional Children, 46*(2), 6–13.

Ward, T. (2009). Voice, vision, and the journey ahead: Redefining access to the general curriculum and outcomes for learners with significant support needs. *Research and Practice for Persons with Severe Disabilities, 33*(4), 241–248.

Ward, T., Van De Mark, C., & Ryndak, D. L. (2006). Balanced literacy classrooms and embedded instruction for students with severe disabilities: Literacy for all in the age of school reform. In *Teaching language arts, math, & science to students with significant cognitive disabilities.* Baltimore, MD: Paul H. Brookes.

Wolery, M., Anthony, L., Snyder, E. D., Werts, M., & Katzenmeyer, J. (1997). Training elementary teachers to embed instruction during classroom activities. *Education and Treatment of Children, 20*(1), 40–48.

Wolery, M., & Schuster, J. W. (1997). Instructional methods with students who have significant disabilities. *The Journal of Special Education, 31*(1), 61–79.

SOCIO-EMOTIONAL SUPPORT NEEDS FOR RE-ENTRY TO SCHOOL AFTER TRAUMATIC BRAIN INJURY

Anne E. Crylen

ABSTRACT

Traumatic Brain Injury (TBI) is the most common brain injury and the leading cause of disability in children in the United States (Schilling & Getch, 2012). In addition to physical and cognitive rehabilitation, a family and their child need socio-emotional supports during school re-entry after brain injury. This chapter presents an understanding of the experience of school re-entry for children with TBI from the perspective of the parents. Their narratives of the preinjury, injury, and postinjury experience are framed in the medical and social models as well as special education. Findings suggest that throughout the process, community is a constant while parents' advocacy roles shift with regard to their child's holistic care. Academic research in this area is limited given TBI is a hidden disability representing a broad spectrum of diagnosis, where the individual may have no obvious physical effects even though the injury may have a significant impact on their behavior and daily life. This

Including Learners with Low-Incidence Disabilities
International Perspectives on Inclusive Education, Volume 5, 159–179

ISSN: 1479-3636/doi:10.1108/S1479-363620140000005009

chapter will propose interventions for educators to use with consideration of cultural and familiar traditions.

Keywords: Traumatic brain injury; school re-entry; school re-integration; acquired disability; special education; low-incidence disability

INTRODUCTION

In 2010, over half a million children ages birth to 19 sustained a TBI (CDC, 2014). In 2012, the United States Department of Education reported there were 24,224 students ranging from 3 to 21 years of age served within the TBI special education category, which represents approximately 0.4% of all special education students served in the nation (OSEP, 2013). Thus, TBI is considered a low-incidence disability (LID). Learners with LID, as a group, make up less than 1 percent of the total statewide enrollment for kindergarten through grade 12 and require highly specialized services, equipments, and materials similar to children who sustained a TBI.

The purpose of this chapter is to probe into the experience and "reveal the meaning" of school re-entry for children with TBI from the perspective of the parents as highlighted in the findings of a research project with parents and professionals in medical, educational, and family services. This chapter builds from these findings to provide supportive strategies and practices for educators working with children with TBI in inclusive settings.

This chapter is guided by three main questions:

- What are the most and least challenging aspects of the school re-entry process, and what makes them so?
- How is a child's identity impacted by TBI, specifically in the social and educational context?
- How can educators and related personnel effectively support children with TBI in the school setting?

CAUSES AND CHARACTERISTICS OF TBI

TBI is "caused by a bump, blow or jolt to the head or a penetrating head injury that disrupts the normal function of the brain" (CDC, 2014). In

Table 1. Characteristics of TBI.

Cognitive	Behavior	Social
• Executive functioning skills – focusing, concentrating, problem-solving with abstract concepts • Processing and memory • Learning and recalling new materials • Speech and language difficulties	• Hyperactivity • Mood swings • Low tolerance/ high frustration • Inattention to tasks	• Feeling isolated from peers • Low self-esteem • Identity as victim, not being understood

Source: Adopted from Schilling and Getch (2012).

2010, 2.5 million people in the United States sustained a TBI, of which, 564,000 were children ages birth to 19. Children, from birth to five, and adolescents, 15–19 years of age are most vulnerable to this injury. According to the Center for Disease Control and Prevention (CDC), of all injuries, TBI is the leading cause of death and disability in children. The causes of TBI in youth ages from birth to 14 are attributed to falls (55%), followed by blunt trauma (24%), motor vehicle accidents (14%), and assault (3%). A quarter of a million are due to sports injuries including football, girls' soccer, and recreational biking.

TBI is not a homogenous term and encompasses a wide spectrum of symptoms ranging from mild to moderate to severe. The severity of a TBI may range from mild (i.e., a brief change in mental status or consciousness) to severe (i.e., an extended period of unconsciousness or memory loss after the injury). Most TBIs that occur each year are mild, commonly called concussions (CDC, 2003). Federal and state special education curriculum only targets the severe range of TBI, leaving many students to fall through the cracks or to be incorrectly categorized. A TBI often impacts functioning in all or some of the following areas: memory and cognition, social skills, emotional regulation, attention, behavior, speech and language, and physical health. Table 1 highlights the most common characteristics of TBI.

OVERVIEW OF LEGISLATION

In the United States, federal legislation protects the rights of individuals with disabilities in the community, workplace, and school as stated in the Americans with Disabilities Act (ADA), the Rehabilitation Act of 1973, and the Individuals with Disabilities Education Act (IDEA). Children with disabilities who qualify for special education are also automatically protected by Section 504 of the Rehabilitation Act of 1973 and under the ADA, enacted by the US Congress in 1990. The ADA is a wide-ranging civil rights legislation that prohibits discrimination based on disability under certain circumstances. Section 504 of the Rehabilitation Act created and extended civil rights to people with disabilities, providing opportunities for children and adults with disabilities in education, employment and various other settings by requiring reasonable accommodations.

A major portion of special education today is driven by the IDEA, which specifies the types of children who are classified as having a disability, the criteria to be so classified, and the procedural guidelines schools must follow. For a student to be placed in special education the student must meet the criteria of one of the disability categories, and there must be evidence that the disability has had an adverse effect on the student's educational achievement. Models of disability have been crafted and are tools for defining impairment and, ultimately, for providing a basis upon which government and society can devise strategies for meeting the needs of people with disabilities. We examine two prominent models of disability and their impact on TBI.

MODELS OF DISABILITY

The medical, family, and school contexts are various spheres of support that are provided for a child with TBI. Each sphere of support follows a different philosophy in their interaction with the child. This philosophy frequently relates to the medical and social models of disability. TBI can be explored through several lenses including the medical and social models of disability, as well as the cross-section of special education with its movement from the deficit to inclusive model.

Medical Model

The medical model of viewing the world currently dominates mainstream special education. In this model, it is believed that disability resides within the individual, the disability can be diagnosed, and diagnosis leads to treatment. IDEA and most of the traditional special education practices follow this model. The medical model embraced by the hospital subscribes to a mantra of "we'll fix you."

Social Model

The social model of disability is a reaction to the dominant medical model of disability. The social model of disability identifies systemic barriers, negative attitudes, and exclusion by society, purposely or inadvertently. The introduction of the social model in the United States in the late 20th century changed public attitudes and promoted legislation to address accommodation and inclusion of individuals with disabilities in society. The social model embraces the idea that "you belong as you are," regardless of ability.

Special Education

Currently, the model of special education in the United States straddles both the medical and social models of disability with the goal of meeting each child's individual needs in school. Building on the cornerstone of the medical model, special education initially focused on deficits and institutionalized the majority of children with disability. With the introduction of the social model, public education recognized the need to provide students with disabilities life skills and vocational training. As the social model influenced legislation, special education gradually adopted an inclusive model with more emphasis on socialization and community participation. All students were welcomed into one classroom regardless of ability.

The contrast of medical and social models of disability is apparent in education due in large part to the structure of special education programs and their legislative accountability. There is a substantial amount of outside monitoring to assure all procedures are followed. Often these models are contradictory and can lead to frustration among families, students, and practitioners. A diagnosis can trigger a specific treatment versus an individualized program or a focus on procedural compliance can divert a focus on outcomes. There is an alternative viewpoint that is gaining support: the notion that disability is a social construct and can be redefined in ways that would provide different (and better) services to people so defined.

SPHERES OF SUPPORT

For a child with TBI and their family, navigating recovery through the hospital, school, and local community can be overwhelming and frequently without coordination among these entities. Reframing these groups as spheres of support opens a dialogue for improved transitional services. Currently, there are inconsistent procedures for transitioning students from hospital to school, and many students with TBI who need support are not identified for special education. As a result, many students do not receive appropriate services when they return to school. One federally funded project is studying a hospital-school transition model, the School Transition & re-Entry Program (STEP), which includes hospital, school, and family components. This holistic framework of support was created by The Center for Brain Injury Research and Training (CBIRT) and identifies three spheres that can serve as supports for children with TBI: hospital staff, school personnel, and parents. The STEP model proposes that hospital staff and school personnel exchange information, who in turn disseminate information to parents through top-down communication rather than through an exchange.

The conceptual framework for the following study is grounded on the STEP model, identifying the same individuals as spheres of support for children with TBI. In addition, the framework identifies the services provided, including the Individual Education Program (IEP) and Rehabilitation Therapies (see Fig. 1).

THE RESEARCH PROJECT

The purpose of this research project was to probe into the experience and "uncover the meaning" of school re-entry for children with TBI from the perspective of their parents. This was a qualitative study grounded in ethnographic analysis of semi-structured interviews with parents and professionals in medical, educational, and family services. Their narratives of the preinjury, injury, and postinjury experience, were framed in the medical and social models as well as special education. Informational interviews were conducted with a hospital educator at a large pediatric hospital in the Pacific Northwest as well as a case manager at a local brain injury advocacy council to understand resources available to families of children with TBI. Purposeful sampling was used in selecting the family participants, and

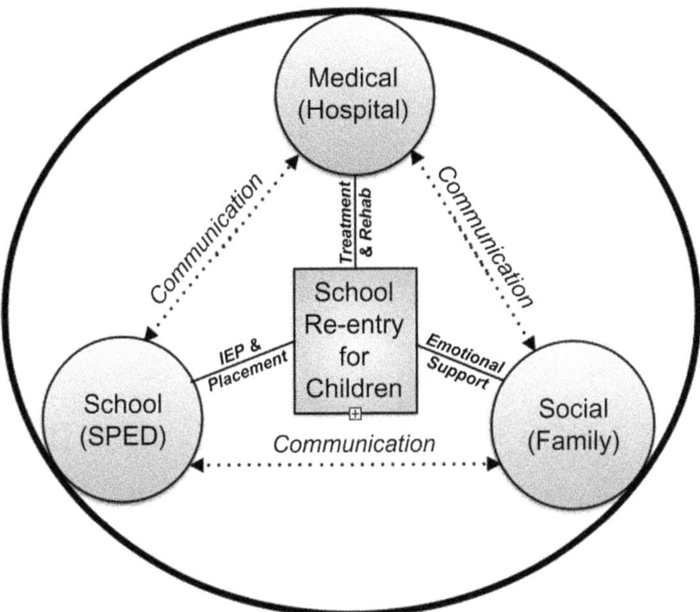

Fig. 1. The Three Spheres of Supports Model Based on the School Transition Re-entry Program and Presented by the Center for Brain Injury and Training (2010).

cognitive interviewing was conducted using a common set of questions. Grounded theory was used to analyze the data through open coding in which several themes emerged.

Participants

The four children with TBI in this study were between 10 and 13 years of age and were involved in a motor vehicle accident or sustained a sports-related injury as indicated in Table 2. The children's names have been changed to respect confidentiality. Three of the children with TBI in this study were in the hospital for at least two months, although not at the same medical facility. Those that stayed in pediatric trauma units were moved to intensive rehabilitation programs and were then "reintegrated" into school with the support of the medical team. Those quickly discharged were left to navigate school re-entry on their own, often resulting in several placement changes among districts.

Table 2. Study Participants Overview.

	Age of Injury	Diagnosis	Cause	Treatment	Home Life
Ben	12 yrs.	TBI paralysis	Hit by car	62-day hospital stay followed by in-patient rehabilitation	Oldest of 4, parents divorced after accident
Clint	11 yrs.	Concussion	Youth sports	Emergency room, no hospital stay, outpatient clinic	Youngest of 4, twin, never admitted to the hospital for treatment
Elise	10 yrs.	TBI	ATV accident	Two hospitals over 3-months	Oldest of 4, parents work within the school district, currently a college freshman
Frank	12 yrs.	TBI	Hit by car	4-month hospital stay	Youngest of 2, media coverage, emancipated self from public school and sought GED

Results

From the parental lens, the relationship of systems is linear and not cyclical as revealed in two findings consistent across the narratives: (1) community is present in each sphere and (2) parent engagement shifts over time. Communication plays a key role in bridging these themes and advancing the need for parental voice of advocacy for the child with TBI as they transition from the hospital to school while continuing rehabilitation therapies. Four themes emerged from the data related to community, social stigma, communication, and advocacy.

Community

The timeline from injury and diagnosis to discharge is mirrored both in the hospital and in school, which respondents of this study framed as a sense of belonging. One mother reflected:

> When you're injured, you leave your community. You literally are rushed into the ER and you are in this beautiful bubble where everyone is focused on saving your life. And then you move to another bubble, and there they are all focused on helping you

through rehab. But it's a world. You are in a community right then, and it's very supportive. And then you leave all that. You go back home. And there's this huge gap between what you may be able to do right this moment and what you were able to do … before your injury. And that gap is the difference between being part of community and not" (Frank's mother).

Before the injury, the child has a routine daily schedule of school and home. In each place they are surrounded by the support of teachers, staff, and friends at school and come home to parents, siblings, neighbors and perhaps even church friends. Yet at the time of injury, the hospital staff replaces the school community.

The child living in the Pediatric Intensive Care Unit (PICU) and their parents receive support from surgeons, doctors, nurses, and social workers. One mother stated that the nurses closely monitor the families' optimism. The nurses know TBI does not end with discharge and they see too many children who are treated and discharged who return for additional complications, known as "frequent flyers." For example:

> Almost every family I know has that experience in some way, someone is trying to save them from disappointment of what we actually know. It's really hard for professionals to see children in that kind of suffering [and] see families hopeful (Frank's Mother).

Perhaps the most powerful supports to parents are the communities formed in the waiting room. Two parents interviewed did not know each other before their children's injuries, yet created a bond in the waiting room. That relationship evolved into a nonprofit organization that serves families affected by brain injuries. The organization now delivers goody bags of supplies, including phone cards, personal hygiene products, and food to families in those same waiting rooms. These waiting room communities extend to include the sharing of resources, such as doctors' names and accommodation plans.

As the child recovers medically, their care is taken over by the rehabilitation staff. Still remaining in the medical sphere, the therapists become the go-to experts in the next stage. Postinjury, the child is still under the consult of the doctors, more frequently at the rehabilitation clinic, and is beginning to return to school. Although the family goes through great stress, the familiar community remains at the side of the child with TBI, especially as the parents seek to find a school that provides the services that will meet the needs of their child postinjury. If the neighborhood school does not have the resources or services, the school must identify and work on transitioning the student to an appropriate school at the cost to the school district.

Social Stigma

Parents of children with TBI report taking on a navigational role seeking resources from both the hospital and the school, which frequently leads to conflicting advice. Each mother addressed the attitude toward invisible injuries like TBI and the frustration in proving their child's disability. This is illustrated by one comment: "after a sports concussion, Clint returned to school and was told by school friends that he was a 'faker' and that he had always had mental problems, but concussion was the excuse." The rumor mill extended beyond students to parents and was further evidenced in teacher emails, making it difficult for Clint's mother to clear her son's name. As Clint's mother later said, "there's dynamics involved, and always this shared bias about invisible injury combined with the rumor mill to make a really serious injustice." The following year the administration convened a meeting with all of his teachers. Clint's mother personally communicated with each instructor about her son's specific strengths and progress on the work they assigned in order to relieve some of the skepticism about Clint's progress. Also, a resolution on how to proceed working with Clint as a student was addressed.

After being hit by a car in a pedestrian walkway, Frank's verbal outbursts became a symptom of his TBI. Considered extremely disruptive in class, Frank was put in a self-contained resource room for students with emotional and behavioral disorders. Expressing discomfort and frustration in that environment, Frank told his mother, "I just want to be back in gen pop." As she explained gen pop refers to general population "which is a prison term actually. But he used to say that. Just put me back in gen pop, Mom." The desire to belong is challenged by symptoms including fatigue and executive function, both diagnosed by physicians, yet the emotional strain on the child with TBI is also invisible.

Frank's mother reflected, "My dad put it really well I think. He said, everyday he walks up those steps he's reminded of what he lost. It's like trying to push him through the eye of a needle, he's just not ready." She continued that it took Frank a long time to trust adults again because he tried to overcompensate and be positive but wasn't understood. Clint's mother expressed a similar sentiment as she reflected: "Healthcare people don't listen to people with concussions, and I find in my experience that teachers don't listen to kids or to the parents either. I think the educational system and healthcare system are really, really biased." Each mother expressed that negative stigma stemmed from adults, yet varied among parochial and public schools and organizations. More research is needed to parse out the differential treatment of children with TBI in these settings.

Communication

Each sphere contains roles and channels of communication. The disconnect between the systems leaves the parents to become as one mother said "the messenger" between the hospital and the school. While medical care takes precedence, it also remains most solid in providing guidance for recovery. The school may be welcoming, yet all mothers expressed concern that the school team did not understand what was happening with their child. This leaves the parent in a difficult position as a protector of their child's academic and emotional well-being. For example:

> I never would have kept that kid in that school except that's where [he] wanted to be. That's where his friends were. His, friends, but they didn't never communicate, never invited him anywhere. But it was really important to him. And people with brain injuries, it's hard enough. But the social part of being a kid with a injury is so huge ... The hardest thing you find is [being] social; it's not the academics. The kid, what he wants and identifies [is] the need socially. And we kept him there [in that school] for that reason (Ben's Mother).

Three of the four parents stated the hospital had not communicated with the school to prepare for the child's re-entry nor were they consulted on the IEP and 504 Plans. Instead, the parents brought binders of information to the school administration and special education team including discharge papers and neuropsychological evaluations. Both Frank and Ben returned to public school and shared that district personnel were present but not engaged in the re-entry process at school leading both children to leave or move schools. Frank's mother commented:

> Before [transition from hospital to school] happened I was hopeful. I had this picture of somehow it would be. And it included some kind of peer support and teachers, you know, that knew how to work with kids with brain injury. Something happy. And it just wasn't like that at all. And the connection between the district and the school itself, as far as I could tell, there was zero. Zero support and input, other than what ended up on the IEP. But there was no, like face-to-face kind of okay, this guy's coming back and let's help you through this. It was all okay, here's the 504, here's the IEP. Go!

Clint's experience at a parochial school was extremely supportive emotionally, but he was not provided with the resources to support his special learning needs. This left the family to outsource therapies, further exacerbating frustration and confusion in the experience of re-entering school.

Elise's family had a completely different and fluid transition due to the hospital's "re-integration" program that worked alongside the school's IEP team and helped facilitate educational meetings with teachers and classmates weeks before returning to school. They also worked with Elise to help understand when, why, and how to self-disclose her TBI to friends. In addition, the school had previous training on TBI as their home state's board of education provides a separate IEP form that is specific to TBI rather than a checkbox on the general IEP form. According to IDEA, TBI is its own category within Special Education; however, educators often group TBI in the category of other health impairment.

While initial re-entry was successful, Elise's mother encountered issues with the special education teacher not monitoring the implementation of her child's IEP. In addition, Elise began to have issues with her instructional assistant. Her mother commented:

> We got lots of stories about her being belligerent, of her being defiant – from the instructional assistant. Our special education co-op actually has what's called a program support person who is actually a behaviorist. She was there a lot at the end of the day and felt like the problem was not with Elise, it was with the instructional.

Given that Elise's parents both work in the school district, they called the principal directly to express their doubt that the instructional assistant was trained in TBI. The parents were suspicious that the IA had experience with autism and was treating Elise as if she was on the Autism Spectrum Disorder. Eventually, the instructional assistant was removed, yet the family continually needed to leverage their positions in the school district to secure Elise's accommodations.

Learning Curve of Advocacy

The data collected in this study illustrate that mothers are highly protective throughout the recovery process. Initially, parents' shock and confusion are silenced by information provided by medical professionals at the hospital. "We were given a manual that had a lot of medical information about TBI from the hospital, a binder. And then I got on websites" (Elise's Mother). As parents become more educated, they ask more questions and become stronger advocates for their child with TBI. Unfortunately, this advocacy voice intensifies as the child goes back to the classroom, as parents perceive school personnel are not as knowledgeable and the burden to educate falls on the parent and the child with TBI. This trajectory continues throughout education into adulthood. Parents do not anticipate this learning curve of advocacy, yet professionals along the route of recovery confirm its reality. This is illustrated by Frank's mother:

> I remember the educator at [the hospital] say to me, you're going to have to be an advocate and fighter for your son. And honestly, I looked at her and said, you've got to be kidding me. I need a fighter for us. I can't fight the world. Aren't you guys going to advocate? Aren't you going to advocate for us? She laughed. No, no, the reality is you're going to have to fight.

All four mothers spoke to the fatigue factor of advocacy. Whether it was calling insurance companies, lawyers, school district, or state vocational agencies, parents logged many hours following varying protocols and lines of communication. While all four children needed physical rehabilitation, Ben was left paralyzed after his accident, resulting in a long battle for home care and accessibility supports. "He was a human shish-kebab … hundreds of stitches on his head. I really felt like he's going to die in that environment of a nursing home. He needs to be around the sights and smells of the chaos of having his three brothers there and the dogs." The doctors continued to say no, a fight compounded by the refusal of the insurance company to provide the needed equipment and home care nurses. Ben's mother said the entire process of advocating takes a great deal of energy from a parent. "The amount of paperwork I have had to put in … is unbelievable. And the amount of meetings that I've had to go to. It just seems like things could be simpler" (Ben's Mother). Elise's mother echoed the sentiment, "TBI parents don't have the knowledge or the time to manage and be sure that the student's IEP is being met. We had a discussion at home about whether we threatened to sue or not" (Elise's Mother). The professionals who were interviewed shared that there are a lot of advocacy groups available to parents, including local, state, and national brain injury associations. Yet, the parents' voice needs to be strong and empowered (Clint's Mother).

DISCUSSION

These narratives highlight the need for better coordination of care across medical and school contexts. In this section, we discuss the findings and suggest directions for the development of coordinated care. This project has generated interesting insight into a small group of mothers' views on their experience and has surfaced many questions and concerns that have implications for improved coordination of care.

Recovery to Transition

Recovery to transition is a critical period in the life of a family and child with TBI when they are in need of specialized supports and services.

Many pediatric hospitals nationwide provide in-house educational programming for patients. These programs are proven effective within the physical structure; yet program continuation is not cost-effective for many hospitals following discharge. A study of the hospital educator at one pediatric hospital revealed the provision of six hours of postdischarge educational follow-up at the hospital's expense, as insurance does not offer reimbursement under the IDEA. However, outside of these consultation appointments, this pediatric hospital program does not have the resources to perform school visits during the child's transition period between hospital and school.

Regardless of the severity of injury, specific special arrangements are legally required by the school for re-entry. However, parents are not as comfortable initiating these accommodations when their child acquires a disability. As first reported by Martin (1988), "The parents of a TBI student are much less likely to be able to advocate effectively for their youngster's special educational needs than the parents of a child born with disabilities who have learned over time how to work with the educational system" (p. 471). Recent work by Ylvisaker, Todis, and Glang confirms that this challenge persists for parents and supports the need for preparation and training for educators before a student with TBI re-enters the classroom.

The CBIRT has recognized "a critical issue in service delivery for students with TBI [to be] the significant discrepancy between the incidence of TBI and the identification of children with TBI for special education services" (CBIRT, 2010, para.1). Employing a mixed methods study, Glang et al. (2008) found that "severity of injury and the provision of hospital-school transition services [e.g., written or verbal communication between hospital and school] were strongly related to being identified for formal services (either IEP or 504 plan)" (p. 482). Further research supports that frequent misidentification of children with brain injuries in school result in an underserved population (Cronin, 2001). Therefore, consistent procedures are needed for transitioning students from the hospital to the school beyond the IEP.

Moving from the medical model to educational policy and practice, Savage, DePompei, Tyler, and Lash (2005) focus on the difficulty of penetrating the special education system in American schools for those students with an acquired disability. In the United States, schools are designed to identify special needs early. These children "grow up" in the special education system (Savage et al., 2005). In the days, weeks, and months following injury, parents of children with TBI are emotionally overwhelmed and confused by the healthcare system, insurance coverage, and special education programs. Pediatric patients who are transferred from trauma hospitals to in-patient rehabilitation centers receive individualized transition plans for their return to school. However, abrupt discharge from a hospital requires parents to take on the role of monitoring and advocating in a new world of disability (Savage et al., 2005).

Communication plays a key role in finding the appropriate classification, placement, and services inside the special education system. As Ylvisaker et al. (2001) identify, there is "extreme diversity of TBI" and disability may evolve over time. Each TBI is unique and assessment may show average knowledge of skills, yet fail to capture difficulties with new learning (Ylvisaker et al., 2001). A consensus opinion is expressed that "All those in the student's treatment and recovery process ... should be consulted in making best decisions for supports and accommodations" (Schilling & Getch, 2012, p.62). Additionally, school personnel must take initiative to seek information resources about TBI. Savage adds the move to inclusive classrooms in the US demands that all teachers, both general educators and special educators, become knowledgeable in TBI.

Medical research on TBI shows that the body is in survival mode during the first 12 months after injury. The individual with TBI begins to gain awareness of their injury and its social implications about 18 months after injury. Also noted, vulnerabilities in intellectual function surface as the individual with TBI is challenged cognitively, and erratic behavior may become symptomatic of such challenges and frustrations. Educators must be aware that TBI is a traumatic event in one's life, and the process of recovery involves grieving, adjustment to new strengths and challenges as well as social identity.

The "RE" Experience

According to Lazar and Menaldino (1995), there are "gaps in communication between rehabilitation and educational facilities, as well as limited resources for this population despite federal legislation designating TBI as a specific category of disability" (p. 56), alluding to further intensification of the problem. There were a great deal of terms describing life after a TBI that began with the prefix "re" throughout these interviews.

The mothers used the terms: rebuild, restart, recover, refresh, rejuvenate, and relieve. This "re" list can be challenging but perhaps the most difficult is the "re-living" of the experience as is done so often by mothers and the child as they repeatedly "re-tell" of the injury to each new group of professionals, whether it be medical, academic, or legal. The school re-entry process may be less distressing if children with TBI and their parents are given thoughtful consideration of the "re" experience of the injury.

The Identity Tug of War

Interviews revealed that consistent with negative stigma, it was common that labels or names are placed on children with TBI following their injury, especially if reported in the local media. The fight for control over personal identity may exacerbate the child's traumatic experience beyond the brain injury. While the medical literature speaks to the recovery of brain function and the school literature addresses the interventions and inclusion strategies in the classroom, postinjury identity needs to rise to the surface of each of the spheres of support.

Historically, the medical model supports the charitable view of disability, within which children with challenges and needs are portrayed as heroes and as poster-children. The terminology used is "survivor" – often illustrated as a super-kid. Yet, every mother interviewed stressed the need for their child to feel like they belonged in their family, their school, and their group of friends. Elise's mother commented:

> I never use the word [survivor]. I just say [she] had a TBI. I don't even say "has" anymore. I know she still has effects from it and she will always have that ....We didn't change our expectations for [her]. We only accommodated. We're telling her we understand she's frustrated and we're offering her help finding how she can deal with that.

School officials understand that brain injury is a disability under the IDEA and that students are eligible for special education services and supports. However, there are no formal regulations guiding the transfer of information or services from the medical to the educational settings during recovery. Many school personnel may not understand the unique needs of a child with TBI, and this lack of coordination between the medical and school context can put the child at risk, preventing them from receiving adequate supports and services.

Focusing on strengths-based instruction, educators should communicate with therapists and parents to ensure the child with TBI gradually re-enters school. This may mean attending school for a few hours for the first phase of re-entry, then half a day, then to a full day with modified physical activities. Like most students, a child with TBI wants to belong to the class community and doesn't like being singled out. Reference made to accident, injury, or absence may make the child uncomfortable. Educators should have a conversation with the child and their parent on if/when/how to refer to the child's TBI. It is important for educators, therapists, and parents to talk about each area of identified challenges and possible supports for the child with TBI. Table 3 highlights common challenges and suggested strategies for the classroom.

Table 3. Challenges, Strategies, and Tools.

Challenges	Teaching Strategies	Environment and Tools
Attention and concentration	Create well-paced routines	Use a concrete visual schedule and timers
Fatigue	Provide frequent "brain breaks"	Designate a quiet space for rest with minimal distraction Not intended for sleep, but perhaps listening to music and flipping through a book
Overstimulation	Limit distractions	Remove extra pencils, books and materials from the student's workspace Avoid situations with loud noise, crowds and flashing lights
Communication	Establish verbal cues and nonverbal signals	Use overt signals such as raising a hand or pointing to a door and saying "break" Gradually taper to independent transitions with flipping an empty cup or other object on the desk/table
Processing information	Ask student to summarize new information	Use graphic organizers for students to fill in during lessons
Organization	Provide step-by-step instructions and practice sequencing	Use individualized checklists and color-coded materials to complete tasks
Following conversations	Guide students to take turns speaking without interrupting others or quickly changing topics of discussion	Use an object for the speaker to hold and then pass when they are done talking
Emotional sensitivity and self-esteem	Encourage journaling and opportunities for the child to express themselves	Give a special notebook to the student to write stories or draw when they have something to share, celebrating their strengths and successes, or feelings of frustration

Source: Gathered from Hibbard, Gordon, Martin, Raskin, and Brown (2001), Lash (2000), and Stahura and Schuster (2009).

CONCLUSION

This study generates interesting insight into a small group of parents' views on their own experiences and has revealed many perspectives that have implications for school re-entry for children with TBI. Clearly, the sample is limited in the extent to which the findings can be generalized to other parents in other contexts and other countries. But it does highlight particular areas of potential interest for those who design and implement hospital to school transition for children with TBI. This research provides an example of how the use of semi-structured interviews to obtain parental insight could contribute to the development of successful contextually specific TBI experiences. Results of this study indicate that this group of parents would benefit from stronger hospital-school communication and transition planning and greater focus on the social identity struggles the child and family face after sustaining a TBI. The International Pediatric Brain Injury Society states, "There must be greater collaboration between health and education services to ensure co-ordination" of services (IPBIS, 2011). As there is different terminology in each sphere of support, using a common framework of areas of cognitive, behavioral, and social needs would be an effective place to start when identifying the child's vulnerabilities postinjury (refer to Table 1).

Brain injury is a hidden epidemic. Physical disabilities are visible, and consequentially, there is a general social knowledge and consideration of individuals with physical impairments. Cognitive disabilities are invisible; thus, general social knowledge is only constructed through personification of diagnoses in mass media, that is, sitcom characters with Down's Syndrome. Yet only the recognized cognitive impairments are included in general social knowledge. Brain injury has been said to be a "silent epidemic." However, recent focus on concussion and head injury in professional sports has raised general social awareness.

The purpose of the study presented in this chapter was to create awareness of the experience of the mothers of children with TBI, to better address the socio-emotional needs of a child with an acquired disability during re-entry to school after brain injury. Easing the transition between the hospital and school is extremely significant to the child's mending and adjustment to life after injury.

We have only begun to scratch the surface of the parental experience of school re-entry for their children with TBI. This disability is indiscernible and encompasses a broad spectrum of diagnosis from the mild forms of TBI like concussion to severe TBI that may include possible paralysis.

Thus, continued research is particularly needed to reveal the perspective of the child with TBI. Their stories needs to be heard and taken to heart across the academic, medical, and social services fields and disciplines.

KEY TERMS

504 plan – A nondiscriminatory accessibility plan that allows individuals to fully participate in all learning activities and environments.

Acquired disability – Impairment in a person's ability to function caused by illness or injury after birth.

Capitalistic frames – a perspective that places value on means of production, distributing, and exchange of wealth. In reference to the field of education, the student must acquire schooling to be a productive member of society; in the field of medicine, the patient must recover to return to work.

Child find – A mandate in the Individuals with Disability Education Act (IDEA) that requires schools to locate, identify, and evaluate all children with disabilities from birth through age 21. The Child Find mandate applies to all children who reside within a state, including children who attend private schools and public schools, highly mobile children, migrant children, homeless children, and children who are wards of the state (20 U.S.C. 1412(a)(3)).

CT – computer processed x-rays to show specific areas of the scanned object providing an image of what is inside the object without making an incision.

Executive function – the complex processing of large information used in goal setting, planning, initiating, self-awareness, self-monitoring.

Glasgow Coma Scale – A neurological scale used to assess levels of consciousness that is used by Emergency Medical Services, nurses, and doctors.

Individualized Education Program (IEP) – Mandated by the Individuals with Disabilities Act, defines the educational goals and objectives of a child who has been identified with a disability as described by federal regulations. Each child's IEP is written specifically for their individual learning needs.

MRI – Magnetic resonance imaging used in radiology to form images of the body for medical diagnosis and staging of disease and injury.

Neuropsychological – the study of brain damage on behavior and the function of the mind.

Pediatric Intensive Care Unit (PICU) – the special unit within a hospital separate from the general population of patients where children receive close observation and continued medical care by specialists.

Parochial school – private educational institutions organized, managed, and connected to religious affiliations or places of worship.

Stakeholders – the person or group that holds an investment in the child with Traumatic Brain Injury including but not exclusive to parents, doctors, therapists, social workers, teachers, and friends.

REFERENCES

Americans with Disabilities Act (ADA). 34 CFR 104.3, (1990).

Center for Brain Injury Research and Training (CBIRT). (2010). *School Transition Re-entry Program (STEP)*. Retrieved from http://cbirt.org/our-projects/school-transition-re-entry-program-step/

Centers for Disease Control and Prevention (CDC). (2003). *National center for injury prevention and control. Report to congress on mild traumatic brain injury in the United States: Steps to prevent a serious public health problem*. Atlanta, GA: Centers for Disease Control and Prevention.

Centers for Disease Control and Prevention (CDC). (June 2, 2014). *Traumatic brain injury in the United States: Fact sheet*. Retrieved from http://www.cdc.gov/traumaticbraininjury/get_the_facts.html

Cronin, A. F. (2001). Traumatic brain injury in children: Issues in community function. *The American Journal of Occupational Therapy*, *55*(4), 377–384.

Glang, A., Todis, B., Thomas, C. W., Hood, D., Bedell, G., & Cockrell, J. (2008). Return to school following childhood TBI: Who gets services? *NeuroRehabilitation*, *23*(6), 477–486.

Hibbard, M., Gordon, W. A., Martin, T., Raskin, B., & Brown, M. (2001). *Students with traumatic brain injury: Identification, assessment and classroom accommodations*. New York, NY: Research and Training Center on Community Integration of Individuals with Traumatic Brain Injury, Department of Rehabilitation Medicine, Mount Sinai School of Medicine.

International Pediatric Brain Injury Society (IPBIS). (2011). *Towards an international model of service provision for children and young people with acquired brain injury: Good practices and recommendations*. Retrieved from http://www.ipbis.org/IPBIS_Good_Practice_Recommendations.pdf. Accessed on August 26, 2014.

Lash, M. (2000). Teaching strategies for students with brain injuries. *TBI Challenge!*, *4*(2). Retrieved from http://www.biaoregon.org/docetc/Resources/children/teaching.strategies.for.students.with.brain.injuries.pdf

Lazar, M. F., & Menaldino, S. (1995). Cognitive outcome and behavioral adjustment in children following traumatic brain injury: A developmental perspective. *The Journal of Head Trauma Rehabilitation*, *10*(5), 55–63.

Martin, R. (1988). Legal challenges in educating traumatic brain injured students. *Journal of Learning Disabilities*, *21*(8), 471–475.

Office of Special Education Programs (OSEP). (2013). *Data accountability center*. Retrieved from http://tadnet.public.tadnet.org/pages/712; http://www.disabilitycompendium.org/docs/default-source/2013-compendium/2013_compendium.pdf?sfvrsn=2

Savage, R. C., DePompei, R., Tyler, J., & Lash, M. (2005). Pediatric traumatic brain injury: A review of pertinent issues. *Developmental Neurorehabilitation*, *8*(2), 92–103.

Schilling, E. J., & Getch, Y. Q. (2012). Getting my bearings, returning to school: Issues facing adolescents with traumatic brain injury. *TEACHING Exceptional Children*, *45*(1), 54–63.

Stahura, B., & Schuster, S. B. (2009). *After brain injury: Telling your story, a journaling workbook*. Youngsville, NC: Lash & Associates Publishing. Retrieved from http://www.brainline.org/content/2010/09/after-brain-injury-telling-your-story_pageall.html. Accessed on August 26, 2014.

Ylvisaker, M., Todis, B., Glang, A., Urbanczyk, B., Franklin, C., DePompei, R., … Tyler, J. S. (2001). Educating students with TBI: Themes and recommendations. *The Journal of Head Trauma Rehabilitation*, *16*(1), 76–93.

SECTION II
INTERNATIONAL PERSPECTIVES ON INCLUDING LEARNERS WITH LOW-INCIDENCE DISABILITIES

THIS IS WHAT WORKS FOR ME: STUDENTS REFLECT ON THEIR EXPERIENCES OF SPECIAL NEEDS PROVISION IN IRISH MAINSTREAM SCHOOLS

Richard Rose and Michael Shevlin

ABSTRACT

This chapter draws upon research conducted in the Republic of Ireland to discuss the views of students who have been identified as having a range of high and low-incidence special educational needs. The data reported within the chapter are taken from Project Inclusive Research in Irish Schools (IRIS), a longitudinal research investigation using a mixed methods approach conducted within the country. The chapter provides evidence that students with a range of needs are able to articulate their views of their learning needs, to comment upon approaches that they find helpful and to reflect upon their personal growth. The authors suggest that the insights that can be provided by students should inform the development of the curriculum and approaches to teaching.

Keywords: Inclusion; empowerment; student voice; special education provision

---

Including Learners with Low-Incidence Disabilities
International Perspectives on Inclusive Education, Volume 5, 183–202

ISSN: 1479-3636/doi:10.1108/S1479-363620140000005011

INTRODUCTION

This chapter discusses the views of students who have been identified as having special educational needs in the Republic of Ireland, on the provision made for them and their perceptions of what helps them to learn. The data reported within the chapter are taken from Project Inclusive Research in Irish Schools (IRIS), a longitudinal research investigation into special and inclusive education provision within Ireland. The project has focused upon gaining data to inform an understanding of the quality of provision, the effectiveness of policy, the experiences of students, teachers and families and the learning outcomes for students in schools throughout Ireland. Field work has been conducted using mixed methods to obtain both qualitative and quantitative data from a variety of sources particularly focused upon service users and providers. The methods deployed included a national survey of all mainstream and special schools in Ireland, focus groups with professionals providing support for children with special educational needs and their families, the construction of profiles of individual students in schools and the development of narrative case studies of 24 schools. This chapter therefore draws upon a large data set but is mainly focused upon qualitative data obtained from interviews with students in schools from across the country.

The authors of this chapter are keen to present the voices of young people and to discuss these in relation to the development of inclusive education provision within an Irish context. In order to achieve this, the following key questions are considered:

1. What are the experiences of children and young people with special educational needs in Irish mainstream schools?
2. What do these children and young people report as being helpful in providing them with access to learning and positive school experiences?

These two questions are addressed through a discussion of the provision made for students with special educational needs in Irish schools and their views of their educational experiences. This discussion is undertaken by presenting evidence selected from interviews with 120 individual students in 24 schools.

THE IRISH EDUCATION CONTEXT

Compulsory school attendance in the Republic of Ireland covers the age range 6–16 years though the vast majority of children are enroled in primary schools by five years of age. Primary education consists of an eight-year cycle comprising infant classes (two years) and first to sixth class with the transfer to postprimary schools normally occurring at age 12. The postprimary education sector comprises secondary, vocational, community and comprehensive schools, which broadly offer similar curricula though due to historical reasons the management structures vary. Postprimary education consists of a three-year junior cycle followed by a two/three-year senior cycle. Students usually begin postprimary education at age 12 and take a national examination, the Junior Certificate, after three years. Senior cycle education provides for 15–18-year-olds, and in the final two years of Senior cycle accreditation is available through a national examination which is taken by the vast majority of students. The Leaving Certificate Applied programme (LCA) taken by a minority of students many of whom have special educational needs has been developed in recent years to cater for those students who were at risk of not completing Senior cycle education or failing the final examinations and aims to accredit these students through a range of assessment measures including a final examination.

A continuum of educational provision has been established for students with special educational needs which include full-time enrolment in mainstream classrooms, special class placement in mainstream schools and full-time enrolment in special schools. Special educational needs are designated as either 'high incidence' or 'low incidence': 'high incidence' refers to those special educational needs that occur with greater frequency in the general student population and consists of borderline mild general learning disability, mild general learning disability and specific learning disability; 'low incidence' refers to those less frequently occurring special educational needs within the general student population such as physical disability, sensory impairment, emotional difficulties, moderate and severe/profound general learning disability, autistic spectrum disorders (ASD) and specific speech and language disorder. Special classes have been established in mainstream schools to cater for particular categories of students with special educational needs including mild general learning disabilities, moderate general learning disabilities, autism spectrum disorders and specific speech and language disorders. Special schools have traditionally been organised according to the 14 disability/special educational need categories recognised in the Republic of Ireland. Since 1998 there has been a significant increase in support teacher and Special Needs Assistant (SNA) provision for mainstream schools.

Research in special educational needs in Ireland has focused for the most part on aspects of support provision and debates surrounding the move towards a more inclusive approach to schooling (Rose, Shevlin, Winter, & O'Raw, 2010). Project IRIS from which the data in this chapter is drawn, is the largest scale investigation into special educational needs provision ever conducted in the country.

LISTENING TO AND LEARNING FROM THE VOICES OF STUDENTS

In recent years there has been an increasing recognition that children and young people can provide unique insights into their own learning experiences (Mortimer, 2004; Porter, 2014). This has led to an increased involvement of students in the assessment of their academic and social performance (Flutter & Ruddock, 2004) in setting learning targets (Morton, 1996) and assisting in the shaping of school policy and ethos through mechanisms such as school councils (Alderson, 2000). Instilling democratic principles in the education of children is an area that has been widely debated, with a belief that giving students greater involvement in decisions related to day-to-day classroom activities and procedures may enable them to accept greater responsibility for the management of their own learning (Fielding, 2001).

However, several writers have urged caution when considering the promotion of participation which can at times appear uncritical unless safeguards are established in respect of why student opinions are sought. Roche (1999) and Lundy (2007) have both suggested that if the voices of students are to be heard and have any impact upon their education, it is essential that adults are clear from the outset with regards to their reason for seeking opinions, and that they uphold a commitment to act upon any findings resulting from interviews or other means of obtaining student voices. We would contend that this view holds well in research as much as in teaching (see Rose & Shevlin, 2010 for a fuller discussion). If the views of children are sought, this must be for a purpose which is clearly stated in making use of these opinions in any publication or public forum. By presenting excerpts from transcripts in this chapter, it is our intention to provide students with an opportunity to illustrate our own findings about school provision by providing authenticity to what would otherwise simply be the opinions of the researchers.

Within discussions and debates around the issue of student involvement, there has been a considerable focus upon the ways in which students described as having special educational needs may be full participants in this process. The obvious challenges that some of these students face in respect of limited communication or social skills have been discussed as a barrier to participation but have nevertheless been addressed through a number of innovative studies and approaches (Lewis, Newton, & Vials, 2008; Rose & Shevlin, 2010). Whilst there are clearly difficulties in ensuring that the voices of students with special educational needs are fairly represented, the imperative to provide them with opportunities to influence their own experiences of education is enshrined within the legislation of some countries (Department of Education, 2014) and reinforced through research evidence that articulates the value of such an approach (Davies & Watson, 2001).

As authors of this chapter, we have long advocated that researchers when considering the education provided for students with special educational needs, should consult with those young people and respect the insights that they can provide (Rose & Shevlin, 2006; Shevlin & Rose, 2003). However, it is necessary to be aware of the challenges that this approach brings and to put in place safeguards to ensure that the opinions obtained are both authentic and trustworthy. Bahou (2011) urges caution in obtaining the opinions of students who may have concerns that this process is in some way tokenistic and worry that they may be misrepresented. Establishing trust and demonstrating to students that their words will be used unchanged and within an appropriate context is an essential part of the process. For these reasons the authors of this chapter have made it a principle to present the words of students exactly as spoken and to ensure that the context in which they were given is clear.

Cook-Sather (2002) has suggested that whilst the voices of young people have often been omitted from research, that these should not become dominant and need to be considered alongside the opinions of others, such as teachers or parents in the research environment. We agree that this is an important consideration and one that needs to be addressed if student voices are to command the respect in research that we feel they deserve. It is with this consideration in mind that where excerpts from transcripts of interviews with students have been used throughout this chapter, as elsewhere in reporting our research, they have only been included where we have been able to verify the statements made. This has been achieved through a process of triangulation as advocated by Patton (2002) which has sought multiple perspectives, including those of student peers, teachers and parents, and used several sources, including school documents and survey data to ensure the trustworthiness of the excerpts used.

The excerpts presented in this chapter are taken from interviews conducted in mainstream schools in Ireland with students who had been identified as having both high- and low-incidence special educational needs. These students were asked to speak about their experiences of school, to identify those interventions that either assisted or inhibited their learning and to provide examples of the challenges that they perceive to result from their learning difficulties. Interviews were conducted in the presence of a known adult and each student was given an opportunity to withdraw statements or complete recordings if they were unhappy with any aspect of the data collection process. The transcripts of interview recordings were verified through a process of multiple source triangulation by comparing the experiences articulated by students with those of their peers, parents and teachers. In situations where it was not possible to establish the trustworthiness of the data, this was discarded from the overall data set.

The excerpts from interview transcripts within this chapter have been used as a means of illustrating the experiences of students and enabling their voices to be heard in our discussion of the two questions identified in the introduction. The discussion woven around these excerpts represents our interpretation of the provision made and the experiences of students with special educational needs in Irish mainstream schools.

THE EXPERIENCES OF CHILDREN AND YOUNG PEOPLE WITH SPECIAL EDUCATIONAL NEEDS IN IRISH MAINSTREAM SCHOOLS

Key themes that emerged from the reports of children and young people with special educational needs included supportive school ethos; positive relationships with school personnel; provision of specialist support groups outside the classroom; and the availability of para-professional support.

The ethos created by staff within a school has seen to be an important factor in determining the ability to foster an inclusive learning environment (Avramidis, Bayliss, & Burden, 2000). The ease with which students settle into school and a sense of belonging within the school environment has been seen as a critical factor in promoting successful learning. Students with special educational needs in Irish schools were asked to comment on their perceptions of how it felt to be a part of their school community. Most recognised the efforts made by teachers and others within the school to make them feel welcome and to settle into their class. A positive opinion of school was the norm with students generally enthusiastic about their attendance.

> I love the subjects and I love the school and I love the helpers because they help me. (Post-Primary Student)

> … the school helps with I suppose your education, that you are finding everything okay and that you are not on top of things and, you know, you can get help like if you want help with that and you can minimise your subjects if you are finding it hard or if you need a study plan you get the career guidance and they'll talk to you if you are finding it hard and they walk through step by step what you can do at home and stuff like that. (Post-Primary Student)

The personalisation of support and reference to positive relationships was a regular feature of discussions with students. They usually perceived teachers to be helpful and recognised that provision had been personalised for them and enabled them to feel comfortable within a range of learning situations.

> It (the school) is very good. Teachers are very nice to me. I learn a lot in school and yes, basically I'm doing fine in school and it's going good for me. (Post-Primary Student)

Being nonjudgemental was a theme that emerged as critical to the provision of appropriate support. Students, including those who had little confidence in their own learning abilities cited instances where teachers did all that they could to bolster student self-esteem. They recognised that teachers would support them once they realised that they were experiencing difficulties with learning and that alleviating anxiety was an important factor in enabling them to work effectively.

> … They (support teachers) just praise me in anything I do, like if I do anything or I don't get on well they say it's alright. That gives me back my confidence. Again, praise me, because if I do anything wrong or something they don't just be like, 'Oh, you're always getting it wrong'. They just say, 'This is one small part here that you have got wrong, don't worry about it'. So that helps. (Post-Primary Student)

Students were often specific in identifying what teachers did that supported them in their learning. They saw the teacher and student relationship as a positive factor that enabled them to succeed and were confident that the support they required would be forthcoming as and when needed.

> … if I'm stuck on a maths question my maths teacher will come up and ask me do I need any help and she'll help me get the question right. (Post-Primary Student)

The importance of support that was pastoral in nature as well as that affording assistance with educational access was seen as particularly important by some students. As an example the following student clearly recognised that the support available was all encompassing and enabled him to feel that all of his needs were being taken into consideration.

> You can go up and talk to them any time you want. If there's anything wrong at home you can go talk to them about it. If you need any extra help you can go talk to them about it any time whenever you want. And then, like, taking an exam they used to help at school as well. (Post-Primary Student)

Whilst discussing the help that teachers provided, students also had a sense of where there were limitations and recognised that assistance needed to be given with a set or rules.

> ... if you're doing tests, if you get stuck on a question, the teacher comes over and they read it to you, and they can't help you with the question but they can read it to you. (Primary Student)

An interesting factor is that some students are able to compare the support they receive in their current situation to that in previous schools. They recognise how schools differ in their approach and the impact that this has upon them as individuals. As one student who had a poor experience in a previous school stated:

> ... the school is grand. It's just like a lot more kinder and more helpful type school. (Post-Primary Student)

The provision of specialist classes or groups within the school was generally viewed as helpful, with students recognising that they received a more personal form of support in these situations. The use of specialist resource teachers is a common feature of the Irish education system and appears for many students to represent a safety net to be used when they believe that they are struggling. The confidence to ask for additional support was a noticeable feature of the provision made for students with special educational needs in mainstream schools, with several expressing the view that this enabled them to feel less dependent than might otherwise have been the case.

> I have my Special Ed classes if I need help with that I'd just ask them. (Post-Primary Student)

> I think it's good the way we get to go out and get extra help with a different teacher. (Primary Student)

This personalisation of support with students feeling some ownership of specialist support teachers was a theme that came through in many of the interviews and may be an indication of how schools have enabled students to feel comfortable with the idea that they cannot always manage to succeed without help.

> I have some of my own teachers to help me in resource so if I get stuck on something I can ask them and they go through it with me again. (Post-Primary Student)

Whilst it has been suggested that being withdrawn from class for additional support in a specialist resource room could have a negative impact upon student self-esteem (Cambre & Silvestre, 2003), there was no evidence of this within the Irish schools visited. Students were clear about the benefits of working in small-group situations and appeared comfortable with being educated in separate groups for part of the school day.

> ... it was better because when you came in here there was only eight people or nine, and it was really good because in like your old classroom it was a big class and you couldn't get much help. (Primary Student)

Some students were more comfortable in the small-group situation and felt that they could express their own anxieties more readily in a group that was less likely to be critical. Whereas they may not have expressed their difficulties in front of a large group of their peers, the security of the specialist class, where others were also experiencing challenges seemed a more comfortable place in which to ask for and receive pastoral support.

> ... putting me in smaller classes so I can, like, get it, talk about problems better and that it's not like crowded and you can get help easier if you are stuck on something. (Post-Primary Student)

They similarly recognised that within the school there were specialist teachers who have the ability to provide them with extra support that is well planned and geared to their individual needs.

> Resource really helps me because at the start of the year I couldn't really read that much but now I got better. (Primary Student)

> I think it's good the way we get to go out and get extra help with a different teacher. (Post-Primary Student)

The image of the resource room and the students who attend for specialist support was discussed by several students. Some had experienced negative comments from their peers with regards to why they went for help, usually with an implication that they were not good enough to manage the work in the mainstream class. However, this was often countered by statements from students who recognised what they saw as the benefits of attending small group support. An example of this was provided by a girl who regularly attends a resource room for additional support with English. She reported a situation where she had encountered some negative comments but where she felt the support provided was vindicated:

> I go out for English and someone said to me that 'oh you go out for extra help, you always get everything wrong'. And then one day someone said that to me and I came back to the classroom like we were filling in the blanks the same as the girls, and the girl that said that to me got three wrong, and I got all of them right. (Primary Student)

In this instance the student clearly felt that she had benefited from the support provided and was happy to outperform a peer who had clearly felt that she was less able than herself. Marston (1996) recognised that the use of withdrawal from lessons to work in more supportive small groups may be a critical factor in enabling schools to retain some students with special educational needs and proposes that this strategy should be considered as part of a mixed method that includes whole class and individual instruction. This appears to be an approach favoured in Irish schools and one that the students we interviewed seemed comfortable with.

The provision of para-professional support in classrooms has become a common feature in addressing special educational needs in mainstream classrooms (Farrell, Alborz, Howes, & Pearson, 2010; Giangreco, Carter, Doyle, & Suter, 2010). In Ireland such support is provided by SNAs who are allocated to specific individual children. The focus of their role is supposed to be on personal care for the student, though it is evident that they are closely involved in pedagogical activities. These paraprofessionals were seen by students as providing a supportive service that enabled them to access learning and participate in whole-class activities.

> I have an SNA that definitely helps specially in the big class ... because you could always ask the SNA like instead of always asking the teacher. (Post-Primary Student)

It was interesting to see that in many instances students felt that they were able to determine when they needed help and to call upon the assistance of an SNA at appropriate times.

> I have an SNA that sits in class with me and another pupil and she's just there to help me if I need help with questions ....I am working well but if I'm confused or I don't understand I just ask her. (Post-Primary Student)

Furthermore, it was apparent that some students acknowledged that they had made such progress in their learning that the necessity for SNA support had diminished as they gained in confidence and independence.

> When I was in first year I needed her (SNA) a lot more than I do today. I needed her in most classes and in second year I only needed her in less classes. Today she's only in one or two of my classes because she knows that because I don't need her as much anymore she goes and spends time in other classes. (Post-Primary student)

This last point is certainly worthy of further investigation at a time when there have been concerns expressed that the allocation of classroom support of this nature may produce dependency and have a potentially negative impact upon learning and the development of independence (Blatchford et al., 2011).

DISCUSSION

The research conducted as part of Project IRIS demonstrated that students with special educational needs can provide valuable insights into their experiences in mainstream schools. We would contend that any attempt to understand the impact of the provision made for students without hearing their voices would be seriously devalued and that researchers need to devote time to understanding the perspectives of these critical service users.

The views expressed by the students during the course of the investigation reveal a number of factors that may be seen as significant for those who wish to provide a more inclusive approach to teaching and learning. These could well form the basis of important discussions with teachers, school principals, parents and of course the young people in receipt of special education support. Furthermore, we suggest that there is a need for further investigation into some of the phenomena identified by students in order to build a profile of good practice that may inform further developments in this area.

The key findings from student reports strongly indicate that attitudes and expectations are crucial in determining whether the student with special educational needs can participate fully within the school. Positive staff expectations of student performance are closely linked to positive student attitudes towards their own learning and engagement with school activities. Strong home-school communication was also regarded as essential in providing targeted support for student academic and social needs. Flexibility of support from teachers and para-professionals was also perceived as critical in ensuring that students were able to access the curriculum and achieve within school.

The students interviewed inform us that the attitude of teachers and other school-based professionals is a significant factor in promoting inclusive schools. A sense of belonging is critical in enabling students to feel comfortable in an environment in which they may previously have been seen to fail and where they may feel apprehensive. Teacher expectations and attitudes have been reported as having a major impact upon the confidence of all children entering school but for those who may see schools as a place where they are likely to struggle or even fail, this factor is likely to take on a greater significance. Young people in previous studies have highlighted the effect that low expectations or negative attitudes can have upon their abilities to thrive in school. In 2003, a European Parliament Hearing of Young People with Special Educational needs, in Brussels provided an opportunity to hear the views of students with special educational needs or disabilities from across the European Union (Soriano, 2005). One of the young representatives from Ireland at this event stated that:

> Some of the difficulties I encountered were access and certain teachers not understanding my full potential.

A further Irish student endorsed the importance of positive attitudes in saying:

> Good experiences would include helping other students to understand that disability is not a negative thing and feeling fully included in the school community.

This second student specifies the need to have a sense of belonging as essential to his ability to learn within a school. This theme has been discussed in the literature and recognised as an important consideration in respect of whether schools succeed or fail in becoming inclusive (Prince & Hadwin, 2013). As Thomas, Walker, and Webb (1998) emphasised, simply placing a child with a special educational need in a school is not enough and is certainly not a guarantee of success. In their study of schools in England, they considered that the raising of student self-esteem was a critical determinant in promoting successful learning and that in some instances this was impeded by the negative attitudes experienced by some students. Skidmore (2004) in developing case studies of schools working towards inclusion found that student attitudes towards their academic work improved considerably when teachers raised their expectations and ceased seeing a special educational need as a reason for poor performance.

The students whose voices were heard as part of the research reported in this chapter endorse the importance of attitudinal factors in determining successful school outcomes. The identification of the importance of praise and encouragement and the knowledge that teachers will offer support at an appropriate level was clearly significant for the students in this study. Equally significant was the fact that several students were able to identify situations where this level of support was lacking and the negative impact that this had upon their performance in school. The notion that a student had entered a *'kinder type of school'* is of particular note as it indicates that this young man was discriminating between a school that was now meeting his needs, as opposed to an earlier experience where he had felt excluded from learning.

The partnership established between home and school was also articulated by the young people in Project IRIS. The fact that teachers were prepared to listen to students and take account of the pressures that they may feel at home was clearly valued by some student respondents. Alur and Bach (2010) identify an understanding of home situations as a vital component of developing inclusive schools. In circumstances where parents and siblings may have a low expectation of the child with special educational needs it may be increasingly important for the school to compensate for this level of negativity. Broomhead (2014) emphasises that a discrepancy in the expectations of parents and teachers can cause confusion in the minds of students with regards to how they are perceived and as a result compromise the effective functioning of a child within school. The student, who reported that if there was a problem at home he felt he could talk about this in school, provides us with an interesting issue in respect to the role that the teacher might play in combating this potential disjunction. The importance of recognising that influences from outside of the classroom impact upon the ability of students to learn and in some cases may lead to significant behaviour issues has been well documented (Barnard, 2004; Hill & Taylor, 2004). The fact that students in this study recognised the importance of this link between home and school may be a factor in their successful inclusion and confidence in the school to respond to their needs.

As part of the research data collection process we discussed the issue of home and school liaison and the perceptions that both parties have of students with the parents of each student that we interviewed. It was interesting to note that many parents gave an honest appraisal of their child's needs and felt able to discuss these with teachers in an open manner. For example, one parent stated that:

> ... they've had a tough time with my son, because he is not an easy with this problem he has, he is a handful, but the school are doing brilliant ....I don't think they could do any more than what they are doing. They're really doing their best for him.

This parent of a student who was described as having challenging behaviours was conscious that her son regularly discussed the difficulties he was experiencing at home, and that teachers listened and cared about what he was saying. The parent had expressed anxieties about the possibility that her son would not cope with school and that his behaviour may deteriorate because of the pressure that she associated with a competitive learning environment. However, she was reassured that the recognition of the challenges faced by her son on the part of teachers and the fact that he felt welcome in the school and able to talk about his fears was an important factor in his inclusion.

The provision of support groups managed by specialist teachers and comprising small numbers of children withdrawn from class and brought together for additional learning support is not without controversy. The impact of withdrawal into groups on the social standing of students and the way they are perceived by their peers have been documented, as has the influence upon their self-esteem (Maras & Brown, 2000). Within an Irish mainstream school context the use of resource rooms to which students are withdrawn for specialist support is a common practice (Griffin & Shevlin, 2007; Shevlin, Kenny, & Loxley, 2008).

The opinions expressed by student in the Project IRIS research were generally favourable of this approach. They believe that working in a small group gives them opportunities to express themselves with greater confidence than may be the case in a whole-class situation. Furthermore, the students interviewed suggested that the specialist teachers managing withdrawn groups were empathetic to their needs and had the skills and the knowledge to structure work in a manner that enabled them to make progress. Comments related to class size indicate that students may feel inhibited at times and that they believe that it is easier to obtain the help that they feel they need in the small-group situation.

This approach to providing support is something of a conundrum within the Irish education system. Travers (2010) has expressed concerns that the predominant use of classroom withdrawal by resource teachers which places a focus upon within-child factors may inhibit inclusion through the perpetuation of a deficit model. However, other researchers in this field

Farrell and O'Neill (2012) suggest that the resource teachers providing this support gain important insights into the needs of individual students that can then be used to inform practice in whole-class situations. It would appear that the necessity to gain further insights into the impact of this approach and to achieve a balance that ensures that students are well supported but assured full curriculum access is a critical point for further investigation in the Irish education system. SNAs within the Irish education system are allocated to individual students with special educational needs following a statutory assessment procedure. As with para-professional support provided in other administrations, the role of the SNA has been debated and remains a topic of some controversy (Rose & O'Neill, 2009). In particular, there are concerns that expressed that the provision of personalised support may inhibit the development of student independence skills and that the role serves to emphasise the inability of a student to cope in classroom situations.

The students interviewed during Project IRIS provided evidence of both the positive and restrictive elements of the SNA support role. As seen from the quotes above, many students acknowledged that having an SNA alongside them in class provided them with opportunities to ask for assistance when required. There is evidence to suggest that the role increases student confidence and that in some instances it enables them to be retained within a mainstream classroom setting. However, it is also interesting to note that as students progressed through the education system they became increasingly self-conscious about having personal support and many saw the phasing out of this provision as desirable.

Interestingly, many of the SNAs interviewed as part of this research recognised that as students get older they begin to distance themselves from the provision of support that singles them out as being different. As one SNA told us, when reflecting upon how her relationship with a student who she had supported over a number of years:

> Absolutely hates it. And I'm sure if you were to interview her she'll tell you I'm the worst in the world. Some days we get on really well and she'll ask me to help her. Other days she just does not want me there, she will argue with me. Very often teachers have to come down to us and say, what's wrong?

The insights provided by students into this particular approach to support are interesting and suggest that it may be advantageous to involve them in reviewing the level and nature of support that they receive. Within the project it was noticeable that it was often parents who campaigned to obtain SNA support in the belief that this would be wholly beneficial to their child. This is, of course, an understandable situation and one to be expected where parents want to ensure that their child has provision that will maximise their ability to cope in a mainstream school. However, it is evident from what we learn by listening to students that the approach to providing personalised support is far more complex than may be assumed.

FUTURE ISSUES FOR INQUIRY

Research in this area suggests that there is much to be learned from seeking the views of students in respect of their own learning needs (Horgan, 2003; Vehkakoski, 2012). The data obtained by listening to students within Irish mainstream schools suggest that there are important matters that should be considered for any further inquiry into special educational needs provision. It is evident that students are acutely aware of the impact that both adult attitudes and the levels of support provided for them has upon their personal learning. We would suggest that the astute comments made by several of the students in this study indicate that many of the standard procedures for supporting students, such as the use of withdrawal into teaching groups managed by specialist teachers or the use of para-professional support, indicates that there are complexities surrounding these approaches that require further investigation. Similarly, the expectations of adults with regards to student potential and performance are clearly seen by students as having a major impact upon their learning. Inquiries that examine how teachers and others develop their expectations of individual students could provide the basis for changing attitudes and raising the level of challenge for students with special educational needs in classrooms.

Alongside these areas for inquiry is the necessity to further consider how the insights afforded by students can be more effectively harnessed for the benefit of teaching and learning. It is apparent that students with special educational needs have much to tell us about their experiences of school. Furthermore, we would suggest that because of the different approaches adopted by schools to address the needs of pupils described as having learning difficulties or disabilities, the lived experiences of these students may be considerably different from those of their peers. If this is the case then an understanding of how these experiences impact upon either their inclusion and participation or their exclusion from the everyday activities in which their classmates are involved may be important in ensuring equity and access to learning.

Listening to the voices of students alone will not bring about change. Teachers and other professionals must make a commitment to make use of the information which their students can provide from a unique perspective. Gaining this information can often be a challenge, particularly where students may lack the sophisticated communication skills of their peers and more especially when as a result of the label of special educational needs attached to them they or others may feel that their opinions are of limited value. Teachers need to adopt a positive demeanour towards such students but also need to consider the ways in which they provide opportunities for students to express their ideas and opinions.

CONCLUSION AND SUMMARY

Researchers and teachers who wish to understand the influences and impact of provision made for students with special educational needs should consider the rich data that can be obtained directly from these students. The body of research into student voice conducted in recent years provides an indication of the value that individuals can add to our analysis of schools as effective inclusive learning settings. However, the collation of trustworthy data from student sources requires careful preparation and management, especially in ensuring that students feel comfortable with the process and are supported through the provision of appropriate means of providing data. Researchers and teachers who collect such data need to be respectful of the rights of individual students and must make a commitment to utilise findings from any such studies to inform and improve the provision and support made available to them.

The students who participated in Project IRIS and gave us access to their data have both confirmed and challenged much of what is written in the literature about creating inclusive schools. They have demonstrated that the current debates surrounding issues such as the use of specialist groups and para-professional support that have often polarised opinions are complex when seen through the eyes of those in receipt of such approaches. These students have played a significant role in challenging our own thinking and identifying these areas as an important focus for further research.

Engaging in discussions with students about their life experiences can enrich our own appreciation of the world in which they live. It will only do so when we are prepared not only to listen to their voices but also to take action to address their concerns and find more effective ways of addressing their needs.

KEY TERMS

Primary schools – Schools designated to address the needs of students between the ages of 5 and 12 years.

Post-primary schools – Schools designated to address the needs of students post the age of 12 years.

Project IRIS – A longitudinal research project investigating the provision made for students with special educational needs in Irish schools.

Resource teachers – Specialist teachers of students with special educational needs working within Irish schools.

Special Needs Assistants (SNAs) – Para-professionals working in schools alongside teachers to support some individual students with special educational needs.

Student voice – The means by which students are enabled to contribute to our understanding of their experiences.

Withdrawal groups – Groups of pupils with similar needs brought together for teaching outside of the main classrooms.

REFERENCES

Alderson, P. (2000). School students' views on school councils and daily life at school. *Children and Society*, *14*(2), 121–134.

Alur, M., & Bach, M. (2010). *The journey for inclusive education in the Indian sub-continent*. London: Routledge.

Avramidis, E., Bayliss, P., & Burden, R. (2000). Student teachers' attitudes towards the inclusion of children with special educational needs in the ordinary school. *Teaching and Teacher Education*, *16*(3), 277–293.

Bahou, L. (2011). Rethinking the challenges and possibilities of student voice and agency. *Educate*, (Kaleidoscope Special Issue), 2–14.

Barnard, W. M. (2004). Parent involvement in elementary school and educational attainment. *Children and Youth Services Review*, *26*(1), 39–62.

Blatchford, P., Bassett, P., Brown, P., Martin, C., Russell, A., & Webster, R. (2011). The impact of support staff on pupils' 'positive approaches to learning' and their academic progress. *British Journal of Educational Research*, *37*(3), 443–464.

Broomhead, K. (2014). 'A clash of two worlds'; disjuncture between the norms and values held by educational practitioners and parents of children with behavioural, emotional and social difficulties. *British Journal of Special Education, 41*(2), 136–150.

Cambre, C., & Silvestre, N. (2003). Students with special educational needs in the inclusive classroom: Social integration and self-concept. *European Journal of Special Needs Education, 18*(2), 197–208.

Cook-Sather, A. (2002). Authorizing students' perspectives: Toward trust, dialogue, and change in education. *Educational Researcher, 31*(4), 3–14.

Davies, J. M., & Watson, N. (2001). Where are the children's experiences? Analysing social and cultural exclusion in 'special' and 'mainstream' schools. *Disability and Society, 16*(5), 671–687.

Department of Education. (2014). *Special educational needs and disability code of practice: 0 to 25 years.* London: Department of Education.

Farrell, A. M., & O'Neill, Á. (2012). Learning support/resource teachers in mainstream post-primary schools: Their perception of the role in relation to subject teachers. *Reach, Journal of Special Needs Education in Ireland, 25*(2), 92–103.

Farrell, P., Alborz, A., Howes, A., & Pearson, D. (2010). The impact of teaching assistants on improving pupils' academic achievement in mainstream schools: A review of the literature. *Educational Review, 62*(4), 435–448.

Fielding, M. (2001). Beyond the rhetoric of student voice: New departures or new constraints in the transformation of 21st century schooling? *Forum, 43*(2), 100–110.

Flutter, J., & Ruddock, J. (2004). *Consulting pupils: What's in it for schools?* London: Routledge.

Giangreco, M. F., Carter, E. W., Doyle, M. B., & Suter, J. C. (2010). Supporting students with disabilities in inclusive classrooms: Personnel and peers. In R. Rose (Ed.), *Confronting obstacles to inclusion: International responses to developing inclusive education.* London: Routledge.

Griffin, S., & Shevlin, M. (2007). *Responding to special educational needs: An Irish perspective.* Dublin: Gill and MacMillan.

Hill, N. E., & Taylor, L. C. (2004). Parental school involvement and children's academic achievement: Pragmatics and issues. *Current Directions in Psychological Science, 13*(4), 161–164.

Horgan, G. (2003). Educable: Disabled young people in Northern Ireland challenge the education system. In M. Shevlin & R. Rose (Eds.), *Encouraging voices: Respecting the insights of young people who have been marginalised.* Dublin: National Disability Authority.

Lewis, A., Newton, H., & Vials, S. (2008). Realising child voice: The development of cue cards. *Support for Learning, 23*(1), 26–31.

Lundy, L. (2007). 'Voice' is not enough: Conceptualising article 12 of the United Nations convention on the rights of the child. *British Educational Research Journal, 33*(6), 927–942.

Maras, P., & Brown, R. (2000). Effects of different forms of school contact on children's attitudes toward disabled and non-disabled peers. *British Journal of Educational Psychology, 70*(3), 337–351.

Marston, D. (1996). A comparison of inclusion only, pull-out only, and combined service models for students with mild disabilities. *Journal of Special Education, 30*(2), 121–132.

Mortimer, H. (2004). Hearing children's voices in the early years. *Support for Learning, 19*(4), 169–174.

Morton, J. (1996). Helping children contribute to their learning plans. *Educational and Child Psychology, 13*(2), 23–30.

Patton, M. Q. (2002). *Qualitative evaluation and research methods* (3rd ed.). Thousand Oaks, CA: Sage.

Porter, J. (2014). Research and pupil voice. In L. Florian (Ed.), *The Sage handbook of special education* (pp. 405–419). London: Sage.

Prince, E., & Hadwin, J. (2013). The role of a sense of school belonging in understanding the effectiveness of inclusion of children with special educational needs. *International Journal of Inclusive Education, 17*(3), 238–262.

Roche, J. (1999). Children's rights, participation and citizenship. *Childhood, 6*(4), 475–493.

Rose, R., & O'Neill, À. (2009). Classroom support for inclusion in England and Ireland. An evaluation of contrasting models. *Research in Comparative and International Education, 4*(3), 250–261.

Rose, R., & Shevlin, M. (2006). Written in the margins. *Prospero: A Journal of New Thinking in Philosophy for Education, 12*(2), 3–5.

Rose, R., & Shevlin, M. (2010). *Count me in: Ideas for actively engaging students in inclusive classrooms*. London: Jessica Kingsley.

Rose, R., Shevlin, M., Winter, E., & O'Raw, P. (2010). Special and inclusive education in the Republic of Ireland: Reviewing the literature from 2000 to 2009. *European Journal of Special Needs Education, 25*(4), 357–371.

Shevlin, M., Kenny, M., & Loxley, A. (2008). A time of transition: Exploring special educational provision in the Republic of Ireland. *Journal of Research in Special Educational Needs, 8*(3), 141–152.

Shevlin, M., & Rose, R. (2003). Encouraging voices: Respecting the insights of young *people who have been marginalised*. Dublin: National Disability Authority.

Skidmore, D. (2004). *Inclusion: The dynamic of school development*. Maidenhead: Open University Press.

Soriano, V. (2005). *Young views on special needs education: Results of the European parliament hearing*. Middelfart: European Agency for Development in Special Needs Education.

Thomas, G., Walker, D., & Webb, J. (1998). *The making of the inclusive school*. London: Routledge.

Travers, J. (2010). The impact of the general allocation model policy on learning support for mathematics in Irish primary schools. *Oideas, 55*, 8–20.

Vehkakoski, T. M. (2012). 'More homework for me, too'. Meanings of differentiation constructed by elementary-aged students in classroom interaction. *European Journal of Special Needs Education, 27*(2), 157–170.

INCLUSIVE EDUCATION FOR STUDENTS WITH LOW-INCIDENCE DISABILITIES IN TAIWAN – WHERE WE ARE, WHAT WE HAVE LEARNED

Pei-Yu Chen and Chun-Yu Chiu

ABSTRACT

The purpose of this chapter is to share the experience and discuss issues that support and hinder inclusive practices in Taiwan. In this chapter, inclusion-related culture and policies are described in the context of Taiwan, followed by the challenges and lessons learned from promoting inclusive education for students with disabilities from the perspectives of general and special education teachers. Some promising strategies applied by teachers are also discussed in this chapter based on the findings of the research literature in Taiwan. Implications for practice and research about inclusion are addressed at the end of this chapter.

Keywords: Inclusive practices; general education; special education; least restrictive environment

Including Learners with Low-Incidence Disabilities
International Perspectives on Inclusive Education, Volume 5, 203–219

ISSN: 1479-3636/doi:10.1108/S1479-363620140000005012

INTRODUCTION

Providing a least restrictive environment (LRE) for students with disabilities is a worldwide trend in the field of special education, including the Republic of China (Taiwan). In 1997, the Ministry of Education officially included the term "least restrictive environment" in the amendment of the Taiwan Special Education Act (TWSE). Since then, more and more students with disabilities have been educated in inclusive settings, including those with low-incidence disabilities. In the 2012 school year, 84% of school-age children with disabilities received special education in general education and resource classrooms or through itinerary education in Taiwan (Ministry of Education, 2013). The trend of inclusion over the course of 15 years indicates that nowadays students with disabilities have more access to general education curriculum and social interaction with typically developing students (Cheng, 2012a; Wang, 2011).

The purpose of this chapter is to introduce inclusive education for students with disabilities in Taiwan, including those with low-incidence disabilities. According to Kirk, Gallaher, Coleman, and Anastasiow (2011), low-incidence disabilities are categories of disabilities that are less than 1% of school population. These categories include students with multiple disabilities, hearing impairments, orthopedic impairments, traumatic brain injury, visual impairments, and students who are deaf and blind (Kirk et al., 2011). While low-incidence disabilities refer to certain categories of disabilities, most of the research on inclusive education in Taiwan was conducted across various disabilities (Wang, 2011). Therefore, we describe issues around inclusive education in Taiwan without emphasizing specific categories of disabilities.

The following four aspects are depicted in this chapter. First, we describe the inclusion-related culture and policies in the context of Taiwan. Then, we discuss the challenges and lessons learned from promoting inclusive education for students with low-incidence disabilities from the perspectives of general and special education teachers. Next, strategies applied by teachers in Taiwan to promote inclusion are addressed. Lastly, implications for practice and research about inclusion will be addressed at the end of this chapter. By sharing the experience of promoting inclusive education in Taiwan, we hope to help researchers and practitioners understand how inclusion for students with disabilities is perceived and carried out in a different culture and context.

IN CONTEXT OF TAIWAN

Demographics and Policies

Taiwan is a democratic nation consisting of a total population of 23 million, with over 95% made up by Han Chinese with a smaller proportion of indigenous groups (Ministry of Foreign Affairs, 2014). Although Taiwan is a relatively homogenous society as compared to the United States, socio-economic and rural-urban discrepancies still exist nonetheless. Additionally, the increased number of immigrants also significantly diversified cultures in Taiwan in the past decade (National Immigration Agency, 2011). The education system in Taiwan was influenced by the policies and practices of various countries. The majority of disability-related policies were drafted with careful analyses of international laws and societal context in Taiwan, including People with Disabilities Rights Protection Act (TWPD) and the two sets of special education policies.

Chronologically, TWPD was originally enacted as the Disability Welfare Act in 1980 and amended in 1997 and 2007 to align with the United Nations Declarations on the Rights of Disabled Persons 1975. TWPD, recently amended in 2009, 2011, and 2013, mandates general protection from discrimination and specifies educational rights for people with disabilities. Notably, Taiwan's Legislative Yuan (equivalent to congress in the U.S.) passed the first reading of the United Nation Convention on the Rights of Persons with Disabilities in June, 2013 and was in the process of ratifying the convention (Cong. Rec. No.1684, 2014). People with Disabilities Rights Protection Act [TWPD] (2013) prohibits educational agencies (e.g., schools, institutions) from rejecting student admission on the basis of disability or the lack of appropriate facilities and resources. It also provides that schools and education programs must accommodate students with disabilities to receive appropriate education services.

The other set of laws was the TWSE, first enacted in 1984 and subsequently amended in 1997, 2004, 2009, and 2013. Similar to TWPD, TWSE (2013) also supports inclusive education by regulating the local authorities to provide accessible environments, free transportation, and scholarships to students with disabilities. It also states that the committee should make placement decisions following the principle of proximity (distance from home to school). TWSE also provides classification for type of disabilities. See Table 1 for the statistics of students with disabilities. The amendment of TWSE in 1997 incorporated the concept of inclusion and emphasized

Table 1. Statistics of Students with Disabilities in Primary and Secondary Education.

Category	Educational Level				Number	
	Preschool	Elementary	Middle school	High school	Total	%
Total	13,664	40,920	26,460	19,770	100,814	100
%	13.55	40.59	26.25	19.61	–	–
Intellectual disabilities	943	11,229	7,719	5,785	25,676	25.47
Visual impairment	49	373	275	298	995	0.99
Hearing impairment	336	1,142	691	688	2,857	2.83
Speech disorders	568	1,233	173	104	2,078	2.06
Physical disabilities	431	1334	988	1,122	3,875	3.84
Cerebral palsy	113	224	126	69	532	0.53
Other health impairment	280	1,377	835	799	3,291	3.26
Emotional and behavioral disorders	57	2,749	1,491	1,252	5,549	5.50
Learning disabilities	0	11,943	9,596	7,018	28,557	28.33
Multiple disabilities	609	2,761	1,491	581	5,442	5.40
Autism	961	5,034	2,709	1,805	10,509	10.42
Developmental disabilities	9,103	0	0	0	9,103	9.03
Other disabilities	214	1,521	366	249	2,350	2.33

Note: The authors used data from multiple spreadsheets retrieved from Special Education Transmit Net (2014) to compile this table. This data excludes students in special schools ($n = 6{,}636$).

providing LRE and offering related services, accommodation for assessment, and assistive technology in general education settings to meet the learning needs of students with disabilities (Wu, 2004). The policies in Taiwan set the stage for providing inclusive education for students with disabilities.

Statistics of Students with Disabilities

In the 2003 school year, 33% of students with disabilities were enrolled in general education classrooms, 31% received special education services in resource rooms, and 6% through itinerary education (Wu, 2007). Overall, 70% of students with disabilities are educated in inclusive settings (Lo & Lin, 2006). As of the 2013 school year, 2.6% of children ranging from preschool to high school in Taiwan ($N = 107{,}450$) were students with disabilities. A total of 85,607 students with disabilities were enrolled in partial or complete inclusive settings (i.e., general education classroom, resource classroom, and itinerary service) in 2013 (Special Education Transmit Net, 2014), which constitutes 79.67% of the student body. Another 21,843 students (20.33%) were served in relatively less inclusive education settings, namely, special schools, home education, or hospital-based programs (see Table 2).

A general education setting refers to a placement where students with disabilities receive appropriate education along with students without disabilities. Depending on the needs that are documented in their individualized education programs (IEPs), they may receive related-services and accommodations, including personal assistant and assistive technology (The Enforcement Rules of the Special Education Act, 2013). In contrast to full inclusive educational setting, the resource classroom and itinerary service, as defined in the Enforcement Rules of the Special Education Act (2013), are classified as partial inclusive setting. The Enforcement Rules regulate students served in a resource classroom who receive education

Table 2. Educational Placement of Students with Disabilities in Primary and Secondary Education.

Category	Educational Level				Number	
	Preschool	Elementary	Middle school	High school	Total	%
Total	13,839	41,649	27,654	24,308	107,450	
% of *N*	12.88	38.76	25.74	22.62	100	
Partial or full inclusive education setting	12,664	35,704	22,344	14,895	85,607	79.67
% of *N*	11.79	33.23	20.79	13.86	79.67	–
General education classroom	5,454	4,920	3,771	6,342	20,487	19.07
Resource classroom	102	27,463	17,714	8,409	53,688	49.97
Itinerary service	7,108	3,321	859	144	11,432	10.64
Less-inclusive education setting	1,175	5,945	5,310	9,413	21,843	20.33
% of *N*	1.09	5.53	4.94	8.76	20.33	–
Self-contained classroom	819	4,629	3,706	4,875	14,029	13.06
Special school	175	729	1,194	4,538	6,636	6.18
Hospital-/home-school	181	587	410	0	1,178	1.1

Note: The authors used data from multiple tables retrieved from Special Education Transmit Net (2014) to compile this table. The total student number includes students in special schools ($n = 6{,}636$), which differs from Table 1.

services primarily in general education classrooms and who are pulled out for special education or related services when appropriate according to their IEPs. Meng (2006) further specified that the amount of time that a student with a disability spent in pull-out services provided by a resource classroom should not exceed 50% of the total hours of a school day. On the other hand, students who are required to receive special education and related services at home, institution or school due to health considerations are visited by itinerant teachers at least two hours per week.

The data revealed that over the course of 10 years, more students with disabilities received special education services in full or partial inclusive settings. However, the increase in the number of students with disabilities in inclusive settings does not ensure the quality of special education provided to these students. Without sufficient preparation and support, implementing inclusive education may have a negative impact on the social and academic development of students with disabilities (Chiang, 2011).

INCLUSION IN TAIWAN

To understand the quality of inclusive education, more than 300 journal articles and 200 theses and dissertations in Taiwan have investigated various aspects of inclusive education, including perspectives on inclusion as well as challenges and strategies to promote successful inclusive education.

Perspectives on Inclusion

As Wu (2004) pointed out, successful inclusive education for students with disabilities is influenced by the interaction of the following factors, including education placement, administrative support, environmental arrangement, classroom management, instruction and assignment modification, curriculum design and adaptation, professional training, peer interaction, and family collaboration. That is, general education teachers, special education teachers, and parents of students with disabilities play important roles in successful inclusive education. However, most of the studies on inclusion in Taiwan did not involve parents of students with disabilities as participants (Wang, 2011). Therefore, in the following section we focused on describing how general education and special education teachers perceive inclusion in Taiwan.

General Education Teachers

Inclusive education has been implemented in Taiwan since the amendment of TWSE in 1997, and one of the factors influencing successful inclusion is educators' attitude toward students with disabilities and toward inclusive education (Wu, 2004). Chiu (2001) surveyed and interviewed elementary ($n = 129$) and secondary ($n = 149$) general education teachers across 10 counties/cities in Taiwan to understand the barriers and their needs in providing services for students with disabilities. Administrators of the department of education in 18 counties/cities were also involved in the survey. The results indicated that only 27% of elementary teachers and 18% of secondary teachers thought students with disabilities should be placed full-time in general education classrooms, and 32% of secondary teachers thought students with disabilities should enroll in self-contained classes. The results also showed that 11 out of 18 administrators of department of education marked "teachers' refusal toward inclusion" as one of the top five barriers they encountered when providing support for general education teachers to help students with disabilities. Wu (2004) compared 1,422 educators, including administrators, general education teachers, and special education teachers in elementary schools in Taiwan about their attitudes toward inclusion. The findings showed that administrators and special education teachers had more positive attitudes than general education teachers did regarding including students with disabilities in general education classrooms.

The attitude of general education teachers toward inclusion seemed to change gradually overtime. Hsu and Chan (2008) surveyed 308 elementary school teachers who were head-teachers of general education classes in Taiwan. They asked the teachers about their perception about inclusion and the extent to which they would accept students with learning disabilities (LD), autism, hearing impairment, and attention deficit hyperactivity disorder (ADHD) to be placed in their classrooms. The scores on the surveys indicated that overall general education teachers showed neutral to positive attitudes toward students with disabilities placed in general education settings. While general education teachers thought inclusion was the right thing to do for students with disabilities, most teachers reported overall low acceptance of having students with disabilities in their classroom, especially those students with autism and ADHD because of their challenging behaviors.

As Chiang (2011) pointed out, general education teachers in Taiwan had great pressure to keep up with the pace of curriculum mandated by their school. Thus, large group instruction and lecture were the most common instructional strategies applied in general education classrooms. Furthermore, (a) the size of the class, (b) the lack of appropriate teaching materials, (c) the concerns and questions from the parents of typically developing students, (d) the lack of professional training in special education, (e) insufficient collaboration between general and special education teachers, and (f) the lack of administrative support were also reported by teachers in Taiwan as challenges that impede inclusion (Chiang, 2011; Hsu & Chan, 2008; Lin, 2011). Overall, the results of studies in Taiwan indicated that in the past decade the attitudes of general education teachers toward the concept of inclusion gradually became more positive. Nevertheless, empowering general education teachers to overcome the aforementioned challenges to promote successful inclusion in their classrooms still requires support from all stakeholders in Taiwan.

Special Education Teachers

Most of the special education teachers highly supported the concept of inclusion (Wu, 2004), but they still expressed concerns about placing students with disabilities in general education classrooms. Special education teachers indicated concern about the influences of inclusive education on the social adjustment of students with disabilities and about collaborating with general education teachers.

Researchers in Taiwan found that students with disabilities are marginalized in general education settings (Chang, 2011; Cheng, 2012a; Lo, 2009). Cheng (2012a) described that many resource room students usually felt that they were ignored or rejected by peers in general education classrooms. Even students without challenging behaviors, such as students with low vision, were excluded by peer groups. Lo (2009) investigated the challenges encountered by a student with visual impairment in a vocational high school and found similar findings. The student with visual impairment felt she was different from and not as good as her peers academically. The findings of these studies showed that without appropriate support, students with disabilities usually had academic and social difficulties in inclusive settings.

Many studies in Taiwan investigated whether interventions developed by teachers would influence peer acceptance for students with disabilities. For example, peer-assisted learning strategies were applied in general education settings to improve academic performance as well as social relationship of students with disabilities (Chiu, 2003; Tsuei, 2006). Yang and Chung (2006) developed a series of activities for 2nd grade typically developing students to increase their understanding about various disabilities. After eight sessions of intervention, the experiment group showed significantly higher acceptance for students with disabilities than the control group. While the intervention showed promising results, the maintenance and generalization of the intervention effects were not monitored after the intervention. Thus, whether the peer relationship of students with disabilities improved as a result of the intervention remained unclear.

Another challenge that concerns special education teachers is collaboration with general education teachers to successfully implement inclusion. Students with disabilities enrolled in inclusive settings spent most of their time in general education classrooms. To ensure that students with disabilities receive appropriate special education services throughout a school day, special education teachers need to collaborate with general education in many ways. The collaboration may include (a) arranging learning environments, (b) modifying curriculum and instructions, (c) managing challenging behaviors, (d) providing assessment accommodations, (e) accessing assistive technologies, and (f) discussing and implementing IEP goals (Cheng, 2012b).

Liu and Tseng (2012) documented the changes of general and special education teachers in the process of their collaboration. They concluded that collaboration did not occur spontaneously, and both general and special education teachers need to develop understanding of each other's needs and expectation. However, based on the authors' observation during school visits, most of the special education teachers felt uncomfortable reaching out to provide "suggestions" to experienced general education teachers. While most of the special education teachers support inclusion and know that collaboration is essential, more collaboration training may be needed as well as more assistance from administrators in working with general education teachers.

Practice of Inclusive Education

Inclusive education refers to having students with and without disabilities to learn together. It emphasizes arranging normalized learning environments, increasing collaboration between general and special education teachers, and providing special education services in general education classrooms (Niew, 2006). Currently, most students with disabilities in Taiwan are educated with their typically developing peers. But the special education services are usually provided in resource rooms or in pull-out settings, and collaboration between general and special education teachers is still uncommon.

Some researchers in Taiwan have introduced a number of strategies developed in the United States to promote inclusion for students with disabilities, such as differentiated instruction, universal design for learning (UDL) (Lee & Tsai, 2009), response to intervention (Hung & Ho, 2010; Lin, 2008), and cooperative learning (Sheu & Lin, 2006; Tsuei, 2006). However, most of these interventions are not integrated into daily practices by teachers, and the effects have not been verified by researchers in Taiwan.

Other researchers have conducted surveys or qualitative research to help understand what strategies were applied by general and special education teachers who had successful experience with inclusion in Taiwan. In a qualitative study by Niew (2006), 32 participants were interviewed and observed to obtain information about strategies promoting inclusion in general education classrooms. These participants were highly qualified elementary educators who successfully implemented inclusion in their classes and were recommended by special education professors, administrators, special educators, and parents of students with disabilities. The strategies were organized in four sections: (a) strategies before school starts, (b) strategies during school year, (c) transition strategies, and finally, (d) additional strategies.

Strategies before School Starts

General education teachers reported that before the students with disabilities entered their classes, they reminded themselves to treat each student differently since every individual is different. In addition, they actively gather information about specific disabilities by attending workshops or by requesting information from special education teachers. Participants also questioned teachers who had taught the students to prepare themselves for the new school year.

To prepare students with disabilities for a new environment, general education teachers introduced all the teachers and environment to the students before the school year. Some teachers had students with disabilities help decorate the classroom and acknowledged their help in front of the class on the first day of school.

Strategies during School Year

After students with disabilities entered inclusive settings, general education teachers applied numerous strategies to help these students obtain successful experience socially, academically, and behaviorally. General education teachers were good at utilizing resources, such as special education teachers, volunteers, and other professionals to help provide social skills trainings, academic modifications, and behavior management.

General education teachers actively communicated with related personnel, including typically developing students and parents of students with and without disabilities to promote social adjustment of students with disabilities. Specifically, general education teachers conducted activities as described by Yang and Chung (2006) to increase students' understanding about certain disabilities and discussed and modeled how to interact with students with disabilities. Teachers shared the change and growth of typically developing students after students with disabilities entered their class to help parents of students without disabilities view inclusion positively.

As to academic adjustment, general education teachers modified instruction, assignments, and assessments to meet the need of students with disabilities. In addition, arranging small group activities and assigning appropriate roles and tasks for each group member, allowing time for one-on-one instruction after class, and setting up the classroom appropriately for students with disabilities (e.g., seat-arrangement, amount of information on the wall/board, or light in the classroom) were common strategies applied by general education teachers. The effects of utilizing small groups to conduct cooperative learning has been verified across studies in Taiwan (Sheu & Lin, 2006; Tsuei, 2006).

In an effort to effectively manage challenging behaviors, general education teachers tried to understand the underlying reason for the behaviors, clearly communicated the standards and expectations of the behavior, discussed the behavior with students with disabilities in private, and modeled appropriate behaviors. In addition, for some students with disabilities, general education teachers provided warnings before transitions or making changes to the schedule, gave extra time to finish tasks, or modified the activities when necessary.

Transition Strategies

When students with disabilities were transitioned to a new environment, general education teachers prepared the students for the new environment by introducing new teachers, classrooms, schedule, campus, and bus route. In addition, general education teachers prepared the teachers in the new environment by sharing experiences and strategies that worked for the students.

The aforementioned strategies demonstrated that general education teachers were capable of implementing strategies in their classrooms that were effective in educating ALL students, including students with disabilities. Thus, if general education teachers had positive attitudes toward inclusion and were aware and responsive to individual differences, they would feel more confident in promoting inclusive education for students with disabilities.

Additional Strategies

The aforementioned strategies align well with practices that are frequently used by special education teachers. In addition to those strategies, researchers in Taiwan also proposed some guidelines of instruction for special education teachers. For example, Cheng (2012a) suggested that teachers provide multiple modalities during instruction to enable students with disabilities to participate in activities in a way that met their learning styles. Lo (2009) reminded teachers who provided special education services in pull-out settings to plan for successful generalization in the general education classroom by arranging multiple exemplars when teaching and by having students with disabilities practice new skills across persons, settings, and materials. Chiang (2011) addressed the importance of providing age-appropriate activities during instruction, such as games played by same-age peer groups, to help students with disabilities to more easily blend in with typically developing peers.

FUTURE IMPLICATIONS

Successful inclusive education requires support from administrators, general and special education teachers, typically developing peers and parents of students with disabilities. Given the current state of inclusive education in Taiwan, a few directions for educators and researchers are proposed to promote inclusion for students with disabilities.

Implication for Education

General education teachers in Taiwan reported not feeling confident in helping students with disabilities in their classrooms, and special education teachers reported they had difficulties collaborating with general education teachers. In order to better implement inclusive education in Taiwan, schools should first conduct organizational reform by considering exceptional students as members of the whole student body, sharing responsibility for helping them be successful in school settings. Specifically, the leadership team of schools in Taiwan should implement school-wide interventions, such as response to intervention and school-wide positive behavior support to provide proactive services for every student. In addition, administrators should set up professional groups that include administrators, general education teachers and special education teachers to discuss specific cases or challenges in their daily practices to promote collaboration. Administrators should also arrange professional development workshops targeting (1) background knowledge as well as intervention strategies of special education and (2) guidelines to successful collaboration among professionals to help teachers overcome existing challenges.

General education teachers should actively attend workshops about special education and collaborate with other professionals to help them provide appropriate learning experiences for students with disabilities in general education classrooms. Special education teachers should step out of their comfort zone by actively helping general education teachers solve their difficulties in modifying instruction, assessments, and assignments as well as managing challenging behaviors of students with disabilities.

Teacher training programs should add more classes related to special education, such as introduction to special education and differentiated instruction for pre-service general education teachers. In addition, practicum experience in inclusive settings should also be part of the training program. As to special education teachers, while the "collaboration with families and professionals" class is usually offered by most of the teacher training programs in Taiwan, the instructors can arrange more learning experiences in the field for the pre-service teachers to obtain a deeper understanding and experience with collaborative practices.

Implication for Research

According to Wang (2011), 53% of the studies on inclusion conducted in Taiwan applied survey methods and 24% applied qualitative methods. Other studies used case studies, action research, and mixed methods to investigate the effects of inclusive education for students with disabilities. Most of the survey studies focused on investigating the attitudes of teachers or peers toward inclusion, current practices, challenges, and coping strategies. Limited studies were available in Taiwan that systematically investigated the overall effects of inclusion and the maintenance of the effects on the academic, social, and behavioral development of students with disabilities. Future research should examine the effects of inclusion for students with different categories and severities of disabilities.

In addition, the effects and social validity of the interventions developed in different cultures and contexts, such as differentiated instruction, UDL, or response to intervention, should also be examined. These interventions could then be adjusted to fit the school culture in Taiwan.

CONCLUSION AND SUMMARY

The concept and practice of inclusive education in Taiwan are at its early stage compared to that in the United States and other countries. While most of the students with disabilities in Taiwan are placed in inclusive settings, such as general education classrooms and resource rooms, the extent to which their needs are addressed in general education classrooms remains unclear. Currently, the education system in Taiwan is undergoing reform, and such change will dramatically change the practices in general education, which will directly influence students with disabilities enrolled in inclusive settings. How these changes would impact inclusive education in Taiwan requires further examination.

KEY TERMS

Inclusive education – Emphases on arranging normalized learning environments, increasing collaboration between general and special education teachers, and providing special education services in general education classrooms.

Inclusive settings – In this chapter, inclusive settings refer to education placements that provide both partial and full inclusive education, including general education classrooms, resource rooms, and itinerary services.

Low-incidence disabilities – Low-incidence disabilities are categories of disabilities that are less than 1% of school population. These categories include students with multiple disabilities, hearing impairments, orthopedic impairments, traumatic brain injury, visual impairments, and students who are deaf and blind.

Taiwan (Republic of China) – Taiwan is a democratic nation consisting of a total population of 23 million, with over 95% made up by Han Chinese with a smaller proportion of indigenous groups. The education system in

Taiwan was influenced by the policies and practices of various countries. The majority of disability-related policies were drafted with careful analyses of international laws and societal context in Taiwan, including People with Disabilities Rights Protection Act (TWPD) and the two sets of special education policies.

General education classrooms in Taiwan – On average there are 30–35 students and one head teacher in a class in the elementary and secondary levels. Each class may have up to three students with special needs. Students usually arrive at school around 7:30 am and leave around 4:00–4:30 pm.

Resource classrooms in Taiwan – The teacher-student ratio is 1:8 in a resource classroom. Each resource classroom usually has two special education teachers in elementary schools and three special education teachers in middle and high schools. Similar to the resource classrooms in the United States, the courses of resource classrooms in Taiwan usually are conducted in small groups and the content of the courses are made to address the students' needs, including academic, social, and behavioral instruction.

Special education teachers in Taiwan – Most of the special education teachers in Taiwan are graduated from a four-year teacher training program of undergraduate level. Providing direct services to students with disabilities and indirect services to general education teachers and families of students with disabilities consume the majority of the work of a special education teacher. In addition, during the child-find process, most of the special education teachers in Taiwan are responsible for conducting standardized assessment (e.g., IQ test), gathering other information, and writing up an evaluation report for the students' IEP team to determine their eligibility for special education.

REFERENCES

Chang, S. (2011). 就讀普通學校聽障學生的自我認同 [Self-identity of students with hearing impairment educated in regular schools]. *Special Education Quarterly*, *118*, 62–69.

Cheng, C. (2012a). 特殊教育從無到有：談障礙學生在普通班的邊緣化現象 [The growth out of nothing in special education: Discussion on the phenomenon of marginalization of students with disabilities in regular class]. *Special Education Quarterly*, *122*, 45–52.

Cheng, C. (2012b). 臺灣普教與特教的現況與未來—繼續統合或行動融合？ [The current and future of general education and special education in Taiwan – still integrated or going toward inclusion?]. *Special Education Quarterly*, *124*, 21–28.

Chiang, Y. (2011). 「不想成為班上的小白兔！」：以符號詮釋自閉症學童在融合教育中友誼建立之挑戰 ["Don't want to be a pet rabbit in class!": Using symbolic interpretation to explore the challenges of friendship building on students with autism in inclusive education]. *Bulletin of Special Education*, *36*, 87–114.

Chiu, M. (2003). 一個自閉症在國小六年級普通班自然科之融合教育 [Inclusive education in science class for a 6-grade student with autism]. *Tai-tung Special Education*, *18*, 26–31.

Chiu, S. (2001). 普通班教師對特殊需求學生之因應措施、所面對之困境以及所需之支持系統 [The coping strategies, barriers, and the supporting needs for the regular classroom teachers with teaching special students]. *Bulletin of Special Education*, *21*, 1–26.

Cong. Rec. No. 1684. (2014). Retrieved from http://lci.ly.gov.tw/LyLCEW/agenda1/03/pdf/08/05/02/01/LCEWA01_08050201_00011.pdf

Enforcement Rules of the Special Education Act. (2013).

Hsu, C., & Chan, S. (2008). 國小教師對不同類別身心障礙學生就讀普通班意見之調查研究 [A survey study on aspects of elementary school teachers toward students with different disabilities in regular classes]. *Bulletin of Special Education and Rehabilitation*, *19*, 25–49.

Hung, L., & Ho, S. (2010). 「介入反應」在特殊教育的意義與運用 [Response to intervention: The implication and application to the special education in Taiwan]. *Special Education Quarterly*, *115*, 1–13.

Kirk, S., Gallaher, J., Coleman, M. R., & Anastasiow, N. J. (2011). *Educating exceptional children*. Belmont, CA: Wadsworth, Cengage Learning.

Lee, W., & Tsai, K. (2009). 融合教育下特殊教育課程設計之探討 [A study on curriculum design in context of inclusive special education]. *Special Education for the Elementary School*, *47*, 39–50.

Lin, G. (2008). 回應性介入(RTI)內涵及其對國內融合教育之啟示 [The implications of response to intervention (RtI)]. *Special Education for the Elementary School*, *45*, 68–77.

Lin, P. (2011). 特殊教育並不特殊：從特殊教育的特殊性談融合教育之現況與未來 [Special education isn't special: The current and future special education]. *Special Education Quarterly*, *120*, 11–18.

Liu, K., & Tseng, S. (2012). 循著中介系統的脈絡來探討特教與幼教老師在自然情境中的合作歷程 [Education teachers and preschool teachers from the mesosystem perspective]. *Bulletin of Special Education*, *37*, 1–27.

Lo, C., & Lin, T. (2006). 融合教育「關注本位採用模式」理論建構及其試探研究 [The pioneer study for inclusive education by concerns-based adoption model]. *Bulletin of Eastern-Taiwan Special Education*, *8*, 1–19.

Lo, F. (2009). 從融合逆走回隔一位視覺障礙學生的學校生活經驗 [From inclusion to separation: The school life of a visually impaired student]. *Bulletin of Special Education*, *34*, 23–46.

Meng, Y. (2006). 資源教室方案—班級經營與補救教學 [Resource classroom: classroom management and remedial instruction]. Taipei: Wu-Nan.

Ministry of Foreign Affairs. (2014). *About Taiwan: Geography and demographics*. Retrieved from http://www.taiwan.gov.tw/ct.asp?xItem=126579&CtNode=3761&mp=1

Ministry of Education. (2013). *102 年度特殊教育統計年報* [*2013 Special education yearly statistic report*]. Taipei: Ministry of Education.

National Immigration Agency. (2011, December). *Foreign spouse population [dataset]*. Retrieved from http://www.immigration.gov.tw/public/Attachment/11121323157.xls

Niew, W. (2006). 國小融合班教師班級經營策略之研究 [The study on strategies adopted by elementary teachers to manage an inclusive classroom]. *Journal of Special Education*, *23*, 147–184.

People with Disabilities Rights Protection Act. (2013).

Sheu, M., & Lin, K. (2006). 合作學習對國小普通班學習障礙兒童數學學習成效之研究 [The effect of cooperative learning upon mathematical learning process of elementary school children with learning disability]. *Bulletin of Eastern-Taiwan Special Education*, *8*, 39–69.

Special Education Act. (2013).

Special Education Transmit Net. (2014). *102*學年度各縣市學前階段身心障礙學生特教類別統計2014/03/20 [Statistics of students with disabilities in school year 2013, dataset 20140320]. Retrieved from http://www.set.edu.tw/sta2/default.asp

Tsuei, M. (2006). 運用同儕協助學習策略於國小融合教育國語文學習之研究 [The impact of peer-assisted learning strategies on elementary students' Chinese language learning and peer relationships in the inclusive classroom]. *Bulletin of Special Education*, *30*, 26–52.

Wang, Y. (2011). 近兩年國內外融合教育之學術論文分析與議題探討 [The discussion and thesis/dissertation analysis about inclusive education for these two years]. *Special Education Quarterly*, *118*, 34–43.

Wu, S. (2004). 融合班之理念與實務 [Ideas and practices of inclusion]. Taipei: Psychological Publishing.

Wu, W. (2007). Inclusive education in Taiwan. *Chinese Education & Society*, *40*, 76–96.

Wu, Y. (2004). 國小教育人員對身心障礙學生融合教育態度差異分析研究 [A study on elementary education practitioners perspectives toward inclusive education]. *Tai-tung Special Education*, *20*, 29–38.

Yang, B., & Chung, L. (2006). 國小二年級學生認識身心障礙同儕活動方案介入成效之研究 [The effectiveness of "introduction for children with special needs" activities B6in the acceptance of children with special needs among 2nd grade student. *Bulletin of Eastern-Taiwan Special Education*, *8*, 71–95.

LOW-INCIDENCE LEARNERS IN SWEDEN – SUPPORTING SYSTEMS AND SOCIAL INTERACTIONS IN EDUCATION

Daniel Östlund

ABSTRACT

This chapter focuses on the participation and social interaction of pupils with low-incidence disabilities in the Swedish educational system with the goal of relating policies and practices in education for learners with low-incidence disabilities. Sweden has a welfare system that ensures that all low-incidence learners and their families receive support in education and in their everyday life. The research section concentrates on studies that focus on participation and social interaction in an educational context (training school), which is an adapted education program for low-incidence learners characterized by its high staff ratio and individualized forms of teaching. Despite legislation, policies, and intentions that Swedish schools shall include all pupils, it is still a challenge for the Swedish school system to provide education for low-incidence learners in inclusive environments. Research shows that low-incidence learners primarily have vertical relations with teachers and assistants in school,

Including Learners with Low-Incidence Disabilities
International Perspectives on Inclusive Education, Volume 5, 221–240

ISSN: 1479-3636/doi:10.1108/S1479-363620140000005014

and that there is a lack of horizontal relationships with peers. The greatest challenge is to create learning environments that contribute to building relationships between low-incidence learners and learners without disabilities.

Keywords: Interaction; intellectual disabilities; participation; policies; vertical relationships; welfare state

INTRODUCTION

Sweden's welfare system guarantees that individuals in Swedish society are assured a certain level of basic welfare services such as shelter, security, food, medical care, and education. The concept of the Swedish welfare state is based on the premise that everyone should have a satisfactory standard of living. Efforts on behalf of low-incidence learners are tax-funded and provided by the public sector. The support given to this group of learners is founded on a system of early intervention that provides help and support to the families as well as to the education professionals that work with LID children. There are several organizations that share responsibility for providing support for low-incidence learners and their families, such as *Mother and Child Health Services*, *Habilitation Centers for Children and Adolescents (CHC)*, preschool, compulsory school and upper secondary school, *The National Agency for Special Needs Education and Schools* (SPSM in Swedish), technical aid centers, and the Swedish Social Insurance Agency. Support can range from professional counseling for parents at *The Child Habilitation Center* (CHC), to physical adaptations to the child's home environment, to occupational therapy or to providing assistance in testing applicable aids. Support may also consist of special educators' supervision of staff at preschools or consultant counseling from *The National Agency for Special Needs Education and Schools* for teachers and principals in compulsory school. The support given by the state, county, and local government is focused not only on the child and the child's family but also on the educational settings where the child obtains his or her education.

There are currently about one million students aged 6–19 in school in Sweden. Schooling is compulsory for all children in Sweden aged 7–16. Approximately 90% of children aged 1–6 years attend preschool which is not compulsory. Upper secondary school is for pupils aged 16–19 and is also not compulsory, but approximately 99% of all students continue their education in upper secondary school (Skolverket, 2014). The Swedish Education Act (2010, p. 800) states that all children should receive their education by attending compulsory schools. Children who are not expected to achieve standard learning goals because they have an intellectual disability (ID) have the right to receive education in compulsory schools for pupils with ID, which is an adapted form of schooling (Grundsärskola is the Swedish term). However, it is important to emphasize that the parents of a child with ID can decide if they want their child to be educated in a compulsory school or in an adapted form of schooling (compulsory school for pupils with ID). Sweden has a long tradition of providing compulsory education for pupils with ID as an independent education program parallel to regular compulsory school. These independent programs include special needs schools for pupils with hearing or visual impairments and Sami school (for indigenous pupils of Sami origin). Currently, about 9,600 pupils receive their education via compulsory schools for pupils with ID and about 500 pupils receive their education in special needs schools for pupils with hearing or visual impairments (Skolverket, 2014). Low-incidence learners are included in the group of pupils with ID who are provided education in an adapted program.

The content in this chapter is based on four major questions:

1. What is the Swedish policy and supporting system for low-incidence learners?
2. How is education for low-incidence learners organized in Sweden?
3. What is the characteristic of the social interactions in education for low-incidence learners?
4. What are the challenges for the Swedish school system in the future from an interactional point of view?

This chapter is organized in response to these four questions in the order in which they appear, together with concluding remarks.

Policies and Legislation to Promote Inclusion for Low-Incidence Learners

In the Swedish context, a high level of societal services for low-incidence learners and their families is mandated by laws regulating general health care (SFS, 1982, p. 763), a law that regulates services for persons with disabilities (SFS, 1993, p. 387), and the Education Act (SFS, 2010, p. 800). Together, these three laws constitute the foundation for the support that low-incidence learners and their families are entitled to in Sweden.

The Salamanca Statement (1994) and the Convention on the Rights of the Child (United Nations, 1989) are also important documents that have influenced the design of the Swedish support system.

From the late 1930s up through today, all children in Sweden have been offered free health care by the County Councils. In 1954, the first child habilitation center was established to meet the needs of those children who contracted polio during the polio epidemic in the early 1950s. The child habilitation centers provide team support to the child as well as to other family members (SFS, 1982, p. 763, 1993, p. 387). The teams consist of special educators, occupational therapists, pediatrician/neuropediatricians, physical therapists, psychologists, speech language pathologists, and social workers who collaborate in transdisciplinary teams in conjunction with the family. The child habilitation centers also provide free-of-charge medical services and aid for children. The children obtain support from the Child Habilitation Center until the age of 18, after which the Adult Habilitation Center assumes responsibility. There is collaboration between the professionals in the child habilitation center and the professionals during the time students attend preschool/school. According to the Swedish Education Act (2010, p. 800), the municipalities have the responsibility of providing support in preschool/school placements, respite care, and in providing any necessary personal assistants if needed.

The Swedish Education Act (2010, p. 800) assumes a great deal of responsibility for students with special needs and mandates assistance for pupils in need of support. The right to an equal education is a central point of the Swedish school legislation. However, it is up to each municipality (290 in Sweden) to ensure that students receive needed support. The support provided can differ from municipality to municipality, in spite of the basic guarantee that schools must be equivalent in Sweden, regardless of where students live, their gender, or disability.

Educational programs for low-incidence learners was established by law in 1944 (SFS, 1944, p. 477), although it has its roots in schools for "educable" pupils with ID, which were established in the late 1800s. The "educable" pupils of that time was a group of pupils that would be labeled today as pupils with mild intellectual disabilities. In the early years, these schools were developed through private initiative, but in the 1900s the county councils took over the schools and organized them under the health care departments. The education for the educable during the period of the 1880s to the 1950s was organized in institutions. Since the concept of separating the educable from the "ineducable" was pervasive, it also created the need to take care of children, adolescents, and adults who were labeled as ineducable. Söder (1981) provides some examples of early initiatives to create asylums (sanctuaries) within the institutions where persons labeled as ineducable could live and receive some care. The asylums were initially operated with very limited resources and were not eligible for any county operating grants until the early 1900s. It is important to point out that the asylums did not offer any education for the people living there; the asylums rather served as institutional storage facilities primarily focused on the daily care of its patients. In the early 1900s, Swedish researcher Nirjes' (1969, 1992) normalization principle was introduced, which greatly influenced the Swedish disability policy. The normalization principle reflected some key methods of providing people with ID, a life similar to others in society. The dissemination of the normalization principle across Sweden and Scandinavia created a flashpoint that led to the closure of large institutions for people with disabilities in the 1960s.

However, the educable–ineducable division remained prevalent in policy documents and in the law until the Care Act of 1967 (SFS, 1967, p. 940) was enacted. Despite the fact that the first child habilitation center (CHC) was opened in 1954, children with intellectual and developmental disabilities didn't have access to these facilities until the Care Act was enacted in 1967. The legislative changes also gave children, adolescents, and adults who had previously been considered as ineducable the opportunity to participate in education. The expansion of eligibility led to the creation of two distinct divisions that are still intact to the present day: the adapted program (Grundsarskola) for pupils with mild ID, with orientation to subjects quite similar to the compulsory school and the training school (Traningsskola) for pupils with severe ID with a modified orientation.

The adapted program (Grundsärskola) teaches more or less the same subjects as in the regular compulsory school but with its own syllabi. The pupils attend school for nine years and receive 6,665 hours of teaching. Compared to the regular compulsory school, the course syllabi is adapted to meet the cognitive challenges of pupils with ID. The classes have less pupils and more teaching resources, that is, the staffing ratio for teachers is higher. Teachers are legally required to have a special teacher's education with a focus on intellectual disabilities. The special teacher's education is a supplementary education for teachers. It is also common that the special teachers work in teams with paraprofessionals. After the nine years in compulsory school, the pupils can pursue further education by choosing a four-year education program in the upper secondary school for pupils with ID. The upper secondary school is intended to prepare pupils for adult life and prepares the pupils to obtain employment. When the pupils have graduated from secondary school, they are guaranteed employment by a law which regulates services for persons with disabilities (SFS, 1993, p. 387).

The training school (Träningsskola) has its own course syllabi and teaches five subject areas: artistic activities, communication, every day activities, motor skills, and perception of reality (a subject area relating to the natural sciences). The training school program is also for nine years and includes 6,665 hours of teaching. The training school consists of a very heterogeneous group of pupils, and the teaching is organized in small classes with a high staffing ratio. Training school teachers are legally required to have a special teacher's education with specialization in intellectual disabilities, which is a supplementary education. The teacher works in teams with paraprofessionals. It is also common that the pupils in training school receive support in school from the professionals at the child habilitation center (CHC). After the nine years in compulsory school, the pupils can pursue further education in the four-year individual program in the upper secondary school for pupils with ID. The individual program teaches subjects similar to the subject areas in training school. After finishing the individual program, the pupils are guaranteed employment or daily activities at an activity center.

PRIOR RESEARCH

Over the last 20 years, research on special needs education has generated a debate that encompasses two different conceptual frameworks for understanding special education needs in Sweden. The individualistic framework, referred to as the categorical or traditional perspective, employs an individualistic approach in both research and in school practices (Emanuelsson, Persson, & Rosenqvist, 2001). This perspective is also described as a compensatory perspective/approach or as a psycho-medical paradigm by Skidmore (1996). The social and environmental framework, referred to as a relational perspective, appears more of an idyllic type in contrast to the more traditional (categorical) perspective (Emanuelsson et al., 2001). From the relational perspective point of view, there is a focus on the interaction between the pupils and other actors in school. This approach focuses on educational intervention in the environment rather than on individuals.

There is a continued push from researchers in Sweden to shift from special education (categorical perspective) to inclusive education (relational perspective) (Persson, 1998; Thomas & Loxley, 2007), where the responsibility for handling educational diversity becomes everybody's business instead of just the special teacher or the special educators. However, research has shown that the traditional/categorical perspective is pervasive in Swedish schools, and that categorization of pupils is the usual way of handling diversity in educational contexts (Hjörne & Säljö, 2004; Persson, 1998). Emanuelsson et al. (2001) explain the differences in the two perspectives (Table 1):

Since the 1980s, participation has been a central concept in Swedish policies for education and research even though it has been refined through various evolving definitions. The Curriculum for compulsory school and Compulsory school for pupils with ID (including training school) (2011) states:

> It is not in itself sufficient that teaching only imparts knowledge about fundamental democratic values. Democratic working forms should also be applied in practice and prepare pupils for active participation in the life of society. This should develop their ability to take personal responsibility (Skolverket, 2011, p. 10)

The concept of participation establishes the overall mission of the Swedish school to educate all pupils about democratic principles, in preparation for becoming citizens who are well aware of their democratic rights and obligations.

Table 1. Consequences for the Special Educational Activities in Schools Depending on the Perspective Chosen (Emanuelsson et al., 2001, p. 22).

	Categorical Perspective	Relational Perspective
Ontology of special needs	Special needs refer to actual characteristics of individuals	Special needs are social construct
Approach to difference	Differentiating & categorizing	Unifying
Major contribution	Mapping and systematizing the field	Problematizing deconstructing the field
Disciplinary basis	Establishing special education as a "scientific" discipline	Establishing special education as a social scientific discipline
Implication for provision	Special provision	Integrated/inclusive provision
Understanding of special educational competence	Superior support directly related to diagnosed difficulties among students	Superior support for incorporating differentiation into instruction and content
Reasons for special educational needs	Students with difficulties. Difficulties are either innate or otherwise bound to the individual	Students in difficulties. Difficulties arise from different phenomena in educational settings and processes

Although participation is a central concept in Swedish disability and education politics, particularly in relation to low-incidence learners, very little is known about the status of participation in the contexts that low-incidence learners encounter (Östlund, 2012a). Some of the research about Swedish compulsory school for pupils with intellectual disabilities is historically oriented (Areschoug, 2000; Barow, 2009), yet some are also based on more contemporary empirical materials (Anderson, 2002; Berthén, 2007; Molin, 2004; Szönyi, 2005; Tideman, 2000) that indicate an increased interest in issues related to learners with low-incidence disabilities, both from a historical and a contemporary perspective. Sweden's educational programs for pupils with ID, including low-incidence learners, have often been questioned by researchers and teachers with an inclusion and participatory approach to education.

Innovative studies on pupils' experiences with participation in compulsory school for pupils with ID and how the pupils' identities are constructed in school have been conducted by Szönyi (2005) and Frithiof (2007). These studies show that being a pupil in compulsory school for pupils with ID has mixed outcomes and can contribute to participation but also to exclusion. Studies of integration and inclusion have been conducted in compulsory school for pupils with ID since the late 1970s, when Söder (1981) investigated integration processes for pupils with ID. A common focus in these studies was interactional processes that involved low-incidence learners and students without disabilities (Karlsudd, 2002; Nordström, 2002). Nordström (2002) studied pupils with ID and their interactions and relationships with students within their own group and in relation to other students in school. It was characteristic for the pupils with ID to interact generally only with each other in the schoolyard. The pupils in the study were clear that in school they had peers to play with but after school and at home they had few peers with which to play.

Research has been conducted in the last two decades on "what is special about the pedagogical work in compulsory school for pupils with ID" (Berthén, 2007; Blom, 2003). These studies link current pedagogical philosophies to those formed by pioneers in the early years of education for educable pupils with intellectual disabilities. Bloms' (2003) study shows that knowledge in basic subjects, social education, strengthening of self-confidence, and motivation of the pupil are important starting points for teachers describing their goals. The teachers in the study describe educational work that was characterized by students in need of more time and preparation in the everyday life activities of school. The pupils were also in need of an individualized education that was both practical and flexible.

Blom (2003) argues that these aspects can be considered specifically with the educational work in compulsory schools for pupils with ID. Berthén (2007) describes the work of the two classes that were studied, one in a class in compulsory schools for pupils with ID and one in a training school class. Berthén (2007) arrives at similar parallels to Blom (2003), concluding that the pedagogical work and starting points that existed in the early years of education were for educable pupils with ID. The results also showed significant differences between the objectives of teaching in training schools and the compulsory schools for pupils with ID. In both cases, teaching was to prepare the pupils for the future. However, teaching in the training school class focused on preparation for adult life, while teaching in the class in compulsory schools for pupils with ID focused on preparing pupils for further studies.

RESEARCH WITH AN INTERACTION FOCUS INVOLVING LOW-INCIDENCE LEARNERS

From an overall perspective, the Swedish research on low-incidence learners moved from studying the group of children from a categorical point of view to conducting studies of the pupils' engagement in social interaction and relationships. Researchers (Björck-Åkesson, 1992; Brodin, 1991; Wilder, 2008) explored the relationships and the interaction between individuals with ID by directly studying interactions between children and caregivers in the home or in preschool/school. Another approach investigated the familial experiences of parenting a child with a disability (Olsson & Roll-Pettersson, 2012; Riddersporre, 2003). Olsson (2006) studied the factors associated with communicative interactions between children with low-incidence disabilities, their parents and staff at preschool. It was found that the contextual conditions (e.g., it's not the child or the adult who has the communicative competence; the quality of their communication is constructed within their dyadic relationship) were more central to the function of the communication than the children's disabilities and their use of communication. This means that the environment and the relationship can be more important for the child's interaction than the child's disability, and the child's functioning in the interaction was more tied to the situation and the dyadic relationship than to the personal characteristics of the child.

Göransson (1995) studied the interpersonal interaction between students in compulsory school for pupils with ID during classroom time.

This empirical study revealed a lack of interaction between the pupils. The interactions between students occurred infrequently and were unevenly distributed in classes. About a third of the students were isolated in their classes. The interaction that pupils with intellectual disabilities may experience during their teacher-led time is characterized as short in duration and primarily with special teachers or paraprofessionals. Anderson's (2002) study examined qualitative aspects of interaction in classrooms for pupils with intellectual disabilities and hearing impairments. The lessons (formal situations) were characterized by a high degree of adult control, while at recess (informal situations) pupils had better opportunities to be agents and in control of the interaction process. Interaction-oriented research on children/pupils with low-incidence disabilities shows that interaction is characterized by asymmetry and imbalance both in the home and in educational environments. Several studies have shown that adults hold a controlling position in the interaction and take up the most space in an interaction (Anderson, 2002; Brodin, 1991; Göransson, 1995; Östlund, 2012a; Wilder, 2008). This means that low-incidence learners are in vertical relationships in school with teachers and assistants, and there is a lack of horizontal relationships with peers (Frønes, 1995).

Östlund (2012a, 2014a, in press) studied the training school, an adapted education program for low-incidence learners. The results show that the classes' everyday life and the pedagogical work were characterized by daily performed activities and routines. The empirical material was produced through classroom observations and by video recordings (40 hours). The data was derived from video observations in five training school classes and altogether 20 pupils (age 8–19, 11 boys and 9 girls) and 28 members from the staff (9 special teachers, 2 music teachers, 1 psychical education teacher, and 16 assistants) who participated in the study. The pupils and their families were connected to the habilitation center. Staff from the multidisciplinary team in the child habilitation center supported the staff in school. For instance, the physical therapist came to two of the classes to work with the pupils once a week. All 20 pupils were low-incidence learners who used alternative forms of communication such as sign language, gestures, gaze, body language, signals, and vocalization. The pupils used different kinds of mobility aids, and the pupils were united in their need for support in their daily lives, in everything from doing schoolwork to eating lunch, transferring within the school, going to the toilet, or partaking in recess time.

Similarly, Östlund's (2012a) interactionist and sociocultural perspectives raise questions about how the pedagogical practice is organized in the adapted program training school. There are contextual conditions that have an impact on the low-incidence learners' participation, learning, and identity formation in the processes in which pupils are involved. Research has shown that low-incidence learners are given less opportunities to take initiative and to interact with peers when they are in educational environments with high levels of adult control (Mahoney & Wheeden, 1999; McCormick, Noonan, & Heck, 1998). Similar results are presented in the Swedish context when it comes to interaction with related parties in dyadic interaction constellations. The guardians often take a more controlling role in the interaction (Anderson, 2002; Brodin, 1991; Wilder, 2008).

General areas, that represent an established feature in the pupils' school days, are areas that in some cases relate directly to the participating classes' schedules (Östlund, 2012a, 2014a, in press). But the general areas can also be a collective term for a variety of activities carried out within the framework of the subject areas covered in the adapted program training school:

- Circle time – These were performed as a part of a daily routine and bore traces of German Pedagogue, Fredriech Fröbel's ideas of togetherness and social belonging. This was an activity performed in the morning in which all pupils and staff in the class participated. Circle time was characterized by a peaceful and harmonious atmosphere, and all pupils were intended to participate and contribute by being active and responsive.
- One-to-one tuition – During some lessons per day, pupils conducted an activity that the staff called "work." The activity was characterized by one-to-one tutoring, made possible mainly due to the high staff ratio in classes. The overall goal of these activities was to develop the pupils' communicative and sensory skills.
- Group joint education – During some lessons every day, all pupils participated together in the teaching. On these occasions, the contained activities were mainly linked to the subjects' esthetic activities and motor skills. The activities performed were often tied to providing sensory experiences for the pupils.
- Snack time/lunch – This constituted situations with elements of nursing and explicit asymmetric relationships between staff (caregivers) and pupils (recipients of care).
- Breaks and play-time – During recess it was common that the pupils were lifted out of their wheelchairs and rested on mattresses on the floor or sat on a couch in the classroom. Different types of play materials were offered to the pupils, giving them the opportunity to explore a toy or a play material on their own.

- Transitions – This activity refers to transfers made between different activities. The transition could in this context mean a movement from the classroom to another room in the school. But it could also be the transition from a wheelchair to another mobility device or a regular chair.

THEMES IN THE PUPILS' POSSIBILITIES TO PARTICIPATE IN THE PEDAGOGICAL PRACTICE

The results (Östlund, 2012a, in press) revealed that there are seven major themes that are related to the varying expectations of students' participation in different situations in the adapted program training school context. Whether the teaching involves more knowledge- or care-oriented activities, relations between the pupils and staff were clearly asymmetric. The asymmetry in relationships emerged in various ways through the opportunities to participate that the pupils are offered during interaction between the actors. The asymmetry can be described as a vertical relationship (Frønes, 1995); in other words, the staff member has an advantage in the interaction with the pupil that often leads to the pupil needing to adapt to the staff member's requirements. On the other hand, horizontal interaction is equal and is usually experienced between peers that have a horizontal relationship or two equal adults. Interaction between different parties is not always purely vertical or horizontal; it may change depending on the context (Janson, 2005). Sometimes the relationship and interaction are horizontal and sometimes it is vertical, and the expected participation of the pupil depends on whether an activity is more knowledge-oriented or more care-oriented. Hence, pupils have different expectations for participation in different situations. Different ways to interact and participate are encouraged depending on the nature of the activity performed. In the school context, the concept of participation had different meanings depending on the context and the interpretation of the concept. This is apparent in the research study of participation.

Three main aspects of the concept of participation emerges when studied in the context of learning environments involving learners with low-incidence disabilities:

- Participation as a subjective experience,
- Participation as communicative action, and

- Participation as a democratic project that is related to ideas of social justice.

This section describes outcomes analysis of social interaction between learners with low-incidence disabilities and the staff (e.g., special teachers and paraprofessionals) in five training school classes. The analysis focused on the opportunities for the pupils to participate in their education, with an interest in the characteristics of social interaction. The outcomes (Östlund, 2012a, 2014a, in press) revealed varied expectations of pupil participation in different situations and context. Because of the high staff ratio in the classes, a vertical relationship between pupils and staff members seems to be an important foundation in the education for low-incidence learners in Sweden.

The results show that there are seven major themes that relate to the varying expectations of pupils' participation in different situations in the context of educational practice for low-incidence learners. The various themes that are related to the pupils are the following:

- *The attentive and responsive learner*: A central starting point for the teams' interactional work is to create joint attention or joint attention focus (Bruner, 1983), which is the most fundamental aspect of interaction between people. With Goffman's (1966) framework this phenomenon is called focused interaction, and the term is used for highlighting the importance of dedication and attention in interaction. In specific terms, it means that someone in the team calls a pupil's attention and that the pupil is expected to respond verbally or to direct their gaze and make eye contact with the person who called them, indicating that they are receptive to interaction.
- *The experiencing learner*: A fundamental point in the classes where the students are encouraged to experience various stimuli (cf. lights; warm or cold objects; sounds; objects with different texture), to create a bond with the positive emotional register of the pupils. Pupils are expected to be happy, interested, and excited but are also involved in communication that aims to help the pupils to reflect over their experiences.
- *The choice making and autonomous learner*: An important starting point in the educational work in classes is to provide pupils the opportunity for making choices. There are embedded elements of choice in most activities that are performed. This is strongly tied to the curriculum's overall goals on democracy and citizenship.
- *The exploring learner*: One to two times per day, activities are conducted in which students are offered the opportunity to independently explore a material, a toy, or some other object. These activities are carried out

generally as a resting activity in the classroom but could also be implemented as part of a lesson. In these activities, the pupils are transferred from their wheelchair to a mat, mattress, or a beanbag on the floor in the classroom to be able to stretch out for a while.

- *The learner that shows inattention*: Pupils are expected to disregard conversations between the staff in the classroom that did not engage the pupils. Students were expected to show inattention and not to engage in the interaction as the staff talked over the heads of the pupils.
- *The learner as a recipient of care*: This expectation can be linked to activities that involve caregiving and are part of a care-culture, which is strong within the training school because of the comprehensive needs of the pupils. Care culture can be defined as primarily providing care for the pupil, with the purpose of satisfying the pupils' physical or emotional needs. If care culture becomes too dominant, there is a risk that the pupils are not challenged enough in their learning.
- *The playful learner*: This involves situations in which pupils are given the opportunity to play with a friend, someone from the staff, or that provides the pupils the chance to have playful and informal conversation with a staff member.

An overall finding (Östlund, 2012a) is that there are intense expectations about how the pupils should participate in a training school. When pupils do not act according to the socially desirable expectations in each situation, the staff puts in considerable effort to guide the pupil toward the expected response and participation. In activities where students resist participation and do not follow expected social rules, the staff puts a great deal of effort into helping the pupils understand that the situation requires them to adjust their interaction.

FUTURE CHALLENGES

Relating with their peers is something that generally comes easily for children. Through their peer relationships, children learn social skills such as teamwork, sharing, and how to handle conflicts. As Frønes (1995) clarifies it, relationships with adults, caregivers, teachers, and assistants in school are vertical. The caregiver is in control in these relationships, and the children are expected to conform. However, when interacting with peers, children have horizontal relationships that are more equal and not built on a hierarchical relationship. A child's interaction with peers influences both immediate and long-term social and intellectual growth as well as their construction of identity.

A challenge for both special teachers and paraprofessionals (cf. student assistants) is how to create learning environments for low-incidence learners that contribute to building relationships between low-incidence learners and children without disabilities. Causton-Theoharis and Malmgren (2005a, 2005b) highlight the problem of too close and familiar relationships between the pupils and the professionals that can create an obstacle to the pupil's participation. Too close vertical relationships may have the consequence of placing the professionals in the roles of teacher, caregiver, friend, and spokesperson for the pupil.

The results of Östlund's study (2012a) raises questions about the need for training and professional development for both teacher and student assistants. Persson (1998) and Emanuelsson et al. (2001) promote both a categorical and relational approach in Swedish schools, with the challenge of promoting inclusion by working with interactional and relational processes within educational programs for all educators. Thus, the professionals and the school organization needs to become more aware of how participation occurs and how learners can be provided more opportunities to enter into pupil-pupil relationships and learning environments that foster horizontal relationships. Jones and West (2009) raised similar questions based on the organization of teacher education in the United States and the skills teachers need to teach pupils with intellectual disabilities. Both the teachers' ability to work in teams with student assistants and their ability to collaborate with parents are defined as core competencies. Sweden implemented a new special teacher training in 2011 that aims to give special education teachers competence in teaching pupils with intellectual disabilities. One concern is that having a special educational program for special education teachers with expertise in intellectual disabilities, when there is an existing adapted program, might contribute to the continued segregation of low-incidence learners.

A challenge for working in the special needs school, and perhaps especially the training school, is to create new relationships with other professionals within the school. Additionally, there is the challenge to change the teaching role outside of the school. Teachers could coordinate with everyone actively working to expand the pupils' participation and influence which would facilitate more opportunity to develop horizontal relationships with peers.

CONCLUSION AND SUMMARY

Low-incidence learners are a very small group in Sweden, less than 1% of the total number of pupils in Swedish schools. One central conclusion is that, despite the virtuous intentions of legislation, creating inclusive learning environments that can meet the needs of low-incidence learners is difficult. The categorical perspective (Emanuelsson et al., 2001) is still prevalent in the Swedish school system and is one of the reasons why the inclusion of low-incidence learners in the regular compulsory school is still an enormous challenge.

It is something of a paradox that low-incidence learners are still not attending school with peers without disabilities; instead, they are offered an education in the adapted program training school. As Hjörne and Säljö (2004) point out, the Swedish school system has a long history of segregating "deviant" pupils; placement in adapted educational programs is the usual way of handling diversity in educational contexts. These views become a barrier for the development of inclusion and are paradoxical in that these perspectives persist despite Sweden's well-developed welfare system with legislation that mandates that all children obtain the support and help they need. The preservation of a special adapted program for low-incidence learners constitutes an obstacle to the inclusion of these students in the compulsory school along with other students in heterogeneous groups. The results from Östlund's study (2012a, 2014a, in press) as well as other studies have demonstrated that low-incidence learners can be involved in and have an exchange of horizontal relationships. However, to make that possible pupils must be offered such contexts and not unilaterally placed within segregated educational settings (Foreman, Arthur-Kelly, Pascoe, & Smyth King, 2004; Simmons, 2011; Simmons & Bayliss, 2007).

More studies are needed to investigate inclusive educational settings that offer both horizontal and vertical relationships involving children, adolescents, and adults with low-incidence disabilities.

KEY TERMS

Categorical perspective – An individualistic framework that promotes a traditional understanding of pupils' school problems and explains the pupils' special needs as a characteristics of the individual.

Horizontal relationships – A relationship that occur between peers and is characterized by equivalence.

Relational perspective – A social and environmental framework that promotes inclusion. This approach focuses on educational intervention in the environment rather than on individuals.

Training school – An adapted education program for low-incidence learners characterized by its high staff ratio and individualized forms of teaching.

Vertical relationships – A relationships that occur between a parent-child or teacher-pupil and is characterized by asymmetry.

REFERENCES

Anderson, L. (2002). *Interpersonell kommunikation: en studie av elever med hörselnedsättning i särskola. [Interpersonal communication. A study of pupils with hearing loss in compulsory school for pupils with intellectual disabilities].* Diss. Lund: Lunds Universitet.

Areschoug, J. (2000). *Det sinnesslöa skolbarnet: undervisning, tvång och medborgarskap 1925–1954. [The feeble-minded schoolchild: Education, coercion and citizenship 1925–1954].* Diss. Linköping: Linköpings Universitet.

Barow, T. (2009). *Kein Platz im Volksheim?: die "Schwachsinnigenfürsorge" in Schweden 1916–1945. [The Care of the Feeble-minded in Sweden 1916–1945 with special regard to educational developments].* Bad Heilbrunn: Klinkhardt.

Berthén, D. (2007). *Förberedelse för särskildhet: särskolans pedagogiska arbete i ett verksamhetsteoretiskt perspektiv. [Preparing for segregation: Educational work within the Swedish special school – an activity theoretical approach].* Diss. Karlstad: Karlstads Universitet.

Björck-Åkesson, E. (1992). *Samspel mellan små barn med rörelsehinder och talhandikapp och deras föräldrar: en longitudinell studie. [Interactions between young children with disabilities and speech and language disabilities and their parents: A longitudinal study.].* Göteborg: Acta Universitatis Gothoburgensis.

Blom, A. (2003). *Under rådande förhållanden: att undervisa särskoleelever – nio lärare berättar Delrapport 2, i projektet "Det särskilda med särskolan." [Under current conditions: To teach pupils with intellectual disabilities – nine teachers stories].* Stockholm: Socialtjänstförvaltningen, Forsknings- och utvecklingsenheten.

Brodin, J. (1991). *Att tolka barns signaler: gravt utvecklingsstörda flerhandikappade barns lek och kommunikation. [To interpret children's signals. Play and communication in children with profound intellectual and multiple disabilities].* Diss. Stockholm: Stockholms Universitet.

Bruner, J. (1983). *Child's talk: Learning to use language.* New York, NY: Norton.

Causton-Theoharis, J., & Malmgren, K. (2005a). Increasing peer interactions for students with severe disabilities via paraprofessional training. *Exceptional Children, 71*(4), 431–444.

Causton-Theoharis, J., & Malmgren, K. (2005b). Building bridges: Strategies to help paraprofessionals promote peer interaction. *Exceptional Children, 37*(6), 18–24.

Emanuelsson, I., Persson, B., & Rosenqvist, J. (2001). *Forskning inom det specialpedagogiska området: en kunskapsöversikt. [Research in the field of special needs education: A review].* Stockholm: Statens Skolverk.

Foreman, P., Arthur-Kelly, M., Pascoe, S., & Smyth King, B. (2004). Evaluating the educational experiences of students with profound and multiple disabilities in inclusive and segregated classroom settings: An Australian perspective. *Research and Practice for Persons with Severe Disabilities*, *29*(3), 183–193.

Frithiof, E. (2007). *Mening, makt och utbildning: delaktighetens villkor för personer med utvecklingsstörning. [Meaning, power and education. Preconditions of participation for persons with learning disabilities]*. Diss. Växjö: Växjö Universitet. 2007. Växjö.

Frønes, I. (1995). *Among peers. On the meaning of peers in the process of socialization*. Oslo: Scandinavian University Press.

Goffman, E. (1966). *Behavior in public places: Notes on the social organization of gatherings*. 1. Free Press paperback ed. New York, NY: Free Press.

Göransson, K. (1995). *De liknade varandra men inte mer än andra: begåvning shandikapp och interpersonellt samspel ["They looked alike, but no more than others do": Intellectual disability and interpersonal interaction.]*. Diss. Stockholm: Stockholms Universitet.

Hjörne, E., & Säljö, R. (2004). "There is something about Julia" – Symptoms, categories, and the process of invoking ADHD in the Swedish school: A case study. *Journal of Language, Identity, and Education*, *3*(1), 1–24.

Janson, U. (2005). Föreställningar om delaktighet. [Conceptions on participation] Stockholms Universitet. Pedagogiska institutionen opublicerad PM.

Jones, P., & West, E. (2009). Reflections upon teacher education in severe difficulties in the USA: Shared concerns about quantity and quality. *British Journal of Special Education*, *36*(2), 69–75.

Karlsudd, P. (2002). *Tillsammans – integreringens möjligheter och villkor – Erfarenheter från ett projekt där mötet mellan särskola och grundskola fokuserats. [Together – The possibilities and conditions of integration]*. Kalmar: Högskolan i Kalmar.

Mahoney, G., & Wheeden, C. A. (1999). The effect of teacher style in interactive engagement of preschool-aged children with special learning needs. *Early Childhood Research Quarterly*, *14*(1), 51–68.

McCormick, L., Noonan, M., & Heck, R. (1998). An exploration of variables affecting engagement in inclusive preschool classrooms. *Journal of Early Intervention*, *21*(2), 160–176.

Molin, M. (2004). Att vara i särklass – om delaktighet och utanförskap i gymnasiesärskolan. Linköpings Universitet – Högskolan i Trollhättan/Uddevalla, Institutionen för individ och samhälle.

Nirje, B. (1969). The normalization principle and its human management implications. In R. B. Kugel & W. Wolfensberger (Eds.), *Changing patterns in residential services for the mentally retarded* (pp. 179–195). Washington, DC: President's Committee on Mental Retardation.

Nirje, B. (1992). *The normalization principle papers*. Uppsala: Centre for Handicap Research.

Nordström, I. (2002). *Samspel på jämlika och ojämlika villkor: om lindrigt utvecklingsstörda skolbarns relationer till kamrater*. Diss. Stockholm: Stockholms Universitet.

Olsson, C. (2006). *The kaleidoscope of communication: Different perspectives on communication involving children with severe multiple disabilities*. Diss. Stockholm: Stockholms Universitet.

Olsson, I., & Roll-Pettersson, L. (2012). 'No no, you cannot say that!' Perceptions and experiences of parents of preschool children with intellectual disabilities in Sweden. *European Journal of Special Needs Education*, *27*(1), 69–80.

Östlund, D. (2012a). Deltagandets kontextuella villkor: fem träningsskoleklassers pedagogiska praktik *[Contextual conditions of participation. Five training school classes' pedagogical practice]*. Diss. Malmö: Malmö högskola.

Östlund, D. (2012b). Om speciallärare med inriktning utvecklingsstörning är svaret – vad är då frågan? [If special teachers with specialization in the field of intellectual disabilities is the answer – then what is the question?]. In Barow, T., & Östlund, D. (Eds.), (2012), *Bildning för alla! En pedagogisk utmaning* (pp.145–158). Kristianstad: Kristianstad University Press.

Östlund, D. (2014a). Pedagogical practices and everyday life for pupils with Profound Intellectual and Multiple Disabilities (PIMD) in Sweden. Paper presented at the 15th International DADD conference Autism, Intellectual Disability, & Developmental Disabilities, Clearwater, FL, January 22, 2014.

Östlund, D. (2014b). Compulsory education for pupils with intellectual and developmental disabilities in Sweden – past, present and future challenges. Manuscript submitted for publication.

Östlund, D. (in press). Compulsory education for pupils with intellectual and developmental disabilities in Sweden – Past, present and future challenges. *Research and practice in intellectual and developmental disabilities.*

Persson, B. (1998). *Den motsägelsefulla specialpedagogiken: motiveringar, genomförande och konsekvenser: delrapport från projektet Specialundervisning och dess konsekvenser (SPEKO). [The contradictions of special education – Motives, practice and consequences]*. Diss. Göteborg: Göteborgs Universitet.

Riddersporre, B. (2003). *Att möta det oväntade: Tidigt föräldraskap till barn med Downs syndrom. [To meet the unexpected: Early parenthood to children with Downs syndrom]*. Diss. Lund: Lunds Universitet.

SFS. (1944). 477. Lagen om obligatorisk undervisning för bildbara sinnesslöa barn. [Education Act on compulsory education for educable children with mental retardation].

SFS. (1967). 940. Lag angående särskilda omsorger för vissa psykiskt utvecklingsstörda.

SFS. (1982). 763. Hälso- och sjukvårdslag.

SFS. (1993). 387. Lagen om stöd och service till vissa funktionshindrade [Act concerning Support and Service for Persons with Certain Functional Impairments].

SFS. (2010). 800. Skollagen. The Swedish Education act.

Simmons, B. (2011). The "PMLD ambiguity": Articulating the lifeworlds of children with profound and multiple learning difficulties. Paper presented at the Nordic Network on Disability Research (NNDR) 11th Annual Conference, Reykjavík, Iceland, May 28, 2011.

Simmons, B., & Bayliss, P. (2007). The role of special schools for children with profound and multiple learning difficulties: is segregation always best? *British Journal of Special Education, 31*(4), 733–745.

Skidmore, D. (1996). Towards an integrated theoretical framework for research into special educational needs. *European Journal of Special Needs Education, 11*, 33–47.

Skolverket. (2011). *Läroplan för grundsärskolan 2011. [Curriculum for the compulsory school for pupils with intellectual disabilities 2011.]*. Stockholm: Skolverket.

Skolverket. (2014). *Beskrivande data 2013: förskola, skola och vuxenutbildning. [Descriptive data 2013: preschool, school and education for adults]*. Stockholm: Skolverket.

Söder, M. (1981). *Vårdorganisation, vårdideologi och integrering: sociologiska perspektiv på omsorger om utvecklingsstörda. [Organization of services, ideologies of care and integration]: [sociological perspectives on services for mentally retarded]*. Uppsala: Universitet.

Szönyi, K. (2005). *Särskolan som möjlighet och begränsning*. Diss. Pedagogiska Institutionen, Stockholms Universitet.

The Salamanca Statement. (1994). The Salamanca Statement and Framework for Action on Special Needs Education. World Conference on Special Needs Education, Salamanca, Spain, UNESCO.

Thomas, G., & Loxley, A. (2007). *Deconstructing special education and constructing inclusion* (2nd ed.). Berkshire: Open University Press.

Tideman, M. (2000). *Normalisering och kategorisering: Om handikappideologi och välfärdspolitik i teori och praktik för personer med utvecklingsstörning*. Lund: Studentlitteratur.

United Nations. (1989). *Convention on the rights of the child*. Geneva: Office of the United Nations Commissioner for Human Rights.

Wilder, J. (2008). *Proximal processes of children with profound multiple disabilities*. Stockholm: Stockholm University.

INCLUSIVE EDUCATION FOR LEARNERS WITH SEVERE, PROFOUND AND MULTIPLE LEARNING DIFFICULTIES IN ENGLAND

Penny Lacey and Jeanette Scull

ABSTRACT

There has been a policy for including pupils with severe, profound and multiple learning difficulties in mainstream schools in England since the 1980s. However, effective inclusive education has proved to be very difficult to achieve in practice. Currently, there is a mixed economy of special and mainstream schools offering inclusive education, and we argue that the place of education is less important than the quality of that education. Ideally, pupils with S/PMLD would be educated in their own local communities, alongside their non-disabled peers, but this situation is not yet established in English schools.

Keywords: Inclusion; severe; profound and multiple learning difficulties; mainstream schools; special schools

Including Learners with Low-Incidence Disabilities
International Perspectives on Inclusive Education, Volume 5, 241–268

ISSN: 1479-3636/doi:10.1108/S1479-363620140000005017

INTRODUCTION

There has been considerable research into the inclusion of pupils with special education needs into mainstream schools, including pupils with moderate learning difficulties (MLD). And although not every school is successful, good inclusive practice is now well established in England (Booth & Ainscow, 2011; Cline & Fredrickson, 2009; Florian, Rouse, & Black-Hawkins, 2007; Mitchell, 2008). There is much less known about the education, and specifically of inclusive education, of children with severe, profound and multiple learning difficulties (S/PMLD). This population is the subject of this chapter, in an English context.

The first half of the chapter provides an analysis of a range of mainly published literature on the inclusive education of children with severe, profound and multiple learning difficulties in England. Whereas the second half is an account of inclusive education in action from a teacher who has experienced both special and mainstream education for learners with S/PMLD in England.

In this chapter, the following questions will be explored:

1. What kind of education is required for children with severe, profound and multiple learning difficulties?
2. Where should this education take place?
3. If it takes place in mainstream schools, what are the factors that contribute to its success?

For the purposes of this chapter, the following definitions will be used to describe children and young people with severe, profound and multiple learning difficulties (SLD and PMLD). These definitions are taken from the DfE website, but it must be noted that these definitions were written when the previous government was in place and there has been no subsequent update since 2011 (DfE, 2011a).

Pupils with SLDs have significant intellectual or cognitive impairments. This has a major effect on their ability to participate in the school curriculum without support. They may also have difficulties in mobility and coordination, communication and perception and the acquisition of self-help skills. Pupils with SLDs need support in all areas of the curriculum. They may also require teaching of self-help, independence and social skills. Some pupils may use sign and symbols but most will be able to hold simple conversations. Their attainments may be within the upper P-scale range (P4–P8) for much of their school careers (that is below level 1 of the National Curriculum).

Pupils with profound and multiple learning difficulties have complex learning needs. In addition to very severe learning difficulties, pupils have other significant difficulties such as physical disabilities, sensory impairment or a severe medical condition. Pupils require a high level of adult support, both for their learning needs and also for their personal care. They are likely to need sensory stimulation and a curriculum broken down into very small steps. Some pupils communicate by gesture, eye pointing or symbols and others by very simple language. Their attainments are likely to remain in the early P-scale range (P1–P4) throughout their school careers (i.e. below level 1 of the National Curriculum). The use of performance scales (P-scales) is statutory when reporting on the attainment of pupils with special educational needs who are working below level 1 of the national curriculum. The P-scales run from P1 to P8 (DfE, 2014c).

PROVISION FOR PUPILS WITH SEVERE, PROFOUND AND MULTIPLE LEARNING DIFFICULTIES

The literature is organised around themes that relate to different aspects of inclusive education. Firstly, there is an attempt to briefly summarise current educational policy in England and how this relates to children with S/PMLD.

Educational provision for pupils with S/PMLD in England began with the passing of the 1970 Education (Handicapped Children) Act (DES, 1970). They were the last group to enter education in this country and almost all went straight to special schools, with the exception largely being in rural areas where no special schools were available. Since that time, the majority of pupils with S/PMLD have been educated in special schools, although the emphasis on inclusive education, since the Warnock Report (DES, 1978), has undoubtedly been influential in the way provision has developed over the last 45 years. However, inclusive education in mainstream schools is not compulsory in the United Kingdom, and there is a great range and variety of provision available across the union.

Special Educational Needs Policy

England has recently experienced a shift in policy for children with special educational needs and disabilities (SEND) with the advent of the Children and Families Act 2014 (DfE, 2014a). Part 3 contains the law in relation to children with SEN. The basic principle of meeting the individual needs of children with SEN is still central to that law, but some of the detail has changed. For example, an education, health and care (EHC) plan replaces the statement of special educational needs and covers young people from birth to 25 years. Parents can have control of a personal budget to buy additional support in the plan and local authorities must produce 'a local offer' of education, health and care services to be available in their area for children and young people up to the age of 25.

The Act has been accompanied by the Special Educational Needs and Disability Code of Practice 2014 (DfE, 2014b) which gives non-statutory guidance on how to implement the new legislation. The Code includes children with low-incidence disabilities such as S/PMLD.

This shift in policy has been more related to detail than to the principles of educating children with SEN, although generally since the Conservative-Liberal coalition, there has been less emphasis on educating all children in mainstream schools and more interest on providing an effective education whether it is in mainstream or special settings.

Pupils with Severe, Profound and Multiple Learning Difficulties

Despite the cautious emphasis on inclusion in mainstream schools for all children with SEN, the vast majority of pupils with S/PMLD in England can be found in special schools. According to the Department for Education 2013 statistics (DfE, 2013a, 2013b), there are a total of 30,440 pupils with SLD of whom 23,845 are educated in special schools. There are 10,525 pupils with PMLD of whom 8,695 are educated in special schools.

The nature of the needs of pupils with S/PMLD has been changing for some time (Baker, 2009; Lacey, 2011; Male, 1996; Male & Rayner, 2007). Pupils with more severe and complex needs are being admitted to special schools, with a rise in the numbers of pupils with autistic spectrum conditions, challenging behaviour and mental health needs (Baker, 2009).

From the Male and Rayner (2007) survey of special schools, just over half of the head teachers reported that up to a quarter of their population could be described as having PMLD, and this is reported as being an increase in the numbers collected earlier by Male (1996). Head teachers also reported an increase in pupils with life-limiting conditions, most of which relate to those with PMLD. Many of their pupils with S/PMLD also have additional needs, such as hearing or visual impairments, speech and language difficulties, challenging behaviour, medical needs, or life-limiting conditions (Male, 1996; Male & Rayner, 2007; Porter & Lacey, 2008). It is suggested that advances in medical science have increased the chances of survival of babies with complex needs (Blackburn & Carpenter, 2012).

Provision for Pupils with S/PMLD

Provision for the group of children with S/PMLD has been in a state of flux for several years and many special schools have been reconfigured, partly in the wake of the inclusion of more pupils with less severe SEN in mainstream schools, and partly to try to reduce the numbers of special schools. Many special schools have become more generic in nature, educating pupils with a range of different needs (Lacey, 2011; Porter & Lacey, 2008).

Other special schools have been relocated onto mainstream sites, and some have been physically placed inside mainstream schools. Where special schools have been co-located with mainstream schools, there has been mixed success in terms of inclusive practice. Some of the co-located special schools have little to do with their mainstream neighbours and thus possibilities for inclusive practice have been missed (Lacey, 2011).

Many of the changes have been at local authority level, with complete reorganisation of all their special schools, including their funding and support. Partnership links with other schools, and extended and outreach services have changed the nature of some special schools, giving them a more prominent role in the whole LA provision for SEN (Baker, 2009; Farrell, 2006). The actual numbers of pupils in special schools have remained more or less the same for several years (Farrell, 2006; Norwich, 2008), as some special schools have closed but others have opened, perhaps incorporating several smaller schools. Some schools have moved to academy status and new free special schools are being opened (DfE, 2013a, 2013b). In England, academies and free schools are similar in status to charter schools in the United States.

The position of special schools in England has been debated for some time. Some people have questioned their right to exist in the trend to move towards inclusion in mainstream schools (Brandon, 1997; CSIE, 2013a, 2013b). In response to this viewpoint, others have considered the extent to which inclusion of all children within mainstream schools is actually possible at the moment (Lacey, 2003; Male & Rayner, 2007). Recently, this position has been supported by both the current and previous governments, which have pledged to retain special schools certainly for the foreseeable future, seeing them as an important component of provision from which parents can choose what is the right education for their children (DfE, 2011b).

Although the majority of pupils with SLD/PMLD attend day schools, some are considered to require residential education. McGill (2008) suggests approximately 3,000 children and young people with learning disabilities attend residential school or other residential placements. Residential school placement is often recommended for family reasons. That is, families are unable to meet the severity of needs presented by their children. There is little written about residential education. However, that which was found in this review is somewhat critical of its existence. For example, McGill (2008) writes that attendance at residential school limits family contact, increase pupils' vulnerability and makes transition into local services post-school much harder to achieve. McGill (2008) concludes that the arguments against residential special schools are clear, and he suggests that pupils with SLD/PMLD would not need to be educated away from home if they had more family support and the capacity and inclusiveness of local services were extended.

Inclusion

Views on educational inclusion for pupils with S/PMLD are mixed. There are some who call for inclusion in local mainstream schools as a right that is achievable now, and there are those who argue for inclusion but recognise the limitations of mainstream schools and the expertise of many special schools.

Interestingly, the concept of inclusion seems to have shifted from relating simply to being educated in mainstream schools to something much more complex. Warnock introduced the concepts of special educational need and integration (later to be changed to inclusion) in the Warnock Report (DES, 1978). Recently, however, she changed her stance, preferring now a concept of inclusion that includes all children learning wherever is best for them (Warnock, 2005). Norwich (2008) suggests that many teachers who work with pupils with SEN share Warnock's views. Sheehy and Duffy (2009) echo this by claiming that staff in special schools use the language of inclusion but from their segregated position. It is no longer necessary to conceive of inclusion as only relating to mainstream schools. Lacey (2011) found similar claims to the provision of an inclusive education from the schools in her survey, the vast majority of which were special schools. Several respondents talked about effective links between special and mainstream schools which enabled children of all abilities to learn together.

Rix's (2011) detailed analysis of the language used by special schools on their school websites suggests that special schools now present themselves as 'specialist, delivering personalised learning, legitimately professing the values of inclusion and a mainstream standards-driven agenda' (p. 274). He is concerned that special schools have 'twisted' the meaning of 'inclusion' 'to comfort those it was supposed to confront' (p. 275), thereby legitimising their segregated position. He is apprehensive that this position will also prevent the further development of inclusion in mainstream settings.

Norwich (2008) presents what is perhaps a more central position as he grapples with the dilemma that exists if inclusion is seen on a continuum that embraces special schools. If pupils with SLD/PMLD are educated in mainstream classrooms, they are less likely to have their needs met. But if they are taught in special school classroom, they are less likely to be known and accepted by their typical peers. The respondents in Norwich's (2008) study saw resolution to this dilemma of where to place pupils as a 'reluctant future for special schools' (p. 142). Norwich also suggests a 'mixed model' (p. 142) of special and mainstream by delivering specialist provision within or side by side with the mainstream school. This allows for a balance between common and separate provision and includes the following:

- Separate school (special school) linked to ordinary school,
- Same class (varying degrees of withdrawal) and
- Same learning group (Norwich, 2008, p. 142).

These mixed models include specially resourced classes in community schools, campuses where special and mainstream share the same site and a 'school within a school', where a special school shares the same buildings with one or more mainstream school. These types of arrangements have been in evidence for some time, although there has been little actual evaluation of their success (Lacey, 2011; Mencap, 1999).

Riddell, Tisdall, Kane, and Mulderrig (2006) suggests that there are some common tensions, such as those between inclusion and special provision, suggesting that in England (and Sweden) questions are being asked about whether inclusion has gone 'too far', placing a strain on mainstream schools. Riddell, Tisdall, Kane, and Mulderrig (2006) suggest that teachers require much better training before they are able to meet the needs of such a wide range of pupils. Other researchers suggest that mainstream teachers generally seem to be least enthusiastic about including pupils with the most severe disabilities (Head & Pirrie, 2007; Konza, 2008; Wolstenholme, 2010). However, Fredrickson (2010) argues that it is easier for respectful, helpful relationships to form between typical children and children with more severe difficulties than with those with milder difficulties.

Some pupils with S/PMLD are already included in mainstream schools, for example, in the London Borough of Newham (2006) where there are several specially resourced primary and secondary schools which were developed following the closure of all but one of the special schools in the authority. There is a support service run by the local authority where visiting teachers are provided.

Not all local authorities have reorganised to accommodate groups of pupils with such severe disabilities in specially resourced schools, but there are examples of individual children being accepted in particular schools. For example, Brandon (1997) wrote about his son Niki's school career in mainstream, demonstrating that it can work, though not without a struggle with 'the authorities'. Simmons and Bayliss' (2007) study of an effective education for pupils with PMLD suggest that mainstream schools may be able to provide a more suitable social setting than special schools. Their observations of pupils revealed more and better opportunities for interaction in mainstream schools than in special.

THE EDUCATION OF PUPILS WITH SEVERE, PROFOUND AND MULTIPLE LEARNING DIFFICULTIES

Although it is clear from an examination of the provision for pupils with S/PMLD in England that there are many different types of placements for individual children, there is some consensus on what makes for effective practice for this group of learners. The following section of this chapter contains an analysis of the evidence available that supports ways of meeting the individual needs of pupils with such severe and complex difficulties and disabilities. The emphasis in this section is not on 'where' the children are educated but on the 'how'. Attention will be paid to issues related to staff, curriculum and teaching approaches.

Staff

Whatever the location, pupils with S/PMLD need access to staff with knowledge and expertise in meeting individual needs that are often very complex. In special schools, there are often classes of 8–10 pupils with a teacher and several support staff. Occasionally, children have a teaching assistant assigned to them if their behaviour is likely to disrupt the class. In contrast, in mainstream classes, children with S/PMLD almost always have a TA assigned to support them specifically and maybe even more than one (Lacey, 2011). In many cases, these TAs have become the primary educators of pupils with SEN in mainstream schools, and according to the research of Webster et al. (2010) and Webster, Blatchford, and Russell (2013), this can lead to a negative impact on pupils' academic progress. TAs are often not well qualified, especially in mainstream schools, and can actually have an effect of separating the pupil from the teacher and the curriculum.

However, if they are well trained and directed, TAs in any setting are vital to the education of children with S/PMLD. Training can be very variable, but researchers have found that if tasks are delegated by the teacher and are accompanied by specific training in both instruction and behaviour, successful outcomes for pupils should ensue (Causton-Theoharis, Giangreco, Doyle, & Vadasy, 2007). It is also important that TAs do not focus on task completion but focus on the process of learning (Rubie-Davies, Blatchford, Webster, Koutsoubou, & Bassett, 2010), and to achieve this they require education in relevant theories of teaching and learning (Radford, Bosanquet, Webster, Blatchford, & Rubie-Davies, 2014).

It is not just TAs who require training. If teachers are to be effective in the classroom with pupils with S/PMLD, they should be knowledgeable and skilled in meeting the needs of learners with complex needs. However, the numbers of teachers trained in S/PMLD is declining. Male (1996) found that half the teachers in SLD schools had a qualification relevant to SLD/PMLD. Ten years later, Male and Rayner (2007) found this had reduced to a third of teachers. Lacey (2011) also found that about a third of teachers had a qualification relevant to S/PMLD. The explanation for such a decline is partly contained in the lack of initial teaching training in SLD/PMLD that ceased in England at the beginning of the 1990s. Teachers who were trained in the 1970s and 1980s have retired or are drawing close to retirement.

The training of teachers in SEN, particularly in S/PMLD, is seen by many writers and researchers as currently inadequate in England. Wedell made this point clear in 2008, but it was made again in Hodkinson (2009) and the Salt Review (Salt, 2010). There are no specialist programmes for teacher trainees who wish to teach pupils with S/PMLD. It is expected the teachers will train to be a mainstream teacher and then add specialist knowledge and skills at a later date. Salt (2010) recommended that student teachers should add six months' training in S/PMLD to their initial training, but there is no evidence to suggest that this is happening. There are university and online private providers who offer modules but only one university, The University of Birmingham, offers a full masters in S/PMLD. Several universities offer a teaching placement in a special school to their trainee teachers, and others are running training programmes specifically in special schools. This is an area of potential development.

Working alongside teachers and TAs in special and mainstream schools is often a group of professionals assigned to working with pupils with complex needs. This group might consist of educationalists, therapists and care staff who may be working together in a multidisciplinary team such as a Team-around-the Child (Limbrick, 2009). Collaboration between these professionals is seen as important, and there is some evidence to suggest that it is effective, at least in the eyes of those involved (Busch, Van Stel, De Leeuw, Melhuish, & Schrijvers, 2013; Pickering & Busse, 2010). There has been a considerable amount of research focused on collaboration, although mostly in health contexts rather than educational, and the factors that seem to support effective joint working are

- good communication,
- joint assessment,
- a facilitator or keyworker,
- trust between stakeholders,
- appropriate funding,
- pooled resources and
- the flexibility to start and complete partnerships according to the need (Cameron & Lart, 2012; Glover-Thomas, 2008; King et al., 2009).

Achieving this kind of joint working can be very difficult, especially in mainstream schools. But even special schools struggle, particularly when education and health services are contracting as they currently are.

Curriculum and Teaching

There has been a considerable interest in the curriculum for pupils with S/PMLD over the 40 years that these pupils have been in education (Aird, 2001; Ashdown, Carpenter, & Bovair, 1991; Imray & Hinchcliffe, 2014; Rayner, 2011; Staff of Rectory Paddock School, 1983). In the 1970s and 1980s teachers struggled to find a suitable curriculum and teaching approaches for this group, and in 1988, the advent of the national curriculum was seen by many as a possible way forward. It was not immediately clear how a curriculum written for typical children could be adapted for pupils with such severe disabilities. But teachers accepted the challenge and worked very hard to suggest how they could provide access to the curriculum that everyone else was studying (Ashdown et al., 1991). All through the 1990s and most of the 2000s, curriculum access to the national curriculum and the literacy and numeracy strategies were central to the curriculum for children with S/PMLD.

Recently, teachers have become more interested in designing a more personalised curriculum that meets specific pupils' needs. Goss (2006) proposed that learning and teaching for pupils with S/PMLD should be based on an identification of what is meaningful to them, as opposed to wholesale adoption of the national curriculum/literacy and numeracy strategies, even when adapted. Attitudes have changed recently, and there is now considerable interest in curriculum development that responds to pupils' needs (Feiler, 2010). Rayner (2011) writes of Stephen Hawking School where the staff have rewritten their curriculum so that it specifically meets the needs of their pupils with S/PMLD. Imray and Hinchcliffe (2012, 2013, 2014) give examples of curriculum design and development from their own experience, suggesting that the content of traditional school subjects are not relevant for pupils with S/PMLD, who need to learn the more basic skills of living, personalised to individual needs.

However, a more personalised curriculum is not yet universal in England. Lacey (2011) posed a question about the nature of the curriculum offered to children with S/PMLD in her survey. Respondents in half the schools said they adapted the mainstream curriculum for pupils with SLD, although more than half said they used a developmental curriculum for the pupils with PMLD. Almost all of the 49 schools included self-care, life skills and sensory stimulation; and 40 schools offered hydrotherapy. There was one mainstream school in the survey that did not offer their one pupil with SLD anything over and above the mainstream curriculum.

In terms of pedagogy, there has been an interest in what constitutes 'special teaching'. Is there a pedagogy that sets special education apart? Lewis and Norwich (2004) come to the conclusion that special and mainstream pedagogy are more alike than different. They suggest that it is conceived of on a continuum from high- to low-intensity teaching, and generally what works for pupils with SEN works for typical pupils. The same seems to be true of curriculum content. Although all pupils can be said to have similar curriculum needs, there is also a continuum of intensity. Pupils with

PMLD, for example, have a need for high intensity of concentration on the very early stages of communication and cognition (Welsh Assembly Government, 2006).

From this brief exploration of education for pupils with special educational needs and disabilities, it can be seen that education for the mostly severely disabled children in England is shaped by a desire to provide an effective education, rather than an emphasis on this education taking place in a particular setting.

The second half of this chapter is a personal view of inclusion from a teacher who has worked in both special schools and inclusive schools in England. The account contextualises the review of the literature above and provides examples of the problems and possibilities of inclusion in practice.

INCLUSION FOR PUPILS WITH S/PMLD IN MAINSTREAM SETTINGS: A SPECIALIST TEACHER'S PERSPECTIVE

The first section of this chapter articulates key issues arising from inclusion. This section is a narrative about the impact on classroom delivery in a mainstream inclusive provision. The narrative is simply presented and a little disjointed, which reflects the reality of delivering inclusion for me personally.

My teaching career has included teaching in mainstream primary, specialist provision (special school), resource provision in an authority with high levels of inclusion in mainstream schools, and for a local authority as an advisory teacher supporting inclusion. I have recently returned to specialist provision (special school) where I am currently working as part of the senior leadership team.

I enjoyed my work at the first special school, but after being a mainstream primary teacher, I had a strong desire to combine both and work in an inclusive setting. I believe that my experience in a special school prior to resource provision gave me a very good grounding in specialist practice. Working in a resource provision for learners with S/PMLD in a mainstream school was exciting and innovative and I had expectations about developing inclusive practice within a busy mainstream school. The school was both successfully inclusive and valued inclusion. However, it was clear that implementing inclusion in a mainstream setting came with challenges that could not be easily resolved, especially when the educational landscape started to become tightly focused around attainment.

The introduction of the Literacy and Numeracy Strategies in the late 1990s was one of the first major changes that altered the dynamics within mainstream inclusive primary schools. This government initiative was based on the desire to raise standards in English state-funded schools, and its impact was considered to be largely successful (DfE, 2011c). However, it was much more difficult for children with S/PMLD to be educated alongside their mainstream peers. There were very prescriptive approaches introduced, with imposed lesson frameworks that promoted specified teaching and learning. The expected three-part lesson structure generally encouraged a level of pace that did not support full inclusion of learners with S/PMLD, and the specific content that was to be delivered was generally inappropriate for meeting their needs.

The conversations about lesson planning with mainstream class teachers began to become more focused on adaptations for children to be slotted in rather than on meeting individual needs.

Scenario 1 – Expectation that mainstream teachers can include learners with S/PMLD in their lesson plans

Teacher's question: This is my lesson topic, can you help me to differentiate the lesson planning for N.

Specialist teacher's question: These are N's identified needs and targets, can you help me to plan strategies in class and find ways to integrate these opportunities into the lesson?

The main offer for students with Special Educational Needs (SEN) is generally through differentiation and always through entitlement to the national curriculum first and foremost. Whilst this may be the right approach for more able children with SEN, it is generally problematic for learners with S/PMLD. For learners with S/PMLD, an appropriate curriculum includes a repertoire of planned approaches that does not always work in synchrony with the pace of learning of mainstream peers. Pupils with more complex learning needs do not make linear progress and need frequent opportunities for practice to ensure developing fluency of skill development, maintenance and generalisation.

Planning for teaching and learning is directly linked to national curriculum content for typically developing learners, which means that appropriate and targeted learning for learners with more complex needs is inserted into a curriculum framework that is not designed to meet these needs.

In my experience, as a specialist teacher in an inclusive school where learners' needs were being met, the paybacks were great, and there was a great deal of good practice. The school was very well resourced in terms of specialist staff. The school went on to develop a role for specialist teachers within the leadership structure and is probably the best example of a school that has prioritised inclusion. However, there were drawbacks. There were incredible internal pressures in a system where mainstream priorities change very quickly. I always felt that I was constantly being a mediator and mentor and often sensed that I was a guest rather than an integral member of the class grouping.

What Needs to be in Place for Inclusion in a Mainstream School to Happen?

Inclusive provision in mainstream schools requires teacher leadership. Children with complex learning needs must have access to teacher time at least equivalent to their mainstream peers. By this I do not mean just the mainstream class teacher. Students with S/PMLD need access to experienced and qualified specialist teachers. There is also a need for adequately trained support staff at all levels. The team who is supporting learners with S/PMLD in inclusive mainstream primary schools needs to be enhanced with the possibility of working under different contracts that include payment for time to liaise and work with mainstream class teachers in the school.

Access to training for staff is vital. The programme of continuing professional development (CPD) must meet the needs of the S/PMLD provision as well as the needs of a mainstream school. There also needs to be a focus on SEN in CPD and in initial training. Perhaps a return to specialist initial teacher training courses (discontinued at the end of the 1980s) would develop both an appropriately skilled workforce but also practitioners who are likely to engage in action research at various points in their careers. This practice would contribute to the knowledge bank and experience in mainstream inclusive provisions.

'Curriculum Dilemma'

There are some consistent challenges to inclusion in mainstream. Wedell (2008) identified 'three basic dilemmas' faced by those trying to implement inclusion. These included identification, curriculum and location. The curriculum dilemma is particularly pertinent as this was the area I had daily issues with when trying to deliver effective inclusive provision for pupils with S/PMLD. This domain also includes assessment and links strongly to organisational issues, which are equally significant.

Effective differentiation can be problematic where schools do not employ sufficiently experienced and qualified specialist teachers, supported by skilful practitioners who not only understand the learning profiles of students with S/PMLD but also can be challenging where they do.

> Scenario 2 – Lesson plan for a mainstream class subject lesson may be handed to me with a theme and set of learning objectives
>
> I worked with a teacher to support planning for a lesson. I recommended clear strategies and approaches to differentiate.
>
> There are two problems with this! Often due to time pressure, the teacher is not sufficiently involved and the child is merely squeezed into the lesson.
>
> In reality, I was often left feeling that I had facilitated differentiation but less convinced that I had been able to personalise and deliver exactly what was appropriate to the learner with S/PMLD being taught in a mainstream classroom. The lesson dynamics for mainstream lessons require a pace and sequence that may not be appropriate for a learner with such complex needs. On occasions failure to fit in has resulted in teachers suggesting that the child has to take part in all sections of the lesson or I should take them out of the room. Even where this approach is not supported by the school, the situation still exists.

Mainstream schools have to cover a large amount of curriculum content in a short time. The pace of learning is very different for learners with S/PMLD who require many more opportunities to encounter the same learning. Successfully revisiting developing skills with less framework support is an opportunity for progress, as is revisiting them in a different context or with different resources. It is often only possible to observe and evidence progress when skills are delivered within a highly structured learning environment.

Where there is a lack of understanding about learners' progress or when support staff are untrained and there is little input from a teacher, the quality of differentiation can deteriorate. Lesson time can potentially consist of keeping a learner with S/PMLD in mainstream lessons visibly busy and gainfully occupied.

Communication

> Scenario 3 – Monitoring use of communication strategies
>
> I am told that staff working with a student with SLD always carry a key ring around with symbols so they can communicate what is going to happen next or what they want a student to do.
>
> My response: How does the student tell you what they want?
>
> Sometimes there has not been an answer, or at least not one I am happy with.

There is a need for staff to understand how to develop expressive as well as receptive language skills. Inclusive mainstream settings very often do not have a communication profile of individual learners with SEN, and the range of need can be diverse. Thus, staff need a wide ranging level of understanding and also the ability to consistently respond and implement advice from speech and language therapists.

Consistent approaches and methods are required in order to develop communication skills. This can be an issue where mainstream schools have not developed a structured approach for the use of symbolic communication across the school. Developing communication for learners with S/PMLD is about consistently supporting students to develop meaning and consistently linking language and communication to experiences. Many of the opportunities to create a communication rich environment for students with S/PMLD are limited by other factors or lack of understanding. Symbols and objects for communication are often missing or remain unused, and the lack of consistency around key vocabulary to support communication needs is a continual challenge.

> Scenario 4 – Understanding the significance of expressive communication
>
> Sometimes when a student vocalised, I would be asked if s/he could stop making a noise. This request can be due to the lack of shared understanding about the communication strategies I was using but

were also about the pressure teachers are under to deliver to mainstream peers. I can understand their position.

Giving time for learners with S/PMLD to respond or initiate communication can be problematic in many classrooms. Background noise and interference can be a barrier to gaining or maintaining a student's focus on the learning. When students respond or initiate vocally, there needs to be an acknowledgement that they are engaged, even if it is not intentional communication. Staff need to be prepared to interact intensively even in the middle of a mainstream classroom, and everyone else needs to understand what is happening and why.

Cognition and Learning

Scenario 5 – Pace of progress

There is a perception from mainstream teachers that learners with S/PMLD are 'coasting', rather than learning new skills and understanding, when they are practising skills or repeating learning. There are also times when I have to wait confidently and attentively for a response. When a response occurs I know the child is engaged with learning and I can see progress, although it is sometimes fleeting. I am prepared to be patient and work consistently for those golden moments of learning.

The milestones in learning that need to be addressed for students with S/PMLD are unique to their development and learning profile. Modelling and scaffolding play a huge part in the delivery of teaching aimed at developing skills, as does allowing time for the child to make connections and respond. The pace appears slower but the depth of learning cannot be underestimated. This is the basic level of delivery needed to meet the needs of learners who have cognitive impairments that include memory and processing difficulties.

Learning for students with S/PMLD is not about catching up, as is the philosophy in mainstream classrooms, but it is about developing emerging skills and learning in a completely different way. The pace and type of development that the mainstream peer group, including those who have mild to moderate additional learning needs, is in no way similar to the way the most complex students learn.

Physical Development and Sensory Needs

It can be difficult to ensure that advice from therapists is successfully integrated into lesson planning and consistently carried out to the degree that it needs to be: often daily. The example below relates to occupational therapy advice around fine motor development.

Scenario 6 – Physical development

Sometimes there are quite simple and practical approaches that are appropriate. Prepared packs or boxed resources are useful for promoting fine motor development. This strategy needs to be planned into the lesson and consistently implemented. It has worked well where teachers have taken ownership of the approach and planned it into the structure of the lesson for the learner or learners who need it. It has worked less well where it has been delegated to support staff to deliver without on-going liaison and monitoring from teaching staff.

The impact of physical development on learning is a major area for monitoring and evaluating in specialist provision, whether we are referring to limb stretches from physiotherapy programmes that need to be integrated into lessons or postural management that is essential to well-being. There also needs to be a clear understanding of the importance of and the need to plan in opportunities for gross and fine motor development consistently within daily routines.

The impact of not following up on physiotherapy programmes or postural management are well known in specialist provision but are perhaps less understood in mainstream inclusive settings. In my current special school, the standard of recommended physio stretches and postural management are often the focus of management monitoring, as they are both integral to the teaching and learning in the school. In a mainstream inclusive school, it is undeniably harder to maintain such a focus.

Behaviour

> Scenario 7 – Perspectives on behaviour
>
> Teacher – He keeps grabbing at things near him (the blinds) and jumping up making noise. I think his parents should be made to pay for the blinds.
>
> Me – have you considered where you have positioned him in the classroom.
>
> Teacher – is that it?

There was actually a lot more to that conversation but its essence was related to sensory sensitivities and an environment the student could not cope with. When not managed, I have seen this situation escalate to behaviour sanctions and labelling. For example, students with autism and SLD who cannot cope with movement in close proximity have been seated near the busiest thoroughfare in a classroom. This positioning may trigger a response that is seen as poor behaviour in the classroom, and this poor behaviour is seen as the fault of the child rather than a reaction to the environment. In one instance that I needed to work through with a teacher, it was difficult to get across the message that equality and inclusion is not about treating everyone the same but about identifying and mitigating individual learning barriers. This is particularly difficult around behaviour as there is a pressure to have 'good' or 'outstanding' behaviour management and the expectation is that learners with S/PMLD should be able to fit into the behaviour expectations of the class.

Developing Independence and Social Skills

> Scenario 8 – Opportunities for learning
>
> We recently had a group of mainstream Inclusion Managers visit our special school. They visited our classrooms to see how we plan for learning and assess using P-levels. The thing they all noticed the most and commented on was structured learning and that we have strategies in place for learning to happen during breaks and at snack time.

They all planned to give more consideration to opportunities for communication at these times. They all commented on how the students seemed to be enjoying communicating about their favourite snacks and how planned opportunities for play and exploration were engaging them.

For students with S/PMLD, the need for organisation and planning for non-structured times in the schools day is as significant as lesson time. Students need to have continued access to learning opportunities or be working towards managing their own activity during these times. This can sometimes remain a challenge within specialist provision and can be at danger of being completely overlooked within mainstream provision. It can be overlooked for several reasons. Firstly, the pace and timetabling of the mainstream school day is developed with a group that learn quickly to respond to routines that have less structure. Secondly, children in mainstream do not require the same level of focus with regards to self-care, eating and drinking.

Progress and Achievement

Scenario 9 – Making good progress

I had a conversation with an assessment manager and a classroom teacher in mainstream when I was an advisory teacher. The assessment manager was angry that a child was in year 5 and was still not at a secure national curriculum level 2. The student had made good progress from P levels, but this was not acknowledged. The class teacher expressed that she felt like a failure and the assessment manager implied that her teaching had failed the student.

Can teachers really assume that the pedagogical principals apply for assessment regardless of complexity of need, or does there need to be a recognition that different assessment tools and criteria apply?

One of the keys to successfully developing assessment is in identifying and using the most meaningful assessment frameworks that are based on the actual learning needs of children who are functioning at an early stage of development. Routes for learning (Welsh Assembly Government, 2006) and quest for learning (CCEA, 2011) are two such assessments and their use has transformed the curriculum and teaching approaches for learners with PMLD in some settings (Lacey, 2011). These assessments also have a range of curriculum materials that support teachers to identify and plan for learning opportunities at a personalised level appropriate to the needs of learners with a PMLD profile.

One of the main issues is that learners with S/PMLD are not and never will be a homogenous group that can be accurately measured in quantitative terms or compared in large statistical groups. The notion that students make consistent progress in a linear and unbroken fashion has distracted people from confidently approaching the issue of assessment for the most complex learners. Schools use a lot of numerical data to support tracking of progress. However, much of the evidence of progress for learners with S/PMLD is more qualitative. These students can progress in very different ways from typically developing learners due to the impact of significant impairments and other fluctuating or even degenerative conditions.

Assessing and measuring the educational progress of learners with S/PMLD can be hampered by the fact that there is no effective or reliable way to reflect fluency of developing skills, generalisation of learnt skills and maintenance of skills, although the MAPP resources developed at The Dales School (2011) tangibly begin to address these issues. Measuring Achievement and Personal Progress (MAPP) is a tool for personalised target setting that enables a school to measure progress in areas such as developing skill fluency, levels of prompting, generalisation and maintenance of skills. The MAPP tools support an in-depth look at development of targeted skills for learners with complex needs. We are currently piloting these tools in our special school and have had a lot of positive feedback from class teachers.

Including data in statistical returns about the educational progress of learners with S/PMLD can be problematic for mainstream schools. These data are often mixed together with data of other learners who are judged as not 'making good or better progress'. These are likely to be typically developing children with temporary or mild to moderate difficulties. There is often little understanding that the progress data of pupils with S/PMLD require specific contextualisation and there is little acknowledgement that individuals in this group learn in ways that are different from typically developing children. The most useful thing about data is that they suggest what questions schools need to ask. There are very few cut and dried answers in school data.

What Are the Barriers to Inclusion?

Ultimately, it does not really matter where the learners are placed as long as their best interests are served and learning needs are met with appropriate teaching and learning. Inclusion in mainstream schools can provide such an environment, but it is very challenging to achieve. Inclusion needs to be defined as benefits from appropriate teaching and learning as well as social inclusion, and schools need to be clear about their duties to provide a quality education for S/PMLD.

Inclusive provision that is not being included strategically in whole school development planning can have the effect of marginalising the inclusive practice within mainstream schools. Where schools have been most successful, it has been because inclusion has a direct line to school leadership priorities or the head and deputy have a strong vision and ability to implement a strategic lead. It was clearly evident in schools I supported as an Advisory Teacher that where there were specialist teachers within the management structure, identified actions to improve provision were implemented. I often made many repeat visits to support the same issues in schools where the SEN teacher worked in isolation.

The quality of teaching and learning in classrooms for learners with S/PMLD can be impacted significantly by failure to identify training needs, resources, and key areas of curriculum and assessment development. Inclusion has become a more complex enterprise in recent years due to changes in both mainstream education and the student population. There is no homogenous or consistent set of learning issues. There is churn and change in the demographic and incidence of complex needs, including those with S/PMLD. What works this year, last year or next year is never a long-term solution.

Where successful, there is well-resourced and effectively implemented inclusion in mainstream schools that is run on parity with the whole school and delivered in the best interests of children and young people with the most complex learning needs. Unsuccessful practice is demonstrated in poor delivery and learners whose needs are not prioritised or met. It is a tragedy where poor practice is normalised due to the lack of understanding in some mainstream schools.

Summary from a Personal Perspective

I have returned to specialist provision specifically to reconnect with specialist practice. My return was prompted by the dramatic change in specialist provisions since my first experience. Whilst I appreciate benefits of well-delivered inclusion, I believe there is a distinct pedagogy for S/PMLD learners. I have benefited from this move and feel that I have a stake in a sector of education where some exciting things are possible.

In 2006 I attended the SEN Support Services Association (SENSSA) conference where Professor Roy McConkey was the keynote speaker. He presented us with an image of the Penrose triangle, a paradoxical 2-D representation of an impossible 3-D shape, as an illustration of the challenges and tensions associated with inclusion. The answer to the paradox of the Penrose triangle, whilst impossible in 3-D, can be glimpsed by a shift in perspective, which transformed my thinking. Instead of concentrating on my own failings, I was able to appreciate more clearly the enormous challenges and realised that the conflicts and tensions were generated by very tangible issues around inclusion in a mainstream classroom.

The disjointed nature of the scenarios illustrated largely reflects the lack of cohesion I experienced. I wanted to deliver an integrated provision, but the reality was often more fragmented.

CONCLUSION

Whatever the perspective on inclusion is as a principle, it is very clear from both the literature and personal experience that including a low-incidence group such as learners with S/PMLD is extremely difficult to implement in practice. Maintaining a good education for this group alongside their mainstream peers is immensely challenging, especially in an educational climate where raising standards is the dominant feature. The two policies of inclusion and standards are largely incompatible. Including all children in one learning community, whilst continually pushing up attainment, do not sit comfortably together.

However, it is not impossible. What is most important is a concentration on the quality of the education of learners with SLD/PMLD. If this is to be achieved in mainstream settings, then senior leaders need to be committed to facilitating the work of specialist staff. These specialist staff require extensive training. They also need to be given time to promote understanding in their colleagues across the school. If the education of learners with S/PMLD is given over entirely to specialist staff, it is doubtful whether inclusion will result. It is a delicate balance between recognising the specialist quality of the education of learners with S/PMLD and facilitating inclusion in the educational world of the rest of their learning community.

Currently in England, there is a mixed economy of special and mainstream schools educating learners with S/PMLD. One system is not better than the other and both would claim to be inclusive in their practice. What is required in the future is for more and varied opportunities for inclusive practice to be developed. However, inclusion is for naught if good practice is compromised.

KEY TERMS

Inclusion – Inclusion is a complex and flexible term in England that describes educational practice, where learners of different abilities and needs are educated in proximity to each other. It does not necessarily mean that all learners are educated in the same classrooms, although that is likely to be so for some of the time.

Severe, Profound and Multiple Learning Difficulties (SLD and PMLD) – Refers to learners in education in England who have severe or profound cognitive disabilities. Each learner is unique, and there are many different syndromes and conditions that influence the thinking and learning capacity of individuals. Children with PMLD learn the basics of communication and cognition and those with SLD learn may go on to learn basic skills such as literacy and numeracy. All these learners will be supported as adults but can and do live fulfilled lives.

Mainstream Schools – In England, mainstream schools are broadly divided into primary and secondary phases, although in addition, there are Early Years settings, sixth form colleges and further education colleges. Schools can be maintained by the state or are privately funded. Some are comprehensive and others are selective. Many maintained mainstream schools are inclusive, in that they educate learners with a wide range of abilities and needs. However, there are few mainstream schools that include learners with special educational needs, especially if the learners have severe, profound and multiple learning difficulties.

Special Schools – These are schools in England that are either maintained or privately funded. Some special schools educate learners with a broad spectrum of needs, whereas others relate to specific disabilities or differences. Special schools for learners with SLD/PMLD could fall into either of these types. Many special schools describe themselves as inclusive, especially if they have strong links with mainstream schools.

REFERENCES

Aird, R. (2001). *The education and care of children with severe, profound and multiple learning difficulties*. London: David Fulton Publishers.

Ashdown, R., Carpenter, B., & Bovair, K. (1991). *The curriculum challenge: Access to the national curriculum for pupils with learning difficulties*. London: Falmer Press.

Baker, J. (2009). Special school headship in times of change: Impossible challenges or golden opportunities. *British Journal of Special Education, 36*(4), 191–197.

Blackburn, C., & Carpenter, B. (2012). Engaging young children with complex learning difficulties and disabilities. *Eye, 14*(2), 39.

Booth, T., & Ainscow, M. (2011). *Index for inclusion: Developing learning and participation in schools* (3rd ed.). London: CSIE.

Brandon, S. (1997). *The invisible wall: Niki's fight to be included*. Hesketh Bank: Parents with Attitude.

Busch, V., Van Stel, H. F., De Leeuw, J. R. J., Melhuish, E., & Schrijvers, A. J. P. (2013). Multidisciplinary integrated parent and child centres in Amsterdam: A qualitative study. *International Journal of Integrated Care, 13*(2), e013.

Cameron, A., & Lart, R. (2012). Revisiting joint working. *Journal of Integrated Care, 20*(2), 89–93.

Causton-Theoharis, J. N., Giangreco, M. F., Doyle, M. B., & Vadasy, P. F. (2007). Paraprofessionals the "Sous-Chefs" of literacy instruction. *Teaching Exceptional Children, 40*(1), 56–62.

CCEA. (2011). *Quest for learning*. Retrieved from http://www.nicurriculum.org.uk/inclusion_and_SEN/assessment/pmld.asp

Cline, T., & Fredrickson, N. (2009). *Special educational needs, inclusion and diversity* (2nd ed.). Maidenhead: Open University Press.

CSIE. (2013a). *FAQ Special schools have been specifically set up to cater for the needs of disabled children. Why deprive these children of such tailor-made provision?* Retrieved from http://www.csie.org.uk/inclusion/faq.shtml

CSIE. (2013b). *Why inclusion*? Retrieved from http://www.csie.org.uk/inclusion/why.shtml

DES. (1970). *Education (Handicapped Children) act 1970*. London: DES.

DES. (1978). *Special educational needs (The Warnock Report)*. London: DES.

DfE. (2011a). *Glossary of special educational needs terminology*. Retrieved from http://www.education.gov.uk/a0013104/glossary-of-special-educational-needs-sen-terminology

DfE. (2011b). *Support and aspiration: A new approach to special educational needs and disability: A consultation*. London: DfE.

DfE. (2011c). *The national strategies 1997–2011: A brief summary of the impact and effectiveness of the national strategies*. London: DfE.

DfE. (2013a). *Number of academies and free schools*. Retrieved from https://www.gov.uk/government/publications/number-of-academies-and-free-schools

DfE. (2013b). *Statistics: Special Educational Needs (SEN)*. Retrieved from https://www.gov.uk/government/collections/statistics-special-educational-needs-sen

DfE. (2014a). *Children and families act 2014*. London: DfE.

DfE. (2014b). *Special educational needs and disability code of practice*. London: DfE.

DfE. (2014c). *Performance – P scales – Attainment targets for pupils with special educational needs*. London: DfE.

Farrell, M. (2006). *Celebrating the special school*. London: David Fulton.

Feiler, A. (2010). The UK 14–19 education reforms: Perspectives from a special school. *Support for Learning*, *25*(4), 172–178.

Florian, L., Rouse, M., & Black-Hawkins, K. (2007). *Achievement and inclusion in schools*. London: Routledge.

Fredrickson, N. (2010). Bullying or befriending? Children's responses to classmates with special needs. *British Journal of Special Education*, *37*(1), 4–12.

Glover-Thomas, N. (2008). Joint working: Reality or rhetoric in housing the mentally vulnerable? *Journal of Social Welfare & Family Law*, *29*(3–4), 217–231.

Goss, P. (2006). Meaning-led learning for pupils with severe and profound and multiple learning difficulties. *British Journal of Special Education*, *33*(4), 210–219.

Head, G., & Pirrie, A. (2007). The place of special schools in a policy climate of inclusion. *Journal of Research in Special Educational Needs*, *7*(2), 90–96.

Hodkinson, A. (2009). Pre-service teacher training and special educational needs in England 1970–2008: Is government learning the lessons of the past or is it experiencing groundhog day? *European Journal of Special Needs Education*, *24*(3), 277–289.

Imray, P., & Hinchcliffe, V. (2012). Not fit for purpose: A call for separate and distinct pedagogies as part of a national framework for those with severe and profound learning difficulties. *Support for Learning*, *27*(4), 150–157.

Imray, P., & Hinchcliffe, V. (2013). *Curricula for teaching children and young people with severe or profound and multiple learning difficulties: Practical strategies for educational professionals*. London: Routledge.

King, G., Strachan, D., Tucker, M., Duwyn, B., Desserud, S., & Shillington, M. (2009). The application of a transdisciplinary model for early intervention services. *Infants & Young Children*, *22*(3), 211–223.

Konza, D. (2008). Inclusion of students with disabilities in new times: Responding to the challenge. In P. Kell, W. Vialle, D. Konza, & G. Vogl (Eds.), *Learning and the learner: Exploring learning for new times*. University of Wollongong. Retrieved from http://ro.uow.edu.au/cgi/viewcontent.cgi?article=1036&context=edupapers

Lacey, P. (2003). The future of special schools. *The SLD Experience*, *35*, 36–41.

Lacey, P. (2011). Developing a curriculum for pupils with PMLD. *The SLD Experience*, *61*(1), 4–7.

Lewis, A., & Norwich, B. (2004). *Special teaching for special children: A pedagogy for inclusion?* Maidenhead: Open University Press.

Limbrick, P. (2009). *TAC for the 21st century: Nine essays on team around the child*. Clifford: Interconnections.

London Borough of Newham. (2006). *Developing curriculum inclusion for pupils with complex needs*. London: Borough of Newham.

Male, D. (1996). Who goes to SLD schools? *Journal of Applied Research in Intellectual Disabilities*, *9*(4), 307–323.

Male, D., & Rayner, M. (2007). Who goes to SLD schools? Aspects of policy and provision for pupils with profound and multiple learning difficulties who attend special schools in England. *Support for Learning*, *22*(3), 145–152.

McGill, P. (2008). Residential schools for children with learning disabilities in England: Recent research and issues for future provision. *Tizard Learning Disability Review*, *13*(4), 4–12.

Mencap. (1999). *On a wing and a prayer*. London: Mencap.

Mitchell, D. (2008). *What really works in special and inclusive education: Using evidence-based teaching strategies*. London: Routledge.

Norwich, B. (2008). *Dilemmas of difference, inclusion and disability: International perspectives and future direction*. London: Routledge.

Pickering, D., & Busse, M. (2010). Disabled children's services: How do we measure family-centred care? *Journal of Child Health Care*, *14*(2), 200–207.

Porter, J., & Lacey, P. (2008). Safeguarding the needs of pupils with visual impairment in non-VI special schools. *British Journal of Visual Impairment*, *26*, 50–62.

Radford, J., Bosanquet, P., Webster, R., Blatchford, P., & Rubie-Davies, C. (2014). Fostering learner independence through heuristic scaffolding: A valuable role for teaching assistants. *International Journal of Educational Research*, *63*, 116–126.

Rayner, M. (2011). The curriculum for children with severe and profound learning difficulties at Stephen Hawking school. *Support for Learning*, *26*(1), 25–32.

Riddell, S., Tisdall, K., Kane, J., & Mulderrig, J. (2006). *Literature review of educational provision for pupils with additional support needs*. Edinburgh: Scottish Executive Social Research.

Rix, J. (2011). Repositioning of special schools within a specialist, personalised educational marketplace – the need for representative principles. *International Journal of Inclusive Education*, *15*(2), 263–279.

Rubie-Davies, C., Blatchford, P., Webster, R., Koutsoubou, M., & Bassett, P. (2010). Enhancing student learning? A comparison of teaching and teaching assistant interaction with pupils. *School Effectiveness and School Improvement*, *21*, 429–449.

Salt, T. (2010). *Independent review of teacher supply for severe, profound and multiple learning difficulties*. London: DCSF.

Sheehy, K., & Duffy, H. (2009). Attitudes to makaton in the ages on integration and inclusion. *International Journal of Special Education*, *24*(2), 91–102.

Simmons, B., & Bayliss, P. (2007). The role of special schools for children with profound and multiple learning difficulties: Is segregation always best? *British Journal of Special Education*, *34*(1), 19–24.

Staff of Rectory Paddock School. (1983). *In search of a curriculum*. Sidcup: Robin Wren Publishers.

The Dales School. (2011). *Mapping and Assessing Personal Progress (MAPP)*. Retrieved from Equals http://www.thedalesschool.org/article/assessment-progression-mapp/275

Warnock, M. (2005). *Special educational needs: A new look pamphlet 11*. London: Philosophy of Education Society of Great Britain.

Webster, R., Blatchford, P., Bassett, P., Brown, P., Martin, C., & Russell, A. (2010). Double standards and fist principles: Framing teaching assistant support for pupils with special educational needs. *European Journal of Special Needs Education*, *25*(4), 319.

Webster, R., Blatchford, P., & Russell, A. (2013). Challenging and changing how schools use teaching assistants: Findings from the effective deployment of teaching assistants project. *School Leadership & Management*, *33*(1), 78–96.

Wedell, K. (2008). Confusion about inclusion: Patching up or system change? *British Journal of Special Education*, *35*(3), 127–135.

Welsh Assembly Government. (2006). *Routes for learning*. Cardiff: Welsh Assembly Government.

Wolstenholme, C. (2010). Including students with personal care and physical needs: A discussion of how attitudes of school and college staff impact on effective educational inclusion. *Support for Learning*, *25*(3), 146–150.

21ST CENTURY INCLUSIVE PRACTICES AND POLICIES IN RUSSIA

Vita L. Jones, Debra L. Cote, Erica Howell and Melinda R. Pierson

ABSTRACT

This chapter chronicles the evolution of Russian academic practices that are designed to support all students in one educational environment. It draws on Russia's time-honored practices and includes the contemporary global push toward inclusive settings. This dialogue examines the theories that lay the foundation for Russia's inclusive transformation. The method of examination for this descriptive qualitative work is a general review of historical educational legislation. The objective is to examine the barriers to inclusion as well as to provide a description of best practices and guiding principles. This historical discussion addresses the foundation of education and builds a context for educators to view the process of embracing inclusion. In this chapter, language, parental views and educational practices are all assessed to comprehend the Russian social nuances that impact change.

Keywords: Inclusion; Russian educational system; historical context; societal beliefs; low-incidence disability; best practices

Including Learners with Low-Incidence Disabilities
International Perspectives on Inclusive Education, Volume 5, 269–287

ISSN: 1479-3636/doi:10.1108/S1479-363620140000005019

INTRODUCTION

The Russian educational system is embracing changes for learners with low-incidence disabilities (Godovnikova, 2009; Morova, 2012). Recent Russian laws mandated inclusion for learners with special needs, yet challenges in implementation still exist as many children with low-incidence disabilities do not receive appropriate special education services. This chapter presents the barriers (e.g., money, training, access, cultural attitudes) to inclusive education practices and policies in Russia for children with low-incidence disabilities in addition to information on the following topics: Russian people's perceptions of learners with disabilities, an introduction to issues and trends in inclusive practices and policies in special education, a description of best practices designed to support learners with low-incidence disabilities, and present supports for Russian parents and communities. The following questions guided the discussion in this chapter:

1. What is the historical context of inclusionary practices in Russia?
2. What are the societal beliefs toward inclusive practices for children with disabilities?
3. In particular, what are some of the 21st century changes occurring in the Russian educational system for learners with low-incidence disabilities?

Historically, the collapse of the Soviet Union and communism greatly influenced changes in Russia's educational, economic, and social systems, basically permeating every structure/system within the Russian society (Agran & Boykov, 2003). This impact had positive outcomes as the Russian education system aimed to adopt successful educational practices from the Western world (Jones, 2003). While these changes have resulted in advances in the way services are provided to students with disabilities, worries about the current education practices remain. Two key concerns surround the absence of oversight in applying services to children with special needs and the fact that children with disabilities are not required to attend school. Therefore, parents bear the burden of advocating for effective and appropriate educational services for their children with disabilities.

The first organized endeavor to establish inclusive practices occurred in Moscow in 2012 with the establishment of the Institution of Inclusive Education (Pierson, Cote, & Jones, 2012). Although Russia is taking progressive steps toward inclusion with the Institute, diverse viewpoints on inclusion are found across the country. For example, inclusion advocates want to integrate all children with disabilities into schools. In stark contrast to this ideology are current educational practices for students with physical disabilities who have limited mobility. These individuals remain home-bound, and the country does not provide support so that they are able to participate in general education school settings. This limits students with disabilities access to an appropriate education and the ability to develop socially with peers.

HISTORICAL AND THEORETICAL CONTEXT OF INCLUSIONARY PRACTICES IN RUSSIAN CULTURE

In order to clearly understand the evolution of Russia's special education system, one must be familiar with the complex history and structure of the Russian government. Russia encompasses over six million square miles with a population of over 140 million people. It is the world's ninth populated country. The diversity of Russia lies in its 160 ethnic groups and over 100 languages. The first schools to serve students with intellectual disability were opened in 1854, and special education services for students with severe disabilities were mandated in the 1900s. The term "delayed psychological development" was coined much later to identify diverse learners (Kornev, Rakhlin, & Grigorenko, 2010).

In the early 1900s, individuals with disabilities were categorized based on their handicapping condition (Grigorenko, 1998). Initially the term defect, or defectology, was used to define or treat individuals with intellectual and physical disabilities; however, the term broadened to include other disabilities such as autism spectrum disorders and reading disabilities. In 1929, Vygotsky, a Russian psychologist, opened a lab named the Institute of Defectology. The long-standing institute was founded on Vygotsky's four theories: (a) rehabilitation, (b) organization of higher processes, (c) modified/individualized teaching strategies, and (d) a zone of proximal development (Grigorenko, 1998). Students of Vygotsky continued to research difficulties in both written and spoken language in the context of defectology (Kornev et al., 2010). "While Vygotsky contributed significantly to instructional practices for all learners, Russian educators and policy makers are still attempting to understand the best fit for these instructional theories" (Alehina, Cote, Howell, Pierson, & Jones, 2014).

Piaget was another psychologist who had a large influence on the world's understanding of child development. He was a contemporary of

Vygotsky and believed that educators should note the impact of each student's developmental levels when planning instruction. Piaget believed that students adapted to their environment based on their innate biological abilities, while Vygotsky focused on the social emotional environment impact on the child. Early Russian educators were well versed in the Piagetian theory, although not completely convinced of its tenets. Piaget contributed to the European thought of predictable milestones that child development follows. Attention to this typical list of milestones allowed educators the ability to identify student deficit areas. Piaget believed that this allowed special educators to determine what specific deficit areas need to be addressed and to provide instruction in corresponding skills for remediation (Santiago-Delefosse & Delefosse, 2002).

Furthermore, Piaget identified a series of sensorimotor, preoperational, concrete, and formal developmental stages that every individual progresses through. He proposed these stages be examined in light of a student's disability. Bruner (1986) also noted the positive impact of having these well-defined stages and the implications for hypothesizing the needed support for children not progressing typically. Clearly identifying the stage in which a child is demonstrating deficits allows the special educator to create individual lessons tailored to the skill level of the student. While scaffolding is a Vygotskian concept, Piaget proposed an alternative cognitive stage of development in which a child learns based on the particular stage he or she is in. As students pass through these stages, they move from disequilibrium, where students attempt to master new skills, to equilibrium, where the skill set is consolidated and generalized.

According to Csapo (as cited in Agran & Boykov, 2003), Russia had many early processes in place to deliver special education services to students with disabilities. These government-sponsored services were mandated as early as 1931, which was much earlier than Canada or the United States. Russia was considered progressive in Europe for providing support to students with disabilities. In spite of these progressive moves, service delivery models have evolved slowly and lagged in cultural perception and implementation. The western thought of individualism and human potential did not match the ideology of Russian special education policy (Agran & Boykov, 2003).

In the 1900s, political mandates governing special education services for severely impacted students began to increase. A prevailing notion of a flawless society was widespread during the 70+ year Soviet Union rule (Agran & Boykov, 2003). Another mark of this rule was the idea that all children be educated and meet the same expectations without any special support. This fueled the philosophy that a model community would provide a holistic, successful lifestyle (Agran & Boykov, 2003). Societal consciousness about disabilities was not viewed as a normal part of Russian culture.

The process of educating students with disabilities received political momentum starting in 1918 and lasting through the 1920s. Due to the civil way, the country was faced with an influx of individuals with disabilities. Russia did not have specific measures in place to support the needs of their citizens with disabilities; thus, these individuals were frequently overlooked by society without any political, social, or educational support (Grigorenko, 1998). Initial services for students with disabilities were designed to service students with deafness, blindness, and mental retardation with St. Petersburg, Moscow, and the Central federal area being identified as having the highest prevalence of people with disabilities. In relation to gender, more women were identified as having a disability than men, a statistic contrary to today (Andreev & Becker, 2010). Russia touts a comparatively high (99.7%) literacy rate among its citizens over the age of 15 (Central Intelligence Agency, 2014). Initial cases of academic deficiencies were noted in the early 1930s as Tkachev documented cases of alexia and agraphia in students in typical classroom settings. In light of the increase of citizens with disabilities, the 1930s were a time of emerging disability etiological theories (Andreev & Becker, 2010).

At the same time, the historical plight of students with disabilities was withheld from public scrutiny as society did not portray them as mainstream figures. The political image of people with disabilities was obscure as they were considered a stigmatizing factor. Public life for individuals with disabilities was riddled with segregated practices (Frohlich, 2012).

RUSSIAN SOCIETAL BELIEFS TOWARD INCLUSIVE PRACTICES FOR STUDENTS WITH DISABILITIES

With the increase of disabilities in Russia and the outlying regions, came evaluation of policies, cost, and beliefs (Twigg, 2005). Russian societal beliefs "toward handicapped people should not be perceived as a given for all time, but as a social construct that can be reconstructed and changed" (Iarskaia-Smirnova & Romanov, 2006, p. 59). With the passage of time, Russian society expanded their acceptance of individuals with disabilities and support of inclusion. A 2006 investigation examined Russian students', parents', and educators' beliefs about inclusive practices and found a majority of participants used positive words when reflecting on inclusion (Iarskaia-Smirnova & Romanov, 2006). One may surmise the positive association was the result of witnessing or experiencing increased daily interactions between individuals with and without disabilities. Curtis and Roza expressed the following: "About 35% of children who have the experience of contacts with disabled people are ready to study together in the same class" (2002, p. 101). Yet Russian students without disabilities were shown to have limited interactions with children with disabilities. This may be due to educational systems that are unequipped, teachers who receive little training in special needs, or limited funding that addresses the inclusion needs of students with disabilities (Iarskaia-Smirnova & Romanov, 2006).

While equality in the educational system for individuals with disabilities resulted in new disability advocacy legislation in Russia, barriers/challenges remained. Specific physical barriers in the educational system included the following: (1) inaccessibility, (2) parent opposition, (3) teacher preparation programs that failed to address disability topics, (4) parents who lacked knowledge of the services for their children with disabilities, (5) inadequate transportation, (6) decreased funding, and (7) fears and biases surrounding disabilities (Curtis & Roza, 2002). It was/is not uncommon for Russian adults and youth to possess engrained fears surrounding mental retardation and biases pointed toward intolerance and nonacceptance. However, Russian advocacy groups for individuals with disabilities identify the need to do more to address equality and to support transformation (Curtis & Roza, 2002).

A key component contributing to transformative changes in Russian beliefs occurs through education. Iarskaia-Smirnova and Romanov (2007) emphasized that most children with disabilities in Russia are/were not included but instructed in segregated settings (i.e., boarding schools). They noted, "The transition from socialism to the market has worsened the conditions of the special school system due to significant decrease in public financing for boarding schools, lack of specialists entering special education on graduation because of inappropriate salary and alternative possibilities of employment in the private sector" (2007, p. 96).

ASSUMPTIONS/PERCEPTIONS OF STUDENTS WITH LOW-INCIDENCE DISABILITIES

Russian culture suggests that having a disability has an inherent spiritual meaning or religious connotation (as cited in Dovey & Graffam, 1987). In early Russian history, persons who were missing limbs were not allowed to participate in religious ceremonies. Oliver (1996) as cited in Dovey and Graffam (1987) noted the negative perceptions of people with disabilities in the 20th century Russia. Individuals with disabilities were portrayed as "pathetic victims of some appalling tragedy or as superheroes struggling to overcome a tremendous burden" (p. 5). This pejorative view marks individuals with disabilities in Russia as socially inept. Selway and Ashman (1998) found that this belief influences how parents and support providers interact and conduct themselves with people with disabilities. In addition to the barriers, Russian encounters in educating children with disabilities, providing support to parents is a current challenge. Information on supports and services offered to parents of children with disabilities in Russia is almost nonexistent (Kaplan, 2010). A 2010 study (Kaplan) investigated the perceptions of 314 mothers of children with low-incidence disabilities (e.g., physical, developmental delays) at a Moscow rehabilitation center. The findings indicated participants encountered multiple challenges in raising children with disabilities with a main theme surrounding frustration due to the lack of financial support for their children's educational treatment. Many participants indicated they received additional financial support from family members or acquaintances. One noteworthy finding was mothers' preferences for their children to be educated in segregated settings (i.e., rehabilitation center). Participants expressed fears of public school settings related to low academic expectations for their children and the potential social isolation. Similar to other cultures, often-Russian mothers assume responsibility for their children's disabilities (Kaplan, 2010).

PARENTAL VIEWS

Russian parents voiced concern about the integration of their children with disabilities in public schools with typically developing peers (Godovnikova, 2009). Noted concerns were in regard to the quality of the educational program from the standpoint of children with and without disabilities. Worries were that integration would decrease the quality of instruction for all students. Russian parents needed more education on the potential benefits of integration for both children with and without disabilities. Generally, Russian parents were unaware of the participation of students with disabilities at their children's school with one study indicating that 32.6% of parents were unaware children with disabilities attended the public school. Furthermore, they were unaware that specific remedial services were being provided to children needing support (Godovnikova, 2009). These findings indicate that education on intrinsic human rights, quality of life issues, and respect for every individual could benefit the educational system and society as a whole. Parents are instrumental in the success or failure of their children with low-incidence disabilities. Without parent advocacy, many of the changes in Russia toward providing supports for individuals with disabilities would not have occurred. When parents are given the knowledge and the needed direction to support their children with disabilities, many make major changes that contribute to their children's success.

ISSUES AND TRENDS

"The Russian Federation is divided into 83 constituent units or federal subjects, 21 of which are republics, of very different sizes and economic specialization" (OECD reviews of innovation policy: Russian Federation, 2011). These various republics were/are impacted by regional public awareness and policies. Gorbachev's open policy enabled changes in state policies and courses of action (Thomson, 2002), which influenced individuals with disabilities. The issues and trends of the rights of individuals with disabilities were examined for improvement.

Thomson (2002) added:

> The focus on child disability is therefore one of prevention and cure – this goes some way to explain the relatively enthusiastic development of services for disabled children and the neglect of adult services uncovered in this study. Concurrent with this there has been recognition of the need to provide for disabled children outside the traditional long-stay residential institutions. Service developments therefore reflect, by and large, a child deficit model of disability where impairment is regarded as a defect and disabled children as a group are regarded as having a negative impact on the population as a whole. The thrust of services is curative and preventive as opposed to inclusive. However, the very fact of these services' existence has a positive social impact both on the children they directly serve and on their families (Thomson, 2002, p. 111).

Communities established support centers that shared information with families on what resources were available for their children with disabilities. They were identified as social service and rehabilitation centers (Thomson, 2002). Social service centers housed psychologists, social workers, and staff skilled in the law. This collection of experts helped families learn their rights and entitled benefits. Conversely, rehabilitation centers supported families in the home setting. For example, professionals presented a holistic approach that included parent training and the emotional support needed when working with their children. Thomson expressed, "However, systematic referral processes were rarely in evidence and where they did exist they were not formalized" (2002, p. 116).

A lack of formalized processes can serve as a barrier to implementing inclusionary practices for children with disabilities. The attitudinal views of educators, administrators, parents, and students on inclusion revealed conflicting views as to whom (e.g., school, government) was responsible for applying inclusive methods (Martz, 2005). "Administrators, teachers, and parents of students with disabilities viewed it as a responsibility of the school, while parents of students without disabilities viewed it as the government's duty" (Martz, 2005, p. 141). Regardless, there remained minimal school accessibility, limited facilities, attitudinal biases, and a lack of government support in spite of the movement from isolation toward inclusive practices (Martz, 2007).

Oreshkina and Lester (2013) reviewed the development of inclusive practices for children with disabilities. They noted the passage of laws intended to promote access to an inclusive education for children with disabilities (e.g., UN Convention on the Rights of Invalid), yet a significant number of children failed to receive an education. Interestingly, Oreshkina and Lester (2013, p. 688) revealed, "State initiatives to restructure the segregated system exist, yet are grounded in the assumption that the degree of inclusion should be determined by the developmental level of a child." One study (Iarskaia-Smirnova & Romanov, 2007) detailed how students with disabilities were portrayed in the Russian media and found that professionals influenced disability issues, in place of children and youth with disabilities. Regardless, as noted in the printed page (i.e., newspapers), a trend became apparent. The rights of persons with disabilities came to the forefront and educators learned the diverse needs of students with disabilities. Research suggests that segregated instruction remains ingrained in the Russian culture; however, public opinion has started to lean toward inclusive education (Oreshkina & Lester, 2013). Current statistics also indicate an increased numbers of children with disabilities with current estimates at over two million children (Alehina, 2012). Some potential reasons for the rise in numbers includes (a) decreased socioeconomic conditions, (b) poor prenatal care, (c) declining environmental situations, (d) deteriorating employment options, (e) uninformed proactive health care choices, (f) reduced newborn primary care, and (g) worsening living conditions and the catastrophe at Chernobyl (Kulagina, 2003; Roudik, 2007).

BEST PRACTICES FOR STUDENTS WITH LOW-INCIDENCE DISABILITIES IN RUSSIA

The United Nations Convention of the Rights of Handicapped People (as cited in Khudorenko, 2011) advocated the following for Russian students with disabilities: (1) a sense of fit and respect in society, (2) ability to reach their full human potential, and (3) support to integrate into society as a whole. It is further recommended that instructors use methods designed to enhance the learning experience while continuing to learn additional strategies in an ongoing fashion. Educators must possess a positive disposition toward students with disabilities and their families so that a sincere shift away from the stigmatization of students with disabilities occurs. The United Nations further recommends fiscal accountability in providing services and the use of research-based practices for all students with disabilities (Khudorenko, 2012).

It is important to begin services for students born with disabilities through the process of early intervention (Pervova, 1998). In the past five years, a steady increase of preschool programs for students with disabilities has emerged. Most of these preschool programs are state run with a few that are privately managed. Early intervention remediates some of the effects of a disability, is more effective, and costs far less than resources provided at a later age. The child's cognitive agility is strengthened during the foundational stages of life (Pervova, 1998). Students not classified as having a low-incidence disability are considered to have "minimal brain dysfunction."

The concept of a learning disability is relatively new in Russia and encompasses students with difficulty reading, calculating, and some emotional-social difficulties. In the 1990s, schools were opened to address the needs of this population as well as minors with communication and behavioral difficulties (Pervova, 1998). Teacher preparation should be adjusted to include strategies for supporting struggling learners in the general education classroom in Russia so that separate schools would not be necessary for students with learning disabilities. In addition, programs for students with learning disabilities should be created within general education schools so that students can attend regular classes as much as possible and receive support with learning strategies as either a pull-out or push-in option. Thus, specialized teachers would be able to support these students by removing them from the general education population for specific subjects that may need remediation. Or the push-in model would allow a specialized teacher to support students with learning disabilities in the general education classroom by offering services within regular classes. Students would then be able to participate fully in the regular program and not feel as stigmatized by being included. Students with learning disabilities would be less segregated this way and would receive a more comprehensive education, which would support them as lifelong citizens of Russia.

While there are plenty of things to improve when it comes to educating students with low-incidence disabilities in each culture, Russia has many practices that are noteworthy to the Western education system. Post (2005) reports most Russian schools house all grade levels in one four-storied building: primary level on the first level, first through fourth grade on the second level, and fifth through ninth on the third level with tenth through eleventh on the upper level. Another best practice is that each teacher must present one lessen each year to his/her colleagues in an open forum (Post, 2005). This practice encourages teachers to remain skillful in their respective craft and allows them the opportunity to receive feedback from colleagues in their field. A great emphasis is placed on this open forum and teachers spend a considerable amount of time preparing for this annual academic presentation.

In Russia, upper division classes are typically divided by subject (i.e., math, science, literature). Students in Russia study math, chemistry, biology, and physics from 7th grade onward. Often beginning in upper level classes, students attend school on Saturdays for a half-day of instruction. Another common practice of Russian schools is that a student begins a foreign language in the fifth grade, usually English or German. Instead of letter grades, students receive numbers beginning (2–5) to indicate scores on academic subjects and a grade may be lowered because of behavior. Scores are recorded in a *daybook* which teachers sign at the end of the week for parents to review. Also, students are with the same group of children from 1st through the 11th grade.

The merging of special education services into the current format is challenging but well worth the effort. According to Cherednichenko (2000), this transformation consists of integrating new types of specialization and supplementary services as well as curriculum with traditional methods of instruction. The best methods for this transformation are shifting the social and cultural context of educating students with disabilities. This is best done with an attitude of social equality and pluralism in education. The philosophy of individually oriented pedagogy is being embraced as well. The thought of Bourdieu's cultural capital (as cited in Cherednichenko, 2000) is now heralded in linking ability with opportunity to learn. It is hypothesized that each student brings to the educational setting a right to be educated (Cherednichenko, 2000).

21ST CENTURY EDUCATIONAL MOVEMENT FOR STUDENTS WITH LOW-INCIDENCE DISABILITIES

Russian students in 2013 began the school year with a new federal initiative designed to implement inclusive practices. The new federal initiative entitled, On Education in the Russian Federation, sets forth the ideals of a free education for all students and strengthens precepts of inclusion. Under this law, students considered *educable* were transferred to general educational settings. The Russian Ministry of Education reports 31.4% of students with low-incidence disabilities have assimilated into general education classrooms. This is the initial exodus of students with disabilities out of segregated settings into general education classrooms (Retrieved on June 9, 2014 from: http://eng.mon.gov.ru). In Russia, general education consists of (1) preschool, (2) primary general education, (3) basic general education, and (4) secondary complete general education.

The inclusion of students with disabilities in Russia is currently widely discussed and considered one of the most advanced practices being considered (Godovnikova, 2009). This national dialogue is regarded as necessary and expedient. Concerns about the inclusion of students with low-incidence disabilities are related to how the public views the entrance of students with disabilities into the general education classrooms. Along with the public view is the collaboration of teachers, educators, and policy makers in defining inclusion and making it a reality (Godovnikova, 2009). To coordinate this assimilation, the Coordination Council was organized to support this integration process. These first efforts were aimed at early childhood programs where it was presumed it would be less obvious (Godovnikova, 2009). In Godovnikova's examination, inclusion was more effective within the preschool settings for many reasons. Firstly, the preschools had the staff resources to support young learners with disabilities. Secondly, preschool programs had a wider group of specialists involved in the assessment process. Finally, the stigma was lessened with preschool students, as the public did not view them with negative perceptions as much as older students with disabilities. It was also noted the assessment procedures for preschool students was more thorough than that of older students (Godovnikova, 2009). Inclusive measures for preschool programs are an important beginning for the overall plan for the implementation of inclusion in the Russian school system.

Godovnikova (2009) also noted that general education classrooms did not have access to resources such as wheelchair ramps or any technical supports for school-aged students; thus, for inclusion to be successful, these resources would have to be provided. One teacher of students with deafness noted a nonchalant attitude when 10 of her students with deafness were enrolled in a general education classroom. This prevailing theme of lack of resources is one challenging aspect of the implementation of inclusion for students with low-incidence disabilities. If access to the school, classroom, and curriculum are not supported, then successful inclusion will not become a reality in Russia.

With President Gorbachev's rise to power in 1986, a new phrase was coined to capture the political milieu of the Russian Federation. The coined phrase, "glasnost," was implemented to shift focus away from the formalized governmental rule to the citizens' voice and social consciousness. Another term used to define Gorbachev's rule was "perestroika." This term denotes the restructuring that took place during his tenure. These two prevailing thoughts opened the door for more advanced policies affecting people with disabilities (Frohlich, 2012). As Gorbachev transformed the Congress of Soviets with the Congress of Peoples' Deputies special education practices began to change gradually. Until the early 1980s, children with disabilities were not acknowledged as legal citizens in the Soviet Union. Only individuals who served in the military received compensation for injuries they incurred in the line of duty. The United Nations Convention on the Rights of the Child addressed this issue and led to a ratification of policy to include services and pensions for children with disabilities.

Vishnikina (1996) purports a society's treatment of its individuals with disabilities is an indication of its civilization. Another political movement was the development of the Ministry of Social Security overseeing the affairs of students with disabilities. This organization formed in 1994 is responsible for overseeing benefits, grants, pensions, and the oversight of data pertaining to people with disabilities. Of the approximately one million Russian students with disabilities, 82.9% or 217,900 have severe cognitive impairments (Vishnikina, 1996). Russia is investigating the need for improved conditions for students with disabilities; one barrier is the lack of longitudinal statistical data about such students. As a result, there are sparse reporting agencies to inform policy makers. What is clear is the need for medical, financial, and educational support for this population (Vishnikina, 1996).

In 1979, children with disabilities began to be accepted and receive services (Children's Rights: International and National Laws and Practice, 2007). Prior to that, limited funding made it difficult for those families and children with low socioeconomic status to access specialized education. Students in specialized settings (i.e., institutions) and those with challenging behaviors or mental disabilities did not receive individualized and age appropriate training (Children's Rights: International and National Laws and Practice, 2007). One monitoring organization for the children of Russia is the United Nations Convention on the Rights of the Child which sets standards on how children are to be cared for, especially adoption policies. This organization began in 1990 and was composed of an international delegation. The standards set forth by the Convention on the Rights of the Child made limited progress in securing resources for students with disabilities, but overall the mandates went unheeded because there was no standardization for implementation of the laws (Children's Rights: International and National Laws and Practice, 2007). This will continue to hurt children with disabilities and their access to inclusive education. A positive outcome of this policy is that over 90% of children are immunized and receive free medical support. Another initiative is that children under three or who have siblings under six receive medication for free. The conflict for implementing these policies is a lack of budgetary backing. The United Nations Convention on the Rights of the Child addressed this issue and led to a ratification of policy to include services and pensions for children with disabilities.

United Nations Children's Fund [UNICEF] (1999) reports that children with disabilities fare better under the transformed political system than in the socialist era where they were often abandoned. Now these children receive services either in institutions or are at home receiving care from family members. These family members receive supplemental income to support the various needs of their children with disabilities. While this is not the ideal, citizens with disabilities, particularly children with disabilities have gained worldwide attention through the international dialogue on the rights of children with disabilities around the world. This international dialogue places Russian policy makers in the position to collaborate with the global community on best practices and methods to better serve children with disabilities.

With over a million students with disabilities, Russia is faced with the task of enforcing the global initiative of implementing inclusive practices within its borders. Although national policies speak to the inclusive movement, it still remains illusive. For example, in 2006, over 13,000 boarding schools housed 170,000 students with cognitive, vision, hearing, and physical disabilities (Children's Rights: International and National Laws and Practice, 2007).

The majority of students with disabilities do not attend public schools, many because of accessibility issues. There are close to 2,000 separate day schools for students with disabilities educating 236,000 students. In Russia, September 1 of each year marks the new school year. In rural areas, students often do not attend school; parents opt to stay, to keep them in the small villages and settlements in lieu of attending understaffed and underfunded local schools. The number of students at home in rural areas is estimated to be roughly 26,200 students (Children's Rights: International and National Laws and Practice, 2007).

In terms of inclusion for students with low-incidence disabilities, Russian educators are forging partnerships with educators in the United States to examine how to create the environment for inclusion to succeed. Educators often feel unprepared to support students with disabilities in the general education classroom. In addition, often there is no financial support for this transition and very little parental support. It appears that teachers are willing but lack the means to implement inclusive practices. The homebound students receive a curriculum session with a classroom teacher a few times a week. Online centers are being developed so that students can access education with the right technology. Both society and citizens need awareness and support to make inclusion a reality.

FUTURE DIRECTIONS

Russian special educators who were influenced by Samuel Kirk theorized that the social environment of a child with a disability greatly impacted their development (Kordunov, Nigayev, Reynolds, & Lerner, 1998). Kirk was also a proponent of adapting Western models of thought and individualizing lessons to benefit each student. He also proposed a national plan of financial support for students with disabilities and their families. While Kirk believed an interest in Western thought is to be considered, it should not be replicated. Kordunov et al. (1998) considered the Canadian special education system as a better model from which to learn inclusive methods, strategies, and curriculum. Canadian special educators place control of special education in the hands of local and regional administrators that replaced the centralization system. This local and regional control allows parents and educators along with their momentary means to influence the services provided for children. With this model, educators and parents in Canada feel that their voices are heard more and they can get appropriate and immediate services for their children with disabilities based on individualization of services (Kordunov et al., 1998).

Another policy to investigate for the future is keeping children with their families instead of placing them in institutions. Empowering parents to care for their children and become involved in the school setting will benefit students in the long run. The institutionalization of students with disabilities is losing popularity and being replaced with parent friendly practices. Kordunov et al. (1998) note that institutional staff rarely has specialized training or equipment to support students with disabilities. These researchers advocate the module model of schooling similar to the Western idea of resource classrooms. With this type of model, students with disabilities have specialized teachers and a multidisciplinary team to support their learning.

A particular focus for the future hinges on training specialists for the field. The revision of training should include behavior methods and teaching strategies unique to children with disabilities. Russian administrators and educators should advocate for additional time for teacher training either from current Russian educators who are teaching children with disabilities or from Western countries that have demonstrated models of teacher training in special education. University partnerships can be created so that faculty and teacher candidates can have reciprocal teaching and learning opportunities. New teacher training curriculum can be developed to support these new specialists in Russia. In addition, general education teachers in Russia will also need added curriculum to better support students with disabilities in their classrooms. This will strongly support the inclusion movement.

Also, new laws governing special education would impact the budgetary issues as well as create a partnership for educators and families to collaborate on issues. Allowing families the freedom of choice between and institution and public schools will make a vast difference in humanizing the process of educating students with disabilities.

Finally, Russia is experiencing a revolution of sorts when it comes to students with special needs. The old system of placing children in institutions is being replaced with a more democratic experience (Kordunov et al., 1998). A focus on early intervention and dignity in language also contributes to the transformation of the special education system in Russia.

The future of special education services in Russia is optimistic as educators, families, and policy makers make training, budget allowances, and collaboration a high priority in the transformation of special education.

KEY TERMS

Cultural capital – Is the system of deeply embedded values passed from one group to another often consistent with ethics (Cherednichenko, 2000).

Defectology – "Is the scientific belief that there is an inherent characteristic of individuals with disabilities, and that individuals can be differentiated by the type or severity of their disability" (Agran & Boykov, 2003, p. 92).

Defectologists – Are those professionals who service "students with disabilities (e.g., psychologists and speech therapists)" These professionals gained their education "through the faculty of defectology." (Agran & Boykov, 2003, p. 92).

Federal Law on the Social Protection for Handicapped People in the Russian Federation – This law became effective in 1995. The goal of the state mandate was to give persons with disabilities an active voice in society and access to the same opportunities as those without disabilities. The policy applied to both adults and children. One emphasis was to put into place comprehensive systems of support (i.e., rehabilitation programs) in hopes of changing societal negative views toward persons with disabilities (Kulagina, 2003).

Inclusion – "Means that that students with disabilities are to be educated in the same classroom at the same school site as their peers without disabilities" (Alehina et al., 2014). Inclusion suggests that the wants and individualized needs of students with disabilities are met by the school and the professionals serving them (Iarskaia-Smirnova & Loshakova, 2004).

Piaget's stages of development – (1) Sensorimotor stage is the stage where infants and toddlers learn through sensory input; (2) preoperational stage is the stage where children learn through pretend play but have not mastered logic and considered another person's perspective and, (3) concrete operational stage is the stage where children begin to have logical cognitive ability although somewhat rigid. Formal operational stage is the stage a child increases in logic and the higher order thinking process (Genovese, 2003).

UNICEF – Is the acronym for United Nations International Children's Emergency F.

REFERENCES

Agran, M., & Boykov, D. (2003). A preliminary survey of professional and student opinion of special education practice in contemporary Russia. *Research & Practice for Persons with Severe Disabilities*, *28*(2), 91–100.

Alehina, S. V. (2012). Inclusive education in Russia: State and development trends. Paper presented to the Ministry of Education and Science of the Russian Federation, Moscow, Russia.

Alehina, S. V., Cote, D., Howell, E. J., Pierson, M. R., & Jones, V. (2014). Trends toward the integration and inclusion of students with disabilities in Russia. *The Review of Disability Studies An International Journal*, *10*(1/2), 95–104.

Central Intelligence Agency. (2014). *Russia. In the world factbook*. Retrieved from https://www.cia.gov/library/publications/the-world-factbook/geos/rs.html

Cherednichenko, G. A. (2000). School reform in the 1990s: Innovations and social selection. *Russian Education and Society*, *42*(11), 6–32.

Curtis, B., & Roza, D. (2002). Access to an equal education for children and youth with disabilities in Russia. *Disability World*, *15*. Retrieved from http://www.disabilityworld.org/09-10_02/children/russia.shtml

Dovey, K., & Graffam, J. (1987). *The experience of disability: Social construction and imposed limitation*. Burwood: Victoria College Press.

Frohlich, C. (2012). Civil society and the state intertwined: The case of disability NGOs in Russia. *East European Politics*, *28*(4), 371–389.

Genovese, J. E. C. (2003). Piaget, pedagogy, and evolutionary psychology. Evolutionary *Psychology*, *1*, 127–137.

Godovnikova, D. (2009). The conditions for the integrated education of children with impaired development. *Russian Education and Society*, *51*(10), 26–39.

Grigorenko, E. L. (1998). Russian "Defectology": Anticipating perestroika in the field. *Journal of Learning Disabilities*, *31*(2), 193–207.

Iarskaia-Smirnova, E. R., & Loshakova, I. I. (2004). Inclusive education of handicapped children. *Russian Education and Society*, *46*(12), 63–64.

Iarskaia-Smirnova, E. R., & Romanov, P. V. (2007). Perspectives of inclusive education in Russia. *European Journal of Social Work*, *10*(1), 89–105. doi:10.1080/13691450601143732

Jones, A. (2003). Editor's introduction. *Russian Education and Society*, *45*(11), 3–4.

Kaplan, R. L. (2010). Caregiving mothers of children with impairments: Coping and support in Russia. *Disability & Society*, *25*(6), 715–729.

Khudorenko, E. A. (2011). Problems of the education and inclusion of people with disabilities. *Russian Education and Society*, *53*(12), 82–91.

Kordunov, V. V., Nigayev, A. S., Reynolds, L. D., & Lerner, J. W. (1998). Special education in Russia: History, reality, and prospects. *Journal of Learning Disabilities*, 31(2), 186–192.

Kornev, A. N., Rakhlin, N., & Grigorenko, G. I. (2010). Dyslexia from a cross-linguistic and cross-cultural perspective: *The case of Russian and Russia*, *8*(1), 41–69.

Kulagina, E. V. (2003). The social and economic situation of families with handicapped children. *Russian Education and Society*, *45*(11), 42–61.

Library Law of Congress, Russian Federation. (2007). *Children's rights: International and national laws and practice*. Retrieved from http://www.loc.gov/law/help/child-rights/russia.php

Martz, E. (2005). An exploratory study on attitudes toward inclusive education in Russia. *International Journal of Rehabilitation Research*, *28*(2), 141–147.

Martz, E. (2007). Facilitating inclusive employment: An examination of the accommodations for and the barriers to employment for Russians with disabilities. *International Journal of Rehabilitation Research*, *30*(4), 321–326.

Morova, N. (2012). Scholar school "Social rehabilitation of disabled children": From founding to modern practice. *International Journal of Academic Research*, *4*(2), 195–197.

OECD reviews of innovation policy: Russian Federation. (2011). doi:10.1787/9789264113138-en

Oreshkina, M. J., & Lester, J. N. (2013). Discourse of segregation and inclusion: A discourse analysis of a Russian newspaper for teachers. *Disability & Society*, *28*(5), 687–701.

Pervova, I. (1998). Children and youth with special needs in Russia, and educational services to meet them. *Education and Treatment of Children*, *21*(3), 412–423.

Pierson, M., Cote, D. L., & Jones, V. (2012, Summer). Special education reform in Kursk, Russia. *Division on International Special Education and Services Newsletter*, *22*(3), 6–7.

Post, B. (2005). A special section on international education-What we can learn from Russia's schools. *Phi Delta Kappan*, *86*(8), 627.

Santiago-Delefosse, M. J., & Delefosse, J. M. (2002). Spielrein, Piaget, & Vygotsky three positions on child thought and language. *Theory & Psychology*, *12*(6), 723–747.

Selway, D., & Ashman, A. F. (1998). Disability, religion and health: A literature review in search of the spiritual dimensions of disability. *Disability & Society*, *13*(3), 429–439.

Thomson, K. (2002). Regional welfare system developments in Russia: Community social services. *Social Policy & Administration*, *36*(2), 105–122.

Twigg, J. L. (2005). The cost of illness, disability, and premature mortality to Russia's economy. *Eurasian Geography and Economics*, *46*(70), 495–524.

United Nations Children's Fund. (1999). *Children at risk in central and Eastern Europe: Perils and promises*. Retrieved from http://www.unicef-irc.org/publications/pdf/monee4.pdf

Vishnikina, S. (1996). There are more than a million handicapped children in Russia. *Russian Education and Society*, *38*(4), 6–17.

INCLUDING LEARNERS WITH EXTENSIVE SUPPORT NEEDS IN SOUTH KOREA

Kyungsook Kang and Young Hyuk Hong

ABSTRACT

This chapter describes the status of past and current special education, inclusive education, and Low-Incidence Disabilities (LID) in South Korea by introducing historical background, legal development, and current trend. Four main areas related to special education in South Korea are highlighted: the historical background and legal development of special education; current laws relating to special education; inclusive education and LID; and the future of LID support in South Korea. This chapter will provide valuable information for those who want to become more knowledgeable about the current status of special education and inclusive education for learners with LID in South Korea.

Keywords: South Korea; special education; history; inclusive education; law; low-incidence disabilities

Including Learners with Low-Incidence Disabilities
International Perspectives on Inclusive Education, Volume 5, 289–313

ISSN: 1479-3636/doi:10.1108/S1479-363620140000005022

INTRODUCTION

Education in general reflects trends in society. Therefore, when discussing education one must first consider the history and the cultural context, which is particularly important to the evolution of services and supports for learners with LID in South Korea. Development and implementation of special education and inclusive education in South Korea reflect trends, especially in the areas of social and legal development.

This chapter will focus on information and data on all Low-Incidence Disabilities in conjunction with an overview of special education and the development and implementation of inclusive education for these learners.

This chapter is structured around these key questions:

1. What are some noteworthy historical moments that led to the development of current special education support systems in South Korea?
2. How were the laws relating to special education developed, improved, and implemented over time?
3. What does the current law related to special education address?
4. How do special educators in South Korea define inclusive education and LID? And how are learners with LID supported within inclusive education settings?
5. What are some successful examples of including learners with LID?
6. What are the future plans to improve special education nationwide?

DEVELOPMENT OF SPECIAL EDUCATION IN SOUTH KOREA

The history of special education in South Korea can be divided into two periods: before and after the establishment of the Special Education Law of 1977. The following sections will detail some significant events and laws related to the development of special education in South Korea.

PRIOR TO THE ESTABLISHMENT OF THE SPECIAL EDUCATION PROMOTION LAW OF 1977

Historical texts report that the government operated an institute to teach job skills to a few selected students with visual impairments as early as

1445 during the Chosun Dynasty in the Korea Peninsula. Previous dynasties also operated similar institutes to educate people with blindness (Kim, Lee, & Kim, 2011).

Throughout the Japanese forced occupation (August 29, 1910–August 25, 1945), there were efforts, mostly led by foreign missionaries, to educate learners with LID who were mainly blind and deaf. In 1894, Rosetta Sherwood Hall, an American missionary, privately taught braille to BongLye Oh, a young female student with blindness in PyoungYang, the current capital of North Korea. This has been cited as the first modern special education movement in Korea. In 1900, Mrs. Hall started a special education class for female students with blindness in JungJin Women's School located in PyoungYang. These students also received general education with typical peers. This was the first recorded inclusive education. Mrs. Hall, other missionaries, and Korean educators opened up a school for the blind, later named "PyoungYang School for Blinds." In 1914, members of the "PyoungYang School for Blinds" organized the Council for Oriental Blind Children and held a conference, "the Benefit of Inclusive Education," in Korea. Additional schools to educate learners who were blind and deaf were subsequently established (Kim & Kim, 2011; Kim et al., 2011).

On August 15, 1948, three years after the Japanese forced occupation ended, the Republic of Korea was established. In 1949, the Korean government enacted "the Korean Law of Education" which included the establishment of special schools and special classes. However, the Korean War broke out in 1950, preventing further development of special education. The Korean war (June 25, 1950–July 27, 1953) resulted in the division of Korea into two Koreas, South and North Korea.

South Korea, which officially carries the name "the Republic of Korea," continued to support the Korean Law of Education and reaffirmed the importance of education in 1959. This law mandated compulsory elementary education. As a result, 96.4% of elementary-aged children enrolled in elementary schools. During the 1960s, the government continued to work on improving the quality of compulsory education by implementing the first and second five-year plans to expand and improve compulsory education (Ministry of Culture and Education, 1988). A small number of schools operated special classrooms to support "sick and feeble children," or "weak eyesight" students. The decision to create special classrooms in regular schools was mostly based on the needs of the school or reflected the educational philosophy of the school administrators (Korean Society for Rehabilitation of Persons with Disabilities [KSRPD], 2006; Korea Society of Special Education [KSSE], 1995).

In 1971, special classes were added to the public elementary schools in a more strategic manner. "ChilSung Elementary school" in KyunSangBukDo was the first school that established a special education classroom for students with intellectual disabilities. In 1972, the central government began to discuss whether to provide or limit special education services to learners with intellectual disabilities and learners with learning disabilities. This national debate and further research paved the way for the establishment of the Special Education Promotion Law of 1977. By 1974, local educational agencies established at least one special classroom within their jurisdiction, totaling 210 special education classrooms throughout the country (KSRPD, 2006).

AFTER THE ESTABLISHMENT OF THE SPECIAL EDUCATION PROMOTION LAW OF 1977

The year 1977 was the pivotal moment for the development and establishment of special education in South Korea. The enactment of "the Special Education Promotion Law" of 1977 (Special Education Promotion Law [SEPL], 1977) and the proclamation of the rules and regulations a year later led to dramatic improvements in special education. SEPL (1977) enabled the establishment of additional special schools and special classrooms resulting in a significant increase in the numbers of students receiving special education. Learners with disabilities were able to receive compulsory education in special schools and special classes in elementary and middle schools.

By 1981, the number of special classrooms in elementary school increased to 411, serving 6,512 students. Special classrooms were added to middle schools in 1985 and the total number of special classrooms was 1,601, serving 22,534 students in elementary and middle schools. The number of special classrooms continued to rise. By 1990, there were 3,181 special classrooms, 2,513 in elementary schools, and a 668 in middle schools (KSSE, 1995).

SEPL (1977) was amended 12 times over the years to meet the demands in the field and changes in society. These amendments also attempted to reflect the latest developments in special education.

In 1994, SEPL (1977) was completely overhauled, amending it with additional research-based support and intervention strategies for special education. One such addition to SEPL was "inclusive education." The reenacted SEPL continued to support the mandate for compulsory education for elementary and middle school aged learners with disabilities. It also extended compulsory education to elementary and middle school and free public education to kindergarten and high school for all learners with disabilities. By 1995, 3,440 special classrooms were operating, 2,777 in elementary schools and 633 in middle schools. By 2004, 4,319 special classrooms were operating, 99 in kindergarten, 3,216 in elementary school, 761 in middle school, and 243 in high school (Ministry of Education, 2013).

Despite the improvements over the years, there were a couple of major limitations to SEPL. First, SEPL mainly addressed elementary and middle school education. As a result, the educational supports for infants, toddlers, and adults with disabilities were not clearly identified. Second, SEPL did not state the responsibilities of the national and local governments in supporting special education, making it difficult to enforce the law nationwide.

Since 1998, the central government developed and implemented special education improvement plans every five years. "The First 5-Year Plan of Special Education Improvement" was from 1998 to 2002. The year 2013 was the first year for the Fourth Five-Year Plan of Special Education Improvement. Each Five-Year Plan was carefully developed and implemented to meet the demands of the time for learners with disabilities. For example, the Second Five-Year Plan of Special Education Improvement strengthened inclusive education by establishing more special education classrooms, promoting disability awareness programs, and implementing facilities for ease of access. The Second Five-Year Plan also diversified learning opportunities by setting up E-Learning[1] for special education and improved the quality of special education by implementing programs to elevate professionalism for special education teachers. Additionally, the Second Five-Year Plan improved special education delivery and support systems by implementing and operating "the Special Education Support Centers"[2] within the boundaries of local educational agencies (Ministry of Education, Science, and Technology, 2008).

In addition to the Five-Year Plans of Special Education Improvement in 2001 and 2006, the government performed a study on "the Prevalence of Students with Special Needs." Results of this study, which documented an increase in the prevalence of students with special needs, helped to further improve special education in South Korea and provided the basis for "The Special Education for Individuals with Disabilities and Others Law" of 2007.

THE CURRENT LAW ON SPECIAL EDUCATION

Special Education for Individuals with Disabilities and Others Law of 2007 (SEIDOL, 2007) is the most recent special education law in South Korea. Basic components of SEIDOL (2007) are discussed below. This law and its provisions have made a tremendous impact on special education, inclusive education, and educational supports for LID.

First, inclusive education is a core component of SEIDOL (2007). The law requires that a special education recipient must be assigned to an inclusive education environment located in a school nearest to their homes. Furthermore, the law dictated that if necessary, "the special education operation committee" can make a determination for the location of inclusive education on behalf of learners with disabilities. The committee considers and evaluates the severity of disability and capacity of the learner and also solicits and considers parents and guardians' input. Based upon the committee's recommendation, school principals or superintendents of the local branch of the Ministry of Education can make the final decision on the location of the inclusive education environment for special education recipients.

SEIDOL (2007) established the legal basis to support successful implementation of inclusive education by describing in detail the responsibilities of school principals for the development and implementation of the inclusive education plan. When a special education recipient is placed in a school, the principal of the school must develop and implement the inclusive education plan, based on the types and severity of disabilities of special education recipients. This plan must address several key areas: curriculum modifications, assistive technology needs, support personnel needs, and professional development for school staff.

When special education recipients are assigned to regular schools where special education classes are not established, teachers from the Special Education Support Center (SESC) can visit and provide supports. The learners with disabilities placed in regular schools can receive services and supports from SESC to enhance their educational experiences in inclusive education setting (Korean National Institute for Special Education [KNISE], 2005a).

Previously, the special education-related services were provided mainly in special schools. With SEIDOL (2007) in place, learners with disabilities were enabled to receive special education-related services in any educational environment that they are placed in, including special schools, special classrooms in regular schools, and regular schools.

Second, SEIDOL (2007) expanded compulsory education to include kindergarten to high school for learners with disabilities. Compulsory education for regular learners is still limited to elementary and middle school education. The law also guaranteed free education for infants with disabilities under three years old. The reason for implementing kindergarten compulsory education was to provide early childhood education as soon as a child was diagnosed with a disability and in need of services. Expanding compulsory education to kindergarten age children has provided such benefits as preventing the development of a secondary disability, decreasing the effects of disability, and supporting parents who exhibit lack of disability awareness to be legally responsible for sending their children to school. Expanding compulsory education to high school provided opportunities for learners with disabilities to experience transitional services including independent living skills and job training.

Third, the Early Child Find system that detects disabilities as early as possible and provides free education for toddlers with disabilities was implemented as a result of the law. Previous laws including SEPL did not support the early child find, which resulted in a delay in detecting disabilities and early intervention. Even when a disability was diagnosed, the previous laws supported only "free daycare" without specialized instructions, leaving parents to rely on private care, which frequently resulted in a financial burden. SEIDOL (2007) enforced the provision of free education for toddlers under three years old and free medical exams to detect disabilities. Because of these changes, any special education recipient at any age can receive "free education" at special schools, at SESC, or at home.

Fourth, the legal basis for establishing and operating SESC was established. SESC was one of the focuses during the Second Five-Year Plan of Special Education Improvement (2003–2007). However, the legal basis to establish facilities and assign personnel did not exist then, limiting special education supports from SESC.

Fifth, SEIDOL (2007) strengthened transitional and occupational education. To support transition of special education recipients to the next phase of their lives after they graduate from schools, principals of middle schools and high schools are required to collaborate with related agencies to provide occupational rehabilitation training and independent living training. Schools are able to establish separate classrooms to directly provide transitional and occupational education, as well as job training classrooms to provide occupation-related training. The law also provided a funding mechanism, which made it possible to supply support personnel and financial support for transitional and occupational education. Public schools can now operate classrooms for occupational rehabilitation training and independent living training that can support learners in transitioning from school to postschool.

Sixth, SEIDOL (2007) provided guidelines for setting up special classrooms and allocating teachers. Kindergarten, elementary school, middle school, and high school can establish special classrooms based upon the number of special education recipients. One special classroom can be established with four special education recipients in kindergarten, six in elementary school, six in middle school, and seven in high school. Fewer students in a special classroom means that they will be able to receive better individualized education based on learners' individual characteristics and capacities. Previous laws only allowed placement of special education teachers in special schools, preventing special education recipients from attending special classrooms and regular classrooms in regular schools. The 2007 law made it possible to assign special education teachers to wherever learners in need of special education are placed.

Seventh, the SEIDOL (2007) defines special education as "an education to fulfill the educational needs of special education recipients by providing curriculum appropriate to characteristics and special education related services." The special education-related services are defined as "providing services, including human resources and material resources, to enable efficient delivery of education for special education recipients." The related services also include family supports and a provision for assistive technology.

SEIDOL (2007) removed therapeutic education services (including occupational therapy, physical therapy, speech therapy, hearing training, fine motor training, psychological and behavioral therapy, walking training, and daily living skills training) for learners with disabilities in the public school system and replaced it with a Voucher System. According to the Voucher System, learners who require therapy treatments receive vouchers to visit therapeutic treatment service providers after school. The logic behind this shift is that the previous regulations allowed one therapeutic treatment service provider to provide all eight therapeutic treatments listed above. This "one teacher providing all therapeutic treatments" cannot always guarantee quality treatments. Additionally, providing therapeutic education services at the same time and same place where instruction occurs was viewed as problematic and inappropriate, with learners losing precious learning time. However, those who supported the idea of providing therapeutic education services in school settings argued that therapeutic treatment services were part of "special services in special education" (KNISE, 2005b). Therefore, removing therapeutic treatment services in a school setting can be viewed as a "reduction in the areas of special services in special education." Only those who hold the national certification or license can provide the therapeutic treatment supports (KNISE, 2007). Additionally, as special education-related services, the law provided the legal basis for allocating assistance staffing, providing instruction materials and assistive technology, and transporting learners to and from school, building and operating dormitories for efficient implementation of special education.

Eighth, SEIDOL (2007) established the legal basis for supporting postsecondary education and continuing education for individuals with disabilities. Since 1995, many universities and colleges implemented the university special entrance program for special education recipients. The number of students with disabilities attending universities and colleges continued to rise (Chung & Lee, 2006). In response, SEIDOL (2007) ensured the establishment of an organization to support students with disabilities to protect the educational rights and to improve educational welfare of students with disabilities attending universities and colleges. Based on this law, "the Student with Disabilities Support Center" is charged with oversight of supports for education and daily living of learners with disabilities who attend postsecondary schools.

The importance of continuing education became apparent, especially for adults with disabilities who missed educational opportunities when they were young because they were not provided with appropriate services and supports. The law enabled the development of a lifelong education curriculum specifically designed for individuals with disabilities, providing education in various settings including regular schools, special schools, and lifelong education facilities for regular citizens.

SPECIAL EDUCATION TRENDS RELATED TO INCLUSIVE EDUCATION AND LID IN SOUTH KOREA

LID and inclusive education became major components of SEIDOL (2007). It should be noted that, unlike inclusive education, LID is not specifically defined in any special education-related law in South Korea. Yet SEIDOL (2007) dictated central government level support to promote and implement inclusive education for learners with LID including but not limited to visual impairment and/or hearing impairment, severe developmental delays, and autism.

In this section, information related to LID and current support trends will be discussed.

DEFINING LID IN SOUTH KOREA

In reviewing the definition of LID accepted in the United States, LID is generally associated with words like "low rate of occurrence," "severe," "significant," "complex," "multiple," etc. Generally speaking, LID includes disabilities that occur at a low rate and at the same time require extensive supports. According to the Individual with Disabilities Education Act (IDEA), P.L. 94.142 in the United States, "the term 'low incidence disability' means (A) a visual or hearing impairment, or simultaneous visual and hearing impairments; (B) a significant cognitive impairment; or (C) any impairment for which a small number of personnel with highly specialized skills and knowledge are needed in order for children with that impairment to receive early intervention services or a free appropriate public education." LID in IDEA specifically includes visual impairments, hearing impairments, and significant cognitive impairment. It leaves the rest of the LIDs open to interpretation (Individuals with Disabilities Education Act [IDEA], 2004). LID also generally includes but is not limited to the following disabilities: autism, significant developmental delay, complex health impairment, serious physical impairment, multiple disabilities, etc.

Despite the absence of the legal definition of LID, the importance of finding, serving, and supporting learners with severe, significant, and/or multiple disabilities are acknowledged by policy makers in South Korea. Based on the list of disabilities and services included in SEIDOL (2007), it is logical to assume that the general definitions of LID developed in the United States can be applied to South Korea as well. In fact, "the 2013 Special Education Yearly Report to the National Assembly" included the specific data on learners with visual impairment, hearing impairment, intellectual disabilities, autism, developmental delay, health impairment, and physical impairment, which are generally regarded as LID. "Low rate of occurrence" of these disabilities is apparent based on the data but not noted in the report.

FIGURING OUT THE LEARNERS WITH LID IN SOUTH KOREA

Based on the data reported in "the 2013 Special Education Yearly Report to the National Assembly, currently only 1.2% of school-age students are identified as special education recipients. The percentage of special education recipients, when compared to total number of students, steadily increased over the last few years: in 2007, 0.80%; in 2008, 0.88%; in 2009, 0.94%; in 2010, 1.03%; in 2011, 1.1%; and in 2012, 1.2%" (Ministry of Education, 2013). It should be noted that compared to other countries, the percentage of special education recipients in South Korea is much smaller. In comparison, in 2010 and 2011 about 13% of the total student population in the United States was identified as students with disabilities (Digest of Education Statistics, 2012).

Researchers provided the following explanations for the lower percentage of identification in South Korea. First, categories and areas of disability are restricted and limited. For example, the percentage of learners with learning disabilities is about 5% of the total number of special education recipients. Learners with learning disabilities in South Korea must exhibit severity and significance of disability in order to receive special education (KNISE, 2010; Lee & Lee, 2004). Second, in order for a learner to receive special education, they must be identified as an individual with a disability, which is assigned by the government based on a doctor's medical diagnosis, instead of the needs of learners with disabilities (KNISE, 2004). Third, when calculating the number of special education recipients, learners receiving special education in educational agencies other than special schools, special classrooms and regular classrooms in regular schools, and the Special Education Support Center are not included in the total (KNISE, 2005a, 2009). Fourth, parents' permission is required to provide special education services. Many parents of children with disabilities are still reluctant to accept the fact that their children have disabilities, thereby requiring special education. These parents are afraid their children will be labeled as having a disability. Part of society viewed disability as a burden and shame, making many parents and guardians of children with disabilities, especially severe and visible disabilities, feel ashamed. As a result, researchers speculated, just as in the early history of special education in the United States and other countries, an unknown number of children with disabilities either stayed at home or were placed in care facilities without a chance of receiving education (KNISE, 2001). This is also related to the culture that disability brings shame to the family. As a result, if disability is not severe and/or more apparent, parents tend to ignore the fact that their children need special education. Because of these reasons, identified special education recipients in South Korea do not typically include learners with mild disabilities, but moderate and severe disabilities, ultimately resulting in more special classrooms and special schools. The ultimate purpose of special education in South Korea, as stated in SEIDOL (2007), is to help individuals with disabilities to achieve "self-realization" and "social inclusion" through "inclusive education" and "(individualized) education." Since 2013, Special education in South Korea has been allocating significant resources in finding, serving, and supporting learners with severe, significant, and/or multiple disabilities to meet this goal.

Most of the special schools serve learners with severe, significant, and/or multiple disabilities that meet the definition of LID. One hundred fifty-five (95.7%) out of 162 special schools serve students with severe, significant, and/or multiple disabilities: 12 special schools for visual impairment, 16 special schools for hearing impairment, 107 special schools for intellectual disabilities, and 20 special schools for physical impairment (Ministry of Education, 2013).

The exact number and percentage of learners with LID in South Korea is not readily available. However, data presented in the latest special education report provide a glimpse of LID's presence. As of 2013, 86,633 students (1.2% of 7,152,702 total students) are identified as special education recipients in South Korea. Following are the list of LID and their percentages compared to the total number of special education recipients. 2.6% of students out of 86,633 special education recipients are with visual impairment, 4.2% are with hearing impairment, 54.4% are with intellectual disabilities, 13% of students are with physical impairment, 10.1% are with autism, 2.5% are with health impairment, and 3.2% are with developmental delay (Table 1).

Therefore, the number of special education recipients identified with LID is 77,866 students, which is 89.9% of total special education recipients, and 1.09% of total number of students in South Korea.

INCLUSIVE EDUCATION FOR LEARNERS WITH LID IN SOUTH KOREA

As described in the history of special education in South Korea, new laws related to special education were developed and enacted, and periodically

Table 1. 2013 Inclusive Education Settings.

			Special Schools	Regular Schools		Special Education Support Center	Total (%)
				Special classroom	Regular classroom		
The number of students	Disability categories	Visual impairment	1,468	311	436	5	2,220 (2.6)
		Hearing impairment	1,053	821	1,774	18	3,666 (4.2)
		Intellectual disabilities	15,172	27,901	4,000	47	47,120 (54.4)
		Physical impairment	3,584	4,214	3,325	110	11,233 (13.0)
		Emotional behavioral disorder	279	1,760	715	–	2,754 (3.2)
		Autism	3,191	4,840	688	3	8,722 (10.1)
		Communication	113	907	925	8	1,953 (2.3)
		Learning disability	38	2,831	1,191	–	4,060 (4.7)
		Health impairment	33	335	1,788	1	2,157 (2.5)
		Developmental delay	207	1,261	1,088	192	2,748 (3.2)
		Total	25,138	45,181	15,930	384	86,633 (100)
	Grade levels	Infants	194	–	–	384	578
		Kindergarten	869	1,394	1,927	–	4,190
		Elementary	6,633	21,087	5,798	–	33,518
		Middle	6,293	12,023	3,925	–	22,241

Table 1. *(Continued)*

		Special Schools	Regular Schools		Special Education Support Center	Total (%)
			Special classroom	Regular classroom		
	High	7,555	10,631	4,280	–	22,466
	Job training	3,594	46	–	–	3,640
	Total	25,138	45,181	15,930	384	86,633
Special schools/centers		162	6,919 (45[a])	7,229	201	10,880
			10,517			
Special classrooms		4,269	9,343	(14,799)	46	13,658
Special education teacher		7,509	9,635	–	302	17,446
Assistance staffing		2,788	7,060	503	–	10,351

Source: Ministry of Education (2013).
[a]45 special classrooms are designated as all day self-contained classrooms.

amended and reenacted with updates to reflect best practices and current researches.

Inclusive education is one such an example. The importance and benefit of inclusive education was discussed and sporadically supported around the country for the past few decades. Though definitions for inclusive education varied among scholars and special educators, most agreed that it is about including children with disabilities in general education environment. It was not until 1994, when the Special Education Promotion Law of 1977 was updated and reenacted, that inclusive education was fully supported by the law and integrated into the existing special education structure in South Korea. The Special Education for Individuals with Disabilities and Others Law of 2007 (SEIDOL, 2007) provided further support for inclusive education. The most notable difference between SEPL and SEIDOL (2007) in conjunction with inclusive education was the purpose of the law. The Purpose Section of SEPL stated that the purpose of the law is to provide "appropriate and fair educational opportunities," and support "development of independent living skills," to help "stabilize the living condition" of a special education recipient and support their "participation in society". On the other hand, the Purpose Section of SEIDOL (2007) stated that the main focus of the law was to "provide inclusive education environment" and "(individualized) education" to help a person with disabilities to reach "self-realization" and "social inclusion" (SEIDOL, 2007). Thus, a greater emphasis has now been placed on inclusive education since the most recent laws provided language to support this movement.

When "inclusive education" appeared in the law for the first time in SEPL, the definition emphasized the location where inclusive education is provided.[3] In SEIDOL (2007), the definition of inclusive education emphasized the educational rights of an individual as much as the location for the inclusive education.[4] The purpose of inclusive education in these two laws was different as well. SEPL stated that inclusive education is implemented to "aid normal development of social skills of a special education recipient." Whereas SEIDOL (2007) stated that inclusive education is in place to support a special education recipient to "receive education appropriate to the individual's educational needs."

The exact number and percentage of learners with LID participating in inclusive education in regular schools can be calculated based on the data from Table 1. There are 6,919 special classrooms in regular schools. Forty-five of them are all day self-contained classrooms (the Ministry of Education, 2013). The remaining 6,874 special classrooms are resource rooms supporting learners with disabilities in regular schools. When combined, special education recipients, whether they have LID or other disabilities, in special classrooms and regular classrooms in regular schools are significantly larger than the number of learners with disabilities in special schools. Following is the list of LID and the percentages of learners with LID placed in either special classrooms or regular classrooms in regular schools compared to total number of learners with each LID category. 33.6% of learners with visual impairment, 71.3% learners with hearing impairment, 67.8% learners with intellectual disabilities, 68.1% of learners with physical impairment, 63.4% learners with autism, 98.5% learners with health impairment, and 92.5% learners with developmental delay participate in inclusive education in regular schools (Table 1).

TEACHER TRAINING AND CURRICULUM ADAPTATION FOR INCLUSIVE EDUCATION

With the number of identified learners with disabilities including LID increasing every year, improving the quality of special education became one of the top priorities. In addition to improving teacher preparation programs[5] at education universities, SEIDOL (2007) dictated that the local and national government must provide trainings and workshops to improve the quality of special education staff. The local and national government were also required to provide special education related trainings for regular teachers in regular schools to improve the quality of inclusive education. In response to the legal requirement, the local and national government have been providing special education-related trainings to special education teachers and regular teachers. According to 2013 Ministry of Education report, at the local level, special education-related in-service trainings were provided at the local department of education and at teacher preparation universities. At the national level, Korean National Institute for Special Education (KNISE)[6] has been providing online and offline teacher training.

Increasing the number of special education recipients also influenced the improvement of curriculum for learners with disabilities. SEPL specifically dictated that the curriculum of inclusive education needed to be the "regular school curriculum," stressing the importance of preparing and providing high-quality inclusive education. The National Curriculum, the legal name for the regular school curriculum, was modified and used to teach learners with disabilities in inclusive education settings.

SEIDOL (2007) redefined the curriculum used in inclusive education setting by asserting that it must provide "appropriate education according to the educational needs of individual." The National Curriculum became twofold: the General Curriculum and the Basic Curriculum. The General Curriculum is used for regular students in regular school. It can be modified for learners with disabilities in inclusive education setting. For example, the General Curriculum can be used for learners with visual or hearing impairments and intellectual disabilities, while modifying Language Art, English, and Physical Education according to the needs of learners. The Basic Curriculum includes alternative curriculum for learners with severe and significant intellectual disabilities (Kang, 2007).

SUCCESSFUL INCLUSIVE EDUCATION CASES FOR LEARNERS WITH LID

This section provides a few examples of successful inclusive education implementation for learners with LID, especially the ones with significant LID. These cases illustrate how special education services and supports were provided in general education settings and/or across different educational settings.

The first case focused on providing inclusive education for an elementary school learner with intellectual disabilities. The special education support team developed the plan not only to include the student physically in regular classroom but also to provide instructional modifications and co-teaching between general education teachers and special education teachers. Through collaboration, the teachers came up with two goals: improving the curriculum inclusion of the learner with intellectual disabilities and at the same time maintaining the rigor of curriculum for regular students. It was important for the teachers to understand the current developmental stage of the learner and the severity of the disability. The result was the development of a curriculum that met both the requirements of general education curriculum and the needs of the learner with intellectual disability. The improved curriculum provided the same assignments to students but required different levels of proficiency from students based on their abilities. This curriculum focused on the learner's abilities and needs but not deficiency (Japan National Special Support Education Research Institute, 2007).

The second case focused on collaboration between a special school and a regular school. This particular special school supported learners with severe intellectual disabilities from kindergarten to high school. To promote and provide inclusive education for its students, the school collaborated with a regular school, and developed and implemented various monthly inclusive education programs. The purpose of the collaboration was twofold. First, they wanted to provide regular students opportunities to get to know disabilities and improve their behaviors toward individuals with disabilities. Second, they would like to provide opportunities for students with disabilities to spend time and to experience positive interaction with peers. Building collaborative relationship between teachers from both schools proved to be worthwhile. They were able to observe the students' interactions and come up with solutions in a timely manner. For example, while running an inclusive activity, teachers noticed that regular students tended to dominate the activities. The reason was because students with intellectual disabilities were slow at understanding the process of the activity and exhibited low functional skills. The team of teachers discussed the ways to improve participation of the students with disabilities. They felt that they need to come up with various activity programs to reflect the interests and capacities of both groups. They also decided to provide preloading for students with disabilities so that they know what to expect from the activities. Preloading within a familiar setting helped the students with disabilities to get used to the contents of the activities and to learn necessary skills. The students with intellectual disabilities noticeably improved their participation during the actual activity (Seoul Jungjin School, 2012; The Korean Association for Special Education, 2014).

The third example focused on inclusive education effort for a learner with visual impairment. A school for visual impairment worked with a regular middle school to provide opportunities for their students to experience inclusive education in regular classrooms. Teachers on both sides received some preliminary training to develop and implement instructional strategies and curriculum for both groups of students. Through the inclusive education experience, the learners with visual impairment gained confidence in their learning and everyday lives. They also made new friends. Additional observation report revealed that students who were reserved tended to be less successful in inclusive education setting. Those who had communication and relationship building skills were more successful in the same setting. Some drawbacks of including learners with visual impairment in regular classrooms included the following: special education teachers felt that they were wasting too much instruction time in order to make inclusive education work; general education teachers were not fully aware of the needs of the learners with visual impairment; and the increased classroom size and the noise level incurred with inclusive education for learners with visual impairment (Kang, 2006).

Providing inclusive education for learners with LID is challenging yet rewarding for all participants including learners, teachers, and other stakeholders. Focusing on learners' needs and abilities will improve chances of success.

FUTURE OF INCLUSIVE EDUCATION FOR LEARNERS WITH LID

South Korea has made tremendous gains in promoting inclusive education for learners with LID; however, the country still has a long way to go. Educators involved in special education and regular education, parents, students, and the society as a whole will need to work together to realize the full potential of inclusive education. Following are some of the major efforts toward that goal.

To ensure the success of inclusive education, South Korea will continue to improve its educational environment in regular schools to build a strong foundation for inclusive education. Current and future efforts are focused on improving and expanding the curriculum, developing instructional materials and tools, and strengthening the sense of responsibility of the general education teachers who work with learners with LID. Furthermore, developing and implementing evaluation systems to enforce the laws related to special education to measure progress will assist in the inclusive education efforts (KNISE, 2011).

A greater emphasis has been placed on the early child find program and the need for early intervention (KNISE, 1999; Korea Institute of Child Care and Education, 2012). In addition, families and educators have a greater awareness of these efforts resulting from the movement to disseminate this information to ensure children are diagnosed and provided with early intervention to improve outcomes. Early childhood teachers are provided with in-service training to ensure they are knowledgeable about the most effective research-based intervention strategies (KNISE, 2003a; You & Park, 2007). Comprehensive inclusive education programs for infants and toddlers with disabilities are being developed and implemented on a wide-scale basis. In addition, a method for transition planning from preschool to kindergarten has been instituted to assist children and families during the process. Curriculum for special education recipients is constantly being evaluated and updated to help these learners achieve their dreams and their full potential (Choi, 2011).

Efforts to improve the teacher preparation programs to effectively teach students with diverse needs are continuing. The teacher evaluation process is being reviewed and updated periodically to improve special education teachers' expertise and professionalism (KNISE, 2013b). More and more teachers are participating in team teaching to improve their skills and to facilitate better inclusive education (KINSE, 2012). The National Government and the Ministry of Education are continually providing disability awareness programs and activities, including developing disability awareness dramas, photo contests, movies, writing contests, and music concerts to create and improve the environment for inclusive education (KNISE, 2003b, 2003c, 2013a). Some additional efforts to improve inclusive education include strengthening special education-related services and after school activities; diversifying special education assistance staffing and improving human resource management structure; improving supports for special education assistive technology; supporting parents and family; supporting safer transportation to and from school; providing career and occupational training; and improving access to higher education (Kim, 2006).

Despite efforts to improve inclusive education, there are still some reports of incidents of discrimination based upon disability. These reports identify the lack of curriculum modification; provision of assistive technology; assignment of personnel to support the needs; and disability awareness of school staff as main reasons for incidents of discrimination. (Kang, Kwon, Kim, & Kim, 2000; KNISE, 2006)

CONCLUSION

In this chapter, we discussed the historical background and development of special education system in South Korea. The special education system in South Korea has made significant gains since the enactment of SEPL (1977). Through reauthorization of SEPL and enactment of SEIDOL (2007), South Korea improved, redefined, and refocused its special education system. One of the most important outcomes of this successive progression of legal development is a greater emphasis on inclusive education for learners with LID.

The popularity of inclusive education has continued since the 1990s. The number of special education recipients attending special classrooms and regular inclusive classrooms in regular schools has continued to rise as well. More special classrooms equated to more opportunities for inclusive education. In 2013, about 70.5% of special education recipients attended regular classrooms and the special classrooms in regular schools. However, increases in the numbers of learners with disabilities attending inclusive education settings does not necessarily mean that the quality of inclusive education is improving.

The direction that inclusive education in South Korea is taking is unique with many ramifications and implications. With more special schools and special classrooms installed each year, thereby providing more educational options for parents and learners with LID, time will tell whether South Korean style of inclusive education for learners with LID will result in better educational outcomes.

KEY TERMS

Early child find system – A system to identify children with disabilities.

E-Learning – Short for "Electronic Learning." The term is used in South Korea to describe "Online Learning." The concept is to enable instruction and communication through Internet to improve learning of participants.

Ministry of Culture and Education, Ministry of Education, and Ministry of Education, Science, and Technology – These are all different names for the government agency overseeing education in South Korea. As of 2014, the name is Ministry of Education.

Occupational rehabilitation training – Training that focuses on learning and improving job-related functions, performance, and skills.

Therapeutic education services – Services including occupational therapy, physical therapy, speech therapy, hearing training, fine motor training, psychological and behavioral therapy, walking training, and daily living skills training. These services were provided in schools before SEIDOL (2007) removed them from school. Learners with disabilities are still able to receive these services after school from outside service providers.

Special education-related services – SEIDOL (2007) defined it as "providing services, including human resources and material resources, to enable efficient delivery of education for special education recipients." The related services also include family supports and a provision for assistive technology.

Special classroom – Same as "resource room." It is a classroom established in regular schools to support learners with disabilities placed in inclusive education setting in regular schools.

Special education recipients – Students and learners who are diagnosed with disabilities, evaluated for educational needs related to the disabilities and selected to receive special education.

Special school – Schools established outside of regular schools to support learners with disabilities. Most of the special schools serve learners with severe, significant, and/or multiple disabilities that meet the definition of LID.

The Special Education Operation Committee – A group that oversees selecting, placing, and providing services for special education recipients. The leader of the committee is selected from the leaders of LEA. Committee members consist of special education teachers, parents, educational public servants, and others who have experience working with learners with disabilities.

The Special Education Support Center – First established during the Second Five-Year Plan of Special Education Improvement (2003–2007) with limited services. SEIDOL (2007) provided a legal basis for the center's operation, enabling it to expand and provide various special education related services for learners with disabilities.

The Student with Disabilities Support Center – Centers established within postsecondary education facilities including universities and colleges to support education and daily living of learners with disabilities.

NOTES

1. "E-learning" is short for "Electronic Learning." The term is used in South Korea to describe "Online Learning." The concept is to enable instruction and communication through Internet to improve learning of participants (Kim, 2012).
2. "The Special Education Support Center" is established within the boundaries of local educational agencies to support early-find of special education recipients and their diagnosis and evaluation. The center also manages data related to the special education recipients and provides special education training, instructions and study supports, special education related services, and itinerant education (Special Education for Individuals with Disabilities and Others Law [SEIDOL], 2007).
3. Section 2, Definition 6 of Special Education Promotion Law Amended of 1994 states "Inclusive education is defined as, educating a special education recipient in regular school environment, or allowing a current student who attends a special

education agency to participate in regular school curriculum, to aid normal development of social skills of a special education recipient."

4. Section 2, Definition 6 of Special Education for Individuals with Disabilities and Others Law of 2007 states, "Inclusive Education means that a special education recipient receives appropriate education according to the educational needs of individual within regular school without discrimination based on categories and/or severity of disabilities."

5. Education universities that provide teacher preparation programs have been improving their curriculum for future teachers. Taking selected special education courses became a graduation and certification requirement for future general education teachers.

6. Korea Nation Institute for Special Education (KNISE) is a government educational agency founded in 1994. KNISE focuses on improving special education. It provides researches, and online and offline teacher training, and develops curriculum and instructional materials related to special education.

REFERENCES

Choi, H. Y. (2011). A review of students concerning instructional adaptations to promote curricular inclusion for students with disabilities. *Special Education Research*, *10*, 5–24.

Chung, C. C., & Lee, H. K. (2006). A base study on the education and living services program for college students with disabilities. *The Journal of Special Education: Theory and Practice*, *7*, 507–533.

Digest of Education Statistics. (2012). Retrieved from http://nces.ed.gov/programs/digest/. Accessed on August 1, 2014.

Individuals with Disabilities Education Act. (2004). 20 U.S.C. § 662.

Japan National Special Support Education Research Institute. (2007). Mokpo Imsung Elementary School: Promoting inclusive education through curriculum support program. Collection of South Korea-Japan Special Education Seminar Resources, Japan National Special Support Education Research Institute.

Kang, K. S. (2006). Education for children with visual impairment in regular schools. *The 9th Asia-Pacific Regional Conference.*

Kang, K. S. (2007). Development and validation of a model for implementing inclusion of students with disabilities in elementary schools focused on curriculum implementation. *Journal of Korean Special Education*, *41*, 107–132.

Kang, K. Y., Kwon, T. H., Kim, E. J., & Kim, S. Y. (2000). *A field study on the implementation and maintenance of inclusive education in three schools.* Seoul: Korean National Institute for Special Education.

Kim, B. H., & Kim, T. Y. (2011). Establishment of East-Asian special education for rebuilding education essentials. *The Journal of Special Education: Theory and Practice*, *12*, 71–92.

Kim, B. H., Lee, K. Y., & Kim, T. Y. (2011). Korean special education and Daegu university: History, phenomenon, and issues. *The Journal of Special Education: Theory and Practice*, *10*, 323–342.

Kim, H. J. (2006). Inclusive education for children with multiple disabilities in Korea. *Journal of Special Education in the Asia Pacific*, *3*, 18–29.

Kim, S. W. (2012). *E-learning 2.0 and education*. Seoul: Yangseowon.

Korea Institute of Child Care and Education. (2012). *The study on advanced supportive ways for inclusive child care and education*. Seoul: Korea Institute of Child Care and Education.

Korean National Institute for Special Education. (1999). *A study of expanding special education for infant*. Seoul: Korean National Institute for Special Education.

Korean National Institute for Special Education. (2001). *A study on strategies for early-find and evaluating infant and toddler*. Seoul: Korean National Institute for Special Education.

Korean National Institute for Special Education. (2003a). *Collaboration strategies among educational agencies to improve education for infant and toddler with disabilities*. Seoul: Korean National Institute for Special Education.

Korean National Institute for Special Education. (2003b). *Disability awareness education for kindergarten and elementary schools*. Seoul: Korean National Institute for Special Education.

Korean National Institute for Special Education. (2003c). *Disability awareness education for middle schools and high schools*. Seoul: Korean National Institute for Special Education.

Korean National Institute for Special Education. (2004). *A study on improving the current structure of finding, evaluating, and placing children with disabilities for special education*. Seoul: Korean National Institute for Special Education.

Korean National Institute for Special Education. (2005a). *A study on operating the Special Education Support Center*. Seoul: Korean National Institute for Special Education.

Korean National Institute for Special Education. (2005b). *A study on the current status and improving therapeutic education*. Seoul: Korean National Institute for Special Education.

Korean National Institute for Special Education. (2006). *A study on the status of students with special education needs placed in regular schools*. Seoul: Korean National Institute for Special Education.

Korean National Institute for Special Education. (2007). *Findings on needs and supports for the special education related services*. Seoul: Korean National Institute for Special Education.

Korean National Institute for Special Education. (2009). *A field study on improving efficiency of the special education support center operation*. Seoul: Korean National Institute for Special Education.

Korean National Institute for Special Education. (2010). *Special education report*. Seoul: Korean National Institute for Special Education.

Korean National Institute for Special Education. (2011). *A study on strategies for early-find and evaluating infant and toddler*. Seoul: Korean National Institute for Special Education.

Korean National Institute for Special Education. (2012). *Guide for general education teachers to utilize inclusive education instructional strategies for infants with disabilities*. Seoul: Korean National Institute for Special Education.

Korean National Institute for Special Education. (2013a). *A study on culture and art education and support strategies for students with disabilities*. Seoul: Korean National Institute for Special Education.

Korean National Institute for Special Education. (2013b). *A study on preparing special education teachers*. Seoul: Korean National Institute for Special Education.

Korean Society of Special Education. (1995). *100-year history of special education in Korea*. Seoul: Special Education Publisher.

Korean Society for Rehabilitation of Persons with Disabilities. (2006). *50-year history of welfare for persons with disabilities in Korea*. Seoul: Yangseowon.

Lee, W. R., & Lee, H. W. (2004). A study on understanding of characteristics of learning disabilities for persons attended at the study and training on special education. *Journal of Korean Special Education*, *5*, 407–425.

Ministry of Culture and Education. (1988). *40 years history of the culture and education*. Seoul: Ministry of Culture and Education.

Ministry of Education. (2013). *The 2013 Special education yearly report*. Seoul: SunMyung Print.

Ministry of Education, Science, and Technology. (2008). *The third 5 year plan of special education improvement to promote self-fulfillment of persons with disabilities and uniting society*. Seoul: Department of Special Education Support.

Seoul Jungjin School. (2012). *A study on active participation of students with disabilities in inclusive education*. Seoul: Jungjin School.

Special Education for Individuals with Disabilities and Others Law. (2007). Pub. L. No. 12127. South Korea.

Special Education Promotion Law. (1977). Pub. L. No. 5440. South Korea.

The Korean Association for Special Education. (2014). *Collection of successful inclusive education*. Seoul: The Korean Association for Special Education.

You, E. Y., & Park, J. Y. (2007). The effects of a teacher training on inclusion on the teachers' personal teaching efficacy and teaching performance. *The Korean Journal of Early Childhood Special Education*, *7*, 1–19.

INCLUSIVE EDUCATION IN POLAND: POLICIES, PRACTICES, AND PERSPECTIVES

Kinga M. Ober, Andrzej Twardowski and Melinda R. Pierson

ABSTRACT

This chapter focuses on the special education system of education in Poland since the transformation of the political system in the late 1980s. The move from segregated settings toward more integrated settings for students with low-incidence disabilities is described along with the new structure of special education identification and classroom settings. Current strategies and support for students with high-incidence disabilities in Poland who are placed in general education and special education are discussed. Ideas on how to improve the existing system are outlined and solutions are presented. Overall, the implementation of educational reforms brought about positive changes in educational settings for most students identified with special needs in Poland. Due to this emphasis on inclusion, more students with high-incidence disabilities have the chance to succeed in integrated schools with adequate support.

Keywords: Inclusion; integration; segregation; Poland; international education

Including Learners with Low-Incidence Disabilities
International Perspectives on Inclusive Education, Volume 5, 315–339

ISSN: 1479-3636/doi:10.1108/S1479-363620140000005024

INTRODUCTION

In this chapter, the contemporary state of the Polish education system is presented, focusing mainly on the services and strategies for supporting the development of children with low-incidence disabilities. The historical background of the reforms that had led to the transformation of segregated educational settings to more inclusive settings are detailed. Subsequently, the structure of special education in Poland is introduced along with current solutions with explanations of available support. In the last two sections, unresolved dilemmas and challenges of special education are addressed. This chapter is guided by two main questions:

1. What kind of support and services are available for children with low-incidence disabilities in Poland?
2. What areas in the field of special education in Poland are still omitted, unresolved, and how we can improve the system using the available resources?

Poland as a developing country has gone through many political and cultural changes. These changes are also visible in the field of education and especially special education after joining the European Union in 2004 and, prior to that, with the 2012 ratification of the Convention on Rights for Persons with Disabilities (CRPD).

PATHWAYS TO INCLUSION

The history of inclusive education for children with disabilities in Poland is preceded by the tradition of building integration education, which dates back to the early 1970s and 1980s. Up until the 1990s, the only available option for children with low-incidence disabilities was enrollment in special schools in fully segregated settings (Holowinsky, 1975, 1981). This idea of integration was popularized by Aleksander Hulek who made a significant contribution to the development of inclusive education in Poland (1977, 1983). The period of political transformation from the communist time to the current democratic system, which began in 1989, brought new legislation that paved a new pathway in Poland's field of special education to restructure all schools for integration. Furthermore, efforts then focused on creating an adequate developmental and educational environment to help children with disabilities fully participate in different aspects of social life.

Practical realization of integration meant that changes were needed not only in the social perception of disability but also must be reflected in the regulations of education law and other political acts (Rudek, 2009).

The educational reforms which assisted in adjusting education for children with low-incidence disabilities from a segregated educational model to a more inclusive one in Poland are The Education System Act in 1991, Reform of School System in 1999, and Core Curriculum in 2002 (Journal of Laws of Republic of Poland (JLRP), 1991, 1999, 2002). The Education System Act (JLRP, 1991) was the first decree that implemented the idea of inclusion to an educational reality, even though the term integration or inclusion is not specifically mentioned in this ordinance. According to the provisions of this act, all children have the right to an education that meets their needs and capabilities. The most important portions of the law that referred to children with disabilities were (1) the opportunity to attend all types of schools according to a student's developmental and educational needs or predispositions; (2) the individualized educational program must be followed so that students with disabilities receive additional support services such as speech and language or occupational therapy support groups; and (3) adjustment of the content, methods, and forms of teaching to address the individual psychophysical abilities of each child.

The significant impact on the development of inclusive educational settings in Poland was also influenced by the School System Reform Act (JLRP, 1999). The requirement of the eight years of primary school was adjusted to six years of primary education followed by three years of gymnasium (lower secondary school) (Fig. 2). After children complete the lower secondary school, they continue their education in academic or vocational upper secondary schools (OECD Education Working Papers, 2010). This act included all children, even those with low-incidence disabilities which then paved the way for this population to be educated in more integrated settings.

These changes in the school structure were accompanied by curricular reform with the introduction to the concept of core curriculum (The Regulation on the Core Curriculum, JLRP, 2002). This gave schools more autonomy in choosing educational programs. Teachers were given the exceptional opportunity to create their own programs. Teachers could then use more inclusive strategies for their students that were struggling learners and those identified as having special educational needs.

Regardless of the criticism of the 1999 reform by researchers and professors in education, especially those pointing to the unpreparedness of schools and teachers (Denek, 2005; Kupisiewicz, 2006; Putkiewicz & Zahorska, 1999), this reform was the first step in creating equal educational opportunities for all children despite their developmental disabilities. All of these initiated reforms focus on the improvement of the quality of education, building early intervention systems, and psychological counseling which facilitates children's development.

MODELS FOR INTEGRATION IN POLAND

These changes were visible not only in the field of educational legislation but also in the theoretical perception and understanding of ideas of integration and inclusion. The term integration (*integracja*) can be understood in three different ways revealing levels of participation of children with disabilities in mainstream education. This way of interpreting inclusion created three separate models of educational setting:

1. *Full integration* – All children with disabilities are to be taught in mainstreamed settings. Full integration in this sense can be perceived as inclusion. Segregated schools for students with disabilities do not exist in this model.
2. *Incomplete integration* – Only students with mild disabilities should be included in the mainstreamed educational setting. Children with severe disabilities are still taught in special schools.
3. *Partial integration* – Children with disabilities can be taught in special schools or mainstreamed schools, but the decision about the school setting is made by taking into account the needs, well-being, and welfare of the child (Krause, 2010; Pańczyk, 1999; Szumski, 2006).

The incomplete integration perspective defines the severity of disability as the main criteria of choosing the educational pathway. This perception of disability is derived straight from the medical model in which all the efforts are concentrated on adapting the person with disabilities to the social reality, without any attempt to change the environment to make it more accessible for one with disability (Wdowik, 2009). This is in contrast to the partial integration perspective, which states that the needs of children with disabilities come first. Knowing the needs of children with disabilities, specialists are searching for the most optimal developmental environment in which children will be able to excel. Differences in understanding the meaning of the term integration presented above do not overshadow its main goal, which is "to counteract segregation and insulation tendencies and to disapprove stigmatization or intolerance" (Dykcik, 1998, p. 330).

From the legal point of view, the current Polish educational policy for children with disabilities fits with the partial integration model because different forms of education (special vs. integration vs. mainstream) coexist together. From history, it is evident that Poland is moving toward an inclusive model of education for students with low-incidence disabilities but more work must be done to make sure this goal is fully implemented.

THE CONTEMPORARY STRUCTURE OF SPECIAL EDUCATION IN POLAND

Special education and support is designed and devoted to students experiencing different developmental difficulties including children with (1) socially maladjusted or with behavior disorders, (2) specific learning difficulties, (3) gifted, (4) speech and communication disorders, (5) chronic illnesses, (6) experiencing crisis or trauma, (7) experiencing educational failure due to educationally deprived environment, and (8) experiencing adaptation difficulties in a Polish school setting after finishing education abroad (The Ordinance of the Minister of Education on the Principles of Providing and Organizing Education and Psychological Counseling, JLRP, 2010).

Definitions and Categories of Special Education in Poland

According to Polish legislation, the definition of a child with a disability is "one in which the doctor has diagnosed abnormal development, inborn defects or disabilities. He/she has a valid certificate of disability, as defined by the Act of Rehabilitation" (The Act on Vocational and Social Rehabilitation and Employment of Persons with Disabilities, JLRP, 1997) and/or a "recommendation issued by the Public Psychological and Educational Counseling Center documenting the need for special education services" (Chrzanowska, 2010, p. 46). The categories of disability, according to the decrees of the Ministry of National Education are as follows: deaf, hard of hearing, blind, visual impairment, motor impairment and aphasia, mild mental retardation, moderate or severe mental retardation, autism and Asperger's syndrome, and multiple disabilities (The Regulation on Education and Care for Children and Youths with Disabilities, JLRP, 2010a,b). In all legal documents, the term intellectual disability is continuously replaced by the stigmatizing term "mental retardation," even though the scientific literature on intellectual disability in Poland does not recommend it (Cytowska, 2002).

For educational purposes, the only legal diagnosis is the one issued by the decision of the Public Psychological and Educational Counseling Center. The certificate of disability is required when parents want to apply for additional help from social services (Leśniewska & Puchała, 2010). In general, the definition of disability in Poland differs from one legal act to another. This situation often can lead to misunderstandings and confusion, especially when parents are trying to gain more appropriate and specialized help (Szeroczyńska, 2008). For example, a child may have a valid certificate of disability issued by the Regional Center for Assessment of Disability, but without the decision and further diagnosis conducted by the Public Psychological and Educational Counseling Center, will not be eligible for additional support in school. Some authors highlight the need of centralizing and delegating responsibility of certification of disability to one institution, which will decide what type of help and support are necessary on all levels of functioning (social, medical, educational), (Wdowik, 2009).

Laws Surrounding the Education of Children with Disabilities

Three decrees issued by The Ministry of National Education regulate the rules of education for children with disabilities:

1. *The Regulation on Education and Care for Children and Youth with Disabilities and Socially Maladjusted* – devoted to education and support offered in segregated educational setting (JLRP, 2010);
2. *The Regulation on Education and Care for Children and Youth with Disabilities and Socially Maladjusted* – devoted to education and support offered in integration and mainstream setting (JLRP, 2010);
3. *The Regulation on the Organization of Remedial Classes for Children with Profound Mental Retardation* – devoted to planning education, rehabilitation and care for children with profound intellectual disabilities (JLRP, 2013).

The system of education for children with disabilities in Poland can be thought of as pluralistic. This means that different paths in education coexist together (Kogut, 2010; Wyczesany & Gajdzica, 2006). It is also known as a "differentiated educational system for everybody" (Głodkowska, 2010, p. 39) or multi – track approach (EADSNE, 2003). Thus, children and adolescents with disabilities can participate in three forms of education: segregation, integration, and mainstreamed schooling (see Fig. 1). These forms of educational settings are available for all children regardless of the disability and the severity of disability.

Description of School Settings

Segregated education is implemented in special schools or special classes (in mainstreamed schools) which are dedicated exclusively for students with a particular type of disability. The number of children in these special classes depends on the type of disability. In classes for children with autism and Asperger's syndrome and for children with multiple disabilities, up to four are placed in each class. In classes for students who are deaf or hard of

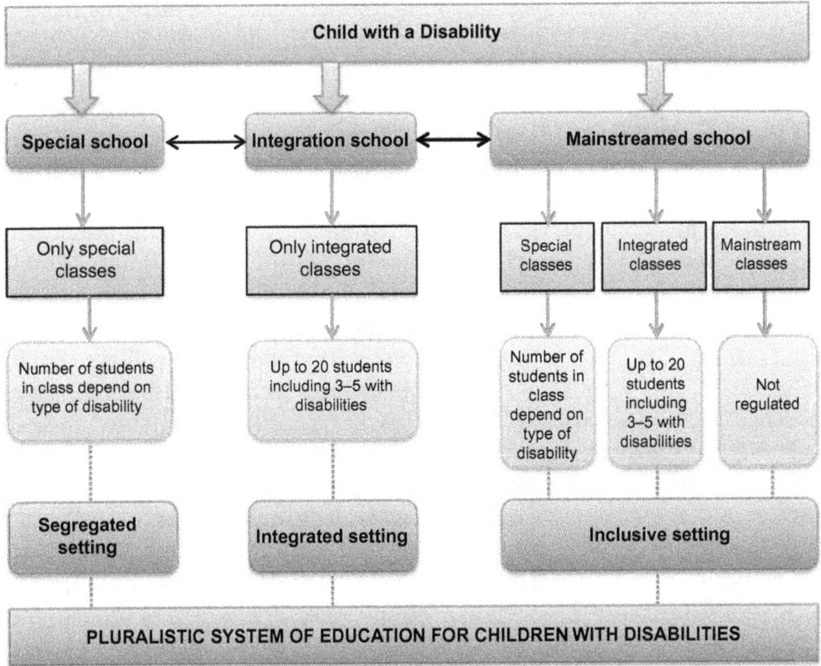

Fig. 1. Structure of Special Education in Poland.

hearing and with moderate or severe disabilities, up to eight students are placed in each class. In classes for children who are blind or who have a visual impairment, 10 students can be enrolled in the class. In classes for children with motor disabilities and aphasia, up to 12 students can be enrolled and for children with mild intellectual disability (learning disabilities), up to 16 total students can be placed in the class (The Regulation on the Framework Statute of Public Kindergartens and Schools, JLPR, 2001). In special settings, all teachers need to have special qualifications enabling them to work with children with disabilities.

Integrated education occurs when children with and without disabilities are placed in the same school or classroom. There are distinct rules which define the educational setting as one that is integrated. Integrated classrooms consist of no more than 20 students and approximately 3–5 children with disabilities. However, children may vary in the type of disabilities in one classroom such as one may have visual impairment, one may have a motor impairment, two may have autism, and one may have an intellectual disability (JLPR, 2001). This rule is directly derived from the Hamburgian integration model which originated in Germany that mandates the integration of children with disabilities into mainstream classes (Gajdzica, 2008). In the integrated classroom, the second teacher who is called the supportive teacher is responsible for providing accommodations and modifications for the students with disabilities (JLRP, 2010b). The supportive teacher must have additional qualifications in special education to work in an integrated class or school.

In the mainstreamed system, which is similar to inclusion, children with and without disabilities are taught in the same classroom. In Polish schools, inclusion is created by merging children with disabilities into a mainstreamed setting. The most problematic point in the mainstreamed system results from the lack of legal regulation that does not obligate mainstreamed schools to employ supportive teachers or any other teachers with special education preparation and does not regulate how many children with and without disabilities can participate in the same classroom.

Students can switch between these types of settings after graduating from each stage of education. For instance, the student can begin his/her education in a special kindergarten and then continue education in an integrated primary school and mainstreamed lower secondary school. In this sense, the multitrack approach can be perceived as elastic and adjusting to students' needs.

In addition to the knowledge of the structure and types of educational settings available for children with disabilities in Poland, it is important to highlight how the structure of teaching and participation is in integrated and mainstreamed setting. The participation is based on the level of one's disability because children with different levels of intellectual disability follow different core curriculum and courses. Children with mild intellectual disability such as a learning disability follow the same core curriculum as children without disabilities. Children with moderate and severe intellectual disabilities follow a separate core curriculum (JLRP, 2002). Because of varying curriculum, children with different levels of disability participate in different courses. In integrated settings, students with moderate and severe disabilities can participate with their peers' full-time, but they follow different curriculum. Because of the presence of the supportive teacher, students with disabilities spend more time in the main classroom. Mainstreamed settings are different because there is only one teacher, very often without qualifications to work with children with disabilities. It is common that students with disabilities have little classroom involvement in mainstreamed settings due to the lack of specialized curriculum.

Students with profound disabilities and frequently low-incidence disabilities do not follow core curriculum, and they are enrolled in specially organized classes. Remedial classes are the activities designed especially for students with profound disabilities to help them participate in as many daily activities as possible. The classes are organized in various educational settings including kindergartens and schools (special or mainstreamed), educational centers, rehabilitation and educational centers, social welfare homes (residential care), healthcare centers, and at home. The form of these classes can be group (2–4 participants) or individual. Individual classes are dedicated for children who for medical reasons cannot participate in group activities. If the child is qualified for group remedial classes, he or she can participate in 20 hours of different activities per week. Students who qualify for individual remedial classes can receive services for 10 hours per week. The goal of remedial classes is to support the student especially in the areas of communication and independence (JLRP, 2013).

Compulsory Education for All

In Poland, education is now compulsory for all children, despite the severity of the disability. Compulsory schooling includes children between age 5 and 18 (JLRP, 1999; see Fig. 2).

Compulsory schooling begins at the age of five with one year of preschool preparation in kindergarten. Afterward, children continue education

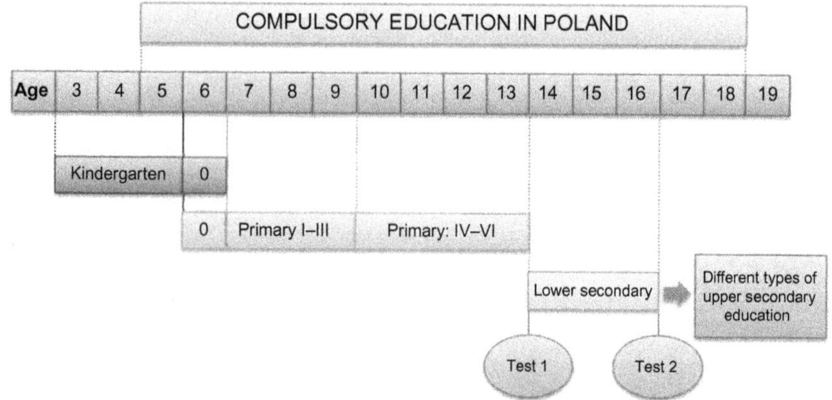

Fig. 2. Compulsory Education in Poland.

in the zero class in schools or kindergartens. According to new regulations, the zero classes will be removed gradually and children will begin primary school at the age of six in year 2015 (JLRP, 2012). Full-time education in primary school is divided in two stages. The first stage comprises classes I–III and offers integrated early school education and is followed by the second stage (classes IV–VI) based on subject teaching. At the end of primary school, students complete an assessment demonstrating their general knowledge. If students test high enough, they will be allowed to enter the general lower secondary school (equivalent to American middle schools). At the end of this school experience, students must pass another mandatory external examination. Children with moderate, severe, or profound intellectual disabilities are exempt from taking both compulsory examinations. Students with other types of disabilities such as blindness or deafness take the placement exams with accommodations. At all levels from kindergarten to lower secondary school, schools can be organized as special, integrated, or mainstreamed (EURYDICE, 2012).

Accessibility to upper secondary education (equivalent to American high school) is more dependent of one's level of disability. Students with disabilities such as physical disabilities, deafness, or blindness can choose between a four-year technical or four-year general (academic) upper secondary school. Students with mild intellectual disabilities can attend four-year basic vocational schools, which lead to obtaining qualification in specific occupations. Students with moderate and severe intellectual disabilities may continue their education in three-year special job training schools which prepare them for independence. Due to psychophysical conditions, some of the students with moderate and severe intellectual disabilities continue their education in occupational workshops, environmental home care centers, or daily activities centers (Klaro-Celej, 2012).

The requirement of compulsory education can be delayed in the case of children with disabilities. This delay can be due to different circumstances. In most cases, it is the consequence of health issues of the child with disabilities but very often is also dictated by the parents' fear that the child is not ready to move from a kindergarten education to a school setting. Students with disabilities can attend primary school up until the age of 18. Similarly, the age limit applies to the lower secondary and secondary schools. Students can attend the gymnasium until the age of 21. Lastly, students can attend upper secondary school until the age of 23. This age limit applies to all three educational settings (special, integrated, and mainstreamed) (JLRP, 2012a,b). The age limit is different in regard to students with profound intellectual disabilities. They can participate in remedial classes between the ages of 3 and 25 (JLRP, 2013).

Tiers of Education for Children with Disabilities in Poland

In Poland, three different tiers of education are available for children with disabilities. Recommendation for a particular type of school is issued by the Public Psychological and Educational Counseling Center. After assessment by a specialist, the most appropriate placement is determined. The final decision about the type of school in which the child with a disability will attend is ultimately made by the parents (according to The Education System Act enacted in September of 1991 [with further amendments], art. 71b, para. 5a). Many authors point out that this choice is often illusory, because mainstream schools refuse to take responsibility of children with disabilities, arguing that it will be better for a child to attend a special setting which is more accessible and prepared for meeting the needs of this group of students (Ciura & Osiecka-Chojnacka, 2013; Lempart, 2012; Wdowik, 2009).

School Attendance Data in Poland

In 2011–2012 in Poland, there were over three million students in primary schools and about 1.2 million attending the lower secondary schools

(Central Statistical Office in Poland [CSO], 2012). Primary schools served 58,500 students (20,400 girls) with special educational needs. They accounted for 2.7% of the overall primary school population. Most of the children with disabilities were educated in mainstreamed school settings (56.9%). The remaining were placed in integration schools (40.8%) or in special schools (2.3%). There were 4,200 children with disabilities, who could not attend school for various reasons, mainly due to health issues. They fulfilled the compulsory education obligation, where individual instruction was given to them at home by teachers. In lower secondary schools, there were 51,600 students (18,800 girls) with disabilities. They accounted for 4.3% of the overall student population attending on this stage. Most of them were educated in mainstreamed school settings (62.1%). The remaining students with disabilities were in integration schools (33.3%) or in special schools (4.5%). There were a total of 2,900 children with disabilities who were given individual instruction at home.

Comparing these two levels of education, one can observe an increasing number of lower secondary-aged children in mainstreamed settings, in conjunction with an increasing number of children in special schools. This demonstrates that the integrated schools are more accessible for students at the primary level of education. It is due to the number of integrated schools which is higher at the primary level than at the secondary level (Dudzińska, 2009; Kummant, 2008). In 2011–2012, only 346 youths with disabilities in Poland were qualified to enroll in upper secondary schools. Most of the youth with disabilities taught on this level of education attended special vocational schools (14,095 students), special job training schools (10,356 students), or special technical schools (586 students) (CSO, 2012). In 2011, 26% of students with disabilities finished their education at lower secondary schools, 41% at basic vocational schools, 6% at general upper secondary schools, 18% at technical schools, and 9% on higher levels (CSO, 2012).

School options for children with disabilities in Poland have shifted throughout the years since the advent of Polish educational reforms. These changes are documented in Tables 1 for primary level of education and Table 2 for secondary level. The open educational setting is more accessible for younger children. At the secondary level in school year 2010–2011 still 55% of children were taught in special schools compared to 39% at the primary level.

In 1990, there was a decrease in the number of children with disabilities in special schools. This process began to slow down and stabilize at about 40% for primary schools and 55% in lower secondary schools. There are

Table 1. Number of Primary School Aged Children with Disabilities in Different Forms of Educational Settings.

School Year	Number of Children with SEN	Forms of Organization[a]			
		Special primary schools	Special division mainstream in primary school	Integration school	Mainstream primary school
1990–1991	101,680	84,317	17,363	X[b]	X
1995–1996	95,806	82,999	6,613	2,036	4,158
2000–2001	100,014	52,020	3,207	6,897	37,890
2005–2006	75,552	33,209	1,450	13,578	28,315
2010–2011	61,211	24,459	1,725	14,539	20,488

[a]Data processed by the *Central Statistical Office in Poland (CSO)* (2011).
[b]Before the school year 1991–1992, children with disabilities were taught only in special schools.

Table 2. Number of Gymnasium (Lower Secondary School) Aged Children with Disabilities in Different Forms of Educational Settings.

School Year	Number of Children with SEN	Forms of Organization[a]			
		Special gymnasium	Special division in mainstreamed gymnasium	Integrated gymnasium	Mainstreamed gymnasium
2000–2001[b]	48,550	30,367	1,672	1,109	15,432
2005–2006	64,075	35,649	1,813	5,225	21,388
2010–2011	53,956	29,733	1,826	7,811	14,586

[a]Data processed by *CSO* (2011).
[b]Reforms in Polish education in 1999 introduced the gymnasium (lower secondary schools).

significant differences in the available forms of education, depending on the size of the village. In rural and suburban areas, education of children with disabilities takes place in mainstreamed schools. In urban areas, students are educated more frequently in special and integrated schools. The number of primary special schools has increased since 1990 from 779 to 786 in 2012, but the number of children with disabilities attending primary schools has decreased by half. Attendance at special lower secondary schools has increased from 753 in 2000 to 830 in 2012. There have been stable levels of children with disabilities in recent years at this stage of education (Ciura & Osiecka – Chojnacka, 2013).

Contemporary trends in Polish special education can be summarized as follows: (1) the number of children with low-incidence disabilities attending mainstream schools is increasing (this change is more visible at the primary stage of education); (2) the number of special education classes in mainstreamed schools is decreasing; (3) the number of children with low-incidence disabilities in special schools is decreasing; and (4) students attending special schools are mostly children with moderate or severe intellectual disabilities (Twardowski, 2005).

SUPPORTING THE DEVELOPMENT OF CHILDREN WITH DISABILITIES

The Main Educational Act, which details the rules for supporting children with disabilities is *The Ordinance of the Minister of Education on the Principles of Providing and Organizing Educational and Psychological Counseling (JLPR, 2010)*. All types of educational institutions in Poland are obligated to support the psychological and educational needs of children who are vulnerable and at risk for disabilities. Parents and teachers can obtain help in the form of consultation in Public Psychological and Educational Counseling Centers. All the support and assistance offered is unsolicited and free of charge (Fig. 3).

The main task of this team is the preparation of the individualized educational program (IEP) and recommendations for additional assistance and support. All IEPs are prepared for one educational stage and should be re-evaluated once a year after the student is re-assessed. This additional support for the student may include the following:

(1) *Therapeutic sessions* – these classes are organized in mainstreamed schools for children with disabilities who need extensive support and special curriculum. The number of children attending therapeutic sessions is limited to 15.
(2) *Programs for gifted children* – teachers utilize active teaching methods in these classes for intellectually gifted children. In each gifted program, no more than eight children can participate.
(3) *Didactic and compensatory classes* – children with learning disabilities who are struggling with core curriculum requirements attend these classes. The number of children attending these classes is limited to eight.

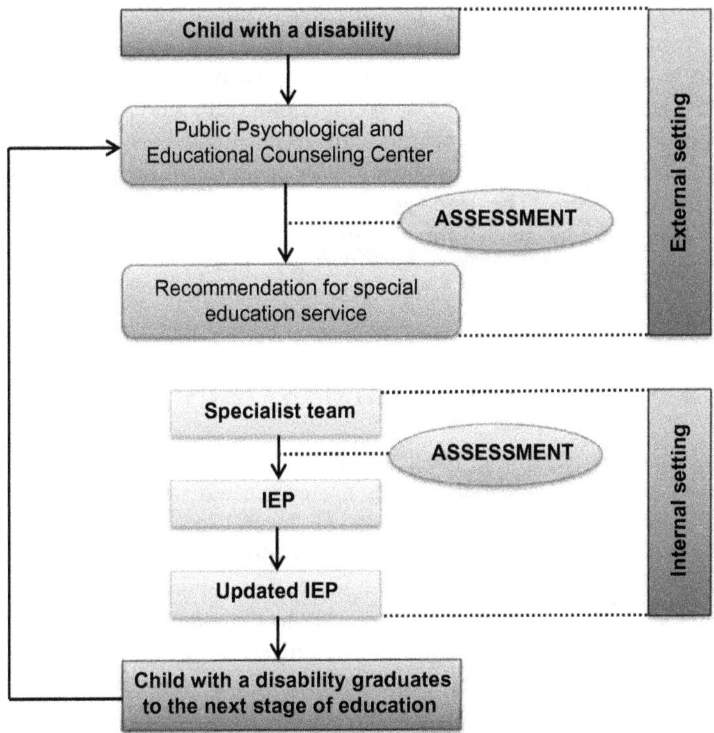

Fig. 3. External and Internal Supportive Settings Available for Children with Disabilities in Poland.

(4) *Specialist classes* – this type of program varies depending on the needs of the child. One option is a correctional class which is organized for groups of five children with developmental delays or specific learning disabilities. Speech therapy is another form of specialized support for a group of four children with speech and language problems. Socio-therapeutic classes are organized for groups up to 10 children with social and emotional disorders (JLPR, 2010).

This support is in addition to the normal school routine and schedule. This psychological and educational assessment is optimal for adjusting the support to the developmentally changing needs of each child.

Apart from special education services, Public Psychological and Educational Counseling Centers may recommend home schooling. In home schooling instruction, children are taught by one or two teachers from a local school who then come to home. Individualized instruction may also occur in a school setting depending on the type of health impairment the child has been diagnosed with. For younger children, who are not obligated with compulsory schooling, centers can recommend early developmental support which is designed for children with developmental difficulties from birth to age seven. The needed support may be provided by Early Intervention Centers or within the primary schools (*The Regulation of Supporting Early Children Development*, JLRP, 2009).

UNRESOLVED DILEMMAS OF INCLUSION

New educational reforms in the 1990s brought many unresolved dilemmas to Polish schools. Most of the issues are connected with the gap between the required regulations and the reality of the Polish education system. All of the legislation describes in detail what support should be provided by the schools to the children with disabilities. Two main concerns regarding these regulations should be highlighted due to their potential harmful influence on the school success of children with disabilities.

The first issue refers to the responsibility of the integration of children with disabilities with peers and society, which is mentioned only in the regulations referring to special schools. Integrated schools and mainstreamed schools are not legally obligated to provide full inclusion. Under this broad assumption, integration may mean "putting all children together" and making the idea of integration "work." It may be difficult for integration in Poland to be successful without the full support of teachers and staff who work with students with high-and low-incidence disabilities.

The second potentially harmful issue refers to the level of support offered in general education classes. Supportive teachers are provided only in integrated schools or classes. Thus, children with low-incidence disabilities in mainstreamed schools do not receive any additional support from a specially trained teacher during the school day. These two issues are often the subject of sharp criticism in Poland: "Effective teaching of students with disabilities in a large classroom (with more than 30 students) with no extra-curricular activities (remedial classes) is a fiction" (Gołubiew, Krause, 2009, p. 37). Very often children are "left behind" and struggle throughout the school day. Supplementary activities, which are provided after regular lessons (e.g., compensatory exercises, psychological support, etc.) to support students may not be enough given the fact that in some mainstreamed schools specialists are not available. Offering opportunities and educational requirements that students with disabilities cannot access in mainstreamed schools may be perceived as discrimination. Discrimination means not only a lack of opportunities but also an underestimation of difficulties and limitations or setting requirements that are impossible to meet (Parys, 2006).

These issues are very controversial based on the fact that Poland ratified the Convention on Rights for Persons with Disabilities (CRPD) in 2012 and as mentioned in Article 24 "State's Parties recognize the right of persons with disabilities to education. With a view to realizing this right without discrimination and on the basis of equal opportunity, State's Parties shall ensure an inclusive education system at all levels and lifelong learning ..." To understand the problem of following the Convention, it is important to discuss its translation. In the Polish translation, the Ministry of Labour and Social Policy use the term "an integrational educational setting" instead of "an inclusive education setting." This mistake or misunderstanding in terminology can lead to keeping the status quo in the Polish special education system, being more prone to integration than to full inclusion (Wdowik, 2008; Kubicki, 2012).

In 2011, the Supreme Chamber of Control randomly chose 40 schools (22 special and 18 integrated) to determine how Polish schools respect new educational ordinances, especially the one assuring psychological and educational support for children with disabilities. The audit found a number of deficiencies. The most important deficiencies related to the education of students with disabilities are as follows: (1) failure to properly integrate students with disabilities in five integrated schools; (2) failure to provide psychological and educational support in eight schools; (3) failure to provide specialists in four schools; and (4) failure to provide accommodations and modifications for children with disabilities in 16 schools (Supreme Chamber of Control [SChC], 2012).

It is important to mention that in this particular audit, children with disabilities in mainstreamed classes were not taken into consideration. In addition, it was determined that special schools spend approximately 760 USD per month for supporting the education of each child with disability. In integration schools, this value was 323 USD and in integration classes only 260 USD. These differences result from the need to determine the best use of funds, that is, architectural barriers or the employment of additional specialists. Paradoxically though, special schools still warrant higher standards of support (Ciura & Osiecka – Chojnacka, 2013). There is still no precise information regarding the support offered for children with disabilities in mainstreamed classes. Knowing that special and integrated schools experience difficulties in meeting the needs of children with disabilities, it would be logical that legitimate concerns exist that mainstreamed classes may have more difficulties.

One Example of Unresolved Issues Related to Integration in Poland

In primary schools in Łódź, the third largest agglomeration in Poland, the following has been determined regarding the education of students with disabilities:

- Twenty-five percent of schools do not control how the recommendations of the Psychological and Educational Counseling Centers are implemented;
- Twenty-six percent of schools do not evaluate results of assessments regarding the needs of the child with disabilities;
- Forty-two percent of the schools did not prepare individualized educational programs for the children with disabilities;
- Thirty-eight percent of schools do not ever modify the established individualized education program; thus, the program is not adjusted as the developmental needs of the child change;
- The regulation requiring the adjustment of the curriculum to match the capabilities and needs of children with disabilities is not occurring in many primary schools;
- Twenty-three percent of students with disabilities do not have access to the whole school area due to architectural barriers while 28% have partial access to the school; and
- In many cases, although the mainstreamed school staff was aware of the regulations and accepted children with disability into the school, they were not able to assure full access to the school. Thus, those children are not able to participate in all school activities, which restricted them from a fully inclusive educational setting (Chrzanowska, 2010).

From the developmental point of view, the special school setting in Poland is perceived as more favorable for children with disabilities because it is an environment which provides additional support and trained teachers. Although developmental aspects should not be placed above the more general goal of integration, the ultimate goal of integration is to prepare the children to be full participants in society. For many years, segregation in Poland succeeded in improving the achievements of children, but after they graduated from the segregated schools, they became "good, rehabilitated, lonely adults – outsiders in the surrounding world" (Krause, 2010, p.72).

The former structure of special education in Poland which was based on segregation-created obstacles are difficult to overcome. The success of inclusion depends on the ability to bridge the segregated setting with the mainstreamed one. Teachers' attitudes toward inclusion are critical to its success. A total of 1,800 teachers were surveyed on their perceptions of inclusion by the Supreme Chamber of Control (SChC, 2012). The majority of the teachers (58%) worked in special schools while 42% worked in integrated settings. Forty-seven percent do not support inclusive education while 25% support inclusive education. Twenty-eight percent of teachers believed that the success of inclusion is dependent on the child's type of disability. Teachers' perspectives were that the group of children who will benefit the most from inclusion are children with motor disabilities (24%), those who are hard of hearing (16%), those with a visual impairment (13%), and those with a mild intellectual disability (11%). Twelve percent of teachers stated that children with disabilities will not benefit from inclusive education. Only 2% of the teachers surveyed were convinced that children regardless of the type and level of disability would benefit from inclusive education. Most of the teachers (75%) believed that children with disabilities should attend special schools, 17% stated that they should attend mainstreamed schools, and 8% reported no opinion.

Reasons why they believed that inclusion will fail include the following: (1) mainstreamed schools are not prepared (42%), (2) children with disabilities will not benefit from participation in the lessons (33%), (3) children with disabilities will make it more difficult for children without disabilities (15%), and (4) children with disabilities will lower the expectations in the classroom (10%). When the teachers do not believe that inclusion will be beneficial for students, it is very difficult to make inclusion a reality.

Inclusion will require many adjustments. Imposing new regulations without working on teacher's attitudes toward inclusion and equipping teachers with tools to work with children with disabilities will not make inclusion work. There are still many children with disabilities in Poland who are "left behind" in the school system. It is important to identify an implementation plan to continue to focus on integration in Poland.

CHALLENGES FOR INCLUSIVE EDUCATION AND FUTURE DIRECTIONS

Recent Polish educational reforms brought positive changes for students with high and low-incidence disabilities but much work is still required. There are many ideas that will lead to the improvement of the quality of education and services delivered to children with disabilities within the existing Polish educational system.

Creating open and inclusive education settings should not be understood and perceived as the exclusion of all specialists working within special schools. The key to successful inclusion is to facilitate contacts and networking between special, integrated, and mainstreamed schools. Throughout the years special schools built up many valuable techniques, materials, and methods to support the development of children with different disabilities. This knowledge must be shared with mainstreamed schools. Special schools could serve as educational and training centers. These centers can play a major role in supporting the development of children with disabilities within the mainstreamed schools by

- providing training to teachers;
- supporting teachers in the course of the lesson;
- working on positive attitudes toward children with disabilities in all mainstreamed setting (including teachers, students, parents and other school staff);
- helping in building up individual educational programs for each child;
- providing assessment and evaluation of the child's development;
- adapting books and other materials for children with disabilities;
- supporting a safe and accessible school environment for all children.

CONCLUSION

Implementing educational reforms brought about positive changes in educational settings for most children with and without disabilities in Poland. A positive outcome of the new reforms is that more children with varying types of disabilities have the chance to succeed in mainstreamed schools with adequate support. Although the regulations in Poland promote integration as an educational solution for children with disabilities, additional work is necessary to create fully inclusive educational settings.

Apart from the legal aspects of inclusion, there are two main areas of concern at the school level. First, there is little data about the support and services available for children with disabilities in mainstreamed schools especially related to individualized educational programs. Another extremely important objective that should guide further changes is bridging the gap with accessibility at mainstreamed schools (Open Society Institute, 2005). Achievements in inclusion in primary education should not overshadow the goal of creating fully inclusive settings at the secondary level.

"The idea of integration comes from the heart, but should be carried into effect, through the intellect and brain" (Obuchowska, 2006, p.15). The more the focus is on using the knowledge of special education teachers and other specialists working with children with disabilities, the better the outcomes will be in Poland. Requiring inclusion by imposing legal regulations, without any "know" and "how," will bring exactly the opposite effect.

KEY TERMS

Inclusion – The term inclusion can be referred to throughout different aspects of life of people with disabilities. In this chapter, the authors refer mainly to educational setting. In this sense, inclusion means that all children (regardless of the type or severity of disability) are taught in regular classes in mainstream schools with other peers. In Polish scientific literature, the term *inclusion* is sometimes replaced by *full integration* to stress that inclusion can be also perceived as a form of integration.

Integration – When referring to inclusion in an educational setting in Poland, the term integration means that children with and without disabilities are placed in the same school or classroom. There are distinct rules that define the educational setting as one that is integrated. Integrated classrooms in Poland consist of no more than 20 students and approximately 3–5 children with disabilities. However, children may vary in the type of disabilities in one classroom.

Segregation – Refers to an educational setting in which education is implemented in special schools or special classes (in mainstreamed schools) dedicated exclusively for students with a particular type of disability. The number of children in these special classes in Poland depends on the type of disability.

REFERENCES

Central Statistical Office in Poland. (2011). *Badanie aktywności ekonomicznej ludności* [*Examining economic activity of population*]. Warszawa: CSO.

Central Statistical Office in Poland. (2012). *Edukacja i wychowanie w roku szkolnym 2011–2012* [*Education in school year 2011–2012*]. Warszawa: CSO.

Chrzanowska, I. (2010). *Problemy edukacji dzieci i młodzieży z niepełnosprawnościa. Regionalna specyfika czy ogólnopolska tendencja?* [*Issues in education of children and adolescents with disabilities. Regional specificity or nationwide tendency?*]. Kraków: Oficyna Wydawnicza Impuls.

Ciura, G., & Osiecka – Chojnacka, J. (2013). Edukacja właczajaca w szkolnictwie obowiazkowym w Polsce. [Inclusive education in Polish compulsory education system]. *Infos*, *9*(146), 1–4.

Cytowska, B. (2002). *Drogi edukacyjne dzieci niepełnosprawnych intelektualnie* [*Educational pathways of children with intellectual disability*]. Wrocław: Instytut Pedagogiki UWR.

Denek, K. (2005). Permanentna reforma systemu edukacji [Permanent reform of educational system]. *Nowe w Szkole*, *7*(8), 83–84.

Dudzińska, A. (2009). *Wszystko jasne. Dostępność i jakość edukacji dla uczniów niepełnosprawnych w Warszawie. Raport końcowy* [*Everything is clear. Availability and quality of education for children with disabilities in Warsaw. Final report*]. Warszawa: Stowarzyszenie "Nie-Grzeczne Dzieci."

Dykcik, W. (1998). *Pedagogika specjalna. Podręcznik akademicki* [*Special education. Academic handbook*]. Poznań: Wydawnictwo UAM.

EADSNE. (2003). Special needs education in Europe. Thematic Publication. European Agency for Development in Special Needs Education.

EURYDICE. (2012). The System of Education in Poland. Polish EURYDICE Unit Foundation for the Development of the Education System.

Gajdzica, Z. (2008). Organizacja kształcenia integracyjnego w Polsce na tle wybranych rozwiazań europejskich [The organization of inclusive education in Poland on the background of other European countries]. In Z. Gajdzica, J. Rottermund, & A. Klinik (Eds.), *Uczeń niepełnosprawny i jego nauczyciel w przestrzeni szkoły* [*Disabled student and his/her teacher in school space*] (pp. 113–121). Kraków: Oficyna Wydawnicza Impuls.

Głodkowska, J. (2010). Model kształcenia uczniów ze specjalnymi potrzebami edukacyjnymi – różnice nie moga dzielić [Models of education od children with special educational needs – differences cannot split]. In *Podniesienie efektywności kształcenia uczniów ze specjalnymi potrzebami edukacyjnymi. Materiały szkoleniowe.* cz. I. [*Improving the effectiveness of education for students with special educational needs, Materials Prepared by Ministry of Education, part I*] (pp. 37–92). Warszawa: Ministerstwo Edukacji Narodowej.

Gołubiew, M., & Krause, A. (2009). Szkolnictwo specjalne – krajobraz po reformie [Special education – landscape after the reform]. In Z. Janiszewska – Nieścioruk (Ed.), *Problemy edukacji integracyjnej dzieci i młodzieży z niepełnosprawnościa* [*Problems of integrational education of children and adolescents with disabilities*] (pp. 77–90). Kraków: Wydawnictwo Impuls.

Holowinsky, I. Z. (1975). Special education in Eastern Europe. Assessment and evaluation in Poland. *The Journal of Special Education*, *9*(4), 435–437.

Holowinsky, I. Z. (1981). Special education in Poland in the 1970s. *The Journal of Special Education, 15*(3), 401–405.

Hulek, A. (1977). *Pedagogika rewalidacyjna* [*Revalidative pedagogy*]. Warszawa: PWN.

Hulek, A. (1983). Changing approaches to methodology of research in special education. *International Journal of Rehabilitation Research, 6*(1), 3–9.

Klaro – Celej, L. (2012). Stan edukacji osób z niepełnosprawnościa intelektualna w Polsce [The state of education of persons with intellectual disability in Poland]. In A. Blaszczyk & B. Imiolczyk (Eds.), *Równe szanse w dostępie do edukacji osób z niepełnosprawnościam. Analiza i rekomendacje* [*Equal chances in access to education for people with disabilities. Analyse and recommendations*] (pp. 35–50). Warszawa: BRPO.

Kogut, A. (2010). Potrzeba i koncepcje kształcenia osób niepełnosprawnych [Need and conceptions of education of people with disabilities]. In I. Sierpowska & A. Kogut (Eds.), *Statut osoby niepełnosprawnej w polskim systemie prawa* [*Statute of the person with disability in the Polish legal system*] (pp. 95–128). Wrocław: Gaskor.

Krause, A. (2010). *Współczesne paradygmaty pedagogiki specjalnej* [*Contemporary paradigms in special education*]. Kraków: Impuls.

Kubicki, P. (2012). Równy dostęp do edukacji osób niepełnosprawnych [Equal access to education for people with disabilities]. In A. Blaszczak (Ed.), *Najważniejsze wyzwania po ratyfikacji przez Polskę Konwencji ONZ o prawach osób niepełnosprawnych* [*The most important challenges after ratification by Poland the ONZ Convention on Rights for Persons with Disabilities*] (pp. 34–40). Warszawa: Biuletyn Rzecznika Praw Obywatelskich.

Kummant, M. (2008). *Raport – tendencje w kształceniu integracyjnym w Polsce w latach 2003–2008* [*Report – tendencies in integrational education in Poland in years 2003–3008*]. Warszawa: Pracownia Wspomagania Rozwoju i Integracji CMPPP.

Kupisiewicz, Cz. (2006). *Projekty reform edukacyjnych w Polsce. Główne tezy i wpływ na funkcjonowanie szkolnictwa* [*Project of education system reform in Poland. Main thesis and its influence on education*]. Warszawa: PWN.

Lempart, M. (2012). Wybrane problemy orzecznictwa w zakresie potrzeby kształcenia specjalnego [Selected problems of the assessment in special education]. In A. Blaszczyk & B. Imiolczyk (Eds.), *Równe szanse w dostępie do edukacji osób z niepełnosprawnościam. Analiza i rekomendacje* [*Equal chances in access to education for people with disabilities. Analyse and recommendations*] (pp. 73–79). Warszawa: BRPO.

Leśniewska, K., & Puchała, E. (2010). *Organizacja procesu wspierania uczniów ze specjalnymi potrzebami* [*Organization of support for students with special needs*]. Warszawa: ORE.

Obuchowska, I. (2006). *Dziecimałeiduże. Jak je kochaćirozumieć.* [*Small and big kids how to love and understand them*]. Poznań: Media Rodzina.

OECD. (2010). The *impact of the 1999 education reform in Poland.* OECD Education Working Paper No. 49, OECD Publishing.

Open Society Insitute. (2005). *Rights of people with intellectual disabilities. Access to Education and Employment in Poland.* EUMAP – EU Monitoring and Advocacy Program, Open Society Mental Health Initiative. OSE Publishing.

Pańczyk, A. (1999). Potrzeby edukacyjne osób niepełnosprawnych i ich zaspokajanie na przykładzie aglomeracji miejskich (na przykładzie Łodzi) [*Educational needs of disabled people on the example of city agglomeration* (cito od Lodz)]. Łódź: Wydawnictwo Uniwersytetu Łódzkiego.

Parys, K. (2006). Pytanie o koncepcje kształcenia uczniów z upośledzeniem w stopniu lekkim [Question about educational concepts of mild intellectually disabled children].

In Cz. Kosakowski, A. Krause, & S. Przybyliński (Eds.), *Pomiędzy teoria i praktyka. Dyskursy pedagogiki specjalnej, tom 5* [*Between theory and practice. Discourse in special education, Vol. 5*] (pp. 30–45). Olsztyn: Wydawnictwo Uniwersytetu Warmińsko-Mazurskiego.

Putkiewicz, E., & Zahorska, M. (1999). *Monitorowanie reformy edukacji. Definicje reformy systemy edukacyjnego i sposoby ewaluowania reformy* [*Monitoring the education system reform. Definitions and evaluation of reform*]. Warszawa: Instytut Spraw Publicznych.

Rudek, I. (2009). Disabled children in Poland – Basic assumptions of social integration. In A. Nowak-Łojewska, A. Olczak, & A. Soroka-Fedorczuk (Eds.), *Education of young child: reflections, problems, experiences* (pp. 161–170). Zielona Góra: University of Zielona Góra.

Supreme Chamber of Control. (2012). *Kształcenie uczniów z niepełnosprawnościami o specjalnych potrzebach edukacyjnych. Raport po wynikach kontroli* [*Education of children with disabilities with special educational needs. Report after the audit*]. Report No. KNO-4101-01-00/2012.

Szeroczyńska, M. (2008). Definicje [Definitions]. In A. M. Waszkiewicz (Ed.), *Polska droga do Konwencji o prawach osób niepełnosprawnych ONZ* [Polish *pathway* to ONZ *convetion* on *rights* for *persons* with *disabilities*] (pp. 12–25). Kraków: Fundacja Instytut Rozwoju Regionalnego.

Szumski, G. (2006). *Integracyjne kształcenie niepełnosprawnych* [*Integrative education of disabled*]. Warszawa: PWN.

The Act on Vocational and Social Rehabilitation and Employment of Persons with Disabilities. *Journal of Laws of Republic of Poland*, August 27 1997, No. 123, item 776.

The Education System Act. *Journal of Laws of Republic of Poland*, September 7, 1991, No. 95, item 425.

The Ordinance of the Minister of Education on the Principles of Providing and Organizing Educational and Psychological Counseling. *Journal of Laws of Republic of Poland*, November 17, 2010, No. 228, Item. 1487.

The Regulation of Ministry of Education of Poland Changing Some of the Previous Education Laws. *Journal of Laws of Republic of Poland*, January 27, 2012, item 176.

The Regulation of Supporting Early Children Development. *Journal of Laws of Republic of Poland*, February 3, 2009, No. 23, item 133.

The Regulation on Education and Care for Children and Youth with Disabilities and Socially Maladjusted in Integrational and Mainstream Kindergardens, Schools and other Institutions. *Journal of Laws of Republic of Poland*, November 17, 2010a, No. 228, item 1490.

The Regulation on Education and Care for Children and Youth with Disabilities and Socially Maladjusted in Special Kindergartens, Schools and other Special Institutions. *Journal of Laws of Republic of Poland*, November 17, 2010b, No. 228, item 1489.

The Regulation on Organization of Activities for Children with Profound Intellectual Disability. *Journal of Laws of Republic of Poland*, April 23, 2013, No. 89, item 529.

The Regulation on the Core Curriculum. *Journal of Laws of Republic of Poland*, February 26, 2002, No. 51, item 458.

The Regulation on the Framework Statute of Public Kindergartens and Schools. *Journal of Laws of Republic of Poland*, May 25, 2001, No. 61, item 624.

The School System Reform Act. *Journal of Laws of Republic of Poland*, January 8, 1999, No. 12, item 96.

Twardowski, A. (2005). Zmiany w sytuacji osób niepełnosprawnych w latach 1989-2005 [Changes in situation od disabled people in years 1989–2005]. In Z. Janiszewska – Nieścioruk (Ed.), *Strefy życia osób z niepełnosprawnościa intelektualna* [*Spheres of life of people with intellectual disability*] (pp. 55–70). Kraków: Wydawnictwo Impuls.

Wdowik, P. (2008). Edukacja i dostęp do oświaty [Education and accessibility to education]. In A. M. Waszkiewicz (Ed.), *Polska droga do konwencji o prawach osób niepełnosprawnych ONZ* [*Polish pathway to convention on the rights of disability ONZ*] (pp. 126–129). Kraków: Fundacja Instytut Rozwoju Regionalnego.

Wdowik, P. (2009). *Dostępna edukacja* [*Accessible education*]. Kraków: Fundacja Instytut Rozwoju Regionalnego.

Wyczesany, J., & Gajdzica, Z. (2006). *Uwarunkowania edukacji i rehabilitacji uczniów o specjalnych potrzebach w rozwoju* [*Backgrounds of education and rehabilitation of children with special educational needs*]. Kraków: Wydawnictwo Naukowe Akademii Pedagogicznej.

ABOUT THE AUTHORS

Vicki Barnitt is the Director of Program Development for the Florida Inclusion Network (FIN), a federal and state funded program that serves school districts in the state of Florida. The mission of FIN is to provide services and supports to districts and schools that ensure all students with disabilities have the same educational, social, and future opportunities as their peers. Vicki holds degrees in Special Education and Rehabilitation Counseling and has worked for over 30 years in the field of Special Education as a teacher, diagnostician, job development specialist, inclusion facilitator, and product developer. She has authored and co-authored numerous publications and training manuals on effective inclusive practices, including those that support inclusion for students with extensive support needs. Vicki also serves on the Board of Trustees for the National Educator Program, an organization dedicated to developing leadership, sustainable school improvement, career academies, high school redesign, and small learning communities.

Jody Marie Bartz is an Assistant Professor of Practice at Northern Arizona University. As a former special educator and the aunt of two nephews with autism, Jody is known as a strong, passionate advocate. Her primary academic interest is instructing and mentoring current and pre-service teachers in evidence-based inclusive educational practices, especially for children with significant support needs. Her research agenda includes studying the effects of family involvement as well as the impact of educational, community, medical, and familial collaboration on outcomes for children with special health and support needs.

Grace I. Blum is a doctoral student in Curriculum and Instruction at the University of Washington, Seattle. She has worked as a bilingual classroom teacher and adult literacy educator in both the United States and in several international contexts. Currently, she works as a teacher educator in preparing teacher candidates to work with culturally and linguistically diverse students. Her research interests include teacher education for linguistic diversity and teacher preparation for inclusive classrooms.

Pei-Yu Chen is an assistant professor in the department of Special Education at the National Taipei University of Education in Taiwan. She received a master's degree in 2005 and earned her doctorate in 2010 in Special Education from the University of Washington. She has held positions as a resource room teacher, practicum supervisor, teacher educator, researcher, and Board Certified Behavior Analyst. Her professional interests include research on examination of evidence-based practices in Taiwan and interventions that promote positive behaviors and social relationships of students with disabilities in school settings.

Chun-Yu Chiu initially pursued special education because she has a brother with significant intellectual and physical disabilities. Knowing that building family capacity can improve individual and family outcomes, she moved from Taiwan to the United States to advance her knowledge and research skills in the areas of special education (particularly students with low-incidence disabilities), family support, and public policy. She received her Masters from Vanderbilt University and earned her Ph.D. from University of Kansas in 2013. Caya returns to Taiwan in 2014 and is currently working as an assistant professor in the department of special education at the National Taipei University of Education.

Debra L. Cote is an associate professor in the Department of Special Education at California State University, Fullerton (CSUF). She received her Ph.D. from the University of Nevada Las Vegas. Her research interests include positive behavior support, evidence-based practices, co-teaching/clinical practice, transition, and cultural linguistic diversity. Dr. Cote currently is the Far West Member for the Council for Exceptional Children – Division on Autism and Developmental Disabilities serving as Chair of the Diversity Committee and President of the Orange County Council for Exceptional Children Chapter 188. In addition, she serves as the Curriculum Coordinator for the PROCESS Project (OSEP grant) and is associated faculty with the CSUF Center for Autism.

Anne E. Crylen is a Fulbright Fellow in Cambodia and doctoral student in the area of Special Education at the University of Washington, Seattle. She received her Masters in Education and Masters of Public Services at DePaul University, Chicago. Prior to her academic pursuits she taught in Chicago Public Schools, served as a Peace Corps Volunteer in Niger, West Africa, and worked at ABC News. Her research interests include school re-entry with acquired disabilities, traumatic brain injury, international education, and disability studies through a cultural context. Ms. Crylen is currently a member of the Comparative International Education Society, the Council for Exceptional Children – Division of International Special Education and Services, and International Association of Special Education. As a champion for students with disabilities, she continues to engage in the debate on the role education plays in international development.

Carol Ann Davis, Ed. D., is an Associate Professor in Severe, low-incidence disabilities at the University of Washington. Her areas of research include assessment and interventions for challenging behavior, developing models of service delivery for students with autism and student with chronic behavior problems, and interventions to promote inclusion and skill development for students with severe disabilities. Dr. Davis is currently the principal investigator for Project BUILD to prepare teachers to work with student with severe disabilities, and Implementing iBESTT a technology tool to assist schools in delivering Tier 3 services. She consults locally and nationally with numerous families, agencies, and schools on the topic of providing appropriate educational programs for students with challenging behavior and serves on several journal review boards.

Robin Drogan holds a doctoral degree in Special Education from Lehigh University. She is an assistant professor and graduate program coordinator in the Department of Exceptionality Programs at Bloomsburg University of Pennsylvania. Robin has presented at national and international conferences and has published multiple articles in peer reviewed journals. Her research and practical interests focus on team collaboration including teacher involvement, family participation, and peer support, meeting the needs of students in inclusive settings, tiered behavioral and academic supports for students, and prevention intervention strategies for young children.

Jeremy Erickson is a doctoral student at the University of Washington and a special education program specialist in the Lake Washington School District. His research interests include implementation of embedded instruction within general education activities and routines, and preparing teachers to train and supervise paraeducators in the use of evidence-based practices.

Michael Gutierrez is a doctoral student at the University of Washington, Seattle, and a board certified behavior analyst. He specializes in the delivery of data-driven behavioral services to children and adults with varying disabilities, teaming with schools and families to deliver best treatment, and the development and implementation of behavior treatment and instructional plans. His primary research interests include best practice in education to ensure inclusion for students with disabilities, the utilization of peer models for young adults with disabilities during post-secondary transition, and evidence-based practices to increase membership and relationships for students with and without disabilities.

Young Hyuk Hong is a special education teacher at Federal Way School District, Washington. He has taught all K-12 grade levels working with students with various disabilities. Prior to teaching, he worked for Microsoft. He decided to become a teacher when his son was diagnosed with autism in 2004. He currently holds Principal and Superintendent Certification in the State of Washington. He is constantly interested in developing effective and efficient classroom and school wide behavior intervention plan. He loves collaborating.

Erica Howell, Ph.D., is an Associate Professor in the Department of Special Education at California State University, Fullerton. She received her Ph.D. from the University of California, Riverside, where she worked as a Doug Flutie Fellow at the SEARCH Family Autism Resource Center. Her research interests include post-school outcomes and transition issues relating to individuals with autism spectrum disorders. Dr. Howell is Co-Director of CSUF's Center for Autism and principal investigator of a grant funded by the National Cancer Institute of the National Institute of Health that equips medical professionals to successfully work with pediatric oncology patients with autism spectrum disorders.

Andrea D. Jasper is an assistant professor at Central Michigan University where she teaches courses on cognitive impairment. Her research interests focus on learners with low-incidence disabilities, issues of diversity, and professional development for moderate/severe educators. She has published articles in several journal outlets and has presented at multiple conferences. She is actively involved in two special interest groups within the Council for Exceptional Children – the Teacher Education Division and the Division for Culturally and Linguistically Diverse Exceptional Learners.

Phyllis Jones is an associate professor in the department of Teaching & Learning at the University of South Florida. Phyllis taught and was a deputy head in schools in the United Kingdom for 15 years before she entered teacher education. She developed and teaches on the masters ASD and/or Severe Intellectual Disabilities program and Curriculum and Instruction doctoral program in the department. She is author and editor of seven books related to teaching and learning and is published widely in international journals related to inclusive practices across all schools, teacher education for teachers of students with severe intellectual disabilities and/or ASD. She is editor of *International Journal of Whole Schooling*, sits of the editorial board of Disability & Society and is a regular reviewer for *British Journal of Special Education, Journal of Child and Family Studies, International Journal of Inclusive Education, Journal of Teacher Education*, and *International Review of Education*.

Vita L. Jones is an Assistant Professor in the Special Education Department at California State University, Fullerton. Prior to this position, she served as a visiting faculty at the University of Nevada, Las Vegas. Dr. Jones 2009 dissertation topic focused on resilience in African American students. She conducted a Delphi study in Las Vegas to determine the characteristics of resilience that led to successful graduation from high school. In addition to this study, she has conducted research on student characteristics of resilience in the township of Kliptown, South Africa, and at the Eton Montessori schools in Beijing, China. She recently presented on the topics of Russian Inclusive Practices as well as Collaboration, Inclusive Education, & Early Childhood Practices in Kursk, Russia, and in Toronto, Canada. She is the author of several articles intersecting resilience, early childhood, and diversity.

Kyungsook Kang is a Professor of Special Education at Wonkwang University in South Korea. She was awarded as an 11th of top 20 South Korea educational researchers based on research citations in 2013. She was a visiting scholar at the University of Washington during 2013–2014. Her research interests include inclusive education, national curriculum development, and teacher education. She is a board member of a number of special education academic societies. She loves collaborating with international scholars.

Jennifer Kurth is Assistant Professor of Special Education at the University of Kansas. Her academic interests include methods implementing inclusive education, including methods of embedding critical instruction within the context and routines of general education as well as methods of providing appropriate supports and services for individual learners. Dr. Kurth's research also examines how teachers, students, and family's interactions support and constrain learning and socialization in general education classrooms. She also studies how teacher candidates develop their dispositions and skills in inclusive practices. Dr. Kurth's research interests in inclusive education also include examining outcomes of inclusion in terms of skill development and quality of life indicators for students with disabilities.

Penny Lacey is a Senior Lecturer at the University of Birmingham, where she runs the 'Severe, Profound and Multiple Learning Difficulties' professional development program. She also conducts research and writes in the area of SLD/PMLD. Penny works as a coach and adviser in a special school for one day a week and as a consultant in many other schools around the country.

Meaghan M. McCollow is an assistant professor in the department of Counseling and Special Education at Central Michigan University. She teaches coursework in special education, specifically in intellectual disability, early childhood special education, and behavior analysis. She has traveled internationally as a faculty leader for study abroad experiences for pre-service special educators. She has spent many years working with children and youth with special needs in many capacities, including teaching assistant, respite care provider, camp counselor, and classroom teacher. Her specific research interests include examining the effectiveness of self-management strategies, promoting teacher implementation of evidence-based practices, and identifying effective professional development for special educators. She is also a board certified behavior analyst.

Kinga M. Ober is an assistant professor in the Department of Child Psychopathology in the Faculty of Educational Studies at Adam Mickiewicz University (AMU) in Poznan, Poland. She obtained her master's degree in clinical psychology and educational counseling and then completed her doctorate in special education at AMU. Her main scientific interests focus on supporting the cognitive development of children with intellectual disabilities, developing evidence-based practices and linking neuroscience with special education.

Daniel Östlund is a Senior Lecturer at Kristianstad University. The general research interests concern interaction, formative learning, and pedagogical relations in educational settings for pupils with intellectual disabilities. Östlund has a background as a special educator and teacher for pupils with intellectual disabilities. Between the years of 2008 and 2012 Östlund was a doctoral student at Malmö University and defended his doctoral thesis "Contextual conditions of participation. Five training school classes' pedagogical practice" in December 2012. Östlund teaches in the special educators, and in the special teachers' education.

Charles Peck is currently professor of teacher education and special education at University of Washington. Cap served as Director of Teacher Education at the UW from 2003 to 2010, during which time the university underwent a major evidence-based program redesign process as part of its participation in the Teachers for A New Era Project (for which he served as Co-Director). Prior to his work at University of Washington, Cap was Director of Teacher Education at University of California, Santa Barbara, and earlier served as Director of the Southwest Washington Educational Partnership for Professional Development – a consortium of 54 urban and rural school districts. Cap's research work over the past decade has focused on policy implementation and systemic change in teacher education. He has been particularly concerned with factors affecting the extent to which programs of teacher education take up opportunities for program improvement that are afforded by new sources of outcome data.

Darlene Perner received her doctorate at the University of British Columbia. Currently, she is a Professor and Chairperson of the Department of Exceptionality Programs at Bloomsburg University of Pennsylvania. She serves as the University's faculty advisor for the Office of Accommodative Services and works closely with students receiving accommodations. Darlene has published books, chapters in books, and journal articles; acquired grants; served as the Canadian Representative for international projects related to early childhood and inclusive education. She also has been an international consultant for the United Nations Educational, Scientific, and Cultural Organisation (UNESCO) and for the Organisation for Economic Co-operation and Development (OECD)/ Centre for Educational Research and Innovation (CERI). Her research, consulting work with government officials, and teacher training in these two organizations focused on children's rights to an education and inclusive education (Education for All).

Melinda R. Pierson, Ph.D., is Chair of the Department of Special Education and the Director of the Center for International Partnerships in Education at California State University, Fullerton. She earned her Ph.D. from UC Riverside while teaching full-time in the public schools and has been a professor for 15 years. Dr. Pierson is an active researcher whose interests include effective interventions for students with mild/moderate disabilities, teacher training nationally and internationally, and issues relating to affective characteristics (self-concept, loneliness, and social skills) of children and adolescents with disabilities. She also directs the Alternative Certification Program for Education Specialists. She has served as a

Fulbright Specialist in both Poland and Germany and continues to develop international partnerships around the world.

Richard Rose is Professor of Inclusive Education and Director of the Centre for Research and Education at the University of Northampton, UK. He has published widely in the field of special education and inclusion and has conducted research in several parts of the world including, India, China, Singapore, and Ireland.

Jeanette Scull – MEd Merit, PGCE, BA (Hons) – Originally Arts trained (Ceramicist). Jeanette has worked in adult residential as a craft instructor then after PGCE taught in mainstream primary, special school, resource provision, and on a central advisory team in a Local Authority with high levels of inclusion. More recently she has worked as an Inclusion Officer monitoring inclusive provision in mainstream schools for students with Complex Needs. Jeanette has delivered NASENCo course as an outreach tutor and provided other training for mainstream schools SEN and Inclusion. She has returned to specialist provision and is currently working as an Assistant Head in a London special school.

Michael Shevlin is Associate Professor in Inclusive Education and Director of the Inclusion in Education and Society Research Centre at Trinity College, Dublin, Republic of Ireland. His research has been published in a range of international journals and books and he is currently involved in a European project examining a life course perspective for people with disabilities.

Jordan Shurr is an assistant professor in the department of Counseling and Special Education at Central Michigan University. He teaches coursework in special education, specifically in intellectual disability, transition, and inclusion. His areas of research specialization include literacy access for students with low-incidence disabilities, technology integration, and critical issues within the profession of teaching students with low-incidence disabilities. He has ten plus years of combined experience as a classroom teacher, teacher educator, researcher, assistive technology consultant, and camp inclusion coordinator.

Daphne Thomas is an Associate Professor in the Department of Special Education at the University of South Florida. She has worked in the field of special education for the past 30 years. She initially served as a School Social Worker and worked closely with a range of families with children at-risk and severely disabled. She has taught courses in general special education, consultation and collaboration, working with families, and urban special education. Her research interests include teacher preparation, family–school partnerships, and building effective cross-cultural relationships. She has published in the area of families of children with disabilities and family–school partnerships. She earned her doctoral degree in Special Education from The University of North Carolina at Chapel Hill and a master's degree in Social Work from Atlanta University.

Andrzej Twardowski is a full professor at Adam Mickiewicz University (AMU) in Poznań, Poland. He received his doctoral degree in psychology (1989) and postdoctoral degree in special education (2002). Professor Twardowski directs the Department of Child Psychopathology at the Faculty of Educational Studies at AMU. His focus areas include education and rehabilitation of children with rare genetic syndromes, support of families with children with disabilities, early intervention strategies and services, and the development of communicative competencies for children with disabilities. Current projects include the early support of the development of children with disabilities in their family environment. Professor Twardowski has published over 90 articles and book chapters, 2 scientific monographs, edited 8 books, and presented at 80 international and national conferences.

Matthew Wangeman has been a disability advocate for over 30 years at the local, state, and national levels. He has a B.S. in Business Administration and a Masters in City Planning from the University of California at Berkeley. Matthew has been invited to speak at various National and State conferences about leadership and he is seen as a leader in disability rights in Arizona. Matthew has a passion to talk to teachers and future teachers about their vital role at ensuring that students of All Abilities have the opportunity to reach their full potential. He is especially proud of his 12-year-old son who he loves and admires! Matthew currently works at the Institute for Human Development as a researcher and an instructor in the Disability Studies Minor at Northern Arizona University.

Elizabeth A. West is an associate professor of special education in the College of Education at the University of Washington. She received her Ph.D. from the University of Washington (2003). Dr. West's research agenda focuses on transforming communities to increase access and to improve outcomes for students with low-incidence disabilities. She has played a vital role in the college as a researcher specializing in severe disabilities with a focus on cultural and linguistic diversity, technology, and teacher preparation; and as an instructor in the elementary and special education teacher education program, as well as the college's doctoral program. She has published numerous journal articles and has presented nationally and internationally. She currently holds leadership positions at the national and international level.

INDEX

CPSIA information can be obtained
at www.ICGtesting.com
Printed in the USA
LVHW060314070623
749124LV00004B/9

9 781784 412517